EDUCATING THE NEGLECTED MAJORITY

# EDUCATING
# THE NEGLECTED MAJORITY

*The Struggle for Agricultural and Technical Education in Nineteenth-Century Ontario and Quebec*

RICHARD A. JARRELL

To Gary and Bev
with best wishes,

D'Arcy, Mymi, Court and Martha
August 16th 2017

McGill-Queen's University Press
Montreal & Kingston • London • Chicago

© McGill-Queen's University Press 2016

ISBN 978-0-7735-4737-7 (cloth)
ISBN 978-0-7735-4738-4 (paper)
ISBN 978-0-7735-9924-6 (ePDF)
ISBN 978-0-7735-9925-3 (ePUB)

Legal deposit fourth quarter 2016
Bibliothèque nationale du Québec

Printed in Canada on acid-free paper that is 100% ancient forest free
(100% post-consumer recycled), processed chlorine free

This book has been published with the help of a grant from the Canadian
Federation for the Humanities and Social Sciences, through the Awards to
Scholarly Publications Program, using funds provided by the Social Sciences
and Humanities Research Council of Canada.

McGill-Queen's University Press acknowledges the support of the Canada
Council for the Arts for our publishing program. We also acknowledge the
financial support of the Government of Canada through the Canada Book
Fund for our publishing activities.

**Library and Archives Canada Cataloguing in Publication**

Jarrell, Richard A., 1946–, author
    Educating the neglected majority: the struggle for agricultural and technical
education in nineteenth-century Ontario and Quebec/Richard A. Jarrell.

    Includes bibliographical references and index.
    Issued in print and electronic formats.
    ISBN 978-0-7735-4737-7 (cloth). – ISBN 978-0-7735-4738-4 (paper). –
ISBN 978-0-7735-9924-6 (PDF). – ISBN 978-0-7735-9925-3 (ePUB)

    1. Agricultural education – Ontario – History – 19th century. 2. Agricultural
education – Québec (Province) – History – 19th century. 3. Technical
education – Ontario – History – 19th century. 4. Technical education –
Québec (Province) – History – 19th century. I. Title.

S535.C3J37 2016          630.71'0713          C2016-902852-6
                                              C2016-902853-4

This book was typeset by Marquis Interscript in 10.5/13 New Baskerville.

To the memory of

*Harold Blackburn Atterbury*

*and Annabel Lee Atterbury,*

*who not only believed in technical education*

*and literacy, but lived them*

# Contents

APPENDICES

# Foreword

The interest of my late husband, Richard Jarrell, in working-class education likely arose from his experiences while studying at Indiana University in Bloomington. In his first year there, 1964, he was admitted to the Residence Scholarship Program, which occupied one floor in an all-male dormitory in Trees Center, a collection of Second World War army barracks. The program provided inexpensive room and board to a small group of high-achieving students who lacked financial backing, in exchange for housekeeping tasks and continuing excellent marks. Richard later told stories of the grandmotherly administrator who helped students whose grades were dipping too low.

After Richard and I graduated, he was accepted into the PhD program in the new Institute for the History and Philosophy of Science at the University of Toronto in 1968. We settled in Toronto and made a life for us and our growing family. Richard graduated in 1971 and became a professor in the field at York University, specializing in the history of Canadian science and technology. He researched the thought and activities of Sir Henry Cole as a probe to study the bureaucratization of education in nineteenth-century Britain and to discover the roots of technical education. This research exposed him to some of the schemes to provide agricultural and technical education in nineteenth-century Ontario and Quebec.

Meanwhile, this interest took nourishment from his conversations with his Uncle Harry and Aunt Ann Atterbury, both firm believers in the value of education. Early in his career, Harry, at Carnegie Institute of Technology in Pittsburgh, had taught a blend of theory and practice to graphic-arts students who would become managers in publishing and printing. Years later, when he and Ann were running the *Hustisford News* in Wisconsin, their editorials encouraged local school boards to empha-size academics over sports – for example, to put books in their libraries rather than uniforms on their athletes.

For Richard, his adoptive and welcoming new land provided the per-fect focus for the abiding interest in working-class education that had emerged from his own background and family and his experiences at Bloomington. He kept finding more and more about a vast and rela-tively uncharted field full of dazzling dreams and often-disillusioning realities: instruction, both formal and informal, for farmers, artisans, and mechanics in Victorian central Canada. To this subject he turned in the 1990s with incredible energy and determination.

Richard had been researching and writing this book for many years and was revising it when he died in December 2013. In particular, he planned further revision of some chapters, which he would have under-taken had he lived. After learning of his passing, McGill-Queen's University Press expressed continued interest in this manuscript.

We in Richard's family wish to thank especially four people for their contributions to this publication: Mark Abley, Richard's sponsoring edi-tor at McGill-Queen's, for his commitment and for providing invaluable information and direction; David Pantalony, curator at the Canada Science and Technology Museum in Ottawa, for suggesting possible readers; Professor Suzanne Zeller, for reading the manuscript and sug-gesting "next steps"; and copyeditor John Parry, for his dedication to what he saw as Richard's extensive and path-breaking research, and for editing, revising, and organizing the manuscript and creating solutions. Each of these people has played an invaluable part in the fulfilment of my husband's objective by completing his work.

Shared circumstances bonded the Residence Scholars at Indiana University, who in 1987 started holding annual reunions in Bloomington. They named themselves the "AHAYWEHS" ("Abandon hope, all ye who enter here," from Dante's *Inferno*), designed a t-shirt with that logo, and set up a website. I hope to celebrate this book with Richard's residence mates at the next reunion, back where this project began to germinate half a century ago.

Martha Jarrell
January 2015

# Preface

The ideologies and institutions of education have finite and sometimes surprisingly short lifetimes. Science and technology are human activities that exhibit more change than stability. The combination of science and technology with education – in the form we now call technical education – has a historical past of rapidly succeeding challenges and responses. This was as true in the mid-nineteenth century as today; just as society is continually facing technological and scientific change, so its educational responses have sought to keep pace. What seems pretty clear, however, is that it does not really keep pace: it only reacts, and so it has always done.

In the extensive literature on Canadian educational history, technical and agricultural education has remained on the periphery. Nor have labour and economic historians paid much attention to this area. No detailed picture exists of the earliest attempts to educate workers to fit into the industrial revolution. In Lower Canada/Canada East (now southern Quebec) and Upper Canada/Canada West (now southern Ontario), the provincial systems of common schools taught basic literacy, but did not offer specialized, and often adult, education. Instead, technical education, under a bewildering variety of names and guises, occupied the thoughts of educational reformers, educators, legislators, manufacturers, and, occasionally, the "mechanics" and "artizans" who might receive it. Agricultural and technical education for farmers and working people was – at least in theory – specialized education as much as training for lawyers or physicians was.

In nineteenth-century central Canada, higher education mostly excluded farmers and workers. Before the 1840s, few of these people had access to any school education; afterwards, more and more would manage a few years of common school. Until nearly century's end, few if any attended the academies, *collèges classiques*, grammar schools, and universities available to the wealthy and to the rising middle class. Although the common schools did produce a literate population, they offered no specialized training for rapidly evolving agriculture and industry. Only a few small-scale efforts addressed this neglected majority, while academic and professional schooling for the middle class grew apace. The few advocates of a broader, more-inclusive vision of education attracted scant notice from authorities and legislators. Even by the 1890s, when the advantages of European and American educational advances were evident, Canada saw only a few limited victories. Ironically, the reformers belonged mostly to the middle class.

Many years ago, while working in the Baldwin Room of the (Metropolitan) Toronto Reference Library, I came on papers concerning the Board of Arts and Manufactures for Upper Canada. It and its ilk – such as the Toronto Mechanics' Institute – have received attention from only a few aficionados, most of them antiquarians. My later work on the growth of technical education in Britain led me back to the central Canadian story, of which it seems a microcosm. But the two countries differed, as both did from the United States, and technical education evolved in distinctive ways in each.

While institutions and state schemes in each society are relatively easy to describe, the thoughts and desires of the working class remain almost inaccessible, as does the efficacy of state programs. For elementary education, literacy figures provide a rough indicator, but the assessment of technical instruction is problematic – indeed, one can hardly speak of a "right" way. Despite all of today's schemes to train and retrain young and old for society's technical requirements, assessing their effectiveness is still a mug's game.

This study began as a paper that I read before the Canadian Science and Technology Historical Association at its Kingston Conference in 1983. I had intended to publish it as an article, but, as so often happens to such plans, one thing led to another, and the project mushroomed. The material was surprising in its extent. Although many observers think that technical education in Canada began with the efforts of the Canadian Manufacturers' Association in the late 1870s, we should start perhaps a half-century earlier.

Various stages of my research received support from the Social Science and Humanities Research Council of Canada and from York University, which I gratefully acknowledge. My thanks also to the helpful staff of various libraries and archives, including the Archives du Séminaire de

Québec (ASQ), the Archives of Ontario (AO, Toronto), the Atwater Library (Montreal), the Baldwin Room of the (now) Toronto Reference Library, the Bibliothèque et Archives nationales du Québec (Quebec City and Montreal), the City of Cambridge (Ontario) Archives, Library and Archives Canada (LAC, Ottawa), the Royal Society of Arts (RSA, London, England), Special Collections at York University, the United Church Archives (UCA, Toronto), the University of Guelph Archives (UGA), and the Victoria and Albert Museum (London). Special thanks, as always, to Martha Jarrell for her editorial eye and enduring support. My editor, Mark Abley, has been always cheerful and supportive. I also owe much to the insights and suggestions of two reviewers of the manuscript.

EDUCATING THE NEGLECTED MAJORITY

# Introduction: Farmer, Artisan, Mechanic, and Technical Education

During the spring of 1910, thousands of Canadian children in classrooms, workshops, and school gardens in all nine provinces were learning to cook, draw plans, fashion metal, sew, turn wood, weed vegetables, and perform a myriad other technical tasks to fit them for future employment. Whereas their grandparents might have learned their trades as apprentices or on the job, they would pass from elementary schools to publicly supported technical high schools and night schools. In June of that year, Parliament appointed James W. Robertson (1857–1930), principal of Macdonald College, McGill University's agricultural faculty, to chair a Royal Commission on Industrial Training and Technical Education. In response to several years of agitation, Liberal Labour Minister William Lyon Mackenzie King (1874–1950) proposed that the commission explore Canadian approaches to technical instruction. The body's massive, four-part report (1913)[1] – much of it a review of foreign experience – paved the way for both the Conservatives' Agricultural Instruction Act of 1913 and their Technical Instruction Act of 1919, which helped launch Dominion/federal transfer payments to the provinces for education.

Since the late 1870s, about a decade after Confederation brought together the Province of Canada, New Brunswick, and Nova Scotia, several constituencies, such as the Canadian Manufacturers' Association, had been lobbying for better technical instruction. Ottawa, however, had interpreted the British North America Act's separation of powers restrictively and saw little need for massive, European-style educational intervention for Canada's low-key industrialization. Mackenzie King had proceeded cautiously, arguing for an information-gathering royal commission only if all the provinces agreed. Also in 1910, Ontario, the most industrialized province, released a report by its superintendent of education, John Seath (1844–1919).[2]

Robert Stamp has written of a thirty-year "campaign for technical education" in the later nineteenth century.[3] If this era constitutes the pre-history of modern technical education in Canada, what about the decades preceding it? Were there no attempts to instruct the working class and farmers, no debates about practical instruction in an industrializing country, no government involvement? In fact, the pre-history has its own five-decade pre-pre-history. Before the union of the two Canadas in 1841, technical and agricultural instruction in central Canada had a low priority – as did public instruction in general – as was the case generally throughout British North America, the United States, and the United Kingdom. Yet as early as the 1830s, British North America had experienced sporadic attempts to raise the educational level and productivity of farmers and the emerging working class.

I restrict this study to the two central colonies/provinces, eventually (southern) Ontario and (southern) Quebec – the emerging agricultural and industrial heartland of what was to become the Dominion of Canada.[4] The existing literature on the subject lacks a comparative framework. Studies dealing with single institutions or single provinces overlook the wider context – educational practices do not arise in a vacuum: institutions borrow or adapt ideas from elsewhere. The quarter-century-long United Province of Canada (1841–67), which many historical studies ignore, shaped much of what was to come in Ontario and Quebec's education.[5]

As well as limiting the geographical purview of this study, I offer a restrictive definition of technical education or instruction. During the nineteenth century, there was no consensus on its domain, beyond its relating to those occupations for which science and technology were central. Both British and continental writers included art instruction, in the sense of ornamentation or design of manufactures. Technology was beginning to influence both manufacturing and agriculture early in the century, and the embrace would tighten as the century wore on. Britain had seen both industrial and agricultural revolutions, which would naturally spread to its colonies.

The definition and approaches of technical education in central Canada evolved through the forces of educational thought and economic events. By the mid-nineteenth century, definition was posing a real problem, because domestic advocates had virtually no practical experience in the field. They shared with their US and British counterparts a strong desire to improve the lot of the working class and farmers through education and, not just coincidentally, increasing industrial production and profits. If they were successful, they would also control the direction of this educational project.

For whom did they intend this instruction? Schemes for agricultural education in Canada spoke of farmers or agriculturists. The driving force behind agricultural advancement in Britain and Ireland had been not farm labourers or cottiers, but wealthy estate owners and substantial farmers – social groups virtually non-existent in Canada until the 1830s' expansion of social and economic diversity produced farmers of substance, some of them open to innovation. Agricultural instruction also required literacy, which was fairly scarce until well into the century.

Advocates framed technical education in crafts, manufactures, or trades as education for "artisans," the "labouring classes," "mechanics," and the "working classes." They aimed it at people who worked for wages, not salaries. The term "artisan" referred usually to a skilled person in a trade or craft, while a "mechanic" performed manual labour. Many people used the various terms interchangeably. British-style artisans were rare in Canada. Later in the century, terms such as "manufacturing" or "industrial classes" referred to men, women, and children working in factories. These terms also shifted with the times and the writers. It is perhaps easier to define this group, with its several overlapping constituencies, by what its members were not: they were *not* professionals, merchants, or shop clerks, nor were they indigents.

To keep this study manageable, I exclude two extremes of technical education – so-called industrial training (the low-level trades instruction that occurred in foundling homes, reformatories, and workhouses) and higher education in engineering. Industrial training was unsystematic and for only a small fraction of society, and engineering matured only at the end of the century in centres such as Montreal's McGill University and the University of Toronto. Although the first steps towards engineering education included the ideal of instructing mechanics – which we look at below – a small group of middle-class men attempting to professionalize and control their practice of engineering soon took it over, moving it outside our area of study.[6]

Between these extremes lies an astonishing array of approaches to educate Canadians to deal with technology. The traditional system of apprenticeship, although it was still extant in some trades, was clearly dying out or never took root in other trades. Most immigrants or native-born Canadians could learn skills on the job without passing through the equivalent of indentured servitude. Although the fluidity of Canadian society militated against the old, often-rigid training methods in use in Britain or on the continent, few observers saw on-the-job training, such as it was, as a reliable substitute.

Therefore, the evolution of ideas about technical education in mid-century Canada responded to both the breakdown of the traditional system of instruction and the challenges of increasing industrialization. Educationists and industrialists would suggest art instruction for factory hands, domestic science for girls, industrial arts or handicrafts for urban children, practical and theoretical agricultural instruction for rural children, and science courses for artisans and mechanics. This wide variety of approaches not only reflects a lack of consensus but also mirrors a shift from the early focus on working-class training to technological instruction for all students in public schools.

How are we to understand this story in its broader context? A growing historiography has pointed to the rise of liberalism and the displacement of toryism as one way to understand nineteenth-century changes to Canadian society. Jean-Marie Fecteau, Ian McKay, Fernande Roy, and others have argued that the century's rise of the Canadian state was about the creation of a liberal social order.[7] The movement for technical and agricultural instruction evolved primarily through the actions of institutions that the state largely created and financed and through voluntary organizations that it often supported. Middle-class men directed almost all of these activities, and most of them hailed from the rising group that believed in social and political reform and the value of the individual. Thus this facet of Canadian educational history could fit comfortably into the liberal-order framework. Yet, as Constant and Ducharme note, "It is not so much the principle of individualism, freedom, or the openness to reform that provides the foundation for the liberal order framework, but rather the question of property and economic equality."[8] This latter view is perfectly congruous with educational reform, so often pitched as a way for the individual to get ahead.

The literature on state formation examines this institution-building. In Bruce Curtis's account of the 1871 census,[9] for example, many of his key figures are active in the push for technical education. An extreme reading of this kind of analysis could lead to a conspiracy view of social control. Did social groups – in this case, the middle class – seek to extend their vision to others? Of course. Yet we need not assume that a reformer such as Canada West/Ontario's very-long-time superintendent of education,

Rev. Egerton Ryerson, was Machiavellian nor doubt the sincerity of his ideals and actions. That groups will attempt to co-opt others if they cannot directly persuade them of their vision seems uncontroversial.[10]

We can also recognize in this story the maturation of Canadians' reliance on the state, either directly or indirectly through financial support, to solve social problems. It is striking, as one reads through even the earliest Canadian parliamentary papers, how often individuals and groups stretched out their hands for money from the state. This is consonant with the liberal-order interpretation, as the state could be the vehicle to allow more citizens to advance.

This is also a story about internal class dynamics and class relations. Working-class people and farming families had their own evolving social visions, and specialized education seems to have formed only a very small part of these visions. The organization of technical and agricultural education by the middle class, however, was entirely in keeping with that group's evolving views of itself and the society it wished to build.[11]

In the realms of agricultural and technical education, we see very little inter-class friction throughout the century. Perhaps working-class interest in specialized education was too slight to generate a point of contention, which the evidence seems to suggest. From the 1870s onwards, as manufacturing grew apace and trade unionism advanced, inter-class friction was often evident, but, as labour historians have documented, the unions' struggles focused on wages and working conditions, not on educational opportunities. For farming populations, the advance from mere survival to prosperity depended on productivity and markets. Again, the interest by most farmers in agricultural education – when it comes at all – emerges quite late in the century.

None of this was peculiar to Canada. In the United Kingdom, the birthplace of many of the ideas that informed Canadian technical education, there was a similar, long evolution where both state and private organizations developed a rich assortment of schemes to educate the working class and to improve manufactures. The Great Exhibition of 1851 in Hyde Park's Crystal Palace had provided a wake-up call for its urgent necessity if Britain were to keep up. In 1884, the Royal Commission on Technical Instruction triggered wide-ranging legislative changes. The intervening thirty years of debates over technical education resembled Stamp's "campaign." Activities to foster technical education during the early period in Canada might seem worthless, and certainly the gestation period was long – Jean-Pierre Charland's "préhistoire interminable"[12] – and replete with missteps and misguided ideas, but it holds much of interest. The state's role in technical education and the surprisingly rapid adoption of British ideas tell us much about mid-Victorian Canada.

The story falls naturally into two parts: before and after Confederation. The earliest attempts to institute technical instruction occurred in the late 1820s, when state intervention or assistance was slight. After the union in 1841, the pace of state involvement picked up slightly, leading to creation of government organizations and institutions for technical and agricultural instruction beginning in the late 1840s and a clear pattern in place by 1860. Confederation divided the parallel but distinct organisms of the two halves of the province. After 1867, the two provincial systems began to diverge, though retaining certain common interests and practices. Until Ottawa struck the 1910 royal commission, it played no role in education in Ontario and Quebec, despite some efforts in the North-West Territories before it created Alberta and Saskatchewan in 1905.

Any study of educational practice presents obvious questions – some answerable, others not. These typically include:

- Who is doing the targeting? What social group is their target, and why? What ideas or methods are they using?
- What outcome do they expect?
- What is the actual outcome?

In nineteenth-century Canada, certain groups argued for organized technical instruction: educational reformers, journalists, legislators, manufacturers, and philanthropists, almost all of them middle-class men. Their targets are not always so apparent, as we saw above, because of the fluid definition. Their methods will become apparent in the chapters below. Their goals were disparate ("increasing our wealth," "improving our manufactures"), that is, without clear-cut means of implementation or measurement. Short-term actual results such as the ability to draw or a specific grade on an examination paper were measurable, but longer-term effects, such as a wealthier society, were almost impossible to quantify. Any discussion of actual outcomes has to focus on short-run expectations and goals; it was and remains almost impossible to isolate eventual societal or economic amelioration from myriad factors that produce change. This last sad reality, however, still does not prevent people from framing educational schemes with assumptions about long-term effects. Such assumptions are not demonstrable; they were and are matters of faith.

Throughout this study, I make a distinction between two types of technical or agricultural education – informal and formal. Informal education is a general catch-all: it includes both self-education, through reading or observing, and learning through such activities as attending lectures, engaging in discussions with a neighbour or co-worker, following the press, participating in organizations, and visiting exhibitions, fairs, or museums. Formal education implies training or instruction, typically in a classroom or workshop setting, or within the context of an apprenticeship. It usually assumes the possibility of some kind of measurable progress, such as passing examinations and obtaining diplomas. In most societies, informal education emerges before formal, but in nineteenth-century Canada they often coexisted. Problems in measuring the outcomes of education only increase for informal practices.

The first chapter below details pre-Confederation efforts in central Canada to introduce scientific and technological information to farmers through informal means, looking in turn at, first, agricultural societies and their activities and, second, the agricultural press. The need to support and organize these efforts at dissemination of agricultural knowledge led governments to create – the third subject – an infrastructure that would later also encompass the urban working class in technical education. Chapter 2 focuses on attempts to create formal means of instruction in agriculture through stand-alone agricultural colleges, specialized schools, and universities. These two chapters close by identifying some modest successes, not unlike those of neighbouring New York and Michigan.

Chapter 3 turns to the education of the embryonic working class. It reviews debates and events in the United Kingdom, along with its export to the Province of Canada of its movement for mechanics' institutes and the colony's creation of a bureaucratic structure to support it. Chapter 4 details attempts to establish classroom programs: for Upper Canada, most of the work fell to the Board of Arts and Manufactures, and its associated mechanics' institutes, from its inception in 1857 to its transfer to Ontario in 1867; in Lower Canada, which also boasted an eponymous board, the linguistic division and financial problems produced different results.

Chapters 5–8 survey the post-Confederation landscape into the late 1890s. Chapters 5 and 6 explore the evolution of agricultural education in Ontario and Quebec, respectively, where, despite very similar formal and informal modes of education, the approaches of the two provincial governments drifted apart. Respective differences in technical instruction for the working class (chapters 7 and 8) show an even sharper divergence.

Observers of Canadian technical education in 1860 and in 1910 would notice a striking contrast. By the early twentieth century, older institutions, such as the mechanics' institutes, had disappeared or been converted into public libraries. The debate on manual training and the idea of stand-alone technical schools had become part of central Canadians' educational vocabulary and, timidly, their practice. These ideas, though partly of European origin, arrived from the United States. Thus the efforts, some lasting into the 1890s, to instruct artisans, farmers, and mechanics, using mostly British methods, emerge and coalesce as the first phase of technical education in Canada. What followed was American in origin. The campaign that Stamp identified was the debate that prepared the way for the second phase.

PART ONE

# Pre-Confederation (1830s–1867)

# Informal Education for the Farmer to 1867

Because agriculture was Canada's paramount industry in the nineteenth century, it is not surprising that the government first financed and managed technical education in the agricultural department. In 1915, Albert Leake (c. 1866–1957), the provincial education inspector for Ontario, observed: "Agricultural education is a phase of the broader problem of industrial education. In current education discussions, however, the term 'industrial education' has been interpreted to mean almost exclusively that form of training which will fit for participation in the mechanical pursuits of the factory and the workshop. In the discussions of education for industrial purposes agriculture has held a subordinate place, but the time has come when this basic human industry must receive adequate consideration."[1]

The Canadian state started intervening in technical instruction, apart from small grants to private organizations, as part of its attempt to rationalize agriculture, but between about 1800 and 1840 Upper and Lower Canada saw little effort to improve agriculture or to educate people about it. The earliest attempts involved local agricultural societies, and it was the activities of these bodies and the related agricultural press that spurred government intervention and organization by 1850.

The Lower and Upper Canadian legislatures did little to encourage agriculture, but the arrival in the late 1840s of responsible government in the Province of Canada and its related administrative machinery spurred state activity, reflecting a shift from a focus on private effort to interest in state direction and accountability. The earlier, conservative, British-style vision was supportive of well-off landowners and their needs. The advent of reformers in government in the early 1840s led to support for informal agricultural education for a wider population. By then, the

Canadian farming community was anything but uniform in economic or social terms, but promoters of proposals and projects seem to have been unaware of this diversity.

There is a substantial literature on agriculture in New France and early nineteenth-century Lower Canada and whether there was a *crise agricole*.[2] More important for this story, profound changes after 1800 created challenges to farmers: a growing rural population in Lower Canada, rapid settlement of Upper Canada, an expanding market economy that included US and British customers, and burgeoning technological change.[3] The literature explores many themes: Did population growth and subdivision of land impoverish Lower Canadian farmers? Did their technological backwardness impede their competition with Upper Canadian farmers?[4] Were transportation cost or climate important factors? It is clear that farmers who survived and thrived adopted appropriate technology and let economic realities shape their decisions on what to grow or raise. Many of the others left the land or the country.

To what extent did people believe that education in agricultural technique would help them to make sound economic decisions? The voices we hear from below are those of promoters, not potential students. Did these various schemes have real success? The evidence suggests very little. Yet, by the time of Confederation, most Canadian farmers were reasonably prosperous, and this could not have occurred by magic.[5]

This chapter examines three dimensions of the efforts to introduce scientific and technological information to farmers through informal means – first, agricultural societies and their activities; second, the agricultural press; and, third, the government's creation of an infrastructure to support and organize this spreading of agricultural knowledge.

## AGRICULTURAL SOCIETIES

Eighteenth-century British, Irish, and American ideas informed the early organization of agriculture in Canada. In that era, Britain and Ireland developed three informal approaches to agricultural education – the competition, the premium, and the model farm. Agricultural societies there provided a venue for the exchange of such new ideas and knowledge. The Royal Dublin Society (founded 1731) and the Society for the Encouragement of Arts, Manufacture and Commerce, or Society of Arts (London, 1754) focused on farming and manufacturing, while the Royal Highland and Agricultural Society of Scotland (1784) dealt specifically with agriculture. Both England and Ireland had national farming societies by soon after 1800. All these organizations published transactions, which included agricultural intelligence from other countries and the results of trials of new techniques and crops. Several members of these societies who emigrated to Canada brought the British "improver" vision with them. Equally influential for Canada was US agricultural organizing, particularly in New York State, where British ideas were current in the years before and after independence.[6]

## The Agricultural Society of Canada (1789– )

In the 1790s, Canadian farmers themselves had begun to set up local societies and held fairs, receiving occasional crown grants for these purposes. Long-time Governor Guy Carleton, Lord Dorchester (1724–1808), founded the Agricultural Society of Canada in 1789, just after a poor harvest, modelling it on the improving societies of Britain and Ireland as a forum for exchanging information on the latest agricultural techniques. Initially, the society had branches in Quebec and Montreal. In 1790, it distributed a bilingual booklet on agricultural methods, *Papiers et lettres sur l'agriculture*, published by Samuel Neilson. The organization's members included francophone seigneurs, their more recent anglophone counterparts, and farmers of means, but virtually no *habitants*.

### District Societies in Lower Canada

Over the next few years, the society broke into district organizations. In 1815, the legislature of Lower Canada (created in 1791) ordered an inquiry into the state of agriculture. The report by chair Jean-Thomas Taschereau (1778–1832) recommended, among other measures, model farms across the province and a bureau of agriculture,[7] but nothing came of these proposals. In 1818, an Act to Encourage Agriculture (58 Geo. III, cap. 6) appropriated £2,000 to distribute among the agricultural societies in Quebec, Montreal, and Trois-Rivières to support their work generally and for prize money specifically.

District bodies catered to well-off farmers; in December 1817, English-born organizer and timber merchant William Sheppard (1784–1867) wrote from his estate at Sillery (now within Quebec City) to nearby local societies – in Ste-Anne de la Grande Anse (later Ste-Anne de-la-Pocatière, and later still La Pocatière) and in Ste-Marie Nouvelle Beauce – to inquire into their activities and whether they would adhere to the Quebec District Society. He also wrote to county officials to encourage formation of county societies to correspond with the district society. The Société d'agriculture de Québec met on 18 March 1818 to adopt rules, including an annual membership fee of one guinea a year, a considerable sum. Sheppard, who hoped to publish the results of experiments conducted by local societies, was later active in scientific work for the Literary and Historical Society of Quebec, which he helped to establish.[8]

The Trois-Rivières district society, whose first president was the seigneur and sheriff Louis Gugy (1770–1840), was slower to organize itself, but it appealed to the same class of farmers. It expended its initial funds on premiums and a grain competition. In his first report (late 1810s), Gugy admitted that "in a country where want of instruction is so generally complained of – The diffusion of useful knowledge amongst the unlettered by means of recommending this or that practice, must necessarily be of low progress." He appears below as first president of the Montreal Mechanics' Institution. Later revisions to the Agriculture Act followed in 1821, 1829, and 1834 and extended the system to include county societies.[9]

### District Societies in Upper Canada

Upper Canadians also organized societies.[10] Shortly after the first immigrants arrived in the new colony (founded 1791), an agricultural society formed in Newark (Niagara-on-the-Lake) in 1793. Its patron and financial supporter was Lieutenant-Governor John Graves Simcoe (1752–1806). Agricultural societies were as much social as educational in purpose, with the annual dinner being a highlight, as it was in the old country, and support of a local fair a major goal. Early on, the Newark body held a fair at Queenston. By 1822, the naturalist Charles Fothergill (1782–1840) reported fairs in York (Toronto), Cobourg, and Port Hope. The Frontenac County Agricultural Society held its first fair near Kingston in 1825. These events focused on livestock sales, aiming to develop a market for cattle.[11]

New Englander Elkanah Watson (1758–1842) championed the annual cattle show, already common in Britain, and the practice grew rapidly in the US north in the early nineteenth century. Such shows facilitated sales and allowed farmers to observe new breeds, compare their qualities, and discuss various methods of animal care and feeding. As these gatherings became more permanent, they grew to encompass competitions for the best examples of grain, ploughing matches, and even essay writing. Towards mid-century, implement shows and domestic manufactures, such as butter, cheese, cloth, and hats, enriched the mix. Rural fairs were a pleasant, sociable means to learn in an informal way, and almost all fairs were organized by societies.[12]

Leaders of local communities seem to have dominated agricultural societies' memberships. Ross Fair concludes that in Britain these societies – there were more than ninety by the 1790s – worked for mutual improvement and to maintain aristocratic hegemony.[13] In Canada, however, he sees no truly equivalent class, so the local societies, at least in Upper Canada, fostered members' positions as gentlemen, as did the provincial organization, whose founders had similar backgrounds. Certainly, agricultural societies helped to socialize rural inhabitants and, in some cases, inculcated a common vision of society.[14]

However, the government subsidized them because of their educational function. The Upper Canada Agricultural Society appeared briefly in 1818 – the Tory government sponsored it as a counterpoise to the agitation of Robert Gourlay (1778–1863). Despite Gourlay's impressive credentials – he was one of the few graduates of the University of Edinburgh's agricultural program as well as an agricultural reformer and experienced farm manager – his radical ideas on agrarian reform shocked the Upper Canadian elite. In the Kingston area, the Midland District Agricultural Society, promoted by Hugh Thomson, emerged the following year. In 1825, well-off farmers in Ontario, Peel, Simcoe, and York counties formed the Home District Agricultural Society.

Further west, the Western District Agricultural and Horticultural Society, based in Sandwich (Windsor), started in February 1837 but did not meet again until later in 1838 because of the Rebellion. Its first president, Major Robert Lachlan, recognized that many farmers saw no need for such bodies and that local jealousies were a problem for them, but hoped that they would foster competition by offering prizes that would generate improvements. New ideas "lead to the direct proof, through the medium of careful *practical results*, of the *real* value of our *supposed* Agricultural *theory*, ending either in decided approval or condemnation, *after* due investigation, – and, therefore, sure to be productive of *some* good results."[15] The society, Lachlan urged, should develop its own agricultural library, but in the interim might purchase copies of good British and American books and deposit them about the district.

From 1830 on, the legislature offered a £100 grant to any district society that could raise £50 by subscription.[16] These grants increased several times, and the new United Province then offered them to county societies when it dismantled districts in the mid-1840s. Only then do we see a concerted effort to establish a hierarchical system, once there were enough township and county societies in the two provinces. In 1845, the legislature replaced the pre-Union agricultural acts and began to organize and fund county societies throughout. The United Province had no umbrella body, and township and county agricultural societies had no connection with one another, which seemed inefficient.[17]

Canadian societies carried on British-style competitions and premiums. They awarded prizes at exhibitions, usually cash (much of it from the state), for the best specimens in particular classes. They believed that people instinctively compete and that encouraging and rewarding that tendency pushed famers to improve. To this day, this belief underlies competitions in agricultural fairs and horticultural societies. Whether knowledge passes to less competitive individuals is an interesting question.

The premium too was a means to inspire excellence and started with the Dublin Society as early as 1738. The premise – a premium for a particular desideratum such as the best bull of a particular breed – was in essence education by bribery. Many observers have noted that it rewarded those who would have innovated anyway rather than assisting those who truly might have benefitted. In Canada, the term "premium" sometimes served interchangeably with "prize."

Canadian observers were certainly aware of American efforts to organize agriculture. In New York, the Society for the Promotion of Useful Arts lobbied for a government agency to assist agriculture; the state responded in 1819 with a Board of Agriculture to encourage formation of local societies and distribute grants to groups that raised funds for premiums and reports. This idea was not novel: Scottish improver Sir John Sinclair (1754–1835) had in 1793 organized Britain's Board of Agriculture, which collected statistical information under the astute eye of its secretary, Arthur Young (1741–1820), the respected author of *A Tour in Ireland*. Until its demise in 1822, the board compiled and published county agricultural reports; Robert Gourlay had been one of Young's informants.

New York's more activist Board of Agriculture was a successful stimulator of activity, with local societies quickly adopting the periodic cattle show. After it lapsed by law in 1825, leading figures in the society movement formed the New York State Agricultural Society in 1832, and it took over distribution of state funds to local societies. By 1841, the state society inaugurated annual cattle shows and fairs, most notably the New York State Fair at Syracuse, which attracted Canadian visitors. Neighbouring states followed a similar path.[18]

During the 1840s, James Bryce Brown lived in both Canada East (formerly Lower Canada) and Upper Canada (Canada West). On returning to his native Scotland, he published two editions of *Views of Canada and the Colonists* (1851): "Agricultural societies and farmers' clubs form already part of the means of agricultural improvement in Canada; and it is gratifying to observe that such associations have made considerable progress, more especially within the last eight or ten years. A general and central association for the whole province, upon the model of the Highland Society of Scotland or Royal Agricultural Society of England would appear to be alone wanting to complete this branch of the course of means."[19] Brown clearly was not aware of the emerging parallel approach to administering the two halves of the united province. When he first lived in Canada there had been no unifying body at all. To that end, in 1843, the Scottish-born farmer and entrepreneur Adam Fergusson[20] suggested in the *British American Cultivator* a central agricultural body – either a society or a government board – for the two Canadas.[21]

### *Sectional Agricultural Associations (Late 1840s–67)*

The Home District Agricultural Society met in Toronto in July 1846 to discuss the proposal; the result was the Upper Canada Agricultural Association. Its new constitution called for "the improvement of Farm Stock and Produce; the improvement of Tillage, Agricultural Implements &c.; and the encouragement of Domestic Manufactures, of Useful Inventions, and, generally, of every branch of Rural and Domestic Economy."[22] The mention of connections between agriculture, manufactures, and technology was not mere rhetoric. Fergusson was a prime mover and became first president. At its first provincial exhibition (Toronto, autumn 1846), Fergusson gave his presidential address: "Agriculture, properly so called, will form the prime and the leading object of attention with the Board, but assuredly neither Flora nor Pomona will be overlooked, whilst the ingenious manufacturer and mechanic will ever receive the encouragement and support, which they so well deserve."[23] The new association's annual, peripatetic exhibitions attracted few manufacturers' displays at the start.

In 1849, the Scot J.F.W. Johnston visited the Kingston exhibition after attending the New York State Fair: "I was agreeably surprised, both at the extent of the preparations I saw making on my arrival, and with the appearance of the town and of the show-yard on the day of the exhibition. The latter was not so extensive nor so crowded as that of Syracuse, but much more numerously attended by well-dressed and well-behaved people, and rendered attractive by a greater quantity of excellent stock and implements than I had at all anticipated."[24] The implements, many of them local products, considerably exceeded the number and variety that Johnston saw at the Highland and Agricultural Society's shows at home. More generally, "Little knowledge of improved agriculture has hitherto been diffused in Upper Canada; and it is, as yet, among practical men, held in little esteem. In revenge, the farming class are not, as a body, regarded with much estimation by the other classes of society. They do not assume their proper position among a community where, if they only knew how to use it, all political power is, in reality, in their hands."[25]

However, the leading lights of the Upper Canada Agricultural Association were thoroughly middle-class and influential. The presidential speech of Edward W. Thomson (1794–1865), younger brother of the Kingston journalist Hugh Thomson,[26] extolled agricultural science and its diffusion, while Sheriff Henry Ruttan (1792–1871) pressed for more home manufactures to trim the provincial debt.[27] Canada was just starting to manufacture agricultural implements when London's Great Exhibition of 1851 provided a showcase for the continental, British, and American agricultural industries and deeply impressed the association's leaders.[28] In 1856, it asked Rev. Egerton Ryerson (1803–1882), superintendent of education 1844–76, to contribute models of the European implements that he had purchased at the Paris Exposition to its own provincial exhibition. These objects remained for many years in the Educational Museum in Toronto.

*Provincial Exhibitions*

The 1850 exhibition in Niagara-on-the-Lake attracted some 7,000 spectators, including many from neighbouring New York State. Transportation was a problem: as the *Canadian Agriculturist* noted, "It is certainly difficult in practice, in a country like this, where distances are great and conveyances subject to interruptions, to be strictly punctual as to time."[29] By the time of the 1860 exhibition in Hamilton, which hosted the Prince of Wales, both the Great Western and Grand Trunk railways were operational, allowing for much easier access.

The organizers of provincial exhibitions were familiar with the idea of stimulating learning through competition, which they fostered in local shows. They had learned by experience that widening their scope could spread awareness of new ideas, methods, implements, and livestock breeds and that competition increased numbers. In the decade between the shows in Niagara (1850) and Hamilton (1860), greater participation and introduction of more breeds increased judging classes from twenty-four to fifty-nine;[30] Niagara presented 100 sheep, and Hamilton nearly 650. The event's industrial section featured a wide variety of domestic manufactures, which had also expanded. An observer in 1850 commented, "The Mechanics' Hall was well filled with a creditable display of the results of Canadian ingenuity and industry; yet we must confess our disappointment at the absence of several important articles of native manufactures."[31] New directions in agriculture were apparent in the 1860 conclave – more fruit, and dairy products had grown to 201 from forty-two in 1850. Table 1.1 compares judging classes, with the number of entries in each category for the 1860 show.

### Specialist Societies

It seems plausible that societies and their shows did stimulate change and improvement. As agricultural produce diversified, specialist societies emerged. The Toronto Horticultural Society formed in 1834 for gardeners, and the Western District Agricultural and Horticultural Society in 1837. The key organization in the Niagara area was the Fruit Growers' Association (early 1859); its greatest activity would come after Confederation. The province also chartered a private company, the Canada Vine Growers' Association in 1866, once demand for local grapes and wine had increased.[32]

Upper Canada's sister province soon followed its 1846 example and in 1847 incorporated the Agricultural Society of Lower Canada[33] for the better class of agriculturalists. Members included agricultural journalist William Evans (1786–1857); senior politicians such as A.-N. Morin (1803–1865), Sir Francis Hincks (1807–1885), L.-H. LaFontaine (1807–1864), and Malcolm Cameron (1808–1876); civil servants such as J.-B. Meilleur (1796–1878); the Catholic archbishop of Quebec and the bishop of Montreal; and several members of the Montreal elite. Life members numbered seventeen anglophones and eleven francophones, and regular members, eighty-two and fifty-seven, respectively.[34] William Evans's newspaper relaunched in January 1848 as the *Agricultural Journal and Transactions of the Lower Canada Agricultural Society*.

### Other Ventures

In Canadian societies, as we saw above, the prize and the premium were common currency. However, there was also a third approach: the model or experimental farm under the supervision of an improving farmer. A few appeared in late-eighteenth-century England, and there were

Table 1.1  Entry classes of the provincial exhibitions in Canada West (1850 and 1860)

### 1850 exhibition, Niagara (24 classes)

Class A Horned cattle
Class B Devons
Class C Herefords
Class D Ayrshires
Class E Grade cattle/fat cattle
Class F Agricultural horses
Class G Thoroughbred horses
Class H Sheep
Class I Pigs
Class J Agricultural implements
Class K Domestic manufactures
Class L Woollen and flax goods
Class M Dairy produce

Class N Cabinet ware
Class O Agricultural produce
  Horticultural
Class P Iron
Class Q Ladies' Department
Class R Fine arts
Class S Pottery
Class T Bookbinding
Class U Indian prizes
Class V Ploughing
Class W Poultry
Class X Foreign stock
  Foreign implements

### 1860 exhibition, Hamilton (59 classes)

I Blood horses (21)
II Agricultural horses (128)
III Road or carriage horse (188)
IV Heavy draught horses (49)
V Horses of all classes (52)
VI Cattle/Durham (153)
VII Cattle/Devons (172)
VIII Cattle/Herefords (19)
IX Cattle/Ayrshires (63)
X Cattle/Galloway (56)
XI Cattle/bull of any breed (21)
XII Cattle/grade cattle (78)
XIII Fat and working cattle/
  any breed (58)
XIV Sheep/Leicesters (176)
XV Sheep/Cotswolds (68)
XVI Sheep/Cheviots (41)
XVII Long-woolled sheep (121)
XVIII Sheep/Southdowns (118)
XIX Sheep/Merinos and Saxons (52)
XX Rams of all breeds (40)
XXI Fat sheep (28)
XXII Pigs – Large breeds/Yorkshires (45)
XXIII Pigs – Large breeds/large
  Berkshire (19)
XXIV All other large pigs (16)
XXV Pigs – Small breeds/Suffolks (28)
XXVI Pigs – Small breeds/
  Improved Berkshires (45)
XXVII Pigs – All other small breeds (23)
XXVIII Pigs of all breeds (11)
XXIX Poultry (279)
XXX Foreign stock (1)

XXXI Grains, seeds (n/a)
XXXII Roots and other field crops (546)
XXXIII Horticultural – fruit (690)
XXXIV Horticultural – garden vegetables (644)
XXXV Horticultural – plants and flowers (142)
XXXVI Dairy products (201)
XXXVII Agricultural implements (226 entries)
XXXVIII Agricultural tools and implements
  (mostly hand use) 153 entries
XXXIX Cattle food, manures, misc. (6)
XL Foreign agricultural implements (2 entries)
DEPARTMENT SECOND
XLI Architectural and misc. useful arts (70)
XLII Cabinet ware and other
  manufactures (120)
XLIII Carriages, sleighs (47)
XLIV Furs and wearing apparel (28)
XLV Fine arts (262) – divided into professional
  and amateur
XLVI Groceries, provisions, oils, etc. (194)
XLVII Indian prizes (4)
XLVIII Ladies' Dept (535)
XLIX Machinery, models, castings, tools (140)
L Metal work, plain and ornamental (89)
LI Miscellaneous (24)
LII Musical instruments (26)
LIII Natural history (50)
LIV Paper, printing, bookbinding (61)
LV Pottery (53)
LVI Saddlery (72)
LVII Shoes and boots (67)
LVIII Woollen, flax, and cotton goods (159)
LIX Foreign manufactures (21)

Sources: Canadian Agriculturist 2 (Oct. 1850) and 12 (1 and 16 Nov. 1860).

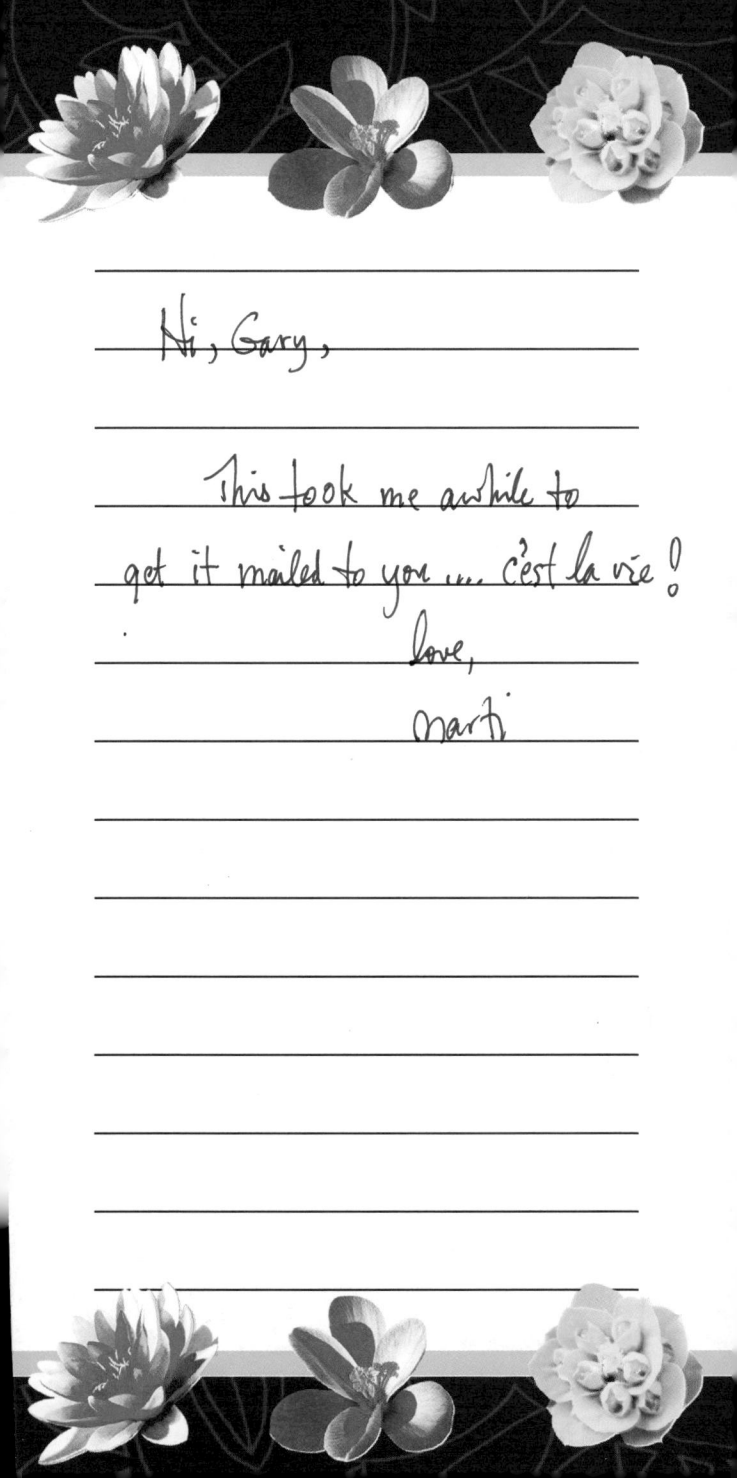

Hi, Gary,

This took me awhile to get it mailed to you .... c'est la vie!

love,

Marti

several attempts in Ireland during the nineteenth. This was education by emulation: a farmer who sees his neighbour's strides, or sends his son to work on a model farm, will be stimulated to adopt new ideas. Continental Europe and the United Kingdom formalized this approach in the model or experimental farm, under an improving farmer or a society. Farmers might send their sons to work and learn there as a form of apprenticeship. Some enterprising farmers or estate agents might take on several youths in what amounted to an informal school. Such experience fitted young men to be farm managers or estate agents, a substantial post in a country with large estates with hired farm labour or tenants. In social terms, this concept would be difficult to translate to Canada.

The first Canadian agricultural school was Bishop Laval's "industrial" school at St-Joachim, which operated between 1670 and 1715 for children of the poor. About 1800, Philipp de Fellenberg (1771–1844) founded a school at Hofwyl, near Bern, Switzerland. This private undertaking provided a literary education to the wealthy and both literary and practical education to poor youths who, in turn, worked on the farm. The idea travelled successfully to Ireland in the 1820s and to the United States, but in Canada most instances had a precarious existence, although the concept informed many discussions about agricultural education.

One other venue for discussion was the farmers' club, which existed in Britain, Ireland, and the United States. Leading Canadian agricultural journalists were well aware of them and carried their reports in their newspapers. Toronto journalist William Edmundson (c. 1815–1852) supported formation of Canadian clubs in an editorial in 1845 and learned to his delight that Newmarket had had one since the previous year. Henry Ruttan made a similar pitch in his *Newcastle Farmer* in 1846, hoping for township-level societies.[35] One of the earliest and most successful emerged in Northumberland County at least as early as 1851 – the Hamilton Township Farmers' Club. By the mid-1850s, clubs had formed in York, Northumberland, Peterborough, Oxford, and Wellington counties. Simultaneous growth of township agricultural societies may have diluted interest in farmers' clubs. An editorial in the *Canada Farmer* in 1864 argued for more clubs: "Every agricultural society has the means within itself, of accomplishing the desired results. If the members or any considerable portion of them, would meet some half-dozen times during the most leisure portion of the year, for the reading and discussing of papers on agricultural subjects, and comparing notes, very valuable consequences would arise."[36].

Farmers' clubs differed from agricultural societies in several ways: they were more local, less formal, and less expensive; they emphasized discussion of current issues rather than exhibitions or premiums; and they received no state aid. In Lower Canada, Evans reported on English clubs regularly in his papers, but wrote nothing on local farmers' clubs. Farmers' clubs emerged in Upper Canada once agricultural journalism established itself. Reading of papers and holding discussions required current knowledge, and that came through the agricultural press rather than from books.

## AGRICULTURAL WRITERS AND THE PRESS

### Books, Pamphlets, and Columns

The British drive for agricultural improvement, discernible in the late seventeenth century, expanded rapidly among well-off farmers during the eighteenth.[37] The "improving" mentality of England and lowland Scotland brought about experimentation with livestock breeding, rotation, manuring, drainage, and new implements, generating a lively literature. British and American immigrants carried this vision to Canada, and in the early nineteenth century francophone settlers took Swiss and French ideas to Lower Canada. Both linguistic groups argued in print for scientific agriculture through experimentation with crops and livestock breeding. "Scientific" here implies not laboratory research but rather the more general empiricism of field trials.[38]

Before the 1830s, only sporadic articles in the regular press in Canada spoke of matters agricultural. In this era of burgeoning journalism of every political stripe, most of the journalists promoting agriculture were progressive, a few even politically radical. Most appear to have fitted comfortably into the emerging liberal and reforming political and social framework. Almost all maintained that individual farmers could adopt progressive ideas and thrive economically and socially, and so the country itself would thrive.

An early example is the Kingston journalist and MLA, Hugh Christopher Thomson (1791–1834), who serialized his observations under the pseudonym "the Prompter" in his *Upper Canada Herald* in 1821.[39] He recognized that Canadian wheat was not as good as American and needed improving; the orchards in the area, despite sad neglect, were nevertheless valuable resources; and farmers ought to use more oxen and grow hops for profit. He exhorted them to support the Midland District Agricultural Society for their own benefit.[40]

Later, improvers such as Evans in Montreal wrote in the agricultural press, while others, such as Adam Fergusson (1783–1862), John Galt (1779–1839), William Hutton (1801–1861), and John Lynch (1798–1884), used the transactions of Upper Canada's Board of Agriculture to preach the British gospel.[41] One of the key concepts of British improvers was the notion that continuous use, particularly by planting a single type of crop, exhausts soil. Certainly, when land was first cleared of forest, soil nutrients were substantial, but farmers in both Canadas recognized that yields of crops such as wheat declined over time. When the noted Scottish chemist and agricultural expert James F.W. Johnston (1796–1855) toured North America in 1849–50, he liked what he saw in Upper Canada and predicted a bright future so long as a "superior class of settlers" would be in place to spread ideas through local societies. In Lower Canada, however, the older generation of farmers, whether French or British, seemed to be carrying on the poor practices of the past, but there were reform-minded spirits in Montreal and Quebec, including Catholic clergymen.[42]

The only remedy for soil exhaustion was to maintain fertility using the European methods of crop rotation and manuring. Evans, Fergusson, and Galt suggested growing green crops or maintaining pastures in a relatively new farm. Hutton even suggested rotation through five crops – turnips or potatoes, barley, clover for hay, clover for pasture, and finally wheat or beans. For most farmers, particularly in Upper Canada, rotation would generate no significant capital; only wheat farming could capitalize a farmer quickly in good times. The message on manuring was also irrelevant: the best way to increase manure was to raise cattle for sale, but no major market for cattle yet existed. The improvers' vision was scientifically sound but economically unviable in Canada.

Beginning in the 1820s, another meaning of scientific agriculture emerged – that of laboratory science in aid of agriculture. Justus von Liebig (1803–1873) and his students developed agricultural chemistry at Giessen and in other German universities, along with Sir Humphrey Davy (1778–1829) in England. The subject studied the application of organic chemistry to soils, manures, and plant and animal nutrition. Davy and J.F.W. Johnston were its champions in the United Kingdom. In Canada, these topics interested not farmers, but urban scientific dilettantes in the Literary and Historical Society of Quebec (1824) and the Natural History Society of Montreal (1827).[43] A.G. Douglas translated Davy's treatise on agricultural chemistry as *Traduction libre et abrégé des leçons de chimie données par le chevalier H. Davy* (1820).

The Montreal journalist Michel Bibaud (1782–1857) published the *Bibliothèque canadienne* from 1825 to 1830 and frequently inserted scientific intelligence from home or abroad. In 1829, he also serialized the notary Valère Guillet's short *Un petit système d'agriculture* (1829).

Lower Canada's best-known agricultural writer in the first half-century was Joseph-François Perrault (1753–1844), whose *Traité d'agriculture pratique* appeared in 1831. He claims to have based the work on twenty years' practical experience at his farm in a Quebec suburb. It was truly a practical handbook, with the first part (*le petit culture*) dealing with gardening, primarily vegetables, and the second (*moyenne et grande culture*), mostly with field crops. Both parts had entries for each plant. The following year, Perrault persuaded the legislature to support an agricultural school in Quebec's Fauxbourg St-Louis.

If a lobby existed for agricultural education, proponents were liberal, sometimes radical. The Swiss-educated Amury Girod (before 1800– 1837), Perrault's associate in the agricultural-school project and designated director of the model farm, had translated or written several agricultural texts, including *Conversations sur l'agriculture, par un habitans de Varennes* (1834).[44] He was one of the *Patriote* leaders at the 1837 battle of St-Eustache, near Montreal.

Journalist Napoléon Aubin (1812–1890),[45] a Swiss who arrived in Canada in 1835 and produced political and satirical writings – authorities arrested him for his views during the Rebellion – gave public lectures on chemistry in Montreal. While a chemistry lecturer at the Quebec Medical School in 1847, he published *La chimie agricole mise à la portée de tout le monde*: "The health of a country grows by the spread of useful knowledge of all kinds, and only when our agriculturists become as enlightened about the theory of their art as they are able and industrious in its practice will they be able to call to their aid and fearlessly risk capital that is now seeking other destinations."[46]

Men such as Bibaud, Perrault, Girod, and Aubin, however, were essentially urban liberal professionals, in effect writing for one another. Even assuming that the average farmer in Canada *could* translate scientific theory into practice, the message was probably not reaching him.

### The Agricultural Press

The authors noted above wrote books, pamphlets, and columns for newspapers. A dedicated agricultural press became a valuable agent for informal education, although societies had a nearly forty-year head start.

The agricultural newspaper or magazine, as Canadians knew it, had its origins in the United States with the appearance of *American Farmer* in Baltimore in 1819. In 1834 in Albany, Jesse Buel (1778–1839) launched the influential *Cultivator*, which exposed Americans to British farming ideas and the new discoveries of agricultural chemistry.[47] It had readers in Canada by the late 1830s, as did the popular *Genesee Farmer*, which Luther Tucker (1802–1873) edited in Rochester until he took over the *Cultivator* in 1839 on Buel's death. *American Agriculturist*, which began in New York in 1842, was perhaps the most influential vehicle, and Canadian journals quoted it. Although the US agricultural press attracted as many as 350,000 subscribers, mostly in the northern states before the Civil War, it appears that few farmers heeded its suggestions.[48]

William Evans effectively founded Canadian agricultural journalism.[49] A native of County Galway, Ireland, he was already an experienced stock raiser when he immigrated in 1819 and began farming in the Montreal area. Essentially self-taught, Evans became an apostle of new agricultural techniques and secretary of the Agricultural Society of the District of Montreal in 1830. His *Treatise on the Theory and Practice of Agriculture* (1835) made liberal use of English and Irish sources. He relied heavily on J.C. Loudon's *Encyclopedia of Agriculture* (1825), which he called "the best work that has been published on agriculture."[50] Evans's *Treatise* was both very complete for its time and also pitched at a high level. Lower Canada's legislature sponsored a French translation (by Amury Girod) and distributed it. Having written articles for the Montreal *Gazette*, Evans in 1838 launched Canada's first, short-lived farm newspaper, the *Canadian Quarterly Agricultural and Industrial Magazine.*

Evans pulled together a series of his letters on agricultural education as *Agricultural Improvement* in 1837.[51] The volume rehearses some standard views. First, if farming is a source of wealth, why wouldn't a farmer find education as crucial as a tradesman does? Second, farming practice in both Upper and Lower Canada was backward and needed schools such as those in Prussia or Fellenberg's Hofwyl, which combined agriculture and general education. Third, model farms would also be valuable. Evans was adamant that farmers work in unison to improve their education, regardless of mother tongue.

Briefly, in 1842, he edited (from Montreal) the Toronto-based *British American Cultivator*. Not wealthy – he always had to farm for a living – Evans believed that a paper would succeed only with government financial support. In 1843, he relaunched his paper, now the *Canadian Agricultural Journal*, and the next year he approached the Canadian assembly for a grant.[52] He had the support of both Governor General Sir Charles Metcalfe (1785–1846) and Reformer Robert Baldwin (1804–1858). MLA Malcolm Cameron, along with William "Tiger" Dunlop (1792–1848), moved to strike a select committee to study the request. In the ensuing debate, Cameron argued for sending Evans's journal, in English and French, to all parishes and for placing a large number with the superintendents of public instruction. In a second attempt to strike a committee, his seconder, Col. John Prince (1796–1870), MLA for Essex, argued: "Sufficient encouragement was not given to Agriculture by the government ... It was not only the source of wealth, but the only true wealth of a nation." According to Attorney-General James Smith (1806–1868), however, "The means proposed to be adopted for the benefit of Agriculture were not the best to arrive at the ends sought; the circulation of a journal through a Canadian population, part only of which could read, would do but little good." The government would do something useful, but "the publication of newspapers which conveyed theory, without the details of practice, was utterly useless." A.-N. Morin responded:

Il [Morin] ne connait pas de meilleur moyen pour disséminer [sic] les connaissances dont nos cultivateurs ont besoin qu'une publication périodique consacrée à la science de l'agronomie. C'est en vulgarisant la science qu'elle devient réellement utile, et cela est vrai surtout par rapport à l'agriculture. L'hon. et savant monsieur reprend M. le procureur-général pour avoir prétendu qu'un journal comme celui de M. Evans ne serait pas utile, dans la supposition qu'il ne serait pas lu; que c'était là une grave erreur, et que les Canadiens, au contraire, le rechercheraient avec avidité.[53]

None the less, the sponsors withdrew the motion.

The *Canadian Agricultural Journal* survived until 1868, with several name changes and occasional French-language editions.[54] With the 1847 formation of the Agricultural Society of Lower Canada/Société d'agriculture du Bas-Canada, Evans became its secretary, and his newspaper the society's official journal the following year. A French version appeared continuously from that time on. Like most papers of its period, it mixed news from agricultural societies with hints for practical farmers and reprints from other journals, both domestic and foreign. When the provincial government formed the Lower Canada Board of Agriculture in 1852, Evans became its secretary, and his journal then became its official organ. In 1856, Evans published another series of letters on agriculture;[55] he reported some progress in Lower Canada, but farmers still not adept at ploughing, drainage, green-cropping, and pasturage as part of rotation – his British-style ideal. After Evans died in 1857, Joseph-Xavier (or -François) Perrault (1836–1905), grandson of Joseph-François Perrault (1753–1844), succeeded Evans as editor and secretary. Under a new title, *La revue agricole* (in 1861), the journal remained in Perrault's hands until Confederation.

In the eastern section of the province, the most important paper was Firmin Proulx's *Le gazette des campagnes* (1861–95), published in Kamouraska and later at the Collège de Ste-Anne-de-la-Pocatière in the Kamouraska region. Whether journals in Lower Canada reached a large number of farmers is doubtful. In 1851, Governor General Lord Elgin distributed 50,000 copies of a booklet on dealing with exhausted soil, but Séguin suspects that low levels of literacy made such efforts of little use: "L'écrit n'était pas, au Bas-Canada, le moyen de rejoindre et de convaincre le paysan."[56]

Upper Canada offers no evidence of agricultural journals before the 1840s.[57] Evans's contemporaries there were William Graham Edmundson, William McDougall, and George Buckland. Edmundson,[58] whose career featured a long series of controversies and financial crises, founded the *British American Cultivator* in Toronto in 1842. He gave editorial backing to progressive ideas such as agricultural societies, clubs, model farms, manual-labour schools, libraries, a chair of agriculture at the Anglican King's College (Toronto), a provincial association, and agricultural education in general. He wrote an editorial in his first issue:

> The great advancements which Agriculture has made in Great Britain, within the last half century, furnish a very interesting example of the improvements of which this science is susceptible. We need only notice the amendments introduced into different sections of these provinces within the last fifteen years by emigrants from the British Isles, to show that much improvement may be made in the general practice of Agriculture. Every available exertion shall be used, on our part, to advance the true interests of the cultivators of the soil, by extending an improved system of cultivation through every portion of the Provinces, and encouraging the more extensive use of articles, the produce of our domestic manufactures.[59]

Edmundson petitioned the legislature unsuccessfully for assistance in 1845. He befriended George Buckland (1804–1885), who toured the province in the early 1840s.[60] Buckland, a member of the Royal Agricultural Society in England, wished to create a model farm and school in Canada. He returned to Canada West permanently in 1847 to become professor of agriculture at King's College; as that position was in abeyance, Edmundson brought him in as assistant editor of the *British American Cultivator*.

The agricultural press and societies had close links in Canada West, as they did in the eastern province. In 1846, Edmundson became first secretary-treasurer of the Upper Canada Agricultural Association. William McDougall (1822–1905), a young lawyer and leading Grit politician, had been an agent for Edmundson in 1842. He founded a rival, semi-monthly paper, *Canada Farmer*, in 1847. Edmundson must have fallen out with his publishers, Eastwood and Company, for in January 1848 he and McDougall created the *Agriculturist and Canadian Journal*, which did not survive the year. Eastwood replied in October with *Farmer and Mechanic*, which, though strongly supportive of scientific farming, was less compelling than Edmundson's publication.

Edmundson, condemned for mismanagement of funds in the provincial association and under a cloud financially, moved to the United States in 1849. In January of that year, McDougall formed the *Canadian Agriculturist* with Buckland; it was the provincial association's official journal until the government reorganized agriculture in 1857, when the Board of Agriculture took over the paper. McDougall dropped out, leaving editorial matters to Buckland and the board's secretary, Hugh C. Thomson (c. 1822–1877), a proprietor of the Toronto *Colonist*. In 1863, the board sold the paper, a financial burden, to George Brown (1818–1880), publisher of the Toronto *Globe*. It expired that year and gave way to Brown's new *Canada Farmer*, with Rev. William F. Clarke (1824–1902) as editor. A rival to Brown's journal appeared just before Confederation, the London-based *Farmer's Advocate*, under farmer and entrepreneur William Weld (1824–1891).

All these journals, and others as well, consistently supported agricultural education and scientific techniques, despite the squabbles among their editors. Because of their greater literacy, Upper Canadian farmers were more likely to read agricultural papers than their Lower Canadian counterparts. While circulation numbers were not substantial anywhere, readership may have been larger.[61] For England 1840–70, Goddard estimates that an average of at least three people read each copy of an agricultural paper.[62] If that was true in Canada, news and new ideas reached perhaps a wider audience than we might imagine.

## THE STATE AND AGRICULTURE

### Feeling Its Way (1841–52)

Before the Union of the Canadas in 1841, the provincial authorities, because of their social and political views, generally ignored agriculture. Funding of agricultural and related activities was scarce and sporadic and tended to favour the well-off farmer. After the Union, these grants grew considerably, and, just as responsible government was coming in in the late 1840s, closer control of this funding became necessary. The emergence in the late 1840s of the two provincial agricultural organizations – the Upper Canada Agricultural Association and the Agricultural Society of Lower Canada – and the 1850 debates over the special committee's report on Lower Canadian agriculture spurred planning of a more structured approach.

The two agricultural societies naturally appealed to more successful farmers in districts with more settlers, but a number of urban members took a keen interest. With their political influence and links to legislators such as Malcolm Cameron and Joseph-Charles Taché (1820–1894), these bodies formed an effective lobby for reform. By 1850, the legislature's only direct connection with agriculture was through grants to local societies and to the two provincial organizations. If the state were to intervene more fully in the agricultural industry or, more specifically, in education, it would have to feel its own way. Britain, the source of so many ideas on agricultural improvement, would seem the first place to seek models but was curiously backward.[63] While Scottish improvers had formed the Highland and Agricultural Society in 1784, only a few years before Lord Dorchester's Canadian society, the Agricultural Society of England appeared only in 1837. Not until 1845 did the private Royal Agricultural College at Cirencester in Gloucestershire open, long before other educational institutions.

After the decennial census and the Great Exhibition in Hyde Park in 1851, the Scot James Caird's *English Agriculture in 1850–51* (1852) argued for more agricultural education. His ideas were out of the mainstream, as the Great Exhibition signalled and triggered improvement of manufactures, not of agriculture. The state apparatus for creating technical instruction – the Science and Art Department – virtually ignored

agriculture until 1878. The British government had nothing comparable to a department of agriculture in the North American sense. The
Board of Agriculture had long since lapsed. The Board of Trade gath-
ered agricultural statistics, and there was a veterinary department; these
two fused in 1883 as the Agricultural Department of the Privy Council.
Only in 1889, in the wake of serious discussion of technical education,
did the government form a Board of Agriculture (which absorbed the
Land Commission) to encourage education.[64] Canadians had to devise
their own model or adapt American ones.

Several US states funded local organizations, but by the 1830s much
of this support had evaporated. Beginning in 1839, the US Patent Office
could spend small amounts on distribution of seed and publication of
reports, but southern opposition was strong. Although the new United
States Agricultural Society called in 1853 for a cabinet-level department,
it was not until 1862, during the Civil War, that Congress created the
Department of Agriculture, which achieved cabinet representation
finally in 1889. The Canadian legislature had to build its administrative
machinery practically from scratch, and by 1867 it had surpassed Britain
and the United States.

In the summer of 1850, the neophyte Rimouski MLA J.-C. Taché
pressed the assembly to appoint a committee to look at agriculture in
Canada East, which it did, and named him chair. To do its work quickly,
the body circularized the province to collect information, as it had few
statistics. William Evans had strong views on public funding: "It is not to
the most skilful and most wealthy of our farmers *alone*, that Legislative
grants for the improvement of our Agriculture should be paid. Let the
poor unskilful farmer derive some benefit from it also; by instructing
and encouraging him to adopt a better system of husbandry. Farming
societies who subscribe their own funds may adopt such regulations as
they think proper for distributing them; but it is not so where public
money is granted to produce improvement rather than reward improvement."[65] Taché's inquiry collected letters, some very thoughtful and
detailed, from a wide constituency.[66] It learned that county agricultural
societies had made a positive impact, although their financial management often made local farmers distrustful. As for informal education,
the committee suggested a change in the awarding of prizes. Societies
typically honoured superior livestock or the best specimens of grain or
vegetables. To encourage better farming, the committee proposed special exhibition societies to award prizes for such categories as best vegetable crops for cattle, most manure applied, most compost produced on

a farm, best producing meadow, or largest flock of cattle fed from the farm's produce.

Several members pushed for model farms and publishing practical treatises, and the committee recommended both. A jargon-free pamphlet, in English and French and distributed widely, would be sufficient, although different literacy rates would have made distribution very uneven. Following the education department's example, the committee proposed hiring two agricultural superintendents who would act as inspectors and teachers. In all, prizes for the proposed exhibition societies, schools and model farms, an agricultural treatise, more funds for the provincial society, and salaries for two superintendents would cost £7,500 a year. Therefore the provincial agricultural society needed more money.

Also in 1850, the legislature set up a Board of Agriculture for Canada West (13/14 Vict., cap. 73), with George Buckland as secretary. The Upper Canada Agricultural Association, in particular Buckland and McDougall, fostered the bill, and McDougall drafted it. The board was to run the Agricultural Association and receive annual reports from local societies. The legislature was probably trying to monitor the spending of government grants, which many North American jurisdictions were trying to do.[67] The board would adopt the *Canadian Agriculturist* as its official publication but in 1856 launched its own *Journal and Transactions*.

Agricultural education would probably fall within the purview of the educational offices. Both superintendents of public instruction, Egerton Ryerson for Canada West and Jean-Baptiste Meilleur for Canada East, wanted agricultural instruction throughout their systems. Canada's rudimentary administration[68] did not represent education offices directly in the executive council, or cabinet (also British practice), but made them administrative units reporting to the provincial secretary. Before the 1850s, in the absence of modern ministries, no one in cabinet could speak for agriculture on a continuing basis.

## A Minister, a Bureau, and Two Boards (1852–67)

Agriculture was, however, the country's largest industry, and it acquired the first modern-style ministry with creation in November 1852 of the Bureau of Agriculture, with Malcolm Cameron as minister. Its creation addressed questions in Taché's 1850 report, and the Upper Canada Board of Agriculture, in its first report, had called for a ministry. The legislation[69] created a dual system of administration: a new Lower Canada Board of Agriculture/Chambre d'agriculture du Bas-Canada

(William Evans, secretary) was to mirror the two-year-old Upper Canada Board. These bodies would guide the provincial associations and handle grants through their offices in Montreal and Toronto, which received mandates to create agricultural museums and libraries. The new organization, headed by a single bureau, would funnel grants downwards through the two boards, provincial associations, and local societies, which would all send annual reports back up the chain. The museums and libraries would stimulate education by collecting and disseminating information about new techniques and implements.

Each of the boards had an annual budget of £2,000, which had to cover the costs of the provincial exhibitions. By 1854, the Upper Canada Board reported a small library in place but no museum. It had set up a small experimental farm in connection with the new chair in agriculture at the University of Toronto with the hope (never realized) of expanding it into a botanical garden. The new Lower Canada Board, in the absence of a functioning Agricultural Society, organized the first provincial exhibition, in Montreal, in 1853.[70] Two years earlier, the correspondent "Quebec" had argued for an annual provincial show: "We certainly have our County and District Exhibitions, but it is too well known these Shows are conducted in a most ignorant and inefficient manner ... Our Agricultural Exhibitions, as at present conducted, are a source of very slight advantage to the country, and afford little more than another proof of our total want of knowledge, in connection with Modern Farming."[71] The solution would be to suppress county societies completely and use their grants to produce better district shows and to hold an annual provincial exhibition. In the mid-1860s, the explorer and educator Henry Youle Hind (1823–1908) saw little to impress him: "The Lower Canadian Provincial Shows have partaken more of the character of an agricultural festival, hitherto, than of a meeting for the purpose of securing the progress of the Science and Art of Agriculture by fair and open competition and peaceful rivalry. In this respect they have differed materially from the same annual expositions in Upper Canada, where astonishing advances in the proper direction have been made."[72]

Once the Bureau of Agriculture was in place, discussion regarding state intervention in agricultural education began anew. Although the Upper Canada Board supported the idea of an experimental farm for the university, it doubted "whether Model Farms, strictly so called, are adapted to the present wants of this young country."[73] Others had no qualms: Charles Treadwell of the Prescott and Russell Agricultural Society and John Ramsay of L'Orignal both petitioned for model farms for eastern Upper Canada.[74]

As minister, Cameron took up agricultural questions with vigour. In 1853, he dispatched McDougall to the New York State Fair to study the agricultural implements. McDougall argued that provincial museums require £400–£500 each for implements if they were to be as useful as the museum in Albany. Indeed, more money was necessary for all projects: "Unless more decisive and thorough measures are speedily adopted, the whole project will miscarry, and not the least of the evils to be apprehended from its failure is the prejudice it will excite in the public mind against all scientific demonstration in the art of Agriculture."[75]

Cameron's first departmental report opined that model farms were a good idea and obviously worked well in Europe. He believed that a Canadian version would have to teach a variety of subjects – as was the case at the French college at Grignon, or at Cirencester or Hofwyl – such as arboriculture, chemistry, geology, horticulture, mathematics, mineralogy, natural philosophy, rural legislation, and veterinary surgery and medicine. And he outlined additional requirements: "A model farm of three or four hundred acres must have buildings to correspond, including the most complete arrangements of the present day, and a literary department, with numerous chairs; the professors for which must be men of the first rank in science. I do not enter into any calculations to shew the expenditure likely to be connected with an institution established on such a scale, believing that it is not adapted to our present necessities."[76]

Cameron believed it made more sense to establish agricultural chairs in existing institutions, such as McGill, and to provide land for experimental work. By 1856, the bureau's annual report claimed that agricultural productivity had increased 17 per cent since 1851, partly because of the encouragement by societies and the board's journals. Results might be better yet if the common schools emphasized agriculture and if "prominent persons" were to lecture across the province.[77]

The man most responsible for organizing the pre-Confederation agricultural department was William Hutton,[78] an Irish immigrant and cousin of sometime-premier Sir Francis Hincks. Settling in the Belleville area, he was an energetic, improving farmer and author of an immigration guide. Entering local affairs, he helped organize the Belleville Mechanics' Institute in 1852 and was the first warden of Hastings County. He became a clerk of statistics in 1852 and then secretary of the Board of Registration and Statistics in 1853. Because of his continuing interest in agriculture, he asked Sir Francis to appoint him secretary (i.e., deputy minister) of the new agriculture bureau. Nothing came of this immediately.

During the winter of 1853–54, Hutton was sent to Ireland to lecture on the advantages of emigration to Canada. With an eye open for educational materials, he dispatched copies of the *Dublin Advocate and Industrial Journal* to Buckland. On his return to Canada, in his capacity as secretary of the Statistics Board, he presented a memo on the bureau's organization to the executive council,[79] which on 20 February 1855 concurred. Although the bureau did not print his report officially, it does survive in manuscript.[80] Adverting to the bureau's duties to "institute enquiries & collect useful facts & statistics" and to disseminate these to improve Canadian farming, Hutton claims that these activities "have been if not wholly neglected, very imperfectly carried out." He believed that the boards of agriculture's agricultural statistics should be readily available to the public and proposed uniting his own statistical board with the agricultural one to collect and publish information – a single secretary (himself) would preside over the joint bureau, with five clerks assisting. He also suggested a quarterly journal similar to that of the Highland and Agricultural Society.

### Reorganization (1857–62)

Most of Hutton's ideas bore fruit in the revised Agricultural Act of 1857.[81] The basic structure of 1852 remained, with the secretaries of the two Boards of Agriculture reporting through the secretary of the Bureau of Agriculture to the minister of agriculture. The secretary for Canada East was still William Evans (who would die in 1857), but Canada West had recently passed from William McDougall, still co-editor of the *Canadian Agriculturist,* to George Buckland, now professor of agriculture at the University of Toronto and later McDougall's successor as editor.

One major innovation in the 1857 act: new Boards of Arts and Manufactures for both halves of the province to deal with *technical* education (see chapter 3, below: section on the act). Board members would also sit on the executive of the provincial agricultural associations, which led McDougall to comment acidly that the Upper Canada Agricultural Association "therefore ceases to be an *agricultural* Association – its original aim – and becomes an affair of Trades, Mechanics, Manufactures, Arts &c. &c. The Association had already extended its arms so as to embrace large portions of these mechanical productions, to the very serious injury of the agricultural objects for which it was established. What it will become under Mr. Vankoughnet's remodelling remains to be seen ... The presidents of all the Mechanics' Institutes, and Boards of Trade *within the country* are made Directors of the Agricultural Society! What are these gentlemen likely to know about agriculture?"[82]

The 1857 act clarified the roles of the various agricultural players. The bureau would collect and publish agricultural statistics from the provincial boards and local societies. The Boards of Agriculture would provide education: establish "model, illustrative or experimental farm or farms" in connection with an educational institution, provide for a museum and library, collect and test new implements and techniques, and publish articles useful to farmers and a monthly journal or adopt an existing agricultural journal. County societies were to disseminate information.

In Canada West, the Board of Agriculture and the Upper Canada Agricultural Association concentrated on the peripatetic annual provincial exhibition. Following the models of the Great Exhibition of 1851 and the Dublin Exhibition of 1853, it erected a "crystal palace" for the 1856 show in Kingston and more crystal palaces in Toronto (1858), Hamilton (1860), and London (1861).[83]

Although the Bureau of Agriculture's reach seemed extensive, in practice it had a low political profile. The premier doubled as minister for agriculture until creation of the Department of Agriculture and Statistics in 1862. In all, by the time of Confederation, ten men had held the post. Only two, Jean-Charles Chapais, *père* (1811–1885),[84] who would become the first federal minister in 1867, and Thomas D'Arcy McGee (1825–1868), had much interest in either agriculture or education. Most of the bureau's energies went into an increasing jumble of administrative functions, including patents, immigration, colonization roads, the census, and statistics.[85]

In 1859, the new Board of Arts and Manufactures approached the Upper Canada Board to cooperate with it, along with the Canadian Institute, the scientific society that Sanford Fleming (1827–1915) had founded in 1849, and others bodies, to form a common museum and library.[86] Nothing came of the proposal. In 1861, Ryerson's *Journal of Education* reported the speech of J. Barwick, president of the Upper Canada Agricultural Association, on agricultural education and the board's decision to erect an agricultural museum in Toronto.[87] The resulting Agricultural Hall opened at Queen and Yonge Streets in 1862, to house the offices of the board, a museum, and a library.[88] Some years passed, however, before the library had books and journals.

### A Full-fledged Department (1862–67)

In 1862, the bureau became a full-fledged department. The minister, François Evanturel (1821–1891), who took more interest than did his predecessors in its operations, admitted that it was a mess due to neglect: "Its organization and internal discipline had been left in a condition so little efficient that the public had begun to doubt the necessity or the importance of keeping it up, under the special management of a Member of the Executive Government. The lengthened absence of certain of my predecessors, and the consequent want of any responsible superintendence and direction, the small number of permanent officers attached to the Department, the too ready admission and dismissal of temporary employees, whose interest in the public weal is of a passing nature, and, to crown all, the death of the Secretary, Mr. Hutton, have with several other circumstances contributed to reduce the Department to a state of disorganization, which is much to be regretted; and for which, when I entered on office, I had, as far as possible, to provide a speedy and sufficient remedy."[89]

Evanturel knew about British and French activity in terms of organization – and thought the French much superior – and the recent US passage of the Morrill Act, which provided support for schools of agriculture and mechanical arts. For Canada, the minister grasped the needs of his bailiwick: "Thus, in 1850, the most serious obstacles to the good working of our system of agricultural organization were perfectly understood, and the preceding suggestions apply with equal force at the present time."

Although Evanturel and his successor, Luc Letellier de Saint-Just (1820–1881), tinkered with the department as best they could, they knew that it needed a full-time deputy minister – they wanted Taché. He had resigned his seat in the legislature in 1856 and after a career in journalism had become chair of the Board of Prison Inspectors. He became deputy minister of the department in 1864 and served with distinction well past 1867.

Yet the Department of Agriculture had few links with the country's agricultural interests. As McGee lamented: "It is to be regretted that the relations between the Department and the two Boards of Agriculture for Upper and Lower Canada, if they ever were intimate, have ceased to be so. The correspondence between my office and these important bodies [is] reduced to mere occasional, strictly official letters, in relations with election of officers or the issuing of warrants for money. Many things could be, and must ultimately be done by the combined efforts of the Department, of the Boards and of the Societies; the ends to be attained, the means of attaining them, have been, and will continue to be, the subject of constant consideration till the plan is sufficiently matured to be safely carried into practice."[90] In contrast, the department had excellent relations with the new US Department of Agriculture, which regularly forwarded its publications, McGee hoped that Canada would eventually be able to reciprocate.

## SUMMARY

Before 1830, informal means of disseminating new agricultural knowledge through discussions, competitions, premiums, fairs, and the agricultural press scarcely existed in either Canadian province. The rise of agricultural societies was slow until government subsidies appeared in the 1830s. Despite class issues, with very poor farmers probably having no connection with societies at all, these bodies did institute local and later provincial exhibitions. In these activities, they followed American as much as British practice. In Lower Canada, francophone farmers were less likely to participate than were their anglophone counterparts.

By the 1840s, the agricultural press was active, but not exactly thriving, and although agricultural journalism was very much a cut-and-paste practice, writers such as Buckland, Edmundson, Evans, McDougall, and Perrault spoke out loudly enough in their editorial columns to prod farmers and government alike. The successes of the Upper Canadian provincial exhibitions and the appearance of umbrella organizations in both halves of the united province before 1850 created pressure on legislators to erect a bureaucratic machinery to deal with their needs. Again, this followed American, not British, models.

Indeed, thanks to pressures of the agricultural community, Canada's construction of a modern liberal state accelerated in the decade before Confederation. A feature of the emerging liberal state in Europe, the United States, and Canada was the gathering and using of statistics, and this was the primary role of Canada's embryonic Department of Agriculture. Collection of data on output was one possible way to monitor the effect of informal education. Knowledge of the contours of the rural population would be equally valuable, and J.-C. Taché presided over both.

# Formal Education for the Farmer to 1867

Informal means of transmitting new knowledge about agriculture origi-
nated in the eighteenth century – as we saw above in chapter 1 – but
formal education in an agricultural school began in the nineteenth.
From its start in Switzerland, the agricultural school concentrated on
manual labour and teaching technique. Science had yet to provide much
of value to agriculture. By the 1830s, however, the new and developing
agricultural chemistry seemed to some observers to be a panacea for
increasing productivity.

In Canada, the idea of combining training in technique with the new
science of agriculture was widespread, but local conditions influenced
the choice of approaches. Upper Canadian promoters had less success
than their Lower Canadian counterparts, but training in agriculture
accomplished little in either part of the pre-Confederation United
Province. A complicating factor was the creation and expansion of public common schools. Who would control agricultural education, and
what form would it take? In social terms, its promoters also supported
agricultural societies and their activities.

## THE IRISH EXAMPLE

Because Canadians had little experience in creating educational institutions, they looked abroad for models. The crucial example for them was
Ireland, which boasted the earliest systematic attempt to provide agricultural instruction to a broad population.[1] Unlike the situation in England,
in Ireland the Board of National Education (created in 1831) directed
non-denominational state schools. In one of its earliest ventures, it set up
a central model school (later, a central normal school) in Dublin to train

teachers, but soon realized that teachers would require agricultural training for such an overwhelmingly rural nation. In 1838, the board opened a model farm in the northern Dublin suburb of Glasnevin for students of the normal school. The farm, later the Albert National Agricultural Training Institution (after Queen Victoria's husband, Prince Albert), soon also took on residential students. The commissioners hoped that teachers would establish gardens or small experimental farms adjacent to rural schools and become "apostles of agricultural instruction and agricultural improvement."[2] By 1851, the Glasnevin farm, with more land, expanded to accommodate 100 residential students, who worked the farm, while both they and teacher-trainees attended lectures on such agricultural subjects as botany, chemistry, geology, and mineralogy. As early as 1842, the commissioners were planning an agricultural textbook for the national schools, but because the subject was not compulsory, individual teachers and school managers made the decision whether or not to include it.[3]

Another Irish innovation had resonance in Canada. At the depths of the famine in 1847, the lord lieutenant of Ireland, George Villiers, 4th Earl of Clarendon (1800–1870), supplied funds for itinerant agricultural instructors whom the Royal Agricultural Society of Ireland was organizing. These "practical instructors" would travel through the worst-hit districts, teaching modern cropping and drainage methods. By 1850, some twenty instructors were active. When Lord Clarendon left office in 1852, the scheme died. This is one of the earliest examples of agricultural extension work anywhere and served as a model for future Canadian endeavours, which inspired many Canadians.

This chapter has three main sections: (1) early attempts at agricultural training: in Canada East, through specialized schools and by teaching agriculture in schools and normal schools, and, in Toronto, in Egerton Ryerson's normal school; (2) involvement by the universities of Toronto, McGill, and Laval in the 1850s; and (3) specialized agricultural education in the 1850s–60s.

## EARLY ATTEMPTS AT AGRICULTURAL TRAINING (1830S–50S)

### Efforts in the 1830s

Lower Canada was much keener to adopt formal education in agriculture than was Upper Canada, perhaps because of its earlier settlement, but also because of the difficulty of farming in the St Lawrence Valley. Two schemes for agricultural schools in the Quebec area surfaced in 1832.[4] English schoolmaster William Henry Shadgett, at Lac Beauport, approached the legislature for a grant to open a model farm and school at Charlesbourg; on 23 January 1832, the legislature refused, citing Shadgett's lack of expertise and the out-of-the-way location. This rejection seemed to be a stimulus for Joseph-François Perrault, the notary and author we saw above,[5] who claimed to have thought of organizing a school as early as 1807. Perrault called a public meeting in Quebec in January 1832 to secure support for a school. To assist him, he chose Amury Girod (see chapter 1), who was a graduate of the Hofwyl school. Perrault's model farm and school opened in the spring of 1832 but attracted only between five and ten students. Without a grant, he exhausted his funds, and the school closed within the year.

The upper province showed its first glimmer of interest in 1836. Reform MLA Dr Charles Duncombe (1792–1867) knew about current practices in France and Prussia, had toured educational efforts in Boston and New York State, and prepared a far-sighted report on education, to which he appended a draft education bill. Duncombe suggested authorizing trustees to "purchase or lease a lot or parcel of land, farming utensils, seeds, grains and grasses for the use, benefit and behoof of that district ... or otherwise employed and occupied, for the profit and instruction of the school or parts thereof, in horticulture, agriculture, or otherwise, growing plants, fruits, grasses and grains."[6] Although the bill passed the assembly in April 1836, the legislative council rejected it.

### Canada East (1840s and 1850s)

WORKING FOR A SPECIALIZED SCHOOL (1849–52)
The Agricultural Society of Lower Canada petitioned the assembly in 1849 to establish agricultural schools and model farms in each district of eastern Canada.[7] The report of Taché's 1850 select committee, noting the cost of agricultural colleges with farms, suggested merely adding farms to a few existing colleges.[8]

In 1851, the society drafted its response (20 May) and forwarded to the assembly its report and responses to a questionnaire it had circulated. Another special committee, again under Taché, reviewed the society's study and reported in August.[9] The society argued that before the government created five model farms, the prospective professors needed training and that, specifically, the province should hire a first-rate man to provide a two-year course in agricultural chemistry, botany, geology, veterinary medicine, and other branches of agriculture. The society applauded the committee's support for distributing publications – Lord Elgin's office had, as we saw above, arranged for the distribution of 50,000 booklets on rehabilitating exhausted soil in 1851 – and promised to provide an agricultural reader. Because of low levels of literacy in rural areas, however, most observers expected only readers with some knowledge of modern technique.

The special committee reiterated some of the arguments of the 1850 report, primarily the call for two agricultural superintendents[10] and textbooks for common schools. There was no easy solution: "Your Committee do not pause to consider other means of encouraging Agriculture, particularly the adoption of Model Schools of Agriculture; finding, as they do, too great diversity of opinion within the narrow bounds of the present grant of the Legislature."[11] The private Catholic *collèges classiques* had exhibited no interest, but in August 1851 the Séminaire de Québec requested one of its staff members, the abbé Edward John Horan (1817–1875), to inquire into establishing a model farm at its property in St-Joachim. Horan was to go to Montreal to speak with William Evans, secretary of the Lower Canada Board of Agriculture, purchase equipment, and then travel to the United States to observe schools and farms there; however, the seminary soon dropped the plan.[12]

In the meanwhile, the provincial society, out of frustration, acquired a five-year lease in 1851 on 500 *arpents* (about 422 acres) at St Philippe-de-la-Prairie, on the Rivière Tortue, several kilometres south of Laprairie. There it established a model farm and the Collège agronomique de la Tortue, which opened in 1852 under Frédéric-M.-F. Ossaye. Unable to obtain a provincial subsidy, the school closed the following year. Ossaye,[13] who came from France in 1850 after supervising a model farm for several years, published a number of books and articles on agriculture during his stay in Canada.

The call for a textbook suitable for common schools inspired the journalist and printer Stanislas Drapeau (1821–1893), who requested aid for *The Cultivator, or Elementary Treatise on Practical Agriculture, designed for the use of the schools in Lower Canada*. Taché tabled his petition in October 1852.[14]

AGRICULTURE IN RURAL SCHOOLS (1840S)
As specialized agricultural schools, or at least model farms, were not a priority for the government, it considered the Irish vision of introducing agriculture into ordinary rural schools. This would require a normal

school with model farm to train teachers, ideally those with some practical experience, in the rudiments of agriculture.[15]

A powerful voice in the educational debate was that of lawyer and later
judge Charles Mondelet (1801–1876), whom Governor General Lord
Sydenham (1799–1841) urged to publicize his views. Mondelet's series
of letters in *Canada Times* later became *Letters on Elementary and Practical
Education* (1841). He proposed that the government and taxpayers
finance a system of schools in both languages. At the top would be normal schools with farms for teaching the theory and practice of agriculture and horticulture. While some of his ideas influenced Lower
Canada's emerging school system, agriculture would appear in normal
schools only after 1860.

By the early 1840s, Superintendent of Public Instruction Jean-Baptiste
Meilleur wished to introduce scientific agriculture into common schools
but knew that that would require normal schools – ideally following the
Irish model of local agricultural schools with a central agricultural normal school – and thought J.-F. Perrault's scheme for a school viable;[16]
indeed, Perrault wanted to expand his agricultural school into an agricultural normal school. In the absence of a training school with agriculture in the curriculum, it is doubtful that more than a few teachers could
have taught the subject even in an elementary manner.

## NEW COUNCIL AND NORMAL SCHOOLS (1856–57)

In 1856, the Province of Canada created the Council of Public Instruction
for Lower Canada, consisting of ten Catholic members and four Protestants,
most of them lay people. The next year, the council established three normal schools – one English (at McGill) and one French (Jacques-Cartier,
for men only) in Montreal, and one French (Laval) in Quebec – but with
little agricultural content, although the abbé Jean Langevin (1821–1892)
taught the subject to boys an hour a week for half the year at Quebec's
Ecole normale Laval. In 1860, at Montreal's Ecole normale Jacques-
Cartier, Frédéric Ossaye offered free agricultural lessons; J.-D. Schmouth
(1842–1917) attended these, took a diploma in the subject, and became
an agricultural instructor at Ste-Anne-de-la-Pocatière.

## VARENNES AND STE-THÉRÈSE (1857–60)

The key promoter of agricultural schools was Joseph-Xavier (or
-François) Perrault, J.-F. Perrault's grandson; J.-X., unlike J.-F., had formal training – from the Imperial Agricultural School at Grignon and
from the Royal Agricultural College at Cirencester. After his return to

Canada in 1857, he sought to open agricultural schools in Varennes (1857–61) and Ste-Thérèse-de-Blainville (1861–63).[17] He tried to convince directors of the local industrial college in Varennes to convert it into a Collège agricole et commercial. In the meantime, the classes there that commenced in September 1860 were practical: "Le cours d'agriculture de la ferme essai de Varennes sera un cours d'agriculture pratique dans lequel les professeurs s'aideront des sciences accessoires le moins possible et seulement dans le but de fair comprendre le pourquoi des différentes opérations agricoles."[18] After a year's operation and one student, the school closed.

### *Egerton Ryerson's Normal School (1844–53)*

In creating a normal school, Upper Canada had a decade's head start, lacking linguistic and confessional differences. In 1844, Superintendent of Public Instruction Rev. Egerton Ryerson,[19] having seen a variety of examples at first hand, became a champion of agricultural education. He remained central to the debates over both agricultural and technical education until his retirement in 1876. A convert to Methodism, he had been ordained in the Methodist Episcopal Church in 1827 and was active in church affairs until education became his focus in the late 1830s. He founded the Upper Canada Academy in Cobourg in 1836 and, having obtained degree-granting powers from the province, opened Victoria University there in 1841. He was briefly principal and in 1844 became superintendent of education in Canada West (a post he would hold – later in Ontario – till 1876). The themes of agricultural and technical education would be a constant throughout his career, and Ryerson sought to dominate them[20] but accomplished little.

As Upper Canada had no agricultural training, Ryerson was open to any applicable models. Agricultural training in Prussia and in Switzerland had impressed him during a study tour in the 1840s. France, with several types of industrial education, did little about agriculture.[21] Ryerson also kept a close watch on US developments. New York opened a state normal school in 1844, and the next year Governor Silas Wright (1795–1847) asked it to teach agriculture. Ryerson thought highly of Ireland's Board of National Education, particularly its central normal school and Glasnevin model farm. Following its example, he argued that agriculture belonged in common schools, but the legislation of 1846 did not mention it.[22]

Ryerson applied the Dublin model to his new provincial normal school in Toronto in 1847. The educational department and normal school started out in the old Upper Canadian parliament building on Front Street, and Ryerson made the grounds available to the new Upper Canada Agricultural Association for its provincial exhibition in 1848.[23] Ryerson brought over a headmaster from Dublin, and to teach mathematics, chemistry, and natural philosophy he chose Henry Youle Hind, an energetic figure who later became controversial.[24]

Son of a lace manufacturer, Hind had studied at the Nottingham Free Grammar School and then for two years at Leipzig's Handelslehranstalt, a technical school. After a year at Cambridge, he studied in France and travelled in the United States before arriving in Toronto in 1846. Although he had no degree, Ryerson hired him in October 1847. He lectured on agricultural chemistry, laid out an experimental garden on the school grounds, and for two years experimented with growing crop varieties and testing wooden drains. He was an enthusiastic convert to agricultural education. In 1848, he wrote four articles on "Agricultural Education in Upper Canada" for Ryerson's *Journal of Education*.[25] He thought that university professorships in agriculture and agricultural schools with model farms would have little impact in Canada and thought it best to focus on common schools. Because of his own background, he believed that the primary topics should be agricultural chemistry and plant physiology, perhaps using Irish school texts, already covering some of this material.

In 1847, Ryerson's *Report on a System of Public Elementary Instruction for Upper Canada* appeared. It stated that he welcomed financial aid to agriculture by the legislature and its encouragement of agricultural societies, even though "experiments without a knowledge of principles will be of little benefit; and improvements in the practice of agriculture must be very limited until the science of it is studied."[26] He had given an address "On the Importance of Education to an Agricultural People" to several audiences during a provincial tour from September to December 1847, in which he asked the standard question of the time: why should the state support education for lawyers, but not for farmers? His view of agricultural progress was distinctly British (he cited Davy), but he was also aware of Jesse Buel's agitation for improvements in New York State.[27]

For Canada West, Ryerson adapted the Irish national school readers, which combined an emphasis on the "vegetable world" with mental culture. For his part, Hind lectured on the latest British practical techniques and the new science of Johnston, Davy, and the French organic chemist Jean-Baptiste Bouissangault (1802–1887). He believed that Canada would benefit from British agriculture only if schools taught agricultural chemistry. Such courses would involve rote learning and no laboratory practice, which was unknown in normal schools. In hindsight, agricultural chemistry lessons would have offered little to a new teacher in a rural school.

During the next two years, the *Journal of Education* included news items and extracts on a variety of topics: new agricultural schools in France, Prussia, Turkey, and the United States; the progress of the Irish agricultural schools; the education of American farmers; and Massachusetts and New York's hopes for their own schools (which did not materialize). After rioters burned Montreal's parliament building and the government moved to Toronto in 1849, the normal school's temporary shift to the Toronto Temperance Hall ended Hind's miniature model farm. On the positive side, Governor General Lord Elgin strongly supported the decision of Canada West's Board of Education to include agriculture in the curriculum. To stimulate interest, he offered two prizes in the amount of £5 and £2 for the best examinations on agriculture in the normal school, which it awarded in April 1849 after an exam on agricultural chemistry, vegetable and animal physiology, and the chemistry of food.[28]

Institutional competition raised its head the following year. In 1849, Robert Baldwin's legislation created the secular University of Toronto, supplanting the Anglican King's College. When a prominent member of the Upper Canada Agricultural Association, Adam Fergusson, wrote to the *Canadian Agriculturist* calling for an agricultural chair, Hind objected.[29] His view was that the normal school, which already taught the subject successfully, was the chair's natural home. A professor would do more good working with the Board of Agriculture than by merely lecturing – a prescient comment. What Hind and Ryerson really wanted was to attach a model farm like Glasnevin's to the normal school.

In 1853, the normal school's new home opened in St James' Square with grounds of some eight acres, two of them for a botanical garden and three for experimental agriculture.[30] Hind had left the year before to become professor of chemistry at the Trinity College medical school, where he had moonlighted since 1851. After his departure, the *Journal of Education* says nothing about experiments or agricultural teaching in the normal school. The ideal of teaching agriculture in the common schools also languished throughout the 1850s.

## AGRICULTURE IN THE UNIVERSITY (1850s–60s)

The idea of agriculture in higher education dates from the same period – the late 1840s – as agriculture appeared in Canada West's new normal school. Although university lectures in agricultural chemistry and rural

economy dated from 1790 at Edinburgh,[31] the idea of formal higher
education in agriculture was still novel in English-speaking countries in
the 1840s. That Edinburgh would support such a chair was something of
a fluke. Upper-class interest in the renewal of impoverished Scottish
agriculture had been high, and the university was the most notable
scientific, especially chemical, centre outside continental Europe. As a
theoretical subject, agriculture initially attracted some thirty students a
year, but the numbers later declined. The 1845 imperial proposals for
the three non-denominational Queen's Colleges of Ireland made provision for agricultural chairs in each.[32] For an overwhelmingly agricultural
nation, which already had local model farms and a national training
institution, higher education for farmers seemed to make sense. The
three colleges, in Belfast, Cork, and Galway, opened in 1849, each with
a professor of agriculture.[33] The two-year course of study, an adjunct to
the arts curriculum, was largely theoretical – no college had a model
farm – and attracted almost no students. At Belfast, the incumbent, Dr
John Hodges (1815–1899), a chemist and former student of Liebig's,
had never farmed himself and typically never had more than five students each year. According to the professors' testimony before a later
parliamentary inquiry, wealthy farmers wanted their sons to become professionals, while poorer farmers' sons had no preparation for university
work. After a decade, when all three colleges had awarded only thirteen
diplomas, the experiment collapsed.

In the United States,[34] Yale University supported a faculty post in agriculture during the mid-1840s. By 1855, Pennsylvania organized a high
school for farmers (which later became Pennsylvania State University),
and the University of Wisconsin offered lectures in agricultural chemistry. At the same time, the Michigan Normal School taught a little agricultural chemistry at Ypsilanti, and so did the University of Michigan at
Ann Arbor.

### Toronto (1840s–Mid-1860s)

Agitation for a chair in agriculture in King's College, Toronto (which
opened in 1843), took several years to succeed.[35] Pressure came largely
from the usual middle-class promoters – journalists and well-off farmers
– not from ordinary farmers. The discussion resonated with contemporary discussions in US agricultural journals. Robert Baldwin supported
higher education in agriculture from the start. During the 1845 debate
over William Evans's request for funds, he told the assembly that Evans's

petition "had his entire approval; no one was more anxious than himself to support the industry of the country, and he thought that Agriculture was a pursuit which called for the first and best intellects the country possessed; with that view he had endeavoured during the last Session, to put that science on a higher footing than it had hitherto occupied, by giving it an academical position in the Toronto College, in order that youth might be trained up to a respect for the occupation of their forefathers."[36]

The agitation came to a head in the late 1840s during the political struggles over the "university question," in which Baldwin was pivotal. As William McDougall noted in the *Agriculturist and Canadian Journal* in 1848: "We said the farmers of Canada have a *right* to claim a direct interest in the University revenue. It may be answered, so they have, and will have the privilege of sending their sons to be educated within its walls, on the same terms as others. But they don't want the *kind* of learning to be obtained there. It is not suited to them, unless they wish to become Lawyers or Doctors – either of which will probably be the very worst use that farmers can put their sons to. No, the farmers of this country, as such, will be practically excluded from the benefits of the University, unless a portion of its funds be appropriated for the support of an Agricultural School."[37]

Equally keen on the subject was McDougall's associate George Buckland. Baldwin and Adam Fergusson had lured him back to Canada in 1847, on the assumption that he would occupy the proposed chair of agriculture at King's College. Because the interminable squabbles over the university's nature made the promise unrealizable, Buckland marked time with journalism. Needless to say, he was not a disinterested observer.

When the secular University of Toronto replaced the Anglican King's College in 1849, the way was clear to create an agricultural department. In the same year, the new Queen's University of Ireland commenced operations. The structure at Toronto strongly resembled that of Queen's, its likely model.[38] Baldwin (whose father was born in Ireland) had spoken of an agricultural chair for Toronto in 1845, just when others were proposing the same for the three Irish colleges. The new University of Toronto's senate was in no hurry to appoint someone, but once the university finally agreed on the conditions of the new chair and surveyed the candidates, it duly named Buckland in October 1851.

Thus, the university was in the vanguard of higher education in agriculture, or so it seemed. Buckland created a small demonstration plot on the edge of the campus for student practice and developed a degree program. Students took his Theory and Practice of Agriculture, along with English and scientific subjects (botany, chemistry, geology, mineralogy, physical geography, and zoology). His was not a full university post – he received $1,200 per annum, half the usual salary – and his classes were very small. Fortunately, he became also dean of residence in 1859, when University College opened where it is today.

Buckland divided the syllabus of his course for 1861 into three sections: history, science, and practice of agriculture.[39] History included ancient, medieval, and modern agriculture. Science covered discussions of soils; plants, including botanical and agricultural chemistry topics; domesticated animals, including breeding and diseases; and climate and farming. Practice, with demonstrations on the experimental plot, dealt with agricultural literature; agriculture as a pursuit; crops, weeds, blights, and harvesting; cultivation; dairy management, butter and cheese making; drainage, including fallowing and rotation; manuring and irrigation; property management and political economy; and stock management and farm buildings. Lectures and textbooks provided the basis for knowledge of almost all these practical topics, as the university had no proper farm.

The university statute had provided for a forty-acre portion of the university grounds, extending north from the university to Second Concession, later Bloor Street, which the Board of Agriculture for Upper Canada would develop as an experimental farm. In 1852, a twenty-five-acre plot was under cultivation but not yet in use; the plan was to provide a place for Buckland to give practical demonstrations and for testing adaptation of plants and foreign livestock breeds to Canadian conditions. The board requested a grant of £500 towards development of the land, which it received in 1853, and the erection of some buildings. A proper experimental farm would have required more land, several buildings, a staff, and annual support for upkeep. None of this happened.[40]

Buckland's reference textbooks were – apart from J.-B. Boussingault's *Rural Economy* (an 1845 translation from the French) – British: J.F.W. Johnston's *Elements of Agricultural Chemistry and Geology*, the *London Encyclopaedia of Agriculture*, David Low's *Practical Agriculture and Domesticated Animals*, John C. Morton's *Cyclopaedia of Agriculture*, and Henry Stephens's *Farmer's Guide*. Some of these books were available from American publishers. This syllabus resembled those of the Irish colleges, and one wonders how much of Buckland's practical knowledge, deriving from English practice and conditions, was applicable in Canada West. Some students attended part time, and very few took a degree or diploma. A sample of the final examination in the course for 1857–58 appeared in the *Canadian Agriculturist* to give farmers an idea of what their sons might learn.[41] The exam consisted of brief questions requiring short written responses, based on rote, with no evidence of problem-solving.[42]

Whether or not a young man would become a more successful farmer with such training was open to serious question – certainly for farmers thinking of sending their sons to Toronto. Buckland had stumbled over the same obstacles as his colleagues had in Ireland. And, like them, he had to face an inquiry by a select committee of the legislature in 1860. He also had to deal with Superintendent Ryerson, who expected to monopolize agricultural education in the normal school and who argued pointedly that agriculture had no place in a university. When the university stopped teaching agriculture in 1864, the government did not train farmers again before Confederation. Buckland, like his counterpart Hodges in Belfast, spent his remaining years as merely titular professor of agriculture.

### J.W. Dawson and McGill (Late 1850s)

University training in agriculture had no greater success in Lower Canada. McGill University, though dating from 1821, was by the early 1850s practically moribund, with little money and few students. Its governing body, the Royal Institution for the Advancement of Learning, underwent a revival in the early 1850s: the new men in charge wanted an English-language, Protestant, and practical university that would serve the province's needs. In a prospectus of 1853 and in statutes of the following year, they spoke of adding architecture and engineering to the curriculum and probably a lecturer in agriculture.

In 1855, Edinburgh-trained John William ("J.W.") Dawson (1820–1899) became principal of McGill. Former superintendent of public instruction of Nova Scotia, with a growing reputation as a geologist and naturalist, he had tried in 1850 to introduce agriculture into the Nova Scotia school act and had persuaded a US publisher to add four pages of his own material to J.F.W. Johnston's *Catechism of Agricultural Chemistry*, which first appeared in 1844.[43] With encouragement from Lieutenant-Governor Sir Gaspard Le Marchant (1803–1874), Dawson wrote *Contributions Toward the Improvement of Agriculture in Nova-Scotia; with Practical Hints on the Management and Improvement of Live Stock, etc.* (second edition, 1856)[44] to stimulate agricultural classes in public schools. This would turn out to be a test run for its applicability in Lower Canada.

Just before moving to Montreal, Dawson had served as a royal commissioner, along with Egerton Ryerson from Toronto, inquiring into the organization of King's College, Fredericton. King's had long cultivated the classical Oxford-Cambridge tradition, but in the rough-and-tumble developing province, pressure for practical higher education – echoing American views – came not only from the press but also from the legislature. Part of the commissioners' task was to discern a way to meet this demand.[45] They did recommend special courses of instruction in addition to the usual collegiate program; these would answer the needs of civil engineers and land surveyors, farmers and businessmen, or navigators. The engineering and agricultural courses they sketched were almost purely scientific, with only English language and literature from the humanities. The commissioners, clearly casting their nets wide, suggested opening individual courses of lectures in scientific and technical subjects to the public: "Thus will the endowment and advantages of King's College be made available to every class of interests and of intelligent and enterprising young men in New Brunswick – to the Mechanic and Engineer, the Farmer and the Merchant, the Manufacturer and the Surveyor, not less than to those who seek the best preparation for any one of the learned professions."[46]

In his inaugural address at McGill, Dawson spoke of democratizing the teaching of practical science: "In the direction of a school of practical science, all that has yet been done is to offer access to any of our lectures to all persons who may desire to attend them without entering themselves as regular students, and the provision of popular evening lectures for the benefit of the public."[47] McGill, he said, would move quickly to institute diplomas in both agriculture and civil engineering. He adumbrated a program very much like Buckland's: "I have no doubt that there are within reach of Montreal a number of enquiring and intelligent young farmers who would gladly avail themselves of such a course during the winter months. It would include the following subjects: – English Literature, Natural History, Natural Philosophy, Surveying, Agricultural Chemistry, Practical Agriculture, and Management of Farm Animals."[48]

Dawson offered to be professor of agriculture without pay and conferred with the Board of Agriculture for Lower Canada to ensure that it would recognize the McGill diploma, which started in 1856. Emulating teaching practices at Edinburgh and Yale, agricultural theory and agricultural chemistry were options in the third or fourth year. The program was a failure; Dawson thought it due to a "lack of scholarships, prizes and other inducements," but Sheets-Pyenson sees other hindrances, such as lack of a library and botanical garden and university supporters whose interests focused more on the extractive industries than on agriculture. Worse, the university had no farm, and presumably no funds to establish, equip, and maintain one. Yet a farm might not have mattered for McGill – having one did Buckland no good in Toronto.[49]

### Laval (Mid-1860s)

The first French-language university, the Université Laval in Quebec, received its charter in 1852. Laval rose on the foundation of the Séminaire de Québec, which had long taught science, and it organized the traditional faculties but excluded technological studies. J.-X. Perrault, as a Séminaire alumnus, was eager to involve the university in teaching agriculture. His election to the assembly in 1863 gave him some leverage; in the following year, he persuaded his colleagues to strike a select committee on improving agricultural instruction. During its deliberations, Perrault asked the university's rector, Elzéar-Alexandre (later Cardinal) Taschereau (1820–1898), whether the arts faculty would eventually teach agriculture; whether, with the aid of a government grant, there would be courses in scientific agriculture; whether students could use a nearby model farm; and how much all of this would cost.[50] Taschereau temporized and then said no, because the science curriculum was for all professions. Perrault held out to him the promise of a professorship in agriculture, which would offer a two-year course, along with an assistant for the model farm. Taschereau, citing a report of the Irish school commissioners who argued for abolition of agricultural chairs at Queen's College, countered that agriculture was an inappropriate subject for higher education. In Canada West, had not the committee of inquiry into the University of Toronto recommended dropping the chair there? Perrault sent along documents to dispute these notions but was unable to budge university officials.[51] Not until after the turn of the century, when the agricultural schools of the Collège de Ste-Anne-de-la-Pocatière affiliated with the university, would Laval teach agriculture.

## SPECIALIZED SCHOOLS FOR AGRICULTURE (1850s–60s)

As we saw in the previous section, even in the 1850s and early 1860s university agricultural training was clearly a non-starter in Canada, just as in Ireland or the United States; the English did not even attempt it. Likewise, the experiment of teaching agriculture in Canada West's normal school in Toronto had ended with Hind's departure for the university in 1852; the failed experiment there would certainly have cooled any fervour for an agricultural college. In this section, we look at US models that inspired planners, veterinary schools in Toronto and Montreal, George Buckland's lecture tours in Canada West, Canada East's new agricultural school, and its select committee on agriculture.

## Looking Abroad

An alternative to university studies was a free-standing agricultural school or college. Such an institution would not grant degrees, would concentrate on the theory and practice of agriculture rather than on literary studies, and might also provide a general education for people with minimal schooling. Such agricultural schools were relatively successful in France, Belgium, and some of the German-speaking states, but less so in the English-speaking world.[52] Several American manual-labour schools, deriving broadly from the Hofwyl experience, appeared in the first half of the century but little influenced the development of agricultural education.[53]

### NEW YORK (1819–53)

New York tried to do the same, in a similar way, but earlier. The effort involved the same class of men, and, as in Canada, such ideas were top-down.[54] The idea of a free-standing agricultural school went back to 1819, when the state's surveyor-general, Simeon DeWitt (1756–1834), argued that farmers deserved an education as much as did the professionals, an argument that surfaced later in Canada. His cousin, Governor DeWitt Clinton (1769–1828), agreed and asked the state assembly for funds to build an agricultural college; it refused because there was no consensus about the nature of such an institution.

In the same era, journalist Jesse Buel was a strong proponent of Fellenberg's model and attracted many sympathizers, because of the popularity of manual-labour schools as a means of educating the poor and of the efforts and ideas of the Swiss Johann Heinrich Pestalozzi (1746–1827), with his farming and industrial school at Neuhof. Buel linked up with the influential Stephen van Rennselaer (1764–1839), who promoted the teaching of agriculture in the common schools, which he believed more appropriate than manual-labour schools. There being no trained agricultural teachers, the two men pressed for a state-supported college. In 1823, Buel sent the New York assembly a report outlining a four-year college program strong in science and suitable for a school with an experimental farm. Despite support from the New York State Agricultural Society, which preferred an elite institution, the scheme failed to interest the government.

Van Rennselaer then opened his own school, later called Rennselaer Polytechnical Institute, in Troy in 1824 and brought in respected geologist and naturalist Amos Eaton (1776–1842) to direct it. Ironically, under Eaton's regime, the school taught no vocational subjects at all – Eaton believed that schools could not teach skills – nor did it train teachers.

Buel and his associates finally persuaded the government to incorporate a state agricultural school in 1836, where "the theory and practice of agriculture shall constitute the paramount study." Unfortunately, the school commissioners could not raise the funds, and the plan collapsed. Finally, in April 1853, the assembly created two agricultural colleges: the New York State Agricultural College and the People's College. Both were failures.[55]

New York finally obtained an operational agricultural college only in 1874 when the private Cornell University was able to tap into the Morrill Act grant (the US legislation of 1862 set aside federal lands to sustain "land-grant" colleges teaching engineering and agriculture). Cornell's Department of Agriculture became a college in title in 1888. From the 1840s onwards, Egerton Ryerson covered the New York story for the *Journal of Education.*

## MICHIGAN (1830S–50S)

While New Yorkers fought among themselves, Michigan farmers acted. Michigan's legislature had intended, as early as 1835, to provide for agricultural instruction in branches of the state university, but nothing concrete resulted. The state agricultural society formed in 1849, three years after Canada West's, and immediately began lobbying for specialized education. By 1855, the legislature agreed and established the Michigan Agricultural College, which opened in East Lansing in 1857.[56] It did not grant degrees or affiliate with the University of Michigan. It would eventually be a model for Canadian educators.

### *Veterinary Schools in Toronto and Montreal (1860s)*

By the early 1860s, Upper Canadians had seen the chair at Toronto fail, and those watching events in New York State could see little hope for free-standing agricultural colleges. Promoters of agricultural education carried on a more limited program. At a meeting of the Upper Canada Board of Agriculture on 8 March 1859, Adam Fergusson proposed that the board set up a veterinary school to serve the farming and general community. Cattle-raising was expanding and needed veterinary surgeons; informal apprenticeship was the only route to knowledge of veterinary medicine. The board corresponded with Professor William Dick (1793–1866) of the veterinary school at the University of Edinburgh – the source of the few trained professionals in Canada – to see if one of its graduates might emigrate.[57] As a result, Andrew Smith, DVM (1834–1910), arrived in Toronto in 1861. By this time, the agricultural chair at Toronto had essentially ceased.

The board conceived of a winter series of agricultural, scientific, and veterinary lectures for farmers. Professors of University College, Toronto, would cover scientific subjects, and George Buckland, agriculture. The board, as it later admitted, organized its first series (winter 1861–62) in a rush and attracted few auditors. The next winter's lasted six weeks, attracted thirty young men from various parts of the province, and covered the anatomy and diseases of domestic animals, the science and practice of agriculture, agricultural chemistry, botany, entomology, geology, and other topics. With this success, the program continued.[58] By 1865, its veterinary portion featured three lecturers: Smith on animal anatomy and diseases; Duncan McNab McEachran (1841–1924) on vertebrate *materia medica;* and Dr James Bovell (1817–1880) of the Trinity College medical school on animal physiology.[59] These lecture series became the basis of the Upper Canada Veterinary School, the oldest in North America, which began awarding the DVM degree in 1866. Smith maintained the specialist school for many years as a highly successful private institution. It eventually became the Ontario Veterinary College in 1897.[60]

The teaching of veterinary medicine began in Canada East at the same time. From 1863 on, a Rivière-Ouelle physician, Dr Ludger Têtu, taught the subject part time at the agricultural school at La Pocatière. Three years later, McEachran, who had graduated from the Edinburgh school the same year as Smith, emigrated to undertake private practice in Woodstock before assisting Smith in Toronto. The two published the first veterinary book for Canada, *The Canadian Horse and His Diseases,* in 1867. McEachran wanted to teach more science and require higher standards for applicants, and because of this he and Smith soon parted company. Moving to Montreal, McEachran interested both Dawson and the Board of Agriculture in the idea of a provincial veterinary school. With funds from both, he opened the Montreal Veterinary College in affiliation with McGill University in 1866.[61] It became a university faculty in 1889; McEachran remained dean until it closed in 1903.

Smith's school in Toronto attracted more students than McEachran's, which Gattinger attributes to Smith's more practical approach – lower requirements and less scientific theory.[62] The Upper Canada Board reported in 1865 that seven regular students attended lectures and demonstrations, along with several occasional students. The first three students had received diplomas, and, "considering the brief existence of the school, the Board believes the results, so far, satisfactory, and as affording much promise of good for the future."[63] Veterinary medicine proved to be more attractive to Canadian youths than collegiate instruction in agriculture – hardly a surprise. Although the DVM degree was not yet available, a graduate of a veterinary school was, in essence, a professional; a rural veterinarian may not have been paid any more regularly than a rural physician, but he did have a standing in the community that a young farmer with a university diploma in agriculture could probably not emulate.

### George Buckland's Lectures (Mid-1860s)

By the end of 1865, George Buckland at the University of Toronto wanted to work more closely with farmers. The editor of *Canada Farmer*, Rev. William F. Clarke, though pleased with Buckland's lectures, wanted local societies to do more to stimulate agricultural progress.[64] Buckland replied that he had more direct connection with the agricultural societies when he was secretary of the Board of Agriculture, and his having become dean of residence at the university in 1859 had removed him from that connection. He now wanted to tour the province, giving lectures to local societies to "excite a greater interest ... in the promotion of agricultural knowledge and improvement" and to collect information on the state of agriculture. Board Secretary Hugh Thomson noted in his 1865 report that the board had commissioned Buckland's lectures, which seemed to have had "encouraging results."[65] At its expense, Buckland spent several months of both 1866 and 1867 on lecture tours, which he reported from time to time in the *Canada Farmer*. His tours were very similar to those of Lord Clarendon's Irish practical instructors of fifteen years earlier and constitute a pioneering effort in agricultural extension.

*Setting Up an Agricultural School in Canada East (1850s)*

By 1867, despite much talk by Superintendent Ryerson and the leading lights of the Upper Canada Agriculture Association, Toronto still had no permanent agricultural training apart from the veterinary school. In fact, Ryerson was almost silent on agricultural matters through much of the 1850s and 1860s.[66] Permanent agricultural schools emerged first in Lower Canada, where educational circumstances were different. We have seen several false starts in the 1830s and efforts in the 1850s – at Varennes and at Ste-Thérèse – but by the end of the 1850s Canada East had a functioning agricultural school at the Collège de Ste-Anne-de-la-Pocatière.[67]

As early as December 1847, a priest of La Pocatière argued, in a local newspaper, for formation of an agricultural school if funds became available. Serious consideration dates from 8 December 1853, when Mgr Pierre-Flavien Turgeon (1787–1867), archbishop of Quebec, who noted the discussion of agricultural education in religious newspapers, published a *mandement* encouraging church involvement.[68] The directors of Ste-Anne in La Pocatière then surveyed the possibilities for such an ambitious endeavour.

The central figure was the abbé François Pilote (1811–1886), who had been a visitor of the provincial society's short-lived school under Frédéric Ossaye.[69] A graduate of the Séminaire du Québec, Pilote arrived in La Pocatière in 1836 and over the next two decades held a series of administrative posts. A strong proponent of colonization, he had pressed for the settlement of the Saguenay–Lac St-Jean region during the 1840s and early 1850s. During discussions on setting up normal schools in Canada East, Pilote enlisted his friends Jean-Charles Chapais, *père*, and journalist and civil servant Etienne Parent (1802–1874) to persuade the new education superintendent, Pierre-Joseph-Olivier Chauveau (1820–1890), and provincial secretary George-Etienne Cartier (1814–1873) to establish a normal school at the college. Failing in this – the normal schools went up in Quebec and Montreal (two) – Pilote thereupon turned to an agricultural school.

A founding member of the Agricultural Society of Lower Canada, Pilote had been supportive of agricultural instruction, and when the society's short-lived school at La Tortue was in operation, he visited often and conferred with Ossaye. He corresponded regularly with instructors at Grignon as well as with members of the New York State Agricultural Society and was thus well aware of the ideas in action in France and the

US struggles to develop agricultural education. In his administrative capacity at La Pocatière, he had already assembled property suitable for a model farm but required money to develop it. Pilote turned again to local MLA Jean-Charles Chapais, *père*, through whose influence Governor General Sir Edmund Head (1805–1868), a keen supporter of improving agriculture, persuaded the government to provide a grant of £250 early in 1858. The Kamouraska Agricultural Society provided an additional £75. Chapais even managed to induce Cartier to divert 2.5 per cent of the annual grants to agricultural societies to the new school.

Pilote had already been searching without success for a professor of agriculture from Europe. In September 1858, he hired Emile Dumais, whom he dispatched to study with Perrault at Varennes. Pilote hoped to provide three levels of tuition: for agronomists, practical farmers, and teachers. To ascertain the latest ideas, he sailed to Europe in February 1859 to see agricultural schools in France, England, and Ireland. After his return, the school opened in October with three students, two years after the Michigan Agricultural College was launched.

In January 1865, the minister requested a full report on the school from Dr Georges Leclère, secretary of the Board of Agriculture for Lower Canada. Leclère found the school fully established and well run.[70] It had five faculty members. The abbé F.-X. Méthot acted as director as well as professor of agricultural arithmetic and surveying; Jean-Daniel Schmouth was professor of agriculture proper – he had replaced Dumais in 1861 – but also taught agricultural chemistry, bookkeeping, and French. His course covered agricultural chemistry, composting, drainage, manures, meteorology, and rotation. Schmouth had studied under Ossaye and later (in 1864) received a diploma from the Board of Agriculture. The abbé Pilote acted as associate professor of agriculture. From 1863 on, two local men offered courses free of charge once a week. Veterinarian Dr Ludger Têtu provided a two-year study of "zootechny," which included the study of horses, the best Scottish and English cattle breeds, diseases, fattening, hogs, milkers, and sheep. The notary F. Deguise taught rural law, including contracts, damages, interest, penalties, and rents. The staff also included superintendents of discipline, the workshop, and practical work.

The two-year scientific course included agricultural physics, chemistry, diseases and discussions of principal breeds, elementary notions of animal anatomy, farming methods, and mensuration and calculation. Students also heard lectures on practical horticulture, saw demonstrations in the barns, and worked with tools and implements in the workshop. Of this program, the *Montreal Gazette* enthused: "The clergy cannot do a better work than to bring their influence upon the improvement of agriculture, especially of the French Canadian population."[71]

The daily routine, consisting of studies and labour on the farm, scarcely differed from that of the Swiss, French, or Irish residential schools.[72] As in Europe, the school at La Pocatière expected students to participate fully in farm chores. In winter, students had four class hours and six study hours; in summer, two class hours, four study hours, and six hours of manual labour. The farm, which had its own labourers and was expected to pay for itself, included a cow-house, hog pens, a sheep-fold, and a stable. The school building provided classrooms, a chemical laboratory, a small library, a museum, and workshops. The school also maintained a collection of implements. To spread knowledge more widely in the region, the college supported the *Gazette des campagnes*, which Dumais founded in 1861. Students' excursions to nearby exhibitions at Kamouraska and St-Roch helped to broaden their knowledge.

Leclère had to admit that, despite the school's sound footing, it attracted very few candidates. The Lower Canada Board set aside $1,000 per annum from 1863 on for twenty half-scholarships for candidates in the twenty judicial districts. By the time of his report, only fifteen districts had made selections, with a total enrolment of only nineteen. Between 1859 and 1867, only eighty-five students attended regularly, an average of fewer than ten annually. These numbers are but a fraction of the pool of potential enrollees, but the Michigan college did not attract more, nor did institutions in Ireland and England.

### The Minister and the Select Committee (Mid-1860s)

In his 1863 report, Minister of Agriculture Luc Letellier called for not only scholarships but also elementary treatises on agriculture as prize books in the common schools. He wanted more state support for education: "This consideration of the moral result of the extension of the cultivation of the soil, which ought to be always present in the mind of the legislator, is too closely connected with the question of public prosperity and of the social and material progress of the people, not to engage all the sincere friends of our country to unite their efforts to secure, by every possible means and at any sacrifice, the progress of agricultural instruction and the maintenance of establishments founded with the view of affording it." But there was also a moral reason for such support: "It is a fact admitted that the family of the farmer, however humble it may be, is surrounded by the nature of his occupations with a purer moral atmosphere than other classes of society; for its daily labor is performed under the eyes of its head, who thus without effort watches over its moral conduct while directing its material labor."[73]

Letellier lauded Pilote's work and recent efforts by the abbés Therrien at Ste-Thérèse and Potvin at Rimouski, along with the part-time teachers at the three normal schools. The result of their work is "the removal of the unfortunate and absurd prejudice which has for such a length of time induced our educated youth to believe that the liberal professions alone offered them a career worthy of their pursuit; and it is with the highest satisfaction that we now see a large number of them devoting their pecuniary means, and the experience resulting from a high education, to the most noble of all the arts."[74] The minister believed that the government did not sufficiently encourage such men; it should make special appropriations for their work.

The assembly revisited the issue of Lower Canadian agricultural education in 1864, with J.-X. Perrault chairing a select committee. Editor in 1861 of the Board of Agriculture's journal *Revue agricole*, Perrault had in January 1863 persuaded the abbé François Therrien, the procureur at the Séminaire de Ste-Thérèse, near Montreal, to form an agricultural school and model farm. Both three-year and one-year courses of study were in the plans. The scientific instructor was Dr Jules-Constant Cazier, who had taught agricultural chemistry at Grignon; abbé Therrien taught practical agriculture. In the following January, the Board of Agriculture offered nine $50 bursaries. With fewer than ten students, the school received no bursaries in 1865 and seems to have disappeared altogether by 1866. At the same time, the abbé Potvin taught agriculture in the new college at Rimouski, which did not operate a full-blown school of agriculture.

The select committee's 1864 report,[75] which it tabled in August, was Perrault's last major contribution to agriculture. Much of the report is a survey of practices elsewhere, especially in France. Lord Clarendon's itinerant-lecturer scheme is its only mention of Irish activity, even though the farm schools impressed many Canadian visitors to Ireland. However, Perrault, as a former student at Grignon, no doubt wanted to champion the French model. Abbé Jean Langevin, in his response to the committee's inquiries, stated that students at his normal school, both boys and girls, received theoretical instruction in agriculture as a means to elucidate science. There was no school garden or farm. Langevin strongly supported the teaching of practical subjects; his *Réponses aux programmes de pédagogie et d'agriculture pour les diplômes d'école élémentaire et d'école modèle*

(1862) earned the approval of the Council of Public Instruction. Langevin added that introducing readers with agricultural lessons into common schools would be valuable, but he did not want also to train agriculture students. The select committee warmly agreed with introducing agricultural readers but *not* with teaching agriculture in the common schools, noting that the three normal schools would instead provide such tuition to future teachers, who would become effective models in schools.

Responses to the select committee from the *collèges classiques* were less supportive. No colleges save Ste-Anne (La Pocatière) and Ste-Thérèse taught agriculture, few thought it advisable to do so, and, while most owned farms, none had set them up for instruction. At Rimouski, which taught some agriculture, the college was moving away from a commercial to a classical curriculum. The principal of St Francis College in Richmond expressed interest – the institution taught some agriculture as an adjunct to science, but it owned no property; it would found an agricultural school a decade later. University-level agriculture at McGill, as Dawson reported, covered just agricultural chemistry, and the program at (the Anglican) Bishop's University in Lennoxville was still a dream for the future. Rector Taschereau told the select committee that Laval taught no agriculture nor did it expect to. In answer to its question on the cost of "the creation of a chair of high agricultural instruction," his tart response was "It is necessary that we should be acquainted with what the Government understands by *high agricultural instruction*."[76] This was, presumably, Perrault's cue to begin private correspondence with the rector. Other evidence included reports on the Ste-Anne and the new Ste-Thérèse schools and from Buckland on the lectures that Upper Canada's Board of Agriculture offered.

The select committee made reasonable recommendations but gave no budgetary figures. Because classical colleges received funds from the government, the committee expected the government to urge them to add agriculture to their science programs. The superior education fund should give the universities resources to complete their courses of study and offer bursaries for promising graduates from the classical colleges. In agreement with the minister and the Board of Agriculture, the committee proposed to create bursaries for agriculture students at Ste-Anne and Ste-Thérèse. Finally, agricultural treatises could be prize books in common schools.

From this list of recommendations, the government only instituted bursaries for agricultural schools. Although Perrault retained his interest in agriculture after Confederation, he directed his energies to his work for l'Association St-Jean-Baptiste de Montréal and for the local Chambre de commerce, and as a Canadian agent for international exhibitions.

CONCLUSION

In the mid-1860s, the ministers of agriculture thought well of the department's educational activities: two schools in Canada East; agricultural courses at Toronto, McGill, and Canada East's three normal schools and a veterinary course in Toronto; local public lectures in Canada West; and the agricultural boards' publishing journals regularly.[77] In the early 1860s, the Upper Canada Board retained John Donaldson, an emigration agent, to teach farmers the methods of flax culture as a substitute for wheat. Progress was encouraging: acreage was expanding, and from sixty to seventy scutching mills, three linen factories, and three linseed-oil mills had opened. The board's library in Toronto grew apace – number of readers unknown – and George Buckland began to lecture all over the province in 1865. By 1866, he was spending half the year touring the agricultural societies, holding eighty-three meetings on dairying, flax culture, intensive cultivation, livestock breeding, and pasturage.[78] The local societies seem to have received him well, although agricultural journalist William Weld noted sourly a few years later that "we have heard it remarked again and again that his addresses are clear and forcible, but never leave much impression – for good or bad on the audience."[79] Whatever Buckland's impact, his lecture tours launched agricultural extension in Canada – a state-supported activity that would prove its value later.

Where informal approaches to agricultural education (see chapter 1) had grown apace in the decades before Confederation, the formal approaches examined in this chapter had a much spottier record. Private agricultural schools or schools focusing on manual training tended to attract few students and funds and die soon. Despite any interest by superintendents of public instruction in agriculture, simply building up the common-school systems in Canadas East and West took all the available energy and money. Secondary schools had no time or interest in agriculture and were preparing students for non-farming careers. Universities were too small, impecunious, and uninterested.

Only in the 1860s do small steps suggest progress in formal education. Perrault, alluding to university education in his 1864 report, lamented: "Unluckily, our country is not enterprising, and follows at a great distance those nations who are most advanced in the race of improvement," and, à propos of the new (US) Morrill Act, "The States of the American

Union, with that intelligent energy which characterizes them, have taught us what can be accomplished by an enlightened people for the benefit of the masses of population compelled to find the elements of prosperity and power in the culture of the soil."[80] This seems to me a disproportionate response. Reasonably wealthy New York had accomplished less than Canada; the Irish system was no longer thriving, the English did almost nothing, and the French were still building their system.

What does emerge clearly in Canada is a pattern of expecting state assistance for local institutions of agricultural education. That even government funding accomplished so little suggests that there was no grassroots demand for such tuition. Certainly, the promoters never spoke of having wide-ranging discussions with ordinary farmers.

# 3

# Mechanics' Institutes and Informal
# Education to 1867

In Prussia and France, the state was supporting rudimentary systems of technical instruction early in the nineteenth century, whereas in English-speaking countries governments tended to leave educational initiatives to private philanthropic and religious organizations. It was a commonplace to early promoters of technical education that a knowledge of science provided the basis for technological advancement. For the average working person, this would have seemed an extremely dubious proposition, but few observers ever questioned it. As with agricultural education, there was both informal and formal technical instruction for the working class.

While agricultural education in Canada derived from a variety of sources, most early efforts in technical education followed British examples. Informal instruction originally meant the passing down of traditional crafts and trades from father to son, mother to daughter. By the nineteenth century, it also included public lectures and private study, which presumed literacy and availability of books. With increasing industrialization, most training was simply unorganized, on-the-job instruction. The formalized training of apprenticeship and its regulation through guilds barely existed in Canada. Thus formal classroom training was the domain of government or the private institutions it supported.

The first three sections of this chapter in turn outline the birth of mechanics' institutes in England, explore the growth and history of the movement in Upper Canada, and examine the situation in Lower Canada, where it faced some competition. The fourth section looks at the Agricultural Act of 1857, which created boards to organize technical instruction in Canada East and Canada West, and at those boards' roots in London's Great Exhibition of 1851 and the impetus it gave to technical education – both formal and informal – in the United Kingdom. A brief fifth section offers census snapshots of the occupational backgrounds and educational levels of mechanics and artisans in Canada about 1830, 1840, and 1860.

## MECHANICS' INSTITUTES IN BRITAIN (FL. 1823–50)

A taste for science burgeoned in the late eighteenth and early nineteenth centuries among England's literate middle class.[1] This taste was a cultural phenomenon relating to entertainment, self-education, or enlightenment, but not a route to a scientific career. Itinerant lecturers were common in the early nineteenth century, although their lectures often descended into pyrotechnics. The middle class in larger towns formed literary and philosophical societies or athenaeums as venues for both one-off lectures and courses of lectures, and in due course these also arose in Canada.

Anyone attempting to provide scientific literature to the lower end of the social scale encountered three hurdles: absence of literacy, of leisure, and of money.[2] While scientific knowledge might have appealed to a very few workers as a form of self-improvement, it little affected social mobility.[3] Although popular science books sold well until the end of the century, particularly in geology and astronomy, the heyday of the popular-science movement was past. Another means for teaching science to the public was the museum. Collections and cabinets, large and small, organized and chaotic, abounded. The British Museum was the greatest of them all. The magnificence of its new building for natural history, which went up 1871–81 in South Kensington, underscored its role as a vehicle for popular education. Botanical and zoological gardens were simply more specialized museums of natural history. "Rational recreation" and self-education were equal functions of the Victorian museum.

The linkages of science and industrial progress took institutional form in the mechanics'-institute movement. Its origins lay in Scotland, which tended to esteem practical knowledge. In 1796, funds from the estate of John Anderson (1726–1796), professor of natural philosophy at Glasgow University, provided for the creation of Anderson's Institution, which would purvey "useful learning" to artisans. In 1799, one of its first professors was Dr George Birkbeck (1776–1841), a Yorkshire Quaker who had recently completed his medical degree at Edinburgh[4] and whose Quaker dissenter views and desire to impart knowledge made him an enthusiastic lecturer. After leaving Glasgow in 1804, he lectured to artisans in

Birmingham, Liverpool, and Hull before settling in London, where he continued to lecture on science at the London Institute for the Diffusion of Science, Medicine and the Arts. One consequence of his Scottish sojourn was the establishment in 1823 of the Glasgow Mechanics' Institute, which included a library, reading room, and lecture series. Birkbeck, with the support of Lord Brougham, then created a similar organization, the London Mechanics' Institution, in December of the same year.

The mechanics'-institute movement saw its most spectacular growth between 1830 and 1850. Its educational programs, which straddled the border between popular science and organized classroom instruction, were a form of adult education.[5] By 1851, some 110,000 members belonged to nearly 700 institutes in England. The typical institute provided the means for self-instruction, through its library and reading room, and for direct instruction, through occasional lectures and courses. This program, however, lacked a system – it had no staged curriculum – and emphasized scientific principles rather than practical application of knowledge. Thus, with no formal and structured teaching, most institutes offered informal education, as did the agricultural societies. The same factors that restricted workers' access to popular literature also kept most of them from the institutes: their lack of leisure, literacy, and money, to which we could add increasing middle-class control.

Widespread support for mechanics' institutes presupposed at least three, sometimes conflicting, goals: first, they would allow the "artizan and mechanic" (usually a skilled person in a craft or trade, and a manual labourer, respectively) to improve himself through formal study; second, they would possess the scientific tools for the worker to improve his skills on the shop floor and thus, of course, increase his employer's wealth; and third, they would serve as inexpensive social control.[6] An alliance of middle-class Whigs, philosophical radicals, and religious dissenters (non-Anglican Protestants) typically directed institutes. A propos of their first, educational goal, they made their earliest science teaching didactic, assuming artisans and mechanics were not intelligent enough for more speculative thought.

As the movement developed, the second, more utilitarian goal – applying scientific knowledge – came into play but seemed too nebulous for most members. Very few manufacturers saw the institutes as increasing their prosperity. With little reward but personal satisfaction, the average worker avoided institute programs. In the early years, serious courses of lectures – up to ninety sessions – focused on single sciences, usually chemistry or natural philosophy. For many reasons, the single lectures that dominated by mid-century were often superficial and on non-scientific topics. A few institutes, particularly those in Cornwall, Lancashire, and Yorkshire, continued to cater to working-class memberships. In Leeds, for example, where workers remained a large constituency during the 1820s–40s, most individual lectures dealt with science or technology.[7] Larger towns, such as Leeds, possessed societies for various classes, with a literary and philosophical group for the upper class, a literary one for the middle class, and the mechanics' institute for the working class.[8]

The consensus is that the mechanics'-institute movement peaked by mid-century but failed to live up to its original aspirations. Its real successes were the evening courses, which gave thousands of workers further elementary education.[9] The key to any scheme attempting to bring science to the working class was literacy. Scotland had long had universal elementary education. Ireland's national schools were under way by the 1830s, but in England elementary education was only for the well-off; universal, compulsory elementary education dates from only 1870. In Canada, artisan immigrants from Scotland were likely to be literate, those from Ireland possibly so, depending on age, and those from England even less likely to be literate, as education there was so hit and miss. Thus the varying literacy levels of British immigrants would shape Canadian approaches to technical education.

## MECHANICS' INSTITUTES COME TO UPPER CANADA

The London Mechanics' Institution (1823) quickly spawned imitators not only in the United Kingdom but also in France and North America: Baltimore, Boston, Cincinnati, Montreal, Philadelphia, Quebec, and St John's had their own by 1830. Generally in the United States, however, the movement – despite its strong culture of self-help and mutual help – gained little traction, as it had to compete with lyceums, which took their name from the gymnasium in Athens where Aristotle may have taught. Josiah Holbrook (1788–1854) had begun the movement in 1826 by setting up a lyceum in Millbury, Massachusetts, to teach natural science to artisans and to improve their moral vision.[10] In Australia, in contrast, mechanics' institutes became widespread.

The impulse in Britain and Canada to establish mechanics' institutes, the reasons for sustaining them, and the attraction they held for individuals varied with both geography and period. They played much the same role for technical education as the agricultural societies did vis-à-vis agricultural education. But while Britain's offered some formal training, their Canadian spin-offs favoured informal instruction. And, like Canada's agricultural societies, they directed their activities and funds primarily to their own members.

*Goals*

In this section, we can make some generalizations about mechanics' institutes in Canada in terms of activities, profile of memberships, and publications. I must admit, however, that we know very little of the detailed history of most of these organizations, despite the many that existed by the third quarter of the century. The surviving documents of several have a numbing sameness about them that may have deterred earlier investigations.[11]

The creation of mechanics' institutes in Canada addressed a number of needs and goals: better training, help with industrialization, education, moral improvement, philanthropy, social activity, and a forum for manufacturers.

BETTER TRAINING,

or the desire to improve manufactures by improving the working man. The common argument, especially in Britain, was that a mechanic who understood the scientific principles of his task or the artisan who had a developed aesthetic sense and artistic training could not only perform a job better, but could also suggest improvements to the product. This would make the manufacturer more competitive in an increasingly volatile market. No one ever commented that this would generate greater profits – or increase the rewards for the worker.

HELP WITH INDUSTRIALIZATION

More specific to Canada was the associated argument that the institutes would help industrialize the country, although exactly *how* was unclear. In Britain, industrialization antedated the movement, but in Canada the opposite occurred. Institute discussions could never replace the organization, markets, capital, and skilled labour of British industry. The institutes typically invoked their value for industrialization when they sought grants from legislatures, but this notion was certainly not demonstrable.

## EDUCATION

Education was, for all institutes, a primary concern. For whom, and the content, varied considerably, although the means of delivery were relatively uniform. The earliest institutes wished to offer instruction for "mechanics" or "artizans" without clearly defining either. Later, programs spoke of the "working class," "working men," "industrial classes," or "labouring classes." We look more closely at this issue at the end of this chapter, but the group designation would change over time. In the 1830s, there was no substantial body of industrial workers as there was in the late 1870s, that is, there were no large agricultural-implement factories, railway shops, shoe manufactories, or textile mills. Also, the level of workers' literacy rose considerably over the four decades, as the colonies/provinces introduced, expanded, and improved their educational systems. As the audience altered, so would the content, as we see below.

## MORAL IMPROVEMENT

Throughout the nineteenth century, the moral imperative survived as a central theme in mechanics' institutes, both in Canada and abroad. Because their directors were from the middle and upper classes, they assumed that their moral vision was not only superior to that of the working class – about which they usually generalized and without any real evidence – but also that the institutes' duty was to impart this vision to its mechanic members. Thus we find a number of exhortations to young men (never young women!) to stay out of taverns and pool halls or off street corners, to obtain education, and to become credits to their families and communities. The institutes would also inculcate the habit of reading good literature. Contemporary religious and temperance societies offered similar messages.

## PHILANTHROPY

For a number of members, particularly before 1867, philanthropy was an attraction. An organization at least ostensibly educating workers would appeal to the same people who supported public clinics, dispensaries, and other charities for the poor. While a number of speeches and articles make allusion to the philanthropic facet, it was probably stronger in larger centres such as Montreal and Toronto, with their visible numbers of poor, working-class people.

## SOCIAL ACTIVITY

For many members, particularly those in smaller towns and villages, the mechanics' institutes functioned as an organized social activity.[12] The

Victorian middle class rarely conceived of leisure time in a frivolous way but rather believed it must be constructive and uplifting. Outside church, there were few cultural, entertainment, or social outlets for the middle class. Music, opera, and theatre made little impact before the last quarter of the century. Politics and private social events – balls, dinners, picnics, skating parties – could not provide the intellectual content that many people craved, even in the villages. The mechanics' institute, with its small library or reading room and its lectures, could, even in the smallest, most backward corners of Canada, link the world of science, technology, and taste with the world of the local clergyman, doctor, and grocer. In a society with sharp divisions of class, ethnic group, language, political party, and religion, the institute offered a relatively neutral venue to pursue a shared value. This was particularly valuable in smaller towns, where a Conservative-voting Presbyterian millwright from the Orange Lodge could meet on relatively equal terms with the French-speaking Roman Catholic notary who supported *les rouges*.

## A FORUM FOR MANUFACTURERS

Finally, many of the mechanics' institutes functioned as local manufacturers' associations, long before the Canadian Manufacturers' Association (CMA) appeared in 1871. This was evident in the very first institute in Montreal in 1828, whose meetings allowed a variety of manufacturers to meet, exchange information, show new products, and debate government policy concerning their industries. Some of these men, particularly those in Hamilton, Montreal, and Toronto, helped organize the country's first industrial exhibitions. Once the Boards of Arts and Manufactures or the Association of Mechanics' Institutes of Ontario set up the institutes, they could act in concert as lobbying agents for the manufacturing interest. Although this was rarely very successful, it was none the less a dress rehearsal for the later activities of the Canadian Manufacturers' Association.

Various of these seven needs and goals featured, as we see below, in the mechanics' institutes that emerged in Upper Canada – in Toronto (1831), Kingston (1834), Hamilton (1839), and other centres.

### *The Toronto Mechanics' Institute (1831– )*

The earliest institutes naturally formed in the proto-industrial centres, with the first in central Canada in Montreal and Quebec (by 1830). Upper Canadians embraced the concept almost as quickly. In the town of York (which became the city of Toronto in 1834) lived English immigrant watchmaker Joseph Bates, who had been a member of the London institute. Circulating notices in November 1830, Bates called a meeting for January 1831, which organized the York (later Toronto) Mechanics' Institute.[13] The body soon attracted more than fifty members, mostly from the upper strata of society. Its first officers were a "who's who" of York society: architect and builder John Ewart (1788–1856), the first president; prominent politician Dr William Warren Baldwin (1775–1844); former army surgeon and Canada Company employee Dr William "Tiger" Dunlop; Home District Sheriff William Jarvis (1799–1864); tanner and philanthropist Jesse Ketchum (1782–1867); businessman James Lesslie (1802–1885); businessman David Paterson; and future rebel Dr John Rolph (1793–1870). Joseph Bates, a tenant of Lesslie's, supported his effort to launch the institute. The first meetings took place in the Masonic Hall on Colborne Street.

Until well into the 1840s, the York/Toronto Mechanics' Institute followed the pattern of its Montreal contemporary with occasional lectures and a library and reading room. In most towns at the time, discussion of scientific and technological topics was central to mechanics' institutes. Curiously, the town briefly had two competing bodies: the York Mechanics' Institute and the York Literary and Philosophical Society, which much the same social group of people formed in 1832.[14] The latter, like many of its kind in England, was oriented towards the middle and upper classes. Some men were directors of both societies, even though the mechanics' institute was for workers.

"Tiger" Dunlop became prominent in both; he had settled in town after his colourful career in Upper Canada as a land promoter. Speaking before the Mechanics' Institute in 1832, he argued that national greatness was due to commerce and manufactures but that a thirst for knowledge was also important. He noted that the institute offered such knowledge to the working class, which in turn could use its ingenuity to assist the economy.[15] Dunlop was also a member of a trio of science promoters, including Dr William Rees (c. 1800–1874), who would become first medical superintendent of the Toronto Lunatic Asylum, and newspaper publisher Charles Fothergill (1782–1840), who attempted to form a "museum and an institute of natural history and philosophy, and of arts and sciences," presumably in connection with the York Philosophical Society. The three men made a second attempt in 1835 to establish a "Lyceum of Natural History and the Fine Arts," with no more success.[16]

Fothergill blamed the failure on "alledged causes as inexplicable, as they appeared to be extraordinary and unsatisfactory" – almost certainly politics. Fothergill, a gifted natural historian and collector from a

Yorkshire Quaker family, lost his job as king's printer in York for his radical political associations and probably had difficulty moving in elite circles. As his one-time employee Samuel Thompson (1810–1886) recounted, "Mr. Fothergill was a man of talent, a scholar, and a gentleman; but so entirely given up to the study of natural history and the practice of taxidermy that his newspaper received scant attention, and his personal appearance and the cleanliness of his surroundings even less so ... His family sometimes suffered from the want of common necessaries, while the money which should have fed them went to pay for some rare bird or strange fish."[17] It is natural that, what with the great stresses of that decade – with the cholera epidemics and mounting political tension – a supposedly neutral, intellectual society would have difficulty accommodating the visions of Fothergill and High Tory Archdeacon John Strachan (1778–1867) at the same time.

The philosophical society soon disappeared, but the Mechanics' Institute soldiered on, though with few members and little enthusiasm by the workers. Its first government grant came in 1835: £200 for "philosophical apparatus" for demonstrations at lectures. Its purchasing agent for apparatus, Dr Birkbeck in London, England, seems to have sent a hodge-podge of equipment, which members never employed effectively. The institute tried to appeal to two quite distinct clienteles; a handbill of 28 February 1835 read: "Toronto Mechanics' Institute, Museum and Library. To the Scientific and Philosophic, this Institute holds out very peculiar and important advantages, both for instruction and rational pleasure; and to the Mechanic and Artizan, its benefits must be evident and even necessary to keep pace with the general improvement in art."[18] The institute announced lectures every Friday at 7 p.m., with the next being that of Mr Durward on "the advantages to be derived from the mechanics' institute."

After the Rebellion ended in 1838, the institute moved into rooms in the market building. At that time, its patron was Lieutenant-Governor Francis Bond Head (1793–1875). When the institute formed, Toronto had a population of only some 5,000; by 1840, when the working-class population would have grown modestly, few appeared on the institute's lists. An institute broadside of 1840 informed working-class youths that, since city businesses closed at 7 p.m. in winter, the institute would remain open until 10 p.m. for their benefit. Because of "the danger to society in leaving so many young men destitute of the means of properly employing their evenings," it would offer them "every means of innocent and instructive amusement," primarily lectures and the library.[19] Despite its goal of presenting useful instruction to the mechanic and artisan, its popular lecture program in the 1840s clearly appealed to a different class and would be of no practical value to a workingman. In 1846, the institute moved into a new fire hall on Court Street, a building to which it contributed more than £465. The institute incorporated the following year.

The Toronto Mechanics' Institute's annual report for 1841 listed the weekly meetings of courses, which included lectures "by the Rev Mr. Lilley on the mind; by the Rev Mr. Leach, President, on education; by Dr. Lang on chemistry; and one by the Rev. Mr. [John] Roaf on geology, for the untiring zeal of these gentlemen, under the depressing circumstances which the Institute has had to struggle with, the Committee tender their grateful acknowledgement." At the time, membership had shrunk to about ninety, and the annual budget was less than £50.[20] Another sign of trouble: an attempt to establish an evening class "unfortunately failed from the unexpected opposition of the persons chiefly intended to be benefited by it." This cryptic comment suggests at least some working-class members. The 1849 winter series of twenty-five lectures – subscription tickets at 2s 6d – offered a more varied fare.[21]

Rev. Egerton Ryerson's address in January 1849 on "Canadian Mechanics and Manufacturers" summarized his view on working-class education: mechanics require the usual school subjects but, in addition, more science, mathematics, and linear drawing because "educated labour is more productive than uneducated labour." He was well aware of American ideas, especially those of Horace Mann (1796–1859), who directed the Massachusetts public schools. Perhaps it was Ryerson's belief in British ideas and disdain for the "Yankee" that led him to ask his audience: "Is adventurous foreign mechanism to do our work? Or avaricious foreign ignorance and cupidity to waste or absorb our resources? Is the Canadian mechanic or engineer to occupy a post of inferiority beside the European or American engineer or mechanic?"[22] Ryerson opined that one solution would be to have a provincial school of arts in Toronto and even elementary schools of art in every district town.

With modest government assistance, the Toronto Mechanics' Institute was able to build up slowly a decent library, containing some 1,300 volumes, by 1850. Mechanics'-institute libraries were meant to be repositories of artistic, scientific, and technical works that mechanics and artisans could consult; however, few workers could afford an annual subscription of 7s 6d. In practice, they became general libraries, reflecting the reading habits of their patrons. A catalogue from 1862 shows that scientific and technical works accounted for less than 20 per cent of the holdings;

more works by Sir Walter Scott stocked the shelves than did all the titles on natural history.[23]

By the mid-1840s, members turned to another means of stimulating mechanical ingenuity: industrial exhibitions. These had become an annual event in France, and in the 1840s the Society of Arts introduced them in England. The first Toronto exhibition, in 1848 in the institute's rooms, mixed manufactures, fine arts, and ladies' work. Open for ten weeks, it generated a modest surplus. A second exhibition in 1849 awarded diplomas and was a bigger success. By 1850, a prize of £12 10s, from the governor general, was available for the best example of mechanical skill. The second largest institute in Canada West, the Hamilton and Gore Mechanics' Institute, also opened an exhibition in May 1865, with noted local naturalist Thomas McIlwraith (1824–1903) as chair.[24] As well, industrial sections became part of the annual, movable Provincial Exhibition, which started in Toronto in 1846.

Still, even with lectures, a good library, and other activities, the Toronto Mechanics' Institute failed to attract much of a constituency. Walter Eales, an English painter who lectured there on 5 February 1851, lamented that an institution with such excellent facilities attracted only 270 members in a city of 30,000.[25] He admired its educational and moral aspects, but these aspects probably discouraged workers. The Toronto institute had never provided systematic, practical education that would assist a mechanic or artisan in his tasks. And surely working-class men resented the middle class's moralizing – its churches generated a surfeit of *that* commodity. None the less the Toronto institute had ambitions: tiring of renting quarters, it purchased a lot at Adelaide and Church streets in 1853 and commenced construction the following year. The provincial government leased the unfinished building for offices, keeping the institute out until 1861.

## The Kingston Mechanics' Institute (1834– )

Upper Canada's earliest mechanics' institutes emerged in the most likely centres, those that actually had mechanics and artisans. Kingston followed Toronto's lead in April 1834.[26] A key mover was William Lesslie, the younger brother of James, who helped found Toronto's institute. The family hailed from Dundee, Scotland, arriving in Kingston in 1822 to establish a stationery and book business. William was a supporter of working-class suffrage, and his partners in forming the institute, Charles Sewell and Donald Urquhart, were also recent immigrants and reformers.

Sewell had been a watchmaker in London, while Urquhart was a Scottish builder, carpenter, culler, and timber measurer.

Most of the institute's earliest members were mechanics and tradesmen, but establishment men joined as well. With an unworkable constitution and political tensions between Reformers and Tories on the board of directors, the organization struggled. Because Kingston already had a library association and a commercial circulating library, building up another library would be difficult. Donations of books led to an early library and hiring of a librarian – Alexander Dawney – who in 1835–36 offered, for a fee, evening instruction in drawing, English, and surveying. The introduction of free classes by the Roman Catholic bishop Alexander Macdonell (1762–1840) trumped Dawney's efforts. In 1835, with thirty-eight members, the institute applied to the legislature for a grant and received £100.

The Rebellion and its aftermath effectively pushed mechanics and tradesmen out of control of the institute, and Lesslie, like his brother in Toronto, ended up in jail. From 1838 on, with the Tories in control, membership doubled with the addition of people such as John A. Macdonald (1815–1891) and, later, Oliver Mowat (1820–1903). Kingston served 1841–44 as capital of the United Province, and the substantially Catholic working class prospered, with the shipyard and construction of fortifications, the general hospital, and the penitentiary. Governor General Lord Sydenham rejected the institute's application for another grant, and the government's move to Montreal crippled it. It could not afford to move into the new city hall and thus had no permanent quarters for its library. When the province introduced grants to institutes in 1847, Kingston's obtained £50 and by 1858 collected nearly £500. By that time, with a 1,200-volume library, its membership had shrunk to eighteen, the smallest of the forty active mechanics' institutes in Canada West. Nevertheless, it survived in an old inn on Princess Street, but by the early 1860s the local school board and Queen's University usurped its role in offering evening classes.

### The Hamilton and Gore Mechanics' Institute (1839– )

In 1839, banker and railway promoter Colin Ferrie (1808–1856) helped to organize the Hamilton and Gore Mechanics' Institute in Upper Canada's second largest town and budding industrial centre. It incorporated a decade later, "for the purpose of diffusing Scientific and Literary knowledge by a Library of reference and circulation; by the formation of a museum of Specimens in Zoology, Geology or other subjects of Nature, Science or Manufactures; by Lectures; by Philosophical Apparatus; by conversations; and by any other method the Committee may judge necessary."[27] It clearly had a more scientific bent than did its Toronto counterpart.

Although the social elite participated in the institute's operation – politician and railway developer Allan MacNab (1798–1862) was a director – one might expect more workers' participation, as Hamilton was not a centre of government and lacked Toronto's range of institutions; but Great Western Railway employees confronted the directors in 1854 over their middle-class bias.[28] The company offered to provide an annual £100 grant to the institute if it would allow railway workers to become members, but the new mechanic members found the fees too high, the library largely irrelevant, the lectures of little value, and no classes. With the company's help, in 1856 they secured lower fees. Evening classes in arithmetic, French, mathematics, mutual improvement, and writing followed the next year, with Great Western workers acting as instructors. In 1866, the employees founded their own reading room, and the company ended its annual grant to the institute.

### Other Mechanics' Institutes

In Brantford in 1836, Dr Charles Duncombe founded an institute, which he and fellow Reformers directed; it collapsed after the Rebellion but was revived in 1840. The Dundas Mechanics' Institute appeared in 1840, although the town already had a lending library as early as 1822 when William Lyon Mackenzie (1795–1861) operated a branch of the Lesslie family business in the town. London (1842), Stratford (1846), and Mitchell, St Catharines, and Whitby (1849) followed suit. A number of minor centres such as Ayr, L'Orignal, Milton, Simcoe, Streetsville, and Waterdown, which must have had few workers, organized institutes during the 1840s and 1850s.

#### BARRIE

One example is the Mechanics' Institute in Barrie. In 1858, one of its directors, James Ardagh, reported that it had offered a lecture program during the previous winter in which chemistry was the only scientific subject. These lectures had been "too desultory" and lacking in scientific content, but Ardagh was realistic: "The chief object of an Institution like ours must be to create and foster a taste for refined pleasure, and for intellectual effort, even where the latter does not immediately appear subservient to the serious business of life."[29]

## OTTAWA

Some towns that did have a working-class base from earlier times were late in forming their own groups. The Ottawa Mechanics' Institute, for example, incorporated in 1853 and first offered public lectures in 1854. "Respectable persons," that is, mechanics, merchants, and professionals, paid membership dues of £1 annually, and all others, 10s – a substantial sum. We can sense the institute's social position: Mayor H.J. Friel (1823–1869) gave the opening address in 1855, and the organization offered little to the working class.[30] With 257 subscribers in 1855, its library already numbered some 1,000 volumes, and its museum – directed by Ottawa-born geologist Elkanah Billings (1820–1876), soon to be founding editor of the *Canadian Naturalist* and palaeontologist to the Geological Survey of Canada – boasted 1,000 specimens. The Silurian Society, the local palaeontology and geology club, met in the institute's leased rooms in Temperance Hall. Two dozen public lectures were on offer in 1855, at a small fee; of the twelve listed for 1855, only two were on scientific or technical subjects, while musical events were numerous. All of this reflects clearly the middle-class cultural and intellectual biases.

## NIAGARA-ON-THE-LAKE

Despite the rhetoric that institutes were designed for working-class education, some were unabashedly middle class from the beginning, as in Niagara-on-the-Lake. Apart from a few tradespeople, Niagara was not a centre of industry or milling. The Niagara Mechanics' Institute formed on 24 October 1848: "That it is desirable to establish an Association in this town for the promotion of scientific pursuits, the advancement of knowledge, and the acquisition of a library and necessary apparatus" (Minute Book 1848–63, Archives of Ontario). No mention of mechanics or artisans, and an admission fee of 5s and monthly subscription of 7½d. None the less, more than 130 people subscribed, and the initial treasury of £52 inaugurated a library in a room in the town hall. The president, first W.H. Dickson, MLA (1769–1846), and then Judge E. Campbell, chaired fortnightly lectures or essay readings. As in so many institutes, its initial fervour did not last, and, although the efforts of stalwarts such as the novelist William Kirby (1817–1906) kept it alive into the 1890s as a library, membership had already dropped into the eighties by 1858 and would shrink even further after Confederation.

## Government Grants (1850s)

Early mechanics' institutes in Upper Canada/Canada West had little connection with government except for the many public officials who were members and held office in them. After 1841, several institutes petitioned the legislature and received ad hoc grants, starting with Toronto and Kingston in 1847 and London in 1849.

In 1851, the Act Concerning the Management of Institutes and Libraries (14/15 Vict., cap. 86) formalized grants and paved the way for incorporation. The assembly then created a subsidy of £50 per annum. With this financial incentive, the number of mechanics' institutes (see Table B1 in Appendix B), libraries, literary and library associations, and Canada East's Instituts canadiens receiving grants leapt from fourteen in 1851 to 131 by 1857, the year of the largest payout. By then, the government realized that it had no effective control over how institutes spent funds, now amounting to some £7,000 a year. Although grants appeared in the 1858 estimates in January 1858, Minister of Agriculture Philip Vankoughnet (1822–1869) wrote to all mechanics' institutes receiving funds and asked for details of their operations.[31]

While mechanics' institutes and similar organizations were not thriving – the average grant was only £50 per year, too little to ensure more than a rudimentary operation – at least a few could operate modest programs of technical instruction. The state was willing to assist these essentially private ventures out of the almost universally accepted notion that knowledge is power or, more specifically Canadian, that it leads to economic development. Because the institutes in Upper Canada/Canada West were in theory strictly for adult education, they did not compete with elementary schooling.

### MECHANICS' INSTITUTES IN LOWER CANADA

#### Early Institutes (Montreal and Quebec, 1820s and 1830s)

Montreal was one of the first cities in the world to establish a mechanics' institute. On 21 November 1828, Scottish immigrant Rev. Henry Esson (1793–1853)[32] organized the Montreal Mechanics' Institution. A graduate of Marischal College, Aberdeen, Esson had come to Canada in 1817 as pastor of the new St Gabriel Presbyterian Church. He and his supporters had ambitious plans for their institute: to collect money, books, and apparatuses through donations; to establish a reference library and reading room; to sponsor lectures; to form a museum of machines and natural history; to found a school for artisans; and to build an experimental workshop and laboratory.

Like Toronto's institute, Montreal's was in the hands of the political and commercial elite. Influential members included Sheriff Louis Gugy as its first president, brewer and industrialist John Molson (1763–1836) as vice-president, and seigneur Louis-Joseph Papineau (1786–1871) and merchant Horatio Gates (1777–1834). Sir James Kempt (c. 1765–1854), who became governor general later that year, acted as patron. The city was more than half British, and virtually none of the institute's perhaps 200 members were francophone, and few were probably mechanics or artisans.[33]

The Montreal Mechanics' Institution, which closed in 1835, managed to form a small library of 500 volumes and offer a variety of lectures on scientific and technological topics. A failed attempt to operate a night class for mechanics in the winter of 1833–34, a cholera epidemic, and rising political tensions created a climate in which the institute became untenable.

The Quebec Mechanics' Institute dated from 1830 and catered to the anglophone middle class. John Neilson (1776–1848), printer and liberal politician, was its first president; with some modest financial support from the legislature, it grew to 150 members within two years and was able to collect a small library and some scientific instruments.[34] By the early 1840s, the library occupied rooms in the parliament house. According to the *Quebec Guide* (1844), "Every exertion has been made by the leading members of the Institute to enlarge the sphere of its usefulness and render it subservient to the benefit of that useful class for whom it was designed"[35] – note the themes of social control and philanthropy. The annual subscription of 10s no doubt deterred artisans from joining, and the early membership lists suggest few mechanic members and fewer francophones, just as in Montreal.

### The Montreal Mechanics' Institute (1840– )

As life settled down after the Rebellion, a new Montreal Mechanics' Institute formed on 11 February 1840 at a meeting chaired by John Redpath (1796–1869), a wealthy investor who would later establish a sugar refinery on the Lachine Canal. By that summer, some 223 members enrolled, including six apprentices. Incorporating in 1845 as the Mechanics' Institute of Montreal, it boasted a thousand members by the mid-1850s and invested £5,236 in the construction of Mechanics' Hall in 1854. Standing at rues St-Jacques and St-Pierre, the hall had an auditorium for lectures and musical events: eight-year-old Emma Lajeunesse (1847–1930) – later Emma Albani – made her debut there in 1856. The space hosted public lectures, on technical topics or more general fare, to members and occasionally to a wider public.[36] The institute's library had grown apace, with some 4,600 volumes by 1854, but its content was non-mechanical; a catalogue of 1869 showed about 13 of the works on mechanics and the arts and another 16 per cent on science, which left two-thirds on non-technical subjects.[37]

EVENING CLASSES

Most institutes discussed, but few put into practice, the evening class for mechanics. British exemplars had offered art training for twenty years, but not evening science classes. The Montreal institute's evening classes had a chequered history. It offered French and drawing in 1847, but "studies of so much importance appear to have been but little attended to during the past season"; adding phonography (phonetic shorthand) the next year made little difference, so classes were dropped in 1849 and 1850.[38] There was an unsuccessful trial with drawing in 1851. Fees discouraged attendance, but even free drawing classes in 1853 attracted few people.

According to the students, employers were not willing "to grant their apprentices the time, when business began to revive about the beginning of March. The Committee would fain believe that such is not the case to any great extent, they can hardly conceive that employers could be so totally blind to their own interest, as to act so inconsiderately towards their apprentices: indeed if it could be definitely ascertained that such were the case, your Committee would recommend parents or guardians in indenturing apprentices, to stipulate that sufficient opportunity be afforded them, to profit to the fullest extent, by the advantages which this Institute affords."[39]

In the following season, 100 applications arrived, and four teachers, including Mr Milln of the steam-engine lectures, provided classes in architectural, mechanical, and ornamental drawing. As three of the four teachers waived their salaries, the courses cost the institute little. "The Committee are confident that if the aims and objects of the Institute were more fully known and understood, it would be appreciated and supported in a corresponding degree, by that large and important class of the community – the working Mechanics – whose interests it is more

especially designed to promote."[40] When the institute decided to levy a
$1 fee for courses, it had to cancel most courses in 1856. Classes in the
1850s covered architectural and mechanical drawing, arithmetic, bookkeeping, French, and writing – essentially what Toronto offered – mostly
adult education, except for drawing, which was technical instruction.

MEMBERS

Members in the Montreal Mechanics' Institute varied remarkably in
background. While leaders came from the anglophone elite, general
members included people from commerce, education, manufacturing,
the professions, and the trades. A listing of 215 life members by occupation for 1841–80[41] serves as the basis for Table 3.1. By the early 1870s, a
life membership cost $20, well beyond a worker's means, although
annual dues were as follows: for master and merchants, $3; journeymen,
$2; and apprentices, $1. The largest group consisted of artisans, mechanics, and tradesmen, with nearly two-thirds of them in the building trades,
a large industry in the city. Only half the life members were "mechanics
and artisans," but tradesmen rather than factory operatives or labourers,
who could not have afforded the fee. Still, half the life members were not
tradesmen, and no single occupational group stands out. This suggests
strongly that members joined primarily to use the library.

*Reception in Lower Canada*

In Lower Canada, the mechanics'-institute movement did not generate
the same enthusiasm as it did in the upper province. Even if potential
members looked to it more to fulfil intellectual and social needs than to
secure technical education, they did not join with alacrity. The increasing estrangement of Lower Canada's two linguistic groups in the later
1830s effectively limited the membership pool, for anywhere we can
document membership we find anglophones in control. So even where
there were enough francophone artisans or mechanics, as in Montreal
or Quebec, they did not join.

One barrier to greater participation may have been the level of literacy
in rural areas, which was higher in rural Upper Canada.

GOVERNMENT GRANTS

During the 1850s, the government's £50 annual grants in Canada East
stimulated creation of new institutes, though not as extensively as happened in the western partner. By the time the grants wound down in

Table 3.1 Mechanics' Institute of Montreal: number of life members by occupation (1841–80)

| | |
|---|---|
| TRADESMEN/MECHANICS/ ARTISANS (101) | Jeweller 2 |
| Builder 22 | Auctioneer 1 |
| Painter 12 | Forwarder 1 |
| Machinist 5 | |
| Contractor 5 | PROFESSIONALS/ CIVIL SERVANTS (34) |
| Printer 5 | Civil engineer 6 |
| Plumber 4 | Gentleman 5 |
| Nailer 4 | Lawyer 4 |
| Bricklayer 4 | Architect 3 |
| Plasterer 4 | Notary 2 |
| Carpenter 4 | Bookkeeper 2 |
| Blacksmith 3 | Dentist 1 |
| Hardware mechanic 3 | Accountant 1 |
| Tailor 3 | Justice of peace 1 |
| Miller 3 | Actuary 1 |
| Baker 3 | Senator 1 |
| Millwright 2 | Customs collector 1 |
| Sadler 2 | Physician 1 |
| Cooper 2 | Geologist 1 |
| Stonecutter 1 | Supt waterworks 1 |
| Gas fitter 1 | Banker 1 |
| Roofer 1 | City surveyor 1 |
| Artist 1 | Teacher 1 |
| Saw miller 1 | |
| Plane miller 1 | MANUFACTURERS (32) |
| Optician 1 | Founder 8 |
| Cabinetmaker 1 | Paper manufacturer 4 |
| Ship carpenter 1 | Brewer 3 |
| Planker 1 | Brick maker 3 |
| Typemaker 1 | Sugar refiner 2 |
| Frame maker 1 | Nail manufacturer 1 |
| Slater 1 | Ship builder 1 |
| Oil miller 1 | Ropemaker 1 |
| Tanner 1 | Soap and candle manufacturer 1 |
| Tinsmith 1 | Boot manufacturer 1 |
| | Lamp manufacturer 1 |
| MERCANTILE/ CLERICAL (46) | Piano maker 1 |
| Merchant 18 | Threshing machine manufacturer 1 |
| Clerk 9 | Pipe manufacturer 1 |
| Druggist 3 | Tobacco manufacturer 1 |
| Grocer 3 | Organ builder 1 |
| Oil/colour men 3 | Cloth manufacturer 1 |
| Insurance agent 2 | |
| Stationer/publisher 2 | OTHER (2) |
| Assigner 2 | Farmer 1 |
| | Pupil 1 |

*Source:* Record of Life Members, Atwater Library, Montreal.

1858, sixty-six mechanics' institutes were receiving funds in Canada West, and fifty-one in Canada East (see Tables B1 and B2, respectively, in Appendix B on mechanics' institutes). In response to Minister of Agriculture Philip Vankoughnet's request for information, only sixteen responded.[42] Numbers had snowballed: thirteen institutes obtained grants in 1855, twenty in 1856, and forty-eight in 1857. In that last year, twenty-eight received their first grants, and another half-dozen their second. Grants dropped in 1858 from £50 per year to £35 (or $140, in the new decimal currency) and then disappeared. One can only assume that few of Canada East's institutes had built up a library of any size and that almost all new institutes must have failed.

It is not easy even to list mechanics' institutes in Lower Canada/ Canada East, as many led a fleeting existence. While several obtained government grants, others seem never to have applied. Lamonde, having combed local sources and parliamentary papers, gives thirty-two at some time between 1840 and 1866.[43] He describes some as "mechanics' institute," others as "institut des artisans." His list does, however, miss another ten (see Table B2 in Appendix B). Almost none of these has left any historical trace.

### Alternatives and Competitors

MECHANICS' INSTITUTES AS CULTURAL CENTRES

A number of these institutes obviously operated as cultural centres rather than as serious institutions for educating workers. Apart from the usual artisans or mechanics one would expect in small towns, such as blacksmiths, coopers, and millwrights, one would not anticipate an incipient industrial workforce in places such as Hemmingford and St-Léon. There was at least one institute catering to an industry: the Grand Trunk Railway Literary and Scientific Society (1857), for employees in Montreal, offered much the same as a mechanics' institute and was still lively in the late 1890s.

Mechanics' institutes in Lower Canada/Canada East failed principally because of competition. Once we understand that mechanics and artisans were never the primary membership – it was the middle class – then we see that francophones would gravitate towards organizations that addressed their own interests. Apart from church-related organizations such as parish *cabinets de lecture*, the focus of such interest lay in the Institut canadien movement.

INSTITUTS CANADIENS

Institutions that the francophone middle class supported rarely, if ever, showed an interest in technical instruction of any kind. The Institut canadien de Montréal (1844), the first of its kind, provided a francophone library and a venue for intellectual and cultural events. Others followed, with a Quebec Institut and a francophone institute in Ottawa in 1847[44] and some twenty other institutes by 1852. A number of factors eventually reduced this number to a core of three – Montreal, Quebec, and Ottawa – in 1858, along with the Roman Catholic Institut canadien-français in Montreal. These organizations had much in common with the middle-class mechanics' institutes and offered libraries, reading rooms, and public lectures.[45] Although Montreal's Institut canadien later became notorious for its outspoken liberal tendencies, its Quebec and Ottawa counterparts were more conservative.

The cultivation of science for directors of the Institut canadien differed from the vision of their contemporaries in the Montreal Mechanics' Institute. In the latter, the teaching of science was a necessary prerequisite to improved technical ability, and any director of a mechanics' institute, be it in Yorkshire, New York, or Toronto, would agree. But the Institut canadien and most francophone intellectuals saw science as just another part of culture. This was evident as early as the 1820s when scientific articles appeared in Michel Bibaud's *Bibliothèque canadienne*. For the Institut canadien movement, science was just one means to raise the intellectual and cultural standards of French Canadians; the end was to unite them in national spirit. The Société de Saint-Jean-Baptiste, formed in 1842, was likewise friendly to science, but only insofar as it assisted the advance of francophones.[46] In none of the francophone institutions was there any mention of educating the working class or pressing for technical instruction. Although there were some francophone industrialists, most directors of societies were professionals or intellectuals who looked out for their own interests.

Lamonde has made a detailed study of Montreal's Institut canadien. When it came into being, the English dominated the city, which had few cultural outlets for francophones. The Institut not only provided a place to hear lectures, discussions, and debates but also housed a library of 10,000 volumes, a reading room, and a natural history and art museum. In a catalogue of books, only 125 volumes – many in English – dealt with science or technology.[47] Despite its (overstated) liberal thought, the Institut was very much like contemporary cultural organizations on both sides of the Atlantic. Professionals and businessmen formed the bulk of the association, attracting many figures who would rise to the top of Quebec society; the leadership was firmly in the hands of lawyers and notaries. Of 926 members between 1855 and 1900 that Lamonde could identify, only fifty-seven could be called mechanics or artisans. Between 1845 and 1871, the Institut offered 391 lectures, essays, and debates for its members; Lamonde's figures show that only 6 per cent dealt with science and technology, not one of which detailed technical matters or technical education.[48]

After 1858, when most mechanics' institutes faded, the Instituts continued to grow. Those in smaller centres reflected the urban institutions. Menard has studied the Drummond County Mechanics' Institute and Library Association/Institut des artisans et association bibliophile du Comté de Drummond,[49] which Jean-Baptiste-Éric Dorion (1826–1866), a key member of the Montreal Institut, set up in 1856 in the village of L'Avenir. It operated, despite its name, like an Institut canadien. The area supported a mixture of farming and extraction, with a mix of anglophones and francophones. Over twenty years, membership fluctuated between seventy-seven and 157, with the mean age of members being about forty years; by 1881, francophones made up three-quarters of the members. Of members' occupations in the 1861 and 1881 censuses, 80 per cent were farmers and farm labourers; tradesmen numbered only 5 per cent. Discussions ranged from local, provincial, and national political matters to agricultural issues. Lectures were rare, and most were nontechnical. The only technical one was on dairying, presented by provincial agricultural lecturer E.-A. Barnard (1835–1898). Before grants ended in 1858, money went into building up a library.

Closer to the metropolis was the short-lived Institut canadien de Longeuil. Lamonde has reviewed its history 1857–60.[50] Membership was entirely male, although women could attend lectures, and mostly from the village. With eighty-five members in 1858 and 130 the next year, it was much more homogeneous than Drummond's institute – francophone and Catholic – with a mean age of thirty-six. The middle class dominated, although the good mix of occupations suggested a proto-industrial town.[51] The discussions ranged over topics such as government, emigration, and business, but not science and technology.

## LITERARY INSTITUTES

When we compare the organizations receiving grants in the two halves of the province, we find a larger number of literary institutes or library associations in Lower Canada. They were able to obtain the same annual £50 subvention as did the mechanics' institutes and the Instituts canadiens. A few were anglophone, such as the Literary and Historical Society of Quebec, which dated from the early 1820s and had accumulated nearly £700 in grants during the 1850s, but most were francophone literary associations. By the late 1850s, some twenty-six literary institutes had received funding from the province, compared with eight in Canada West. In 1857, the year of the largest total payments to groups, literary organizations in Canada East obtained £950 and mechanics' institutes £2,400 (in Canada West, amounts were £400 and £2,900, respectively). It is clear that mechanics' institutes had significant organizational competition in Lower Canada.

## THE AGRICULTURAL ACT OF 1857 AND TECHNICAL INSTRUCTION

### Upping the Ante

As early as 1850, the Canadian mechanics' institutes felt the need for greater cooperation with each other. After the local industrial exhibition that took place as Canada prepared to participate in London's Great Exhibition of 1851, a deputation from the Toronto Mechanics' Institute appeared before the Montreal Mechanics' Institute, suggesting that they and their counterparts throughout the Province of Canada coordinate their efforts and widen their usefulness.[52] In 1854, Montreal's institute petitioned the legislature for more resources to extend its programs to a wider community, possibly through a free reference library and a model room. Although the MLA John Young (1811–1878) had the petition printed and circulated, it elicited no response. Yet a gestalt shift in hopes for improving the situation of mechanics and artisans would lead to innovative provisions in the Agricultural Act of 1857.

In 1855, with Canadian participation in the Paris Universal Exposition heightening interest in technical matters, the Montreal institute pressed for free reference libraries in both Montreal and Toronto. Alfred Perry, the superintendent for the Canadian exhibitors in Paris (and correspondent for the *Gazette*), visited Paris's Conservatoire des arts et métiers and reported: "I am of the opinion that such an institution ought to be founded forthwith in Canada, or such a collection commenced; placing, as it would do, the increasing scientific attainments, for the successful presentation of his art, within the reach of the humblest artizan."[53]

Montreal's institute pushed hardest for more technical education. On 1 August 1856, its members addressed Governor General Sir Edmund Walker Head (1805–1868), already their patron, mentioning how extensively the French and British governments supported technical instruction: "We venture to express a hope that the time is not far distant when the Mechanic may have his College in either section of the Province, not less than the professional man, and when his ingenuity will be judiciously fostered by rewards, as the labor of the Canadian Agriculturist is today." Head found the institute's proposal a "good object," but reported that the state of public funds, rather than ill-will, blocked the government.[54] In December, Perry was in Toronto conferring with institute officers there about cooperating to seek more funds from government and take control of the industrial sections of their respective provincial exhibitions.

The agricultural bill, though complex, proved non-controversial. The new ministry of Etienne-Paschal Taché and John A. Macdonald first tipped its hand in Sir Edmund's speech from the throne on 26 February 1857: "You have ascertained by experience the usefulness of the prizes offered by the Agricultural Societies of *Upper* and *Lower Canada* – I shall be glad if you can extend the same principle of encouragement to arts and manufactures, and can stimulate the ingenuity of our mechanics and artizans by distinctions of the same character."[55] Although Sir Edmund had already done likewise while lieutenant-governor of New Brunswick,[56] he knew that prizes for clever mechanical inventions (like agricultural societies' premiums for essays) were not enough. In the debate on the throne speech, the legislative council (upper house) agreed without demur.[57]

And the Montreal institute responded quickly too: by early March 1857, Perry's subcommittee had drawn up a petition to government for aid in the "advancement of Arts & Sciences in Canada" and had moved to send a delegation to the institute in Toronto (the capital) immediately to discuss how to press for mechanics' claims. Secretary A.A. Stephenson wrote to the Toronto institute to suggest a joint deputation "to the end that measures may be secured to carry out the advancement of an act for the encouragement of the Mechanical Industry of the Province."[58] We do not know to what extent the institutes' input shaped the resulting bill.

The bill that Agriculture Minister Vankoughnet introduced into the legislative council said nothing about prizes for artisans, which had disappeared in the ministry's revamping. Vankoughnet told the council that the proposal for Boards of Arts and Manufactures (rather than Agriculture) "was of material importance to enable the Government to obtain statistical information relative to the progress or retrogression of the country in industrial pursuits."[59] This echoed the ideas of the influential "improver" and statistician William Hutton (whom we met above) and his recent ideas on reforming the ministry. In his 1856 departmental report, Vankoughnet alluded to complaints about the narrow focus on agriculture; hence the broader reference to "arts and manufactures."[60] The bill went through three readings in both council and assembly within a week with virtually no debate. How did the Agricultural Act of 1857 affect technical instruction?

### The Act and Technical Education

For Canada West, at least, technical education became the central issue, not statistics or prizes for artisans. We need to look at the origins of the two Boards of Arts and Manufactures. It is not evident whose idea they were. On the one hand, they were, like the Boards of Agriculture, to stand between the government and the relevant parties – here, groups following "industrial pursuits." Vankoughnet had had little contact with the subject. The same was true for Sir Edmund, too, although his earlier career in England as a Poor Law commissioner would suggest interest in a bureaucratic/state solution rather than private technical education. The most likely originator would be William Hutton, who spurred reorganization of the ministry.

When the new Agricultural Act became law, Montreal's institute, like Toronto's, held a special meeting to discuss its implications. As the council reported to the membership at year's end, the new boards would allow the government to assist all existing mechanics' institutes without privileging Montreal or Toronto's.[61]

While there were no North American precedents for the new boards' activities, Europe had two: the Conservatoire des arts et métiers in Paris and the Science and Art Department of Britain's Board of Trade.[62] The Conservatoire was a depository for industrial materials, but much broader in scale than that of the Patent Office Museum (1857), which Bennet Woodcroft (1803–1879) had assembled in South Kensington and which forms part of the Science Museum. However, none of the principals – Sir Edmund, Vankoughnet, and Hutton – knew much about the French approach. Those most *au courant* with technical instruction – who may well have lobbied for the boards – were leading members of the largest Mechanics' Institutes, those in Toronto and Montreal. The latter institute was firmly in *anglophone* hands, and only Alfred Perry, while in Paris for the 1855 exposition, had shown a keen interest in the Conservatoire and its relevance for Canada. In both cities' institutes, many leaders were immigrants from Britain who maintained close ties there. Thus, by default, the British model is more likely to have played a role.

Which contemporary British activities would have had an effect on Canadian initiatives?

### The Great Exhibition, the Science and Art Department, and Technical Instruction

The origins of the Science and Art Department in Britain's Board of Trade exhibit some parallels with Canada's Boards of Arts and Manufactures that the Agricultural Act of 1857 engendered. Before 1851 in industrial education in the United Kingdom, the government had operated only metropolitan and provincial art schools – "schools of design" – in the 1830s[63] to shape industrial, not fine artists, following the French lead. The Board of Trade was its agent, such as it was, for encouraging industry. The private Society of Arts, nearly a century old, brought together industrialists, businessmen, and artists but had become ineffective.[64] Reorganization in the mid-1840s began to give it some purpose, and very soon a ginger group under Henry Cole (1808–1882),[65] an artist and reformer of the public records, dominated its council. Cole's friends, most of them with utilitarian sympathies, hoped to spark industrial creativity in Britain. Prince Albert (1819–1861), German-born husband of Queen Victoria (1819–1901, reigned 1837–1901) had vague notions about industrial education and, as president of the society, came into close contact with Cole. Among his ideas was setting up a series of national exhibitions of industrial products, again à la française. This series of increasingly popular events culminated in the Great Exhibition of 1851.

The brilliantly successful exhibition at the vast Crystal Palace in Hyde Park had several significant consequences. Not the least of them was a small fortune in revenues, with which Prince Albert and his commissioners purchased land in neighbouring South Kensington to house metropolitan institutions of science and art (including the Science and Art Department). The so-called Albertopolis stretched south down Exhibition Road from Kensington Gardens, next to Hyde Park, and emerged as one of the world's great cultural and educational complexes.

#### ORGANIZING TECHNICAL EDUCATION
In 1848, the Central School of Design had called in Cole to help with internal reforms. His reorganization and the curricular changes by his

friend painter Richard Redgrave (1804–1888)[66] placed the school on a workable footing. Redgrave stayed on as a master, while Cole and other Society of Arts allies, particularly Edinburgh chemist Lyon Playfair (1818–1898), helped plan the Great Exhibition. Once the event ended, the government took its first steps in "science and art" education: its 1852 creation of the Department of Practical Art under the Board of Trade, with Cole and Redgrave as joint administrators to operate and expand the network of provincial schools of design.

In the Queen's 1853 speech from the throne, Prime Minister George Gordon, Lord Aberdeen (1784–1860), promised to organize technical education. The government modelled the new Science and Art Department on the year-old Department of Practical Art. It was the brainchild of a group of prominent politicians. Among them were three crucial figures: Henry Labouchère (1798–1869), president of the Board of Trade during Cole's reform of the Central School of Design and the creation of the Department of Practical Art; Granville Leveson-Gower, Lord Granville (1815–1891), Labouchère's assistant; and Edward Cardwell (1813–1886), president of the Board of Trade when it formed the new department. The department would have joint secretaries: Cole, to administer the art schools, and chemist Lyon Playfair.[67] Playfair moved over from the School of Mines in Jermyn Street to establish a parallel system of science schools for the new department. Cole, Granville, Labouchère, and Playfair had all been commissioners or executive members of the Great Exhibition, and all were active in the Society of Arts. Thus, by 1853, the separate strands came together, with Cole at the centre of the connections.

The Committee of the (Privy Council's) Council on Education had loose control of primary and secondary education. Lord Granville, as president of the council, was responsible for education and wanted the committee to take over the new Science and Art Department, but, by the time of Canada's agriculture bill of 1857, the takeover was under way. Cole, along with Playfair, soon to leave for an academic post at Edinburgh, had strongly urged the change. But the structure and function of the Science and Art Department had already emerged outside the context of official educational policy and operation. In Canada, the only official contact between the Boards of Arts and Manufactures and educational establishments was the boards' ex officio seats for superintendents of public instruction.

STRATEGIES: SCHOOLS AND A MUSEUM

The Science and Art Department concentrated on two strategies to improve workers' scientific and artistic abilities: formal education and, more informally, a museum. First, it created schools of art and schools of science throughout the kingdom, sometimes in existing schools, sometimes in non-school venues.[68] Following Cole and his political masters' laissez-faire views on education, the science and art schools were to be self-sustaining. The department would provide a curriculum, a building and its appliances, and awards for students; and masters were to offer the courses, typically at night for artisans, and receive pay entirely from fees.

In the early 1860s, department schools became test cases for payment by results, which Robert Lowe (1811–1892) had championed in public education when he was in the Privy Council office. The department extended the scheme to elementary education in 1862. This approach, which many observers saw as disastrous, often produced 'crammer' courses to pass examinations instead of systematic courses of study. The planners meant it to spur attendance at science and art schools by ensuring that both teacher and student could profit from academic success. Cole, by 1859 sole secretary in the department, was enthusiastic. The government had to provide support, however, because the programs generated little interest. This facet of the system would have distinct echoes in Canada.

Second, the Science and Art Department created the massive South Kensington Museum.[69] With Cole in charge, it opened in 1855 in a cast-iron building in the South Kensington estate as a national repository of science and art in the broadest sense. Cole intended the collection, which had expanded with purchases at the international industrial exhibitions of London (1851), Dublin (1853), and Paris (1855), to introduce the working class to aesthetic industrial design. Its long-term goal was to propel British industry forward to catch and overtake its continental rivals. Already by the late 1850s, Cole and his allies could point with pride at the growing numbers visiting and revisiting the museum. Members of the working class had attended the Crystal Palace exhibition of 1851 in droves, and reduced rates, free evenings, and the novelty of gas-lit galleries retained their interest in the new museum. To strengthen the link between industry and art, the government moved the collection of models over from the Patent Office Museum to stimulate prospective inventors. Needless to say, the South Kensington Museum – the Victoria and Albert since 1899, and one of the gems of "Albertopolis" – rapidly became a "must see" for visiting colonial promoters of technical education and industry, including Canadians.

## CENSUS SNAPSHOTS OF MECHANICS AND ARTISANS

At mid-century, many Canadians assumed that mechanics and artisans using libraries and evening classes extensively would increase their scientific knowledge and artistic ability, which in turn would translate to better design in manufactures and economic success. But Canada was behind Britain in industrialization, and there were essential differences in work and workers. Before Canada's industrial census of 1871, we can use only proxies to guess at industrial development – early censuses and several other surveys.

Upper Canada undertook a rudimentary census in 1830, and Lower Canada in 1831. This was the period that saw formation of the very first mechanics' institutes. Upper Canada had only grist mills (274) and sawmills (551); Lower Canada's more complete enumeration included barley, fulling, grist, oatmeal, oil, and saw mills; distilleries; foundries; iron works; pot and pearl asheries; and seventy-six items "other." Clearly, almost all the industries in both Canadas related to land clearance and agricultural products. Lower Canadian iron works (102) and foundries (eighteen) were the closest Canada would come to contemporary British industry. While much of the ironwork would have been for mundane purposes, it could also be surprisingly sophisticated: the Molsons' steamboats' engines, for example, were manufactured in the Trois-Rivières area.

The Province of Canada ordered another census after it came into being in 1841. The manufacturing sectors in the two halves of the province appear in Table 3.2,[70] which compares the data for 1842–44 and for 1860–61. Again, the needs of the agricultural sector (and in Canada West, of pioneering farmers) were paramount. That more foundries and trip hammers existed in Canada East underscores its industrial lead. "Other manufacturies" – not even reported for Upper Canada – could have included a wide variety of trades and industries, most of them in the Eastern Townships.

*Lovell's Montreal Directory for 1842–43* provides an index of urban trades and manufacturing establishments in Canada's largest and most developed city.[71] Most practitioners acquired these trades and manufacturing operations in the shop, not through formal apprenticeships. A similar list for Toronto for the same period would have omitted luxury consumer goods, which came in from elsewhere.

In the decade of Confederation, the 1860–61 census shows industrialization (Table 3.2), especially in the shift from "frontier" industries to

Table 3.2 Industrial censuses of Canadas East and West (1842–44 and 1860–61)

| | Canada East | | Canada West | |
|---|---|---|---|---|
| | 1844 | 1860–61 | 1842 | 1860–61 |
| Grist mills | 422 | 450 | 414 | 502 |
| Saw mills | 911 | 810 | 897 | 1,164 |
| Barley mills | 45 | n/r | 41 | n/r |
| Oatmeal mills | 108 | 12 | 63 | 18 |
| Fulling mills | 153 | n/r | 144 | n/r |
| Carding mills | 169 | n/r | 186 | n/r |
| Carding/fulling mills | n/r | 89 | n/r | 62 |
| Woollen mills | n/r | 47 | n/r | 85 |
| Threshing mills | 469 | n/r | 996 | n/r |
| Oil manufactures | 14 | n/r | 48 | n/r |
| Foundries | 69 | 60 | 22 | 124 |
| Trip hammers | 18 | n/r | 10 | n/r |
| Nail manufactures | 6 | n/r | 6 | n/r |
| Distilleries | 36 | 5 | 147 | 53 |
| Breweries | 30 | 16 | 96 | 90 |
| Tanneries | 335 | 214 | 261 | 271 |
| Paper manufactures | 8 | n/r | 14 | n/r |
| Pot/pearl asheries | 540 | n/r | 1,021 | n/r |
| Other manufactures/factories | 86 | 493 | n/r | 1,047 |
| Totals | 3,419 | 2,196 | 4,366 | 3,416 |

Source: Statistics Canada, www.estat.statcan.gc.ca, accessed 4 July 2013.

those of a settled country: carding, foundries, fulling and woollen mills, and "other factories" (in Canada West, most pot and pearl asheries, so prominent in the early 1840s, had disappeared). Some categories changed and are not directly comparable, but consolidation appears in distilling and brewing; the smaller numbers certainly do not suggest lower alcohol consumption.

Another proxy is a list of immigrant occupations. Emigration agents from Canada were long active in the United Kingdom and may have influenced some people with certain skills to move to Canada. Table 3.3 enumerates the male immigrants into Canada for 1864 by stated occupation.[72] The largest groups (three-quarters of the total) consisted of agricultural workers and labourers, most of them probably with minimal or no education. Some of the agricultural group might have benefited from limited agricultural instruction available in Canada. Most members of the two groups may have emigrated because they lacked a job at home or expected to find one in Canada. If we assume that most immigrants expected to obtain work in their occupations, the list of immigrants' occupations does not suggest an industrial country requiring

Table 3.3  Occupations of male immigrants, Province of Canada (1864)

LABOURERS (2,976 = 38%)
Domestic servants 4
Drain layers 1
Labourers 2,962
Navvies 1
Porters 5
Sawyers 1
Storemen 2
Warehousemen 3

AGRICULTURE (2,937 = 38%)
Farmers 2,908
Gardeners 9
Grooms 8
Land stewards 4
Ploughmen 3
Shepherds 4
Trappers 1

INDUSTRIAL WORKERS (504 = 6%)
Blockmakers 1
Brass founders 1
Braziers 2
Engine fitters 1
Factory operatives 42
Firemen 2
Ironmongers 3
Machinists 20
Manufacturers 2
Mechanics, not specified 350
Millers 13
Millwrights 3
Moulders/foundrymen 5
Puddlers 1
Shipwrights 3
Smiths 51
Tenters 1
Tinmen 2
Turners 1

TEXTILE AND CLOTHING
INDUSTRIES (493 = 6%)
Cloth lappers 2
Cotton yarn dressers 1
Curriers 1
Dyers 5
Furrier 2
Glovers/hosiers 2
Hatters 2
Shoemakers 70
Skinners 1
Spinners 1

Tailors 51
Tanners 9
Umbrella makers 2
Weavers (handloom) 344

BUILDING TRADES (232 = 3%)
Architects 1
Bricklayers 2
Builders 1
Carpenters/joiners 160
Contractors 3
Masons 21
Painters and glaziers 26
Plumbers 11
Slaters 2
Stonecutters 5

MINING (224 = 3%)
Colliers 4
Miners 220

CLERICAL AND COMMERCIAL
(150 = 2%)
Clerks and accountants 78
Drapers 5
Commercial travellers 8
Grocers 12
Leather salesmen 2
Peddlars 2
Salesmen 4
Seedsmen 1
Shopkeepers 9
Stationers 2
Traders 27

TRADES (116 = 1%)
Basket makers 1
Blacksmiths 10
Bookbinders 3
Brickmakers 1
Brushmakers 1
Cartwrights 7
Carvers/gilders 5
Chandlers 1
Cigar makers 2
Coachmakers 1
Coopers 15
Coppersmiths 1
Cork-cutters 1
Cutlers 1
Engravers 3
Farriers 1
Goldsmiths 2

Grainers 1
Hairdressers 1
Lithographers 1
Locksmiths 7
Musical instrument makers 2
Papermakers 4
Potters 1
Printers 14
Ropemakers 1
Rulers 1
Saddlers harness-makers 7
Sailmakers 1
Tinsmiths 11
Watch/clockmakers 4
Wheelwrights 1
Working jewellers 1

TRANSPORTATION (76 = 1%)
Carriers 2
Carters/cabdrivers 5
Coachmen 4
Mariners 64
Shipmasters 1

FOOD TRADES (49 = <1%)
Bakers 25

Brewers 4
Butchers 10
Confectioners 2
Fishermen 6
Maltsters 2

PROFESSIONALS (14 = <1%)
Doctors 1
Land surveyors 3
Lawyers 1
Preachers/missionaries 5
Schoolmasters 3
Veterinary surgeons 1

OTHER (61 = 1%)
Artists 3
Engineers 20
Fiddlers 1
Gipsies 5
Musicians 4
Policemen 3
Postmen 2
Soldiers 17
Students 3
No stated occupation 3

---

Source: Province of Canada, *Sessional Papers* (1865), No. 6, 101–2.

technical education. "In the United Kingdom, the science and art schools' primary foci were drawing, modelling, mathematics and general physical science. Industrial design improvements were associated with, for example, machinery manufacture, agricultural implements, carriages, clothing, fabrics and wallpaper, ceramics, glassware, decorative metalwork and furniture. Looking over the immigration groups, we do not find many immigrants with skills in those areas who might have benefited from night classes at mechanics' institutes; the number of industrial workers, in fact, is quite modest."

## CONCLUSION

From its beginnings in England in 1823, the mechanics'-institute movement spread remarkably rapidly, especially in England. Within only five years, it reached Canada and entrenched itself more firmly there than in the United States, which was taking to the new lyceums. While the Rebellion of 1837–38 and the ensuing raw political climate slowed the movement's growth, new mechanics' institutes, especially in Canada

West, began appearing in the 1840s. While governments in both Lower and Upper Canada had supported agricultural societies for many years, they provided the early mechanics' institutes only sporadic, one-off grants. Only by the early 1850s was the movement sufficiently strong that its spokesmen could press government to provide regular support. This allowed for the expansion of institutes to smaller centres.

Our patchwork knowledge of individual institutes suggests that libraries were their main attraction and that these libraries did not focus particularly on "science and art." Occasional lectures on scientific and technical subjects were another attraction, but organized technical instruction through evening classes was neither widespread nor particularly effective. Because of the relative size and education levels of the working class at the time, this is not surprising. Although the provincial government in 1857 created Boards of Arts and Manufactures to foster technical education, its provision of so little funding ensured instead failure of the system.

# 4

# Formal Technical Education to 1867

When the Canadian government made its first small steps in support of formal agricultural education in the late 1850s, it also began thinking about formal technical instruction. The dual administrative machinery that the United Province of Canada forged during its creation in 1840–41 almost ensured that the eastern and western halves of the province would diverge in their goals and means, despite laws that spelled out uniformity. While the Agricultural Act of 1857 established parallel structures for agricultural societies and mechanics' institutes, it had become evident in the 1840s that unitary legislation would not work for education. Sectarian demands clearly complicated educational politics in Canada West, but no one church was strong enough to derail non-denominational schooling. In Canada East, the dominant Roman Catholic church opposed the movement for non-denominational national education, just as it had in Ireland. The linguistic divide added another complexity: most anglophones were Protestant, but while most Catholics were francophones, there were many anglophone Irish. And, although the Catholic church would not truly flex its muscles on educational matters until after Confederation, the province had to accommodate its wishes. Integration of technical education into the regular educational system would be easier in Canada's western sector than in its eastern.

When the assembly approved the Agricultural Act in June 1857, the government set up two Boards of Arts and Manufactures to provide technical instruction to mechanics and artisans. But, as happened in so much else the United Province did, two sets of identical machinery operated quite differently. Because their operations and goals diverged almost immediately, and because they had little contact, we may treat their histories separately.

First in this chapter, the legislature in 1857 creates Boards of Arts and Manufactures for each part of the United Province, but assigns them a vast array of responsibilities. Next, we look in turn at the activities of the boards in Canada West and in Canada East, and a brief section then assesses their results. The chapter's final three sections turn to art instruction in Canada West ("Ryerson's Dream"), to hopes for technical education in schools in Canada East, and to engineering at the University of Toronto and McGill.

## A TALL ORDER FOR THE BOARDS (1857–67)

As their subsequent histories will show, the Boards of Arts and Manufactures "for Upper Canada" and "for Lower Canada" of 1857 seem to have taken their cues from Britain's Science and Art Department (see chapter 3, above) for some of their activities, but their organization borrowed from the earlier Canadian Boards of Agriculture. The British department had its home strictly within the civil service, answerable to a minister and having no advisory body. Its relationship with the organizations educating workers in matters technical – mechanics' institutes and art schools – was one way. It expected them to provide a venue and funds for schools, as masters and students typically came from their ranks; it also set the ground rules, provided inspection, and paid teachers on results. That system was not democratic.

In Canada, such a system was impracticable, both politically and organizationally. Few mechanics' institutes existed, and, of those that did, even fewer had any vigour. If institutes were to play a role for the working class analogous to what agricultural societies purportedly did for farmers, then there would have to be many more of them. The Agricultural Act of 1857 intended to democratize the boards. All institutes – including the new ones it facilitated – could elect delegates, as could boards of trade, ensuring the support of commercial interests. There were seats as well for any professors of physical science in provincial universities and colleges and (ex officio) the superintendents of public instruction, with the minister of agriculture ex officio on both. The boards thus became far more democratic and responsive than are any modern provincial boards, but they almost never had the ear of government.

On paper, the two boards were potentially unwieldy, but their meetings usually attracted very few members. Boards of trade rarely sent delegates. Each mechanics' institute could send its president and one delegate for every twenty paid members – *real* mechanics or manufacturers who had paid at least 5s ($1) in dues – but also had to contribute to the board one-tenth of its own annual provincial grant of $200 ($140 beginning in 1858), a considerable sum for small institutes. One suspects that most institutes had few mechanics or manufacturers. Board meetings took place in either Toronto or Montreal, so only easy railway access would allow more distant delegates to attend. Therefore few institutes sent delegates, and, when the province withdrew the annual grants in 1859, a number of them ceased to exist. A few professors showed up occasionally, superintendents of public instruction infrequently, and the minister almost never. Members of the Toronto and Montreal mechanics' institutes dominated the two boards from first to last. While this was not a drawback, it did give them a disproportionate influence.

The legislation left affairs in the boards' hands, with little direct connection to the ministry. So long as the boards met at least quarterly and maintained a subcommittee to handle affairs during the year, they could make their own rules, expend their funds as they saw fit, and buy and sell real estate. But what did the government expect of them? The list of functions was imposing:

- "to collect and establish at Toronto and Montreal respectively, for the edification of practical mechanics and artizans, museums of minerals and other material substances and chemical compositions, susceptible of being used in the Mechanical Arts and Manufactures"
- "model rooms appropriately stocked with models of works of art, and of implements of husbandry and machines adapted to facilitate agricultural operations"
- "free libraries of reference, containing books, plans and drawings, selected with a view to the imparting of useful information in connection with Mechanical Arts and Manufactures"
- "to take measures to obtain from other countries new or improved implements and machines, not being implements of husbandry or machines specially adapted to facilitate agricultural operations"
- "to test the quality, value and usefulness of such implements and machines, and generally to adopt every means in their power to promote improvement in the Mechanical Arts and in Manufactures in this Province"
- "The Minister of Agriculture may cause duplicates or copies of models, plans, specimens, drawings and specifications [to be] deposited in the Patent Office."
- "to establish in connection with their respective Museums, Model Rooms or Libraries, Schools of Design for Women, on the most

approved plan, and furnished and supplied in the most complete and appropriate manner"

- "also to found Schools or Colleges for Mechanics, and to employ competent persons to deliver lectures on subjects connected with the Mechanical Arts and Sciences or with Manufactures"
- "from time to time publish, in such manner and form as to secure the widest circulation among the Mechanics' Institutes and among Mechanics, Artizans and Manufacturers generally, all such Reports, Essays, Lectures and other Literary compositions conveying useful knowledge."[1]

Each board received only $2,000 per year plus any tithes from affiliated institutes, so the list of functions must have seemed rather daunting. It covered many of the same responsibilities as the Science and Art Department in South Kensington.

The boards, whose goal it was to establish museums, looked to impressive models in the United Kingdom and the philosophy that inspired them: the Museum of Irish Industry in Dublin, the new Scottish Industrial Museum in Edinburgh, London's Museum of Economic Geology in Jermyn Street, and the new South Kensington Museum, which housed a growing collection of fine-art models and manufactures. The purpose of these institutions was to provide the mechanic and artisan examples to imitate or surpass. Museum going was to be an active exercise – educational in the broadest sense. Henry Cole believed that a people's taste could improve only through contact with finer design and *objets d'art*. Subsequent activities by the Canadian middle class indicate that it fully agreed with him. The act's model rooms, as well, emulated the new Patent Office Museum in South Kensington.

The Agricultural Act mandated an agricultural museum for each board to exhibit farm machinery. The boards were to collect models of non-agricultural machinery – presumably items such as sewing machines or steam presses – for educational purposes. The inquiring workman or manufacturer could, at first hand, see improvements by foreign designers and manufacturers. Canada's odd patent laws allowed a British subject to patent any item, no matter how he or she obtained the design, in Canada.[2]

Low on the list of the act's priorities was establishing technical schools, which institutions the British and French esteemed. Canadians put less emphasis on specialized education for workers, perhaps because their public, elementary education was fledgling at best; secondary education was rare in Canada West, although Canada East had a growing number of *collèges classiques;* and the vexed university question, which had recently resulted in the creation of the secular University of Toronto, still troubled many people in the upper province. Thus technical education was unlikely to attract much attention. The act's language echoes British attitudes – "schools of design" for women and separate "schools or colleges for mechanics." The schools that the Science and Art Department supported before 1860 taught the sexes separately in the art schools and in the Irish lace schools. The department intended its proposed science schools essentially for men. Despite its meagre resources, the board in Canada West made a valiant effort on all fronts, while its eastern counterpart practically bankrupted itself at the start and then limped along as best it could.

## CANADA WEST'S BOARD

We may usefully divide the efforts of the Toronto-based Board of Arts and Manufactures for Upper Canada into two areas that reflect its own priorities: assistance with mechanical progress and manufactures (through mechanics' institutes and reading material) and efforts to foster working-class technical instruction. The board's history intertwines with that of its host, the Toronto Mechanics' Institute. The institute, some of whose members must have complained to the government about its preferment of agricultural interests, must have approved of the new act, yet was initially lukewarm about the boards: "Your Committee, although not anticipating any immediate benefit to the Institute, from association with the Board, yet at once took the necessary steps to entitle the Institute to representation therein, considering it to be their duty to join in any movement calculated to promote the manufacturing interests, and develop the industrial resources of the Province."[3] Subsections below explore the headquarters, institutes and grants, reading material, exhibitions, the mid-1860s' push for change, and examinations.

### *Headquarters*

The Board of Arts and Manufactures for Upper Canada (BAMUC) had as its secretary first Robert Edwards, then his brother William, both prominent long-time members of the Toronto institute. The institute also provided a physical home for the board in its new, capacious building at Adelaide and Church streets. The government's lease and occupation kept the institute out until 1861, but the board, being a government agency, could move in, creating an office-library-boardroom and an adjacent model room and gallery on the second floor. When Deputy Minister of Agriculture J.-C. Taché inquired in 1865, William Edwards reported that the rooms, which the institute rented at $240 annually, were sufficient.[4] In day-to-day operations, Edwards was in effect "the Board": maintaining the reference library and keeping it open Tuesdays and Fridays from 10 a.m. to 4 p.m. and, "specially for the accommodation of the working classes" from 7 to 10 p.m.; acting as treasurer and keeping accounts, along with handling correspondence; and editing the board's *Journal* after Henry Youle Hind resigned as editor. On his own time, he acted as secretary to the Toronto City Agricultural Society. For all of this, he received $750 per annum. Thus his salary and the rent used up half the annual government grant, limiting any other activities.

### Institutes and Grants

During its first year in 1858, the board had yet to settle on its goals. The museum function in the act came to the board by default. Minister of Agriculture Philip Vankoughnet informed the governor general early in that year that the Bureau of Agriculture's offices had no room for the patent office's library and model collection, and he recommended distributing them to the two boards, thereby giving mechanics access to the reference books.[5] It was this collection that formed the nucleus of the board's museum until Confederation. The board's first president was Dr John Beatty (1810–1898), a Cobourg physician, mayor, professor of chemistry at the town's (Methodist) Victoria University, and mainstay of its mechanics' institute. His first annual report of January 1859 noted that only nineteen institutes had affiliated with the board (it wasn't compulsory),[6] bringing it more revenue for its activities. The government had distributed grants to sixty-seven during 1858, totalling some $10,800,[7] so nineteen affiliating was not a good showing. In fact, the government cancelled grants for 1859 to cut costs. Despite a sharp depression, it perhaps found the grants ineffective. When Vankoughnet requested reports on activities, fewer than half of the 118 mechanics' institutes replied.

The boards and most institutes strongly objected to the loss of grants. For the board in Toronto, which hoped to form a provincial school of design and mechanics' college and to offer a system of examinations, the resulting loss of revenue from mechanics' institutes hurt. Had grants remained at $200 and all institutes contributed 10 per cent, the income would have amounted to $1,340; but with only nineteen adherents and smaller grants, it would receive a mere \$266. In 1859, it was zero. In his annual report for 1861, Minister of Agriculture Narcisse Belleau (1808–1894) admitted that "the general condition [of the boards] appears to be satisfactory, but the withdrawal of all Government aid from the Mechanics' Institutes appears to have resulted in the failure of some of them, and in crippling, materially, the usefulness of others."[8]

The Toronto board, like its Montreal counterpart, soon recognized weaknesses in the 1857 act. Both wanted to sponsor lecture series outside the cities, not one of their formal functions. Mechanics' minimal participation in institutes was also an issue; the Toronto board's canvass of institutes found that only about 40 per cent of the members were mechanics or artisans.[9] Its correspondence with the government constantly referred to its financial problems and the institutes'.[10] Reinstatement of institute grants in 1863 came too late. By 1864, only the institutes in Toronto, Cobourg, Dundas, Hamilton, London, and Whitby had a connection to the board.

### Reading Material

Many institutes wanted to create libraries, which were apparently their primary attraction in central Canada. The free library of reference in Toronto had nearly 1,300 volumes by the mid-1860s, but local institutes possessed only a few books on technical subjects. Many of their reading rooms lacked science and art journals. In 1855, the Society of Arts, Britain's foremost organization devoted to manufacturing, science, and arts, announced that it would offer colonial institutes discounts on books and periodicals available through its secretariat. The Toronto institute therefore affiliated in 1857,[11] and the board followed suit about 1860. William Edwards soon found, however, that affiliation was more trouble than it was worth.[12]

While institute libraries were useful tools of instruction, the literate population had a variety of ways to obtain information.[13] Subscription libraries or library associations dated from the very early nineteenth century in Canada. Alongside these were a significant number of local literary societies. Imported English and French books were expensive and not readily available, but by the 1840s, inexpensive US editions of British volumes (and of course American books) were easily obtainable for those seeking self-education. Publishing was growing in both parts of the province, as was the circulation of newspapers. We saw above in the second section of chapter 1 the role of the agricultural press, but the few publications for mechanics had short lives and failed. On the local level in Canada West, the Sunday school libraries and township school libraries that Egerton Ryerson began fostering in the 1850s were competitors. School libraries could purchase only books that the Education Office officially sanctioned, but they could do so at a discount from the Book Depository.[14]

## Publications

The Agricultural Act had suggested publications by the boards themselves. The Board of Agriculture for Upper Canada had inaugurated its own *Journal and Transactions* in 1856, which reported on its and the Upper Canada Agricultural Association's activities. This later gave way to the *Canadian Agriculturist*, which had little for the mechanic or artisan apart from reports on agricultural implements or the industrial portion of the annual provincial exhibitions. The Board of Arts and Manufactures for Upper Canada therefore decided in 1860 to launch its own *Journal*, which appeared as a monthly in January 1861 under the editorship of Henry Youle Hind, by then chemistry professor at Trinity College. The public knew him best as the leader of the provincially supported Assiniboine and Saskatchewan exploring expedition in 1858, a voluminous report of which had appeared in print.[15] Further, his journalistic experience as founding editor of the Canadian Institute's *Canadian Journal* stood him in good stead.

Although never financially secure, the *Journal of the Board of Arts and Manufactures for Upper Canada* was remarkable for its time and place. It was foremost a creditable imitation of the *Journal of the Society of Arts*, which that body created when Henry Cole chaired it in 1852. Following the model of its British namesake, it combined hortatory editorials with useful reprints from American and European journals, patent information, science and art news, reports of British North American institutions, and official notices from its board. It also provided an official voice for Lower Canada's board, which could never afford its own publication. Its monthly preparation of copy must have been time-consuming, as one person did it. By 1864, the board, spending $700 per year on the *Journal* and distributing 1,250 copies, was losing money. Hind resigned his teaching post in May 1864 and moved to New Brunswick to undertake a geological survey, thus killing the journal.

"Science and art education" (i.e., technical education) was one of the board's foci, but had been a grey area with no clear state or institutional champion. At the time the board's *Journal* first appeared in January 1861, at least three other periodicals in Canada West dealt with some aspects of the subject: Egerton Ryerson's *Journal of Education for Upper Canada* (since 1849), the *Canadian Agriculturist* (since 1849), and the Canadian Institute's *Canadian Journal of Science, Literature and History* (since 1852).[16] The board's journal, despite its considerable value, expired along with the board in 1868, and the new Ontario government did not resurrect it when it reorganized the mechanics' institutes.

## Exhibitions

The original legislation gave the Boards of Arts and Manufactures no specific duties regarding either international or provincial exhibitions; but, as major participants in the two provincial agricultural organizations that *did* organize provincial exhibitions, both had to pay some attention. Lower Canada's was far more active in this realm. The Toronto Mechanics' Institute began sponsoring small industrial exhibitions in 1848, virtually contemporaneous with the Society of Arts' first national exhibitions in England, with modest success. The annual, peripatetic provincial exhibition was predominantly agricultural, though from the start featuring a manufactures section, apart from agricultural implements. The 1863 revision to the Agricultural Act added a clause enjoining both boards to hold fairs or exhibitions for manufactures, possibly in conjunction with the provincial ones. It was this clause that forced the board in Canada West to concern itself directly with the provincial exhibition. In its 1864 report, it included the recommendations of a special committee seeking ways to involve more manufacturers.[17]

On the international stage, Canada had always participated in an ad hoc manner by appointing a commission. After its success at the first international exhibition in London in 1851, later such events created wide interest; the board helped plan the displays for Dublin in 1853 and Paris in 1855.

## Pushing for Reform (Mid-1860s)

By the mid-1860s, the negotiations for Confederation were absorbing politicians' time and energy, deflecting them from dealing with the board. The provincial government's transfer to its new quarters in Ottawa also spelled problems for the board. In January 1866, Taché informed Edwards that he intended to move the patent-office models and library to Ottawa, although he was willing to pass along to the minister Edwards's plea to retain them in Toronto.[18]

Despite the new uncertainties, the board continued to press for action on technical education. First, it wanted to ease the financial plight of the mechanics' institutes. As the *Journal* noted in 1867, the board's deputation to Finance Minister Alexander Tilloch Galt (1817–1893) in 1859 had demanded reinstatement of annual grants. He assured them that grants would resume on a better plan "soon." They were still waiting eight years later.[19]

The board had a wider vision. Its subcommittee, in its 1865 report, taking note of an article in the Montreal *Gazette* on the United Kingdom's science and art schools, agreed that its Science and Art Department had great value and that "what was done in Britain may be done here, with a proportionate success."[20] Richard Lewis, like his father, hotelier Rice Lewis, a prominent member of the Toronto Mechanics' Institute, picked this idea up in a letter to the *Journal*. He agreed that the government should establish a similar department. This would ensure creation of a school of design.[21] The editor followed up in July with an article on "Art Education in England."

During the last year of the board's existence, a heated controversy on the state's responsibilities filled the *Journal*'s pages. In July 1867, "Canada – Her Educational and Industrial Future" argued that too much money was going to agriculture and to professional and liberal education, and none to working-class education; Canadians had too much higher education and too little of the practical sort. Extracts from British editorials on technical education buttressed this view.[22] The chief combatant, "S.R.," joined the fray in August, claiming that government schemes never worked, and cited failures of the Science and Art Department's programs and Irish agricultural education; he was willing to support the board's more modest plans.[23] In September, "Artificer" accused mechanics' institutes of providing only light entertainment rather than intellectual substance; not only were workers unable to realize the potential benefits of education, but even the "patronising classes" needed education about what was of quality and worth. Their lack of knowledge "leads them to ignore many good things at home, and to make their purchases in foreign markets. The only criticism upon which they can rely is whether or not the article *takes* in New York, Paris or London, and the only estimate they can make of an object, is, that it costs so many dollars."[24] If neither the working nor the middle class had a clear view of its educational and manufacturing potential, "S.R." argued, neither did the state. For him, "technical education" was nonsense that Cole and company at South Kensington pushed, on the assumption that British manufactures were inferior to foreign (not proven) and that, *if* they were, it was because of technical education abroad (for which there is no evidence).[25]

Yet editor William Edwards kept inserting articles on French art education, extracts from the *London Engineer*, and Robert Lowe's remarks in Edinburgh on education, as reported in *The Times*. A duel between "A Worker" and "S.R." ensued, the former reminding readers that Canadian elementary education, though superior to England's, nevertheless required better inspection. "A Worker" also claimed that grammar schools could be excellent bases for technical education if they did not waste so much time on academic subjects. "S.R." replied that British higher education was superior ("irrelevant," the editor inserted), that technical education was just the quackery of South Kensington and Whitehall, and that all that was needful was to pay teachers well and leave them alone. Edwards summed up by saying that "S.R." had shown neither that British technical education was bad, nor that more was needed. Just as "S.R." wound up for a reply, the *Journal* folded.[26]

### Examinations

A valuable initiative by the board was its examination scheme. By mid-century, the British were warming up to their "examination mania" by taking the models of the Cambridge mathematics tripos and extending exams to many groups of society, particularly the civil service.[27] Technical education was another area ripe for such a process. Those in charge of organizing it related closely to each other through the Liberal Party, the Society of Arts, and the Royal Commissioners of the Exhibition of 1851, the last two under Prince Albert's presidency, and ideas moved freely from one arena to another.

An example was the examination system of the Society of Arts. Mathematician and divine James Booth (1806–1878), as a graduate of Trinity College, Dublin, had imbibed the concept of comprehensive examinations and broached the topic at the society. Harry Chester (1806–1868), a clerk in the Education Office, took it up as a new member and quickly became chair of the council.[28] In 1854, the society launched nation-wide examinations on a variety of subjects in technical education. There was little initial response, but over the next few years more and more metropolitan and provincial mechanics' institutes and similar institutions began offering courses following the society's syllabi.

In 1859, Henry Cole launched an exam system from the Science and Art Department that, to his friend Chester's dismay, competed directly with that of the society. Both systems, with some mutual accommodations, slowly increased in popularity. The Science and Art Department was attracting thousands of examinees annually by the 1880s, and the Society of Arts system flourishes to this day.

Canadians were aware of the Society of Arts program. The board in Canada West announced by circular in January 1859 that it would set exams parallel to the courses in the mechanics' institutes. In January 1860, it struck a Committee on Examinations with five members: Scottish-born physician Dr William Craigie (1790–1863) of the Hamilton and Gore Mechanics' Institute, along with four Toronto residents – lawyer and University of Toronto registrar Patrick Freeland, architect William Hay (1818–1888), shipping agent John E. Pell, and William Sheppard. An 1860 report by the committee outlined the program and noted that 641 candidates from seventy-nine local schools sat the Society of Arts exams in 1859.

Unfortunately, in July 1861 *no* candidates had come forth for the Canada West examinations: "This probably is not to be wondered at considering the short notice given, and the difficulties experienced by Mechanics Institutes in this country in establishing class instruction amongst their members."[29] A notice about the program in the board's *Journal* caught the attention of the *Canadian Agriculturist*, which suggested having exams for agriculture, although "its promoters must not be discouraged if it should progress but slowly. It took many years in England before a similar plan became general and efficient in its working."[30] "R.S." told the *Journal*'s editor in September 1861 that no one had appeared for the board's examinations because there were no inducements – no certificates and no prospect of better jobs or advancement.

In the United Kingdom, exams were widespread, esteemed, and competitive because people knew about and respected the central institution. Of course, the Toronto board had earned neither notice nor respect, and the institutes' loss of provincial funding was only exacerbating the problem. The exams committee's report of 14 January 1862 noted: "The withdrawal from the Mechanics' Institutes of all Government aid, has resulted in the total failure of some, and the paralyzing of the efforts of many others of these institutes, and will no doubt in a great measure account for the absence of a more general co-operation on their part with the objects of this Board. Your Committee look upon these institutions as Schools or Colleges, for the adult mechanical and industrial classes of the community, affording them means of instruction, and of healthful recreation, so essential to their well-being, and such is not to be obtained by them through any other agencies now in existence; and are therefore justly entitled to legislative aid corresponding to that given to societies for the encouragement of agriculture, and for the purposes of general education."[31]

Perhaps taking to heart the letter from "R.S.," the exams committee announced in January 1862 an incentive of $10 for any mechanics' institute providing three months' instruction in one of the board's subjects. In addition, the top 20 per cent of students who passed the May exams would receive silver medals. Response was feeble. Annual reports show seven candidates (all Toronto students) in 1863, seventeen in 1864, and nine in 1865. For 1865, Edwards drew up a circular on the "Annual Examination of Candidates ... to encourage, test, attest and reward efforts made by the industrial classes for self-improvement."[32] In the end, the decisive factor was the perilous state of mechanics' institutes. In his 1864 report to the minister, Dr Beatty reiterated: institutes have no funds; they do not affiliate with the boards; and the boards cannot fulfil their goals. Only the return of funding would solve anything: "Your Committee cannot but remark, that while liberal public provision is made for the education of persons intending to follow the various learned professions, they cannot see that it is less important that the working classes should be provided for."[33]

## CANADA EAST'S BOARD

The Agricultural Act of 1857 established a Board of Arts and Manufactures for Lower Canada/Chambre des arts et manufactures du Bas-Canada on the same basis as the upper province's equivalent. The board, in Montreal, would have the same grant and same goals and would draw its members from the same types of constituencies. Leadership throughout its decade or so of existence resided largely with the influential, energetic, and very ambitious directors of the (1840) Montreal Mechanics' Institute. These men – from the city's commercial, financial, and industrial elite – clearly had a different outlook than did their Toronto counterparts, and the two bodies' activities soon diverged.

### Membership

Once the board was operational during the winter of 1858–59, it boasted many more members than its twin. While boards of trade in Canada West ignored the Toronto board, both railway entrepreneur and Liberal politician Luther Holton (1817–1880) of Montreal and James Gillespie, president of the Quebec Board of Trade, took seats on Montreal's. The membership numbers of mechanics' institutes gave them thirty-four delegates, twenty-one of them from Montreal, including president and woollen manufacturer George W. Weaver (1808–1881), David Brown, sugar manufacturer John Redpath (1796–1869), and newspaper publisher Lt.-Col. Alexander A. Stevenson (b. 1829). All became active in board affairs. The institutes of Chambly, Chatham, Iberville, Lachute, St Andrews, St-Césaire, St-Hyacinthe, and Sorel sent their presidents or other delegates, most of whom were anglophones.

The act had also allowed seats for all professors of the physical sciences in colleges and universities. Because Lower Canada had three universities – Bishop's (in Lennoxville), Laval, and McGill – and a system of *collèges classiques*, many more men could participate.[34] But because few of these people attended board meetings – distance being a barrier for many – the anglophones had a majority of those present, giving the anglophone Montreal Mechanics' Institute and McGill members a clear field.

### An Active Executive

The executive ("sub-committee") met first on 30 September 1857 with John Redpath as president; David Brown replaced him in 1858. In the first months, the board agreed on three projects. First, it dispatched firefighter Alfred Perry and foundry owner and city councillor William Rodden to visit the exhibitions in both halves of the province and to purchase models. They were to keep an eye open for materials for an industrial museum, one of the act's expectations.

Second, Principal William Dawson of McGill headed a lecture committee to ask professors in Canadas East and West to speak at mechanics' institutes on applying science to industry. Dawson himself was one of them. In the first public lecture for winter 1858, in Montreal, Bishop's Professor Henry Hopper Miles (1818–1895) talked about ventilation, and the text appeared in print later that year. In the following winter, Edward Kendall, professor of mathematics at Trinity College, Toronto, gave an address: "The Connection between Experiment and Theory in the Progress of Scientific Discovery."

Third, the board would offer evening classes. By November 1858, a circular to affiliated institutes laid out the rules:

1 Classes must run for at least three months.
2 Reading, writing and arithmetic could be taught.
3 Instruction could also be provided in book-keeping, mechanical drawing, mathematics, grammar, English, French, chemistry, natural philosophy.
4 Institutes should arrange with employers to allow apprentices to attend.
5 Examiners for the courses would be approved by the Board.

A problem soon surfaced: institutes seemed reluctant to affiliate with the board. Only two – in Montreal and Lachute – had offered night classes. In January 1858, the subcommittee noted that some institutes did not like the affiliation rules, while others simply had no money.

The board meeting of 4 January 1859 attracted twenty-two members – about one-third of its complement – none of them ex officio from outside the Montreal area.[35] Only one francophone, education superintendent P.-J.-O. Chauveau, attended. Brown was president, Chauveau vice-president, and Brown Chamberlin (1827–1897) secretary. The subcommittee's report on 1858 revealed its interest in a wide range of activities in the act.

By the spring of 1859, nine mechanics' institutes – Chambly, Chatham, Iberville, Lachute, Montreal, St Andrews, St-Georges de Henryville, St-Hyacinthe, and Sorel – had affiliated, but only three were offering night classes under the board's aegis. As in Canada West, this was a poor showing – fifty-one institutes had received government grants the previous year.[36] Of course, most of them were relatively new, and many had probably already disappeared. Montreal's had run classes from January to March with ninety-five students, and Chambly and Lachute's also offered courses. Subcommittee members hoped to supervise and inspect affiliates, although the act did not specify such powers; they had ambitious ideas but received little respect from the government.

The board also wanted to form a union of institutes, similar to the Yorkshire Union in England, which made use of the Society of Arts' exam program. To that end, it invited the affiliates in Quebec, Sherbrooke, and Trois-Rivières to form corresponding committees but heard nothing back. The subcommittee asked the legislative assembly for a larger grant to build up a museum of domestic industry (presumably like those in London and Dublin), a better library, a model room, and a school of design for women. No assistance was forthcoming. But the revised Agricultural Act of 1862 allowed mechanics' institutes to group in unions, which in turn could affiliate with the boards. Following the pattern of the provincial agricultural boards, any grants to institutes would pass through the two boards first, not go directly to the institutes, so that these boards too would definitely obtain their tithes. Changes in the act were moot: no unions or grants materialized.

## Technical Instruction

It was natural that Canada East's board would pursue technical education, as Montreal had Canada's most extensive manufacturing and largest working class. Board members Chauveau and Dawson were firm supporters of technical instruction. Another key player was secretary Brown Chamberlin. A native of Frelighsburg in the Eastern Townships and the son of a physician, Chamberlin took his law degree at McGill in 1850, became proprietor of Montreal's *Gazette*, was a founding member of the Art Association of Montreal, and in 1867 won a seat in the new federal Parliament.

Chamberlin was keen for the board to expand its activities; to that end, he suggested in 1859 that he visit major science and art institutions on a forthcoming trip to Britain and the continent and report back.[37] He sought models that might work in Canada. In Dublin, Edinburgh, and London, he saw the popularity of the museums, which he thought an invaluable educational tool for the poor and working class. The Science and Art Department's art schools and the Society of Arts' examinations and classes in affiliated mechanics' institutes he found particularly attractive. He attended a meeting of the society, spoke with its officers, and read its collection of articles on the lessons of the Great Exhibition. He recognized that Canadians had many educational opportunities but felt that "we need also, under the immediate supervision of this Board, an Industrial University with affiliated Working-men's Colleges in each considerable town or city in the Province."

Chamberlin then set out an ambitious program: the board should create classes in affiliated institutes, museums, and reference libraries, and urge the Board of Agriculture to provide for agricultural education. This, of course, would require more money and direct inspection of institutes. To initiate the program, he had written to Henry Cole in South Kensington for models and designs but, as Cole was ill, received no reply; a request to Sir Roderick Murchison (1792–1871), director of the British Geological Survey, resulted in a shipment of books; and the Conservatoire des arts et métiers in Paris offered its assistance. The ultimate goal of all this effort, for Chamberlin, was financial gain and dignity for the Canadian worker and Canadian competitiveness in manufactures.

### Montreal's "Crystal Palace" (1860)

These ideas were welcome to the board and, indeed, echoed the thoughts of its Toronto counterpart. It was then, in 1859, that the board made what seems a major tactical error – a speculative venture – to erect a massive hall in Montreal to host the provincial exhibition of 1860. As Prince Albert's son Albert Edward, Prince of Wales, was visiting Canada that year, perhaps he might open the structure officially. Thus, at a cost of nearly $44,000, the Crystal Palace rose on Ste Catherine street, between University and Cathcart, and, during the exhibition, the heir to the throne opened it officially on 25 August 1860.[38]

The board envisioned its Exhibition Building as the site of its offices and museum of industry and assumed that it could rent out much of the space and that other events would follow the exhibition. Unfortunately, this did not happen, and the board had to carry a large mortgage, which severely crippled its activities. Continuing pleas for government assistance or a larger annual grant (still only $2,000) were to no avail. The board had had hopes of publishing a journal, but that was now out of the question. As a result, the *Journal* of the Canada West board published its minutes and reprinted articles on technical education from the Montreal press. In 1863, editor J.-X. Perrault offered the board column space in the Board of Agriculture's *Revue agricole*, but it declined because of its "inability."

In 1861, the Board of Arts and Manufactures for Lower Canada was still sanguine about creating a national museum of industrial resources, similar to those in Dublin, Edinburgh, and London, in its Exhibition Building. Although the Montreal Mechanics' Institute seemed to be healthy – with a claim of 440 "mechanic" members – no francophone delegates attended board meetings.[39] The free annual lecture series survived, with Dawson giving the opener in February; Chamberlin reprinted it in the *Gazette*.[40] Contraction was inevitable. In its 1864 report to Minister of Agriculture Thomas D'Arcy McGee (1825–1868), the board noted that Montreal's institute was the only one in Canada East in affiliation. The board maintained a small library and obtained 100 volumes of text and plates from Britain's Patent Office, and Montreal's institute enrolled some 100 students in architectural and mechanical drawing, as well as English.[41]

The Exhibition Building remained problematic: the militia had occupied it during 1861–62, the board could not persuade the Board of Agriculture to rent quarters there, and a contractor had won a court judgment against the board. The board was still paying a large mortgage plus annual ground rent of $1,200 and would be essentially bankrupt unless the government purchased the facility. When it approached Attorney-General (Canada East) Louis-V. Sicotte (1812–1889), he promised to take its case before the executive council (cabinet). A year passed and nothing happened, except for a leaking roof. During 1864, the board suspended its only evening classes because of repairs under way to Mechanics' Hall.

At its January 1866 meeting, the subcommittee admitted that it was still seeking government help with its debt. On 14 August 1865, Chamberlin had put to McGee the same case as Canada West's board, that with the state supporting the upper and middle classes and agriculture, "the artizans or manufacturing classes in that case would, alone, seem to be utterly unworthy of any care or assistance."[42] McGee was sympathetic. He knew that the Crystal Palace albatross was long overdue for solution and that a $2,000 annual grant was nowhere near adequate for the board to fulfil the act's mandate. He thought that Canada's rising manufacturing sector called for more technical instruction and government aid; however, he observed,

while concurring in this view, I yet feel it my duty to observe that it seems most undesirable to have institutions of this description dependent on the Government alone, or even principally, for their pecuniary means. In England, to whose example we are frequently referred by complainants on this subject, all such institutions depend mainly on local subscriptions and only partially on Parliamentary grants. Such is the fact in relation to Mechanics' Institutes, Science Schools, Evening Schools and Schools of Design. The English government, indeed, does much: its Committee of Council on Education, and its Science and Art Department, have effected great things for Arts and Manufactures since the attention of the State was fairly challenged to those important subjects in 1851. The Government of Canada ought unquestionably to do much more than it has done to promote similar objects and interests, but without liberal and continuous local co-operation, the desirable results never can be reached.[43]

The board was becoming more desperate. Early in 1866, Brown Chamberlin, acting on behalf of the Art Association, suggested that the board sell the Exhibition Building to the association for use as a gallery and school of art and design. That organization had first sent delegates to the board in 1866 after changes to the Agricultural Act. It would donate $250 for materials and organization of the school and then an annual $500 if the board would match it. At the next meeting, the sub-committee resolved to inform the government that if there was no solution for the board's financial difficulties, a full board meeting would "consider the propriety of transferring over the property of the Board to the Government, with a view to its dissolution, feeling the impossibility in its present embarrassed condition of properly discharging the functions of the Board." It sent the resolution to McGee. By November, after a deputation to Ottawa to confer with the minister, the government agreed to pay the board for the militia to use the Exhibition Building for five years.

By early 1867, the board's fortunes seemed to be looking up,[44] with the government's finally having settled much of its debt. President Henry Bulmer, brick maker, inventor, and former city councillor; Vice-President George A. Drummond (1829–1910), manager of Redpath's mill (and the owner's brother- and son-in-law); Secretary A.A. Stevenson; and Treasurer former alderman Norton B. Corse, along with an all-anglophone subcommittee, were making plans to move the Library of Reference to the Mechanics' Institute. The library consisted only of British patent records, there having been no funds for other purchases. A school of design again seemed a possibility for the Exhibition Building.

### Other Activities

Preparations for Canadian participation in international exhibitions also absorbed much of the board's energies, unlike its Toronto counterpart. The Paris Exposition of 1867 required substantial effort, but at least a special grant was available to purchase items for it. The following year saw the provincial exhibition, and the board's meagre resources went to assist night classes at the Montreal Mechanics' Institute and the Institut des artisans canadiens (see chapter 8, below). Just over 130 students enrolled in algebra, architectural and mechanical drawing, arithmetic, bookkeeping, dictation, mathematics, and writing. Courses and enrolments the next year were much the same.[45] Throughout this period, as the board's correspondence with the provincial secretary for

Canada East shows,[46] most of its dealings with the government centred on three topics: changes to patent laws, organization and funding of exhibitors to international exhibitions, and requests for a larger annual grant and for relief from "continuing financial embarrassment."

## WHAT DID THE BOARDS ACCOMPLISH?

On 1 July 1867, most of British North America – Nova Scotia, New Brunswick, Canada East, and Canada West – federated as the Dominion of Canada. Unfortunately, no one had bothered to inform the Board of Arts and Manufactures for Upper Canada what its role was to be in the new order. On 11 July, the board struck a committee to examine its future and relations with government and the mechanics' institutes regarding promotion of technical education.[47] Secretary William Edwards wrote to Ottawa asking about the disposition of the following year's grant; a clerk in the agricultural ministry replied that the "Minister of Finance has decided that your application must be addressed to the Local Government of Ontario."[48] Dutifully, Edwards applied to Sir John Carling (1828–1911), who was to be commissioner of agriculture and public works for Ontario,[49] but the new province's cabinet had other matters to deal with. Finally, at its January 1868 meeting, the board, having learned that the government intended to create a separate agricultural library and museum, agreed to wind up its activities. For the hardworking and loyal William Edwards, there was the promise of becoming secretary for public works in the new Ontario Bureau of Agriculture.[50] Edwards would carry on the groundwork that the board laid within a new framework, the Association of Mechanics' Institutes of Ontario.

What had the Board of Arts and Manufactures for Upper Canada accomplished? One would have to judge its results as limited, but useful. It faced many obstacles from the beginning. The government paid little attention to it – not surprising in the light of the divisive political climate in the decade before Confederation. Also, because Canada had not yet industrialized, the place of the working class and its needs was not a mirror of its British equivalent. A simple comparison of the funds Canada West devoted to agriculture and to arts and manufactures speaks eloquently of the government's priorities.[51] There *was* a manufacturing interest, but during the early 1860s it had much less clout than the agricultural, and the government responded accordingly. The small, unorganized, and dispersed working class had few voices in either mechanics' institutes or publications ostensibly for its benefit. In Canadian society, it was largely invisible. Board members meant well but had good educations and were proudly middle class, representing primarily Toronto's commercial and, only marginally, manufacturing interests. Its members and policies were a faithful colonial reflection of the men and ideas of the Society of Arts and the Science and Art Department in London.

The evidence does not indicate whether the model room in the board's suite in Toronto inspired prospective inventors or manufacturers. William Edwards claimed that the reference library had a lot of use, but presumably not by mechanics and artisans from budding industrial centres such as Brantford, Hamilton, or London. In addition, there is no measure of the impact of its excellent journal. Had the board never existed, the history of early technical education in central Canada would have been only a little different. Yet the board's debates, its lobbying the government, and its continuous efforts to establish permanent institutions for technical education, which we explore below in chapter 7, did at least introduce the vocabulary of the issue and set the stage for provincial action, which would come later.

The Board of Arts and Manufactures for Lower Canada had been much less successful. With few financial resources and minimal support from virtually all its mechanics' institutes, it could supply little in the way of a library, museum, and model room. It had no journal, no school of design, and few classes. It saddled itself with an unproductive piece of real estate and, though in Canada's pre-eminent financial and industrial city, did not achieve as much as its Toronto counterpart. Successive ministers, while sympathetic, did little to aid it.

There are several reasons for the Montreal board's poor record. First, it built almost no bridges to the francophone community. Second, francophone college professors displayed no interest in it, as the kind of education they themselves purveyed was so different. Third, P.-J.-O. Chauveau was too busy as superintendent of education. Fourth, the Montreal Mechanics' Institute, which had provided leadership throughout the board's existence, represented concerns quite different from the needs of a francophone working class. Fifth, the slowly emerging group of French-Canadian industrial and commercial entrepreneurs felt no attraction to the essentially anglophone mechanics' institutes, and the Institut-canadien movement eschewed technical instruction altogether.

In the end, what had the board accomplished? Apart from the white-elephant Crystal Palace, it had participated in exhibitions and had supported public lectures and evening classes for mechanics, but almost all of this activity it had in effect usurped from the Montreal Mechanics' Institute. Of course, as the same men ran both organizations, it just meant that the funding came from a different pot.

## RYERSON'S DREAM (1849–67):
## AN ART SCHOOL FOR CANADA WEST

Curiously, before Confederation, most of the discussion on the need for art instruction took place in Canada West; it was only in the 1860s that awareness grew in the lower section of the province, which we consider below in chapter 8. It may be that Upper Canadians were more in tune with contemporary British ideas.[52] Canada West offered no systematic instruction in art, whether fine art or for industry.

As early as 1848, the Toronto Mechanics' Institute must have seen discussions about an art school, and schools superintendent Egerton Ryerson added his support in an address to the institute in early January 1849. J.E. Pell and other mechanics petitioned the legislature to create a school of design and persuaded the Toronto MLA and former premier Henry Sherwood (1807–1855) to introduce it into the legislature in January 1849.[53] No action followed. At the same time, Henry Youle Hind, having studied in a technical school in Germany, sketched out a curriculum for a practical arts school that would include linear drawing in all three years.[54]

Ryerson approved of the idea and believed that the legislature should support such a school. He had visited London's Central School of Design at Somerset House but understood that it taught ornamental, not practical, art. For most of the 1850s, Ryerson was silent about art teaching in his *Journal of Education*. When the normal school had to leave its original home, Ryerson ensured that a new building included space for both a provincial school of art and design and a museum. When the structure opened in May 1852, however, it had no school of art, no museum, and no funds to finance either. The following year, the Supplementary Common School Act (16 Vict., cap. 185) provided Ryerson with £500 per annum for purchases and £500 to establish a school of art and design. When Ryerson learned that the new University of Toronto was contemplating a chair of civil engineering, he suggested connecting the school of art with that chair rather than with the normal school. When the university dropped its idea for this plan, Ryerson reverted to his original scheme.[55]

The earliest purchases for the art school included old books, stuffed animals and birds, birds' eggs, and a geological collection that it purchased from John William Dawson, then Ryerson's counterpart in Nova Scotia (and later principal of McGill). George-Etienne Cartier (1814–1873), provincial secretary for Canada East, named Ryerson to the Canadian Commission for the 1855 Paris Exposition. Ryerson and his daughter planned to spend a year on the continent and in England, and he purchased materials illustrative of education with the assistance of Alfred Perry (whom we met above), curator of the exposition's Canadian Department. Clearly, £500 would not go far in the purchase of original works of art.

Fortuitously, in London Ryerson soon met his old acquaintance Col. John Henry Lefroy (1817–1890), who had recently retired from directing the Toronto Magnetic and Meteorological Observatory. Lefroy suggested purchasing copies of paintings and casts of statues. With approval by key members of the government, Ryerson scoured first London and then Paris for possible additions. After the exposition closed, he obtained a significant collection of items, then moved on to Belgium, Germany, and Italy. In the end, he amassed some 150 paintings (mostly copies), engravings, casts of statues, and models of German agricultural implements. He shipped them all home, and by early 1857 the Educational Museum, crowding into a too-small area of the normal school, opened to the public.

This was the same year that the South Kensington Museum opened, and Ryerson followed in Henry Cole's footsteps: "The Educational Museum is founded after the example of what is being done by the Imperial Government as part of the system of popular education – regarding the indirect, as scarcely secondary to the direct means of training the minds and forming the taste and character of the people."[56] During another trip to London in the autumn of 1857, he met twice with Cole in the vain hope of finding a drawing master.[57] In an effort to keep interest alive, Ryerson reprinted in his *Journal of Education* an article of Lord Granville's on the reasons for establishing art schools with state support.[58]

Soon afterwards, the Toronto Mechanics' Institute petitioned the Board of Arts and Manufactures for Upper Canada to stimulate the teaching of mechanical drawing and practical mathematics in other institutes. In January 1859, the board announced that it would award prizes for drawings in local classes.[59] In January 1858, architect Frederic Cumberland (1820–1881) had reminded the board that the Agricultural Act had called for an art school "for persons engaged in Industrial Art," and he moved to send a subcommittee – including himself, furniture manufacturer Robert Hay (1808–1890), former sheriff William Jarvis, and J.E. Pell – to confer with Ryerson on creating a school of design and its potential use of the new art collection in the normal school. Ryerson told the delegation that the collection would be available and that a school of art and design would open "at an early day." With this assurance, the board sent a circular to mechanics' institutes in February 1858 announcing the superintendent's intentions to open the school and thus "to afford instruction, as far as these are of practical interest to mechanics, artizans and manufacturers."[60]

In 1858, the normal school expanded into a second building, freeing up space for the school of art and design. As the *Journal of Education* noted in February 1861, "The ground work of this school of Art and Design is laid upon an extensive scale. The apartments allotted to its use are spacious and convenient, and it already exhibits a fine display of works of art in sculpture, painting, &c."[61] There was, however, no school in operation, although Ryerson was still claiming in 1862 that it was ready to open its doors. The Toronto *Globe* weighed in on the subject in 1863, noting that Canada had a few outstanding artists such as Théophile Hamel (1817–1870) and Paul Kane (1810–1871) but few qualified drawing instructors; what it needed was a proper school of design: "Dr. Ryerson once cherished a scheme for connecting such an institution with the Normal School ... His idea has never borne fruit, nor is it likely to do so ... The Mechanics' Institute of this city has in operation a drawing class which, we understand, is well taught and fairly attended. It seems to us that this might form the nucleus of a larger establishment in connection with the Institute."[62] The *Globe* believed that even one school could serve as a model for other locations, using the monies the government saved by withholding grants to mechanics' institutes.

The Board of Arts and Manufactures for Upper Canada, in its annual report of January 1864, admitted that there was still no school of design and that Ryerson had yet to accomplish anything "for some cause unknown." The board had no money and could only hope the legislature would assist. Later that summer, the board struck a committee to inquire into the problem. H.E. Clarke, Henry Langley, and William Sheppard reported in October that the province required a school for both science and art, as there was no provision for working-class education. The board re-appointed the committee to supply a plan,[63] which appeared in the annual report for 1865. It went beyond an art school by encompassing science and mathematics, a scheme not unlike what Hind had proposed sixteen years previous.[64]

This scheme fell on deaf ears. In its January 1866 report, the board lamented the great expenditure on agriculture ($100,000) and for the learned professions through support to the university and colleges. While mechanics could attend such schools, it would not benefit their own work. A year later, the board disbanded, and no formal art training beyond occasional night classes was in sight. Curiously, when Ryerson made another museum purchasing trip to London in the winter of 1867, he took William McDougall through the South Kensington Museum and art schools and had a long discussion with him on a school of art.[65] There is no doubt that Ryerson wanted an art school and did much to prepare for it, yet some kind of paralysis gripped him. As it turned out, he would accomplish nothing further in this direction before his retirement in 1876.

In retrospect, the desire for an art school as early as the late 1840s and early 1850s seems to have been premature in the light of the state of Canadian society. Had a school of art and design emerged, where would the instructors have come from? They might have been former students of one of the English schools of design, but those were, by the late 1840s, under severe attack for their inefficiency and poor quality. Worse, where would graduates of a Toronto school find employment? Positions in industrial design in Canada were vanishingly small at the time. One could return to Britain, although competition for positions there would be stiff.

## TECHNICAL INSTRUCTION IN CANADA EAST'S SCHOOLS

### J.-B. Meilleur and Technical Instruction

Jean-Baptiste Meilleur (1796–1878), the first superintendent of public instruction for Lower Canada, was ideal for the position. After a secondary education in both French and English in Montreal, he studied science and medicine in Vermont and received an MD from Middlebury College in 1825. He settled in L'Assomption, working as a physician, writing scientific and medical articles, and sitting in the assembly 1834–38. He already had a great interest in education – schools in Lower Canada were deplorable – helped to found the Collège de l'Assomption in 1834, and wrote the first Canadian scientific textbook, *Cours abrégé de leçons de chymie* (1833). When John George Lambton, Earl of Durham (1792–1840), arrived in Canada as governor-in-chief in spring 1838, he set up several commissions of inquiry, and the group on education learned of Meilleur's ideas on the subject; Durham's famous report of 1839 helped lead to the union of Upper and Lower Canada in 1841. When the United Province's Education Act came into force in 1841, Meilleur was an obvious candidate to become superintendent for the new Canada East.

As an MLA for L'Assomption, Meilleur had sat on the education committee, where he had argued that all teachers must have scientific as well as moral qualifications.[66] He had repeated this, with more emphasis, in his influential letters on education in *Le populaire* of Montreal and *Le canadien* in Quebec in 1838. As well, he staunchly opposed the influx of American textbooks and teachers, as Ryerson did, on the grounds that they would undercut Canadian political and cultural development. Once Meilleur was superintendent, he faced a host of problems far more pressing than those of technical education. For his contemporaries in the mechanics'-institute movement, the teaching of elementary physical science and mathematics was a preliminary to, if not the essence of, technical instruction for the working class. Meilleur, in contrast, thought of science in different terms. He was a physician by training and, being a liberal professional, a full member of the francophone élite. For most of that group, science was an intellectual end in itself, not necessarily a means to a practical end. He supported agricultural education but effected little in that direction. To introduce science into elementary schools, he brought in the texts of the Irish national schools; these books, even the elementary readers, were perhaps the best introduction to science then available.[67]

### Education in Canada East

During the 1840s and 1850s, several parallel streams of education flowed in Canada East. The state-supported common schools suffered from both sectarian and linguistic divisions, and Meilleur's reports indicate little progress in either mechanical or agricultural instruction. Three forms of private school also existed: anglophone institutions, many of them "academies," which would multiply over the next few decades; francophone, Roman Catholic *collèges classiques*; and several Catholic-run specialized schools. Neither the academies nor the *collèges* offered any technical instruction, because both were for the upper and middle classes.

We know much more about the *collèges*,[68] and their records, graduates' careers, and surviving textbooks and lecture notes show them preparing students for the priesthood or the liberal professions.[69] Their fathers may have been farmers, millers, or founders, but they expected their sons to enter medicine, law, the priesthood, or teaching. In fact, many also chose careers in politics or journalism.[70] This pattern merely followed the widespread belief that francophones could not enter other callings, such as commerce and industry, and could forge ahead only in

the liberal professions. As we see below, this assumption, which long out-
lived the reality, truncated later efforts to expand technical instruction
for the emerging francophone urban working class. Although the *collèges*
made science an integral part of secondary education, they concentrated
the physical sciences and mathematics in the last two years (*philosophie*),
a course that only a minority of students followed. Scientific instruction
was first class in some of the *collèges*.[71]

What technical instruction we find during this period was almost exclusively for the poor.[72] The government's creation of schools for the same
class of students had to wait for the 1880s. One limited means of promoting technical education was through a normal school. This was Ryerson's
strategy in Canada West, first with agriculture and later with drawing.
Because of a variety of circumstances and political reasons, Canada East
created no normal schools until 1857. All three normal schools –
Montreal's McGill and Jacques-Cartier and Quebec's Laval – offered
elementary science and mathematics but no agriculture or drawing.[73]
Even in the normal schools, not all pupils studied science and mathematics, and the francophones in particular ignored these subjects.

## TECHNICAL EDUCATION IN THE UNIVERSITIES
## (LATE 1850S)

Before 1850, the profession of engineering in Canada was something of
a grey area: not quite a profession like law or medicine, but obviously
more than a trade. Until later in the century, when the chemical, electrical, and mining industries required engineering specialists, "engineer"
meant civil engineer. Civil engineers, like architects and surveyors, were
much in demand for Canada's growing towns and public works. The
British army's well-trained Royal Engineers had designed and built early
major works, such as the Rideau Canal (1826–32), but civilian engineers
soon became the primary source of expertise. Until about 1850, many of
Canada's finest engineers had trained on the job.[74] Almost all architects,
engineers, and surveyors learned on the job under the supervision of an
experienced person. Lawyers and physicians trained the same way until
professional schools were fully operational and licensing boards turned
against such informal education.

The training of military engineers dates back many centuries, but
schools for civilian engineers started with the foundation of the Ecole
polytechnique in Paris in 1794. In the early nineteenth century, France
and German states created a number of schools to train civilian engineers.

In the United Kingdom, the tradition of on-the-job training persisted, although universities began to show an interest in the subject with the creation of programs at University College, London, in 1828; King's College, London, in 1838; the University of Glasgow in 1840; and Trinity College, Dublin, in 1842. None met with much success. In the United States, the West Point military academy trained army engineers from 1802 on, while the Rensselaer School in Troy, New York, started offering a degree in civil engineering in 1835. Within a decade, many American universities had established engineering education. In Canada, the University of Toronto and McGill began to plan for engineering instruction in the 1850s, with results we now explore.

### Toronto

In Canada West, civil engineering was one of a list of professorships proposed for the University of Toronto in 1851. The creation of a chair in agriculture was the result of several years of discussion and lobbying; supporters of civil engineering seem to have been much quieter. Scientific and mathematical instruction, a staple of university engineering education, could come from regular faculty members, but practical knowledge only from an engineer with experience. As Young relates, much wrangling and politicking ensued, but in the end, Toronto appointed no one to civil engineering.[75]

None the less the university pressed on, publishing regulations for a two-year diploma in 1855, but no engineering lectures were on the horizon. Although the program was ready in 1857, no students appeared until the following year. Local engineers came in as examiners, but there was never a professor. With no professor, a diploma could serve only as a qualification for someone already studying privately with an engineer. Toronto kept its engineering diploma on the books for twenty-six years and in that time awarded seven diplomas.[76]

### McGill

In Canada East, engineering education appeared to have a more favourable outlook. McGill's appointment of John William Dawson as principal in 1855 was a signal that the directors of the Royal Institution for the Advancement of Learning were serious about the university's developing a more practical bent. Although the Faculty of Arts barely existed, the medical school had thrived for some years; any science at McGill was there. In his 1855 inaugural address, Dawson held out the possibility that anyone wanting technical instruction might obtain it without enrolling in a full program: "To secure wide usefulness, collegiate institutions should be prepared to give the preparatory instruction demanded for the learned professions, and special courses of practical science suited to the circumstances of those who, while they desire instruction in some of the departments of college study, do not require to attend to all."[77]

To that, the university would add further outreach: "In the direction of a school of practical science, all that has yet been done is to offer access to any of our lectures to all persons who may desire to attend them without entering themselves as regular students, and the provision of popular evening lectures for the benefit of the public." [78] Dawson envisaged virtually the same program as one that King's College, Fredericton, was considering: special courses in agriculture, civil engineering, and commercial education. In practice, however, the hurdles McGill had to clear just to establish a viable Arts Faculty were so many that in the end it launched only the civil engineering courses.

To drum up interest, Dawson, civil engineer Thomas Coltrin Keefer (1821–1915), and others offered public lectures in 1856–57. A prospectus for a two-year course leading to a diploma in civil engineering appeared in 1857. Mark Hamilton became professor of civil engineering. Although the program began well, an economic downturn cut into enrolments, which declined to one student by 1862–63. Hamilton's position was then terminated. Although the program remained on the books, it was in abeyance from 1864 to 1871.[79] It had awarded only sixteen diplomas. At McGill, as in Toronto, the introduction of professional engineering education was simply premature. By the late 1870s, as the country industrialized rapidly, engineering would thrive in both universities; however, it was clear for Dawson and his associates that professional training within the university was not the same as technical training for the working class.

Someone of Dawson's stature and energy was much in demand in Montreal, and we soon find him a central figure in both the Montreal Natural History Society and the Mechanics' Institute. Through his public lecturing and willingness to sit on committees and councils, his activity was salutary to both institutions, which had been flagging by the mid-1850s. In both, he was part of the middle-class, anglophone establishment of Montreal, and these two institutions, along with McGill, served the needs of that community. Thus technical education in the form of agricultural and civil engineering courses at McGill almost necessarily excluded working-class youths. And, while an increasing number of francophones enrolled in its programs during the next half-century, the linguistic and social barriers remained formidable.

## CONCLUSION

The Province of Canada had rationalized government support for agricultural activities tolerably well, with two viable provincial organizations, stable local societies, local and provincial exhibitions, and the first tentative steps towards formal education. The same was not true for working-class technical instruction. While the vision that the 1857 act laid out for the two Boards of Arts and Manufactures was broad, the boards could not in any way realize it. Those who served on and directed the two bodies had experience and meant well, and most of them were middle class, but the state did not give them enough money. While the board in Toronto had only feeble links with the mechanics' institutes, Montreal's had almost none. In most of the institutes themselves, their activity, which was at a low level, only worsened when their grants evaporated. Although, at least, the Toronto Mechanics' Institute took evening courses seriously, the board's examination scheme was a dead loss. The Montreal institute also provided evening classes, but the board in Canada East usurped them. That board also sank itself financially with the construction of the Crystal Palace. One bright spot was the Toronto board's *Journal*, but it lasted less than a decade, and we will never know how many artisans and mechanics read it. As for art education, then an important facet of technical instruction, there was much talk but no action, except for Ryerson's museum. Finally, in the public-school sector, school systems in both parts of the province focused too much on elementary education to concern themselves with technical education for the working class.

PART TWO

The Campaign (1867–1900)

# 5

# Agricultural Education in Ontario

Before July 1867, the Province of Canada's Department of Agriculture funded most of the educational activity the government aimed at the farming population. The imperial Parliament's British North America Act of 1867 assigned education strictly to the new provincial governments – including Lower Canada's (now Quebec) in Quebec City and Upper Canada's (now Ontario) in Toronto – but section 95 of the act divided agriculture, allowing either provinces or the new Dominion government in Ottawa to enact laws respecting agriculture or immigration, so long as provincial laws did not conflict with federal statutes. In practice, the division of powers proved straightforward and non-controversial.

The Department of Agriculture under the former Union had been a grab-bag of disparate responsibilities: agriculture, the census, colonization roads, immigration, patents, and statistics. Agriculture and colonization roads, the costliest, passed to Quebec and Toronto for funding. Agriculture, properly speaking, had included grants to the provincial agricultural associations, funds for local societies, and small grants for educational purposes. Under the 1867 division of powers, the federal Department of Agriculture had no true *agricultural* responsibilities at all. With the Dominion's purchase of Rupert's Land (about 1½ million square miles) in 1870 and the promise of a vast agricultural region in the west, the federal department would slowly resume this function, offering grants for societies and exhibitions in the North-West Territories as settlers moved in. Animal health and creation of the experimental-farm system would become major activities for it in the last quarter of the century, but neither was educational. The new provincial departments of agriculture in Ontario and Quebec appeared similar to each other in structure and in scope, but differing political cultures and farming needs would quickly distinguish their practices.

In this chapter, we look in turn at how the new and industrializing province of Ontario organized agricultural activity at the provincial, regional, and local levels, including agricultural societies and education; at the rocky emergence of the Ontario Agricultural College in Guelph, its growing reputation, and its influential work in agricultural extension; and at the vexed issue of agricultural instruction in schools.

## AGRICULTURE AND ITS ORGANIZATION

### Industrialization

By 1867, central Canadian agriculture, though heterogeneous, was in the process of a major shift; two areas for diversification were dairying and fruit growing. Both had been small-scale facets of mixed farming from the earliest days, but for home consumption. Orchards had long existed on Lake Ontario and in the Niagara peninsula, and the collapse of the wheat crop due to pests in 1863 turned many Niagara farmers into fruit growers – Canada's first agricultural specialists, leading the way in education. In dairy production, many farms in central Canada had one or two milk cows to provide fluid milk, butter, and possibly cheese. Butter production, in particular, was labour-intensive with the hand churn, the province of the farm wife. Butter was for only home or local consumption, because refrigeration, quality control, and hygiene were lacking.

The industrialization of dairying in the nineteenth century began with cooperative dairies in Switzerland and Denmark. In Denmark, government support for training soon made its dairy industry a market leader, particularly in the large British butter market. Americans were quick to follow; cooperative dairying began in Oneida County, New York, in 1851, with co-op cheese-making in 1852.[1] The idea spread rapidly. Harvey Farrington (1809–1879) of Herkimer County, New York, settled in Oxford County in Canada West in 1863 and opened a cheese factory in North Norwich Township the following year, piquing local interest. In response to a request, Professor L.B. Arnold from Utica gave three lectures daily for one week in Ingersoll. The factory system of cheese-making spread quickly, with new factories opening in Northumberland and Hastings counties by 1866. Cheese soon became a small-scale export item.[2]

Urbanization and industrialization were altering the countryside, with new railways carrying commodities to distant markets and manufactured goods to local centres. By the mid-1850s, many small implement manufacturers existed, but curried only to the local market. By late decade, the arrival of railways spurred implement manufacturers to locate along the lines; most were in Canada West and very few east of Montreal. During and after the US Civil War, Canadian farms began snapping up mechanized equipment – most of it American in design and manufactured under patent licence or simply pirated. According to McCalla, implement production rose six-fold in value during the 1860s. The 1871 census reported Ontario farmers owning 37,000 reapers and mowers.[3] Ontario agriculture had changed radically since the Union of 1841.

### Running the Show

In organizing the administration of both education and agriculture in 1867, John Sandfield Macdonald's Liberal-Conservative coalition in Ontario simply left the Canada West offices in place. With Rev. Egerton Ryerson remaining superintendent, education had no direct representation in the Cabinet. Agriculture combined with public works under a non-Cabinet commissioner. Headquarters staff was minimal: George Buckland carried on as secretary of the Bureau of Agriculture; William Edwards left the defunct Board of Arts and Manufactures to become secretary for Public Works; and agriculture had a librarian and an assistant secretary.

Over the next three decades, innovation in agricultural education depended on the commissioners of agriculture and public works. Fortunately for the farm lobby, the first commissioner, John Carling, was an activist.[4] He grew up on a farm near London and took over his father's brewery in 1849. From 1857 on, he served with little distinction in the legislature. After Confederation, he served as a member of the new provincial Parliament (MPP) and commissioner until Sandfield Macdonald's coalition went down to defeat in 1871. He was also an MP in Ottawa during the same period, although dual representation ended the following year. Carling later returned to the House of Commons to serve as federal minister of agriculture from 1885 to 1892, a period of great growth in that department.

The election of 1871 launched thirty-four years of Liberal rule under Edward Blake (premier 1871–72), Oliver Mowat (1872–96), Arthur Hardy (1896–99), and George W. Ross (1899–1905). Archibald McKellar took office in 1871 as commissioner but became embroiled in the scandals of the founding of the Ontario School of Agriculture, and Samuel Casey Wood replaced him in 1875. A quiet activist like Carling, Wood served with distinction until 1883. Two relative non-entities, James Young and Alexander M. Ross, followed him. In 1888, Premier Mowat raised the post to Cabinet level and chose Charles Drury as first minister of agriculture. Drury was active in agricultural organizations and worked to reform the Ontario Agricultural College but lost his seat in the 1890 election. John Dryden became the most energetic incumbent since 1850 and served as minister until James Whitney's Conservatives came to power in 1905.

In 1867, both the Upper Canada Agricultural Association and the Upper Canada Board of Agriculture remained in place, with George Buckland continuing as secretary to both. As a lover of rural life and strong supporter of agricultural interests, John Carling set the tone for agricultural development. First, he asked for advice about tweaking operations from both the provincial Agricultural Association and the mechanics' institutes.[5] Ontario's revised Agricultural Act (22 Vict., cap. 32) of 1868 abolished the Board of Arts and Manufactures for Upper Canada and the Board of Agriculture and set up a new Bureau of Agriculture and Arts to deal with both farming and mechanical interests. The Agricultural Association became the Agricultural and Arts Association of Ontario (AAAO), with its own council. The council included the commissioner of agriculture, the superintendent of education, any professors of agriculture, the presidents of both the Fruit Growers' Association and the new Association of Mechanics' Institutes of Ontario, and twelve district representatives that agricultural societies elected. Horticultural societies could now receive grants directly, on the same basis as agricultural societies, and grants to mechanics' institutes reappeared. The Bureau of Agriculture had a library but a museum still in progress, despite years of promises. The museum (on the third floor of the Agricultural Hall at Yonge and Queen streets in Toronto) did not impress *Farmers' Advocate* proprietor William Weld when he visited it early in 1867.[6]

Recognizing the pressing need for both agricultural labour and capital, Buckland suggested to the Agricultural and Arts Association of Ontario and the Bureau of Agriculture and Arts that he proceed to England to urge immigration. Carling agreed, and Buckland sailed to England in April 1868 to visit agricultural exhibitions, buy seed, inquire into new kinds of implements, gather publications for the library, and give talks on emigration to Ontario.

*Agricultural Societies*

Agricultural societies in Ontario included some sixty-three at the county or electoral-district level and 260 at the township level. Annual provincial grants to the county groups were typically $800, although some received less; just as before 1867, the new bureau deducted 10 per cent for administration (i.e., for the association) and 2.5 per cent for education and information, for a net typically of $700, which the government would match. In 1867, society members paid $40,412.94 in fees, and government grants totalled $50,869.00. Ten years later, society grants were the same, but now eighty-eight societies received more than $59,000[7] and were spending about $100,000 annually. The government still believed that these bodies' activities, particularly shows and premiums, would spur advances in agriculture.

The Agricultural and Arts Association of Ontario, though now also representing mechanics' institutes, still focused on fairs and exhibitions. It wished to foster relations among township, county, and provincial agricultural societies to encourage "the agricultural and industrial interests of the Province."[8] It was becoming increasingly difficult to coordinate their events so that local shows preceded county ones, which then fed into the provincial exhibition. The guiding ethos was educational: "Our agricultural organizations should aim at becoming, in no restricted sense, 'Mutual Improvement Societies,' by diffusing popular and useful knowledge on the subjects they embrace, by holding meetings for discussing them, by making experiments and carefully recording their results, and by circulating among their members agricultural papers and books, of which, happily, there is, in the present day, no lack of supply."[9]

In the association's view, there could not be too many societies, but there were definitely too many shows. It sought instead fewer shows with more competition, better entries, and larger crowds. The first provincial exhibition in Toronto in 1846 had attracted 1,150 entries and offered $1,600 in prizes, while at London in 1869 nearly 7,649 entries vied for $13,400 in prize money. By 1873, the association's president, Sheriff Gibbons, would boast that Ontario's exhibition was nearly as good as that of the Royal Agricultural Society in England and better than any in North America, save the St Louis Fair.[10]

## Agricultural Education

Carling, however, was thinking more broadly: although the agricultural societies were doing much good, "comparatively little has yet been done towards imparting to the youth of our rural districts, systematic instruction in the theory and practice of a pursuit which constitutes the foundation of our material wealth and progress."[11] As well, a new education bill would require the normal school to offer a course in scientific agriculture and rural schools to teach agriculture, to which end Egerton Ryerson, "our venerable and most efficient Chief Superintendent of Education," had just prepared a textbook for the courses he had long sought. Carling in 1869 dispatched Rev. William Fletcher Clarke to investigate US agricultural colleges. An Ontario Agricultural College was beginning to crystallize, and Carling's views were still fluid – perhaps it should start humbly at two or three sites across the province. Provincial farms could provide sound elementary teaching in chemistry, farm architecture and engineering, natural history, and natural philosophy, with possibly an ordinary English education for "those pupils whose early mental training might have been neglected."[12] There would be experiments, breeding and managing livestock would be key elements, and students would work on the farm. This model was much closer to the Board of National Education's farm schools in Ireland than to the contemporary American land-grant colleges.

## THE GRANGE MOVEMENT (1870S)

The Agricultural and Arts Association of Ontario was not the only general farm organization in Ontario, however. The broadly based Grange had a brief influence in Canada in the 1870s. The US government in 1866 commissioned Oliver Kelly (1826–1913) to survey the devastation of the post–Civil War south and to consider ideas for its reconstruction.[13] In the following year, with other people at the US Bureau of Agriculture, he drew up the principles of the Grange, or the National Grange of the Order of Patrons of Husbandry, which stood for cooperation among farmers and healing the North–South division. The first grange appeared in Fredonia, Chautauqua County, New York, in 1868, and the idea spread rapidly; by 1873, some 27,000 granges had more than 500,000 members.

Canada's first grange surfaced in Quebec in 1872. The enthusiastic advocacy in Ontario of William Weld, publisher of the *Farmer's Advocate* in London, soon led to formation of the Dominion Grange in that city in 1874. The council of the Agricultural and Arts Association of Ontario watched its development with interest; in his address to the association in 1876, its president, Ira Morgan, reeve of Osgoode Township in Carleton County, acknowledged the Grange's rapid rise but noted that "some are afraid of its efforts, other[s] see in it the salvation of the farming interests of Ontario. We wish God speed to every effort put forth to improve and foster the farming interests."[14] The Canadian granger movement, which peaked in 1879 with some 31,000 members, operated as both a non-partisan lobby for agriculture and a local group that fostered social interaction among farm families. On a local level, it exerted political influence. Both Weld's newspaper and the *Globe Weekly* were platforms for Grange views.

In the United States, education was a key issue for many grangers: the Grange blasted the land-grant college system in an 1875–76 report, calling it irrelevant to its needs and calling for farmers to control the colleges.[15] Because education had not been a central theme in the Ontario granger movement, the movement was never a threat to the status quo. Although the Grange faded away – more quickly in Canada than in its neighbour – in Canada it anticipated the emergence of general advocacy organizations, such as the Ontario Farmers' Union of the twentieth century.[16]

FARMERS' CLUBS (1870S– )

Farmers' clubs remained active in some parts of the province, acting locally and not aligning themselves with the county-level societies. As discussion and social groups, they did not provide premiums or hold general exhibitions; individuals keen about those activities would join township or county societies. A typical example: the Township of Puslinch Farmers Club organized in Aberfoyle, south of Guelph, in May 1874 "for the mutual improvement of its members and the advancement of the agricultural interests of the community."[17] While agriculture was its primary concern, any topic that had a bearing on the community's interests was open for debate, save religion and politics. Meetings took place the last Saturday of each month, at 2 p.m., and annual dues were 50 cents (later reduced to 25 cents). Members proposed topics and would then lead the discussions, with others following.[18] Outside speakers were rare; but as the club was only 5 miles (8 km) from the fledgling Ontario Agricultural College, it welcomed as speakers professors Brown, Johnston, Mills, and Panton. It enrolled about sixty members most years, held an annual seed fair, and survived until at least 1896.

THE OTTAWA EXHIBITION (1869–75)

What about the traditional agricultural societies, of which county and many township versions had existed for decades? A new one was the City of Ottawa Agricultural Society, which Carleton County Warden John Holmes formed on 18 January 1868.[19] A county society already existed, but the new one centred on the city's environs. The most prominent members were long-time president, lumberman James Skead (1817–1884), and Ira Morgan, both of whom became presidents of the provincial association. Archibald McKellar, later to be commissioner, was also active. The minutes show from the outset that the society's raison d'être was its autumn exhibition. It purchased ordnance lands (now Lansdowne Park) on the Rideau Canal and put up buildings, which were ready in 1869; its first Agricultural and Industrial Exhibition, with $2,500 in prizes and "open to all the world," was a success. As a local newspaper noted, "The Exhibition, under the auspices of the Society, took place on the 5th, 6th and 7th October, and was successful beyond anticipation; exhibitors came from the distance of Montreal, Lachine, Plantagenet, Morrisburgh, St Lawrence Co., N.Y., and many other distant places, and from them we had the assurance of satisfaction at coming, and their intention to visit us again." The fair attracted 200 competitors, who showed 1,217 entries, and it sold 5,420 tickets. The event continued annually until 1875, when the grounds became the site of the provincial exhibition.[20] Despite rocky finances, the society staggered along until the Central Canada Exhibition Association took over operations in 1888. With the demise of provincial exhibitions, the Ottawa fair became an important regional event, which still takes place at Lansdowne Park.

## THE RISE OF SPECIALIST SOCIETIES

As for informal education, the key element of change in Ontario in the last third of the century – the rise of specialist societies – reflected the increasing differentiation of agriculture. The first of these bodies was the Ontario Fruit Growers Association (1859). It grew rapidly during the 1860s as more Niagara-area farmers moved into fruit cultivation, both the usual orchard crops such as apples and pears, but also tender fruits such as apricots, cherries, grapes, peaches, and plums. Fruit farmers had little guidance, beyond Windsor nurseryman James Dougall's *The Canadian Fruit-culturist; or Letters to an Intending Fruit-grower* (1867), the first Canadian book on the subject.

The Fruit Growers Association, under Secretary Delos White Beadle (1823–1905), produced compendious and valuable annual reports, sometimes hundreds of pages long, with the latest information on cultural techniques, experiments, fruit varieties, marketing hints, and pests; Ontario's Bureau of Agriculture printed these reports as part of the province's *Sessional Papers*. Secretary Beadle's own *Canadian Fruit, Flower, and Kitchen Gardener* (1872) was the country's first general gardening book. In 1878, the association launched *Canadian Horticulturist* with Beadle as its editor; it carried articles on vegetable gardening and, very occasionally, on ornamental horticulture, but its central focus was fruit growing. St Catharines' nurseryman Linus Woolverton (1846–1914) succeeded Beadle as secretary and editor.

The 1860s saw three elements of a dairy industry emerge in Ontario: a factory system to produce butter and cheese, the producers and manufacturers' Canadian Dairymens' Association (Ingersoll, 1867), and a rival Ontario Dairymens' Association (Belleville, 1872). Samuel Casey Wood (agriculture commissioner 1875–83) convinced the rivals to amalgamate on promise of a grant, but the union soon fizzled, leading in 1877 to two Dairymens' Associations of Ontario, one eastern and one western. Their annual reports, like those of the Fruit Growers' Association, informed their constituents, the rapidly expanding population of dairy farmers and operators of creameries and cheese factories. By the late 1880s, both societies had secured paid cheese-factory inspectors, with plant owners paying the societies for this service.

A key figure in the western region was Thomas Ballantyne (1829–1908),[21] a Perth County teacher and farmer, who visited pioneer Henry Farrington's operation in North Norwich Township, toured northern New York State to see cheese factories there, and then opened the Black Creek cheese factory. He helped set up the Canadian Dairymens' Association and was president of the Dairymens' Association of Western Ontario for several terms. An award-winning cheese maker who thoroughly embraced science, Ballantyne was the first to employ the Babcock test for grading milk. On the education side, he supported the unionization of cheese-factory workers and apprenticeship programs. He was active in direct education, establishing a cheese-makers' school in Tavistock in 1891.

Horticultural societies, which dated from the 1830s, had withered away with the loss of provincial grants but increased in number – to fifty-one by 1900 – with later support from the Ontario government. Unlike their Quebec counterparts, which focused on fruit growing, Ontario's concentrated on vegetables and ornamental horticulture. In 1906, with the province reorganizing funding, they formed the umbrella Ontario Horticultural Association. Other specialist groups emerged: a Poultry Association in 1875, where dominance by western breeders, such as dairymen, led to separate eastern and western portions in 1884, and an Ontario Bee-Keepers' Association in 1880. Their meetings and publications informed specialist farmers about the latest methods and technologies. Various livestock organizations did the same about cattle, horses, pigs, and sheep.[22]

The proliferation of specialist organizations, reflecting the heterogeneous development of agriculture in different parts of the province, was a challenge to the primacy of the Agricultural and Arts Association of Ontario, its local affiliates, and their traditional activities. When he became commissioner in 1875, Wood expected more value for taxpayers' money. In his annual report in 1876, he argued: "Farmers need to be reminded that the holding of an exhibition is only one function of an Agricultural Society, though an important one; and that its members, by having only a few meetings during our long winters for considering their local agricultural wants and resources, comparing notes founded on individual experience, and fostering a higher taste for acquiring scientific information in relation to the art of culture, and the raising and management of live stock, these societies would eventually become the means of diffusing an ever-increasing amount of sound knowledge in regard to the theory and practice of agriculture, and of rural matters in general."[23]

### REGIONAL EXHIBITIONS

Such activities would keep young men interested in their livelihood. Local societies producing increasingly larger shows also threatened the Agricultural and Arts Association of Ontario's hegemony. In 1878, the association hosted its first Dominion Exhibition, which Governor General the Marquess of Lorne and Princess Louise opened in Ottawa. The association thought it "somewhat suicidal" to hold at nearly the same time a provincial exhibition, an industrial exhibition at Toronto, and major regional shows in Guelph, Hamilton, and London; it could not be allowed to happen.[24] Wood had other ideas. In his 1879 report, he argued: "In my last report I took occasion to remark, with regret, that comparatively few of the Ontario Agricultural Societies do more than hold an annual exhibition, and although I desire not to disparage the value of these shows, when efficiently managed and with sufficient amount of competition, those persons who are acquainted with the rather stereotyped characters of too many of them, will coincide in the opinion that they would bear a good deal of stimulating."[25]

Now that regional shows were becoming successful, expenses for the provincial show and the association's other budgetary needs were becoming onerous. Good local shows would be, perhaps now, sufficient in Wood's view. He threatened to amend the act to end provincial shows altogether and to strengthen regional exhibitions but made allowances for large "Dominion" shows occasionally.[26] Wood was thinking not just about exhibitions: "The fact that the old Provincial Association, established some thirty-five years ago, has done an invaluable work is readily admitted on all hands. It may be regarded as the parent of most, if not all, our agricultural organizations. But there has been for some time a growing feeling in the public mind that several important modifications have now become necessary in order to increase or even sustain its efficiency, and to adapt it to changed conditions and modern requirements. Its working management has become unwieldy and too expensive compared with the work performed."[27]

END OF THE SHOWS

None the less the association soldiered on with its provincial exhibitions, but in 1882 its new president, Charles Drury, admitted that such events were no longer compulsory and that the association might look into alternative activities to promote agriculture; after all, "the object of an exhibition is instruction, not amusement,"[28] and amusements such as horse racing were now a staple part of any exhibition. The provincial exhibition, in Kingston that year, had a national character, with exhibitors from the Maritimes and Manitoba, but also new local activities. One was the awarding of prizes to best-managed farms (a practice of the Royal Agricultural Society in England) and for essays, which then appeared in the association's reports. Annual publication of herd books was another association function. More directly educational was the distribution, in 1883, of 500 copies of a booklet on butter production, in the belief that creamery butter needed improvement. President John C. Rykert (1832–1913), MP for Lincoln and Niagara, defended the association in his 1889 address,[29] claiming that others were trying to move into its territory. He believed that the provincial exhibition was still valuable, even if the Toronto *Globe*, which used to defend it, now attacked it and asked: had not the association fostered the Ontario Veterinary College, assisted in the formation of the Toronto Industrial Exhibition, and been the first to aid the Entomological Society? His arguments were to no avail; 1889 saw the last one.

John Dryden (minister of agriculture 1890–1905) did not support the exhibition, although he strongly favoured the fat stock show in Guelph, which the association would help sponsor in 1892. A revision of the Agriculture Act in 1895 ended the Agricultural and Arts Association of Ontario on 1 January 1896, after fifty-three years of existence. Probably only its executive lamented its passing.

By 1899, Ontario counted 432 county and township agricultural societies,[30] most of which were active, receiving grants, and participating in local and regional fairs and exhibitions. Sufficient criticism over the years suggests that they were not particularly effective conduits of new ideas. In late century, more formal education, through the Ontario Agricultural College and its extension activities, would make the educational work of societies, except the newer specialist organizations, largely obsolete.

### THE AGRICULTURAL PRESS

As more and more Ontario farm families became literate, the agricultural press could provide the latest knowledge and information to them. When the *Canadian Agriculturist* folded at the end of 1863, it gave way to George Brown's commercial *Canada Farmer*, edited by William F. Clarke.[31] Clarke was a practising Congregational minister and farmer in Guelph who had written agricultural articles for the Montreal *Witness*. After four years in Brown's employ, he left and established the rival *Ontario Farmer* in 1869. It survived only two years, but by that time Clarke was helping to create a provincial agriculture school. The *Canada Farmer* continued until 1877, when it merged with the Globe's weekly paper as the *Weekly Globe and Canada Farmer*. William Weld launched *Farmers' Advocate* in 1866, and it became a serious rival. Under various titles, and later part of the London *Free Press*, it survived well into the twentieth century. Specialist journals were also available, including the Globe's short-lived *Canadian Poultry Chronicle* (on poultry and pigeons, 1870–72); *Canadian Poultry Review* (Strathroy, 1877–1975); *Canadian Bee Journal and Poultry Weekly* (Beeton, 1885– ); and *Canadian Live-stock and Farm Journal* (Hamilton, 1886–95), edited by Thomas Shaw.

### THE ONTARIO AGRICULTURAL COLLEGE AND AGRICULTURAL EXTENSION

By 1867, the only agricultural school in central Canada was the abbé Pilote's school at the Collège de Ste-Anne-de-la-Pocatière, which, despite receiving provincially funded bursaries, was a private school; a similar school at the Collège de Ste-Thérèse had disappeared. In Ontario, despite much talk, no dedicated school for farmers was on the horizon, but promoters of the idea watched events south of the border with increasing interest. There the formation of such facilities had been a slow and demoralizing process. The only schools to survive the Civil War were the Farmers' High School in Pennsylvania (1855, later Pennsylvania State University), Maryland Agricultural College (1856), and the Maryland Agricultural College (1857), none of which attracted many students.

When Michigan's college opened in 1857, Senator Justin Morrill (1810–1898) of Vermont introduced a bill to set aside public land for agricultural and mechanical colleges; sale of the land would generate funds for investing, with the interest available to states to create such schools. Although the bill passed, southern opposition led President James Buchanan to veto it. Morrill remodelled the legislation and reintroduced it in 1862, and it was successful. This scheme set aside in every state 30,000 acres of public land for each of its (two) senators and representatives (roughly by population). Each state government would have to provide lands and buildings for a college. The existing colleges took up Morrill Act funds, and new "land-grant" institutions emerged, such as the Massachusetts Agricultural College in Amherst (1867), the University of Wisconsin's agricultural school (1868), and the Ohio Agricultural and Mechanical College (later Ohio State University, 1873). Soon, most states had similar institutions; however, as Cochrane points out, they had great difficulty in attracting students – wealthy farmers wanted their sons to attend "real" colleges, and poor farmers' sons, with no secondary education, were not admissible.[32]

### Looking and Planning (1867–73)

Canada never had a Morrill Act. The US legislation of 1862 remained in limbo until after the Civil War, and so did not soon generate models that Canadians could study. The latter of course spent the early 1860s in a series of political crises and negotiations with the Maritime colonies leading towards Confederation. Even had the provincial government wanted a Morrill-type scheme, it had very little good agricultural land remaining to sell for investment. By the time Ottawa acquired a vast stock of undeveloped western land with its purchase of Rupert's Land in 1870, Confederation was a fact, and education the domain of the new provincial governments.

The educational establishment in Canada West took more note as the US land-grant system began to show signs of life.[33] In 1866, William F. Clarke, writing in his *Canada Farmer*, affirmed that the few US agricultural colleges such as Cornell, Massachusetts, and Michigan were not going well and were much more difficult to organize than one would have supposed.[34] But by 1869 Ryerson's educational journal noted that Morrill funds were now supporting colleges in sixteen states. Clarke, in his paper, published news, notes, and extracts throughout the 1860s, arguing that Canada should emulate England – which had almost no agricultural training.

When Commissioner of Agriculture John Carling was ready to take action, he asked Clarke to investigate at first hand. Clarke's brief tour took him to the two colleges in Massachusetts and Michigan and to the US Department of Agriculture in Washington, DC. He concluded that Ontario should have a free-standing institution with no relationship to a literary institution like a university. He knew of Buckland's experience: "As with the Professorship of Agriculture in our own Provincial University, though filled by one of the ablest agriculturists of the age, the one word *failure* gives the history of all such arrangements."[35] Clarke wanted a site either near a good-sized country town that could provide society, markets, and commerce or, even better, in a town along a rail line on the edge of settlement. Wherever the institution might settle, US experience showed Clarke that it would be expensive – at least $50,000 for facilities and $10,000 annually for salaries and operations.

He also looked to Michigan Agricultural College, in East Lansing, which expected students to work, as the model for Ontario. Its four-year course covered the elementary branches it thought useful to future farmers:

Year 1:  algebra, bookkeeping, geology, geometry, history, practical
         agriculture, surveying, and trigonometry
Year 2:  analytical chemistry, botany, elementary chemistry and
         entomology, English literature, and horticulture
Year 3:  agricultural chemistry, animal physiology, inductive logic,
         physics, and rhetoric
Year 4:  astronomy, civil engineering, entomology and meteorology.
         French, horticulture, landscape gardening, mental philosophy,
         moral philosophy, political economy, practical agriculture,
         stock-breeding, and zoology.

The curriculum at Michigan was essentially a blend of high school and non-classical elements from contemporary academic colleges. Because of the curriculum's breathtaking scope, one can imagine the teaching was at a superficial level. Clarke also believed that the province needed to do more by introducing textbooks into the public schools, expanding its activities to broadcast useful information to farmers, and undertaking entomological research.

William Weld vociferously opposed the college project. Although he strongly supported agricultural education in general, he had been in open warfare with Clarke and his *Canada Farmer*. In 1867, Weld had encountered Clarke at the Michigan State Fair and offered his hand, say-ing "Good morning, Mr Clarke," but received the response, "Do you think I shall shake hands with you?" Weld claimed he was not afraid of Clarke or his boss (George Brown).[36] Weld's stance was atypical for the time, as there was now solid government and popular support for a pro-vincial school. Although Clarke argued for a Morrill-type endowment, Commissioner Carling moved to purchase a farm site outright and called for tenders for construction.

As Buckland noted in his Bureau of Agriculture report in 1871, the new school, with a small staff and accommodation for 100 students, would be ready in the spring of 1873. Its basis would be "Economy with efficiency," and its motto, "Practice with Science," Buckland's old refrain.[37] In reality, the proposal was extravagant for a cash-poor govern-ment: nearly $46,000 for the land at Mimico Station, west of Toronto, $48,000 for buildings, and nearly $45,000 for additional improvements. Arrangements were just crystallizing when John Sandfield Macdonald's government fell to the Liberals. Carling's successor, McKellar, immedi-ately had to deal with Clarke's strong, reasonable opposition to the Mimico site. After much correspondence, the hiring of consultants from Michigan Agricultural College, and the appointing of committees, the government obtained a far superior site south of Guelph.

### A Rocky Start (1873–79)

The high hopes with which the new Ontario School of Agriculture and Experimental Farm opened in the autumn of 1873 soon dissolved into almost comic opera.[38] The makeup of the staff was a recipe for disaster. McKellar hired Henry McCandless, a graduate of the Albert National Agricultural Training Institution in Glasnevin, to head the school. McCandless had failed to mention that Cornell had recently fired him. He was an incompetent martinet who immediately clashed with the headstrong Clarke, who was in charge of the residence. Among the staff were a number of political appointees. McKellar himself would have an affair with a staff member, whom he later married. McCandless and Clarke bickered, staff left, and the students eventually petitioned Liberal Premier Oliver Mowat to make changes or they would go home. By July 1874, Mowat fired McCandless; Clarke had already resigned.

The new principal, Charles Gay Roberts (born 1838), a graduate of the Royal Agricultural College in Cirencester, could not take the posi-tion immediately and had a nervous breakdown while visiting Guelph.

In the meantime, a new rector was to replace Clarke. Scottish-born William Johnston (1848–1885) grew up near Cobourg, taught in rural schools, studied at Knox College in Toronto and the Universities of Edinburgh and Toronto, and took his degree from Toronto in 1874. That August, with no agricultural experience, he became not only rector but also, in Roberts's absence, de facto principal.

Johnston's lectures covered botany and practical agriculture, but there was no formal curriculum, as he was the only instructor. He proposed a three-year course (differing from Michigan's four-year, non-degree program and Massachusetts Agricultural College's four-year degree program):

Year 1: agriculture, chemical physics and inorganic chemistry, elementary geology and physics, elements of animal anatomy and physiology, elements of botany and zoology, English literature, farm bookkeeping, geography, horticulture, and veterinary surgery and practice

Year 2: agriculture, animal anatomy and physiology with veterinary surgery and practice, drawing, elementary political economy, elements of land surveying, English literature, entomology, horticulture, laboratory practice, mensuration, organic and elementary analytical chemistry, structural and physiological botany, and zoology

Year 3: agricultural chemistry, agriculture, animal anatomy and physiology with veterinary surgery and practice, economic and field botany, English literature, entomology and meteorology, horticulture, laboratory practice, mechanics and land survey, and political economy.

In each year, students would also undertake practical work in the fields and in the horticulture, livestock, and mechanical departments. The curriculum straddled high school and university and, like Michigan's, covered a very broad range of subjects and so could not deal with scientific topics in depth. Fortunately, by the end of the year, Johnston was able to obtain William Brown as professor of agriculture and farm manager. He was a Scottish immigrant farmer with much practical experience but no academic training in agriculture. Johnston brought in other instructors for chemistry, horticulture, mechanics, and veterinary practice. It was clear that a three-year program would not work out, so in 1875 Johnston substituted a plan for a two-year, but still-crowded, curriculum:

Year 1:  animal anatomy and physiology with veterinary surgery and
practice, bookkeeping, chemical physics and inorganic
chemistry, elementary geology and physical geography, English
literature, horticulture, mensuration, practical agriculture,
structural and physiological botany, and zoology
Year 2:  agriculture, animal anatomy and physiology with veterinary
surgery and practice, economic and field botany, English
literature, entomology, horticulture, land survey, mechanics,
meteorology, and zoology.

A student's average daily labour was five hours at ten cents an hour.[39] Any
scrupulous student, even after paying expenses, might leave after two years
with $50 in his pocket. Johnston and his chemistry instructor from 1878
on, James Hoyes Panton (1847–1893), strove to impart the basic science
they deemed an educated farmer should know, but this clashed directly
with Professor Brown's no-nonsense, no-science approach to practical
agriculture. To make matters worse, Brown answered directly to Premier
Mowat, not to Johnston.

## A Commission of Inquiry (1879–81)

In 1879, Commissioner Wood proposed an agricultural commission of
inquiry, which started up the next year. He wanted a comprehensive
snapshot of the sector, including agricultural education and societies,
their grants, and their shows. After taking a great deal of testimony, the
commission said little about education, despite a detailed and optimistic
view of the sector. The Ontario Agricultural Commission published much
of the material as a "how-to" guide: *Canadian Farming: An Encyclopaedia of
Agriculture being the Report of the Ontario Agricultural Commission* (1881).
As for societies, grants, and shows: "While there is, undoubtedly, at the
present time a very considerable feeling in the public mind in favour of
some alterations and modifications of the present system, no radical
change should be made without the most careful inquiry and the utmost
deliberation."[40]

On education, most of the evidence from William Brown, William
Johnston, and James Mills ended up in an appendix.[41] James Mills
(1840–1924) trained at Victoria University and was a high school principal when he succeeded Johnston as principal of the Ontario
Agricultural School in 1879, and he later became president of its successor college. Mills and Brown concentrated on operations and teaching,

noting the lack of a proper chemical laboratory and museum. Mills believed he could fill every space in the college and more, especially with middle-class British immigrants with some capital who wanted to farm in Ontario. He knew that Britain had five agricultural training institutions – none receiving government grants – but "I don't think their teaching is so practical as that in our Ontario college."[42]

Mills (and Johnston agreed with him) followed Ryerson in insisting on an agricultural textbook for elementary schools: "That has been done in some States of the Union. Even if it were not well taught, farmers' sons would get valuable ideas from the mere reading of such a book; it could cause them to think of the subject of farming, and to see that it is a subject which requires thinking ... I would make no distinction between boys and girls; both should study it."[43] Mills believed that provincial high schools were not appropriate places for agriculture and should in fact wean young men off the farm. An alternative that might prove very popular would be agricultural schools similar to Ireland's but without attaching farms. Good students could progress to the college on graduation from these schools. Mills admitted that such schools would be costly, as in Ireland, but worthwhile for Ontario's largely agricultural economy.

Brown knew of no decent textbooks and no serious Canadian farm journal. Johnston sketched the general situation: "Agricultural education is a branch of technical education, and like all technical education has a two-fold aspect. It is in the first place the giving of a higher education (in the sense in which I have defined the word education) to those about to become farmers, by adding on to the elementary branches taught in the public schools subjects directly pertaining to agriculture, and teaching them; and in the second place, it is the training of young men for that particular business or occupation."[44]

Johnston looked to continental European and American practices – not to Britain – for an appropriate model for Ontario. Ireland's three-level system was the best-developed scheme in the United Kingdom and trained peasant farmers. The French system was similar, and to Johnston, superior to the Irish schools. At its lowest rung were *fermes écoles* in each *département* with a knowledgeable local farmer in charge; most had orchards, gardens, and nurseries, and the state provided board and clothing. Next up, the provincial agricultural colleges – Grignon was the oldest and best-known – focused more on science. At the top, the Institut national agronomique, open only since 1876, provided a two-year course. German states, especially Prussia and Bavaria, maintained excellent academies. The American land-grant colleges, in contrast, failed to impress Johnston. A number of universities had simply added agricultural departments, all of which had failed. Most graduates did not even go into farming. Only the Michigan and Massachusetts colleges seemed functional, because they taught only agriculture. Johnston also felt that the English model, whose main purpose was to train farm managers, was not of much use to Ontario.

So what would be best for the province? Johnston recognized that manufacturing was on the rise and farm produce could now reach the world market: "The times are changing and we must keep pace with the change. The watchword of agricultural progress in Ontario to-day should be educate! Educate! Experiment! Experiment! And both are now going on as rapidly as in any country that can be named. By our agricultural societies and exhibitions, by our grange societies when rightly conducted, by our agricultural periodicals and agricultural departments of newspapers, and by this Commission itself, the work of education is going on."[45]

Johnston's recommendation was that, apart from introducing agriculture into elementary schools, the government should establish regional agricultural middle schools, perhaps a half-dozen, each with a farm. These would be a cross between the French *fermes écoles* and the German academies. Boys would study from one to three years, following the curriculum of the Ontario Agricultural College but with a practical emphasis. The sale of shares or the support of local agricultural societies might underwrite the schools. On a more local scale, prize farms throughout the province might take boys on as a form of apprenticeship, with the college examining them periodically. Each year, the Agricultural and Arts Association of Ontario selected prize farms.

A number of observers considered the two-year program at Ontario Agricultural College insufficient. In 1887, the college added a third year but, unlike its US counterparts, offered only diplomas, not degrees. As the provincial Cabinet was loath to create free-standing degree-granting institutions, affiliation with the University of Toronto was a possible option. In the same year, Toronto became the institution awarding the agriculture diploma. In 1888, the college and the university arranged for the latter to provide examinations and to award the bachelor of science in agriculture (BSA) degree, the same accreditation that several US land-grant colleges gave to students completing three years. Most American agricultural colleges were faculties within a larger university, but for the Guelph college, affiliation did not imply any control by the university – it remained independent until it became the University of Guelph in 1964.

The Toronto Veterinary College was a private school that Andrew Smith owned, so it remained in Toronto and had not connected with the Guelph school; its students took courses at the University of Toronto's School of Practical Science until it finally affiliated with the university in 1897. It would not move to Guelph until 1922. While many complained that it had lower standards, less science, and a less-intensive program than US or British schools or even McEachran's school in Montreal, it still graduated many students – 3,365 between its opening in the mid-1860s and 1908 – whereas McEachran's graduated only 315 between 1866 and 1902.[46]

### Guelph's "Model Farm"

What the new college in Guelph lacked – indeed, just like its American counterparts – was research to improve farm products and practices. Johnston told the legislature's commission of inquiry the recent history of agricultural research – almost entirely in Germany – and suggested linking such research stations to his proposed regional middle schools. The idea of a free-standing agricultural research station had just taken root in the United States at the agricultural colleges in Connecticut and North Carolina and at Cornell. Johnston argued that Brown's experiments at Guelph over the previous four years were an equivalent operation but felt that the work needed physical and administrative distance from the college.

Agricultural research stations first emerged in German-speaking countries in the 1850s, growing from Liebig's pioneering work in agricultural chemistry. Although both Canadian and American writers endorsed Liebig's endeavours, particularly on "soil exhaustion," neither country had the resources or personnel to follow suit. Land-grant colleges did not have researchers, and neither governments nor philanthropists would provide funding.[47] Passage of the Hatch Act in 1887, however, created US federal funding for research stations, although Connecticut had funded a modest state facility as early as 1875. It was not until the 1890s that the idea took material form in many states.

In the same period, the Canadian government began to consider agricultural research. The House of Commons struck in 1884 a select committee under G.-A. Gigault (1845–1915) on Canada's agricultural resources. To obtain more information, the minister wrote on 2 November 1885 to William Saunders (1836–1914), a pharmacist in London, Ontario, a key figure in the Entomological Society of Canada, and former president of the Ontario Fruit Growers' Association, asking him to visit agricultural colleges and institutions and to suggest what Canada might do. He visited the Michigan and Ontario agricultural colleges, as he indicated in his *Report on Agricultural Colleges and Experimental Stations, with Suggestions Relating to Experimental Agriculture in Canada* (1886).[48] The only experimental information available in Ontario came from the Entomological Society and the Fruit Growers, who sent out trees and vines for trial. Saunders concluded that Canada should emulate Ireland's Glasnevin school to turn out agricultural teachers: "The effect on agricultural progress would be very marked in a single generation."[49] His report spurred creation of the experimental farm system.[50]

The opening of the Central Experimental Farm in Ottawa in 1886 – the first in a nation-wide chain – with Saunders as director was the federal department's first major agricultural enterprise.[51] Focusing on research rather than on education, the Dominion Experimental Farms could provide useful information for agricultural schools and organizations without interfering with provincially supported institutions. A Canadian version of the Hatch Act was now unnecessary. Unlike Canada's, the US Department of Agriculture concentrated on the consumer side of agriculture with its division of chemistry and Bureau of Animal Industry.[52]

Although the Ontario Agricultural College had the suffix "and Experimental Farm," that did not mean it was an agricultural research station. William Carroll Latta (1850–1935), a graduate of Michigan's college, passed through Guelph about 1881[53] and thought the "model farm" there a disappointment, covered with rocks and weeds. He thought the two-year course too scientific for a practical farmer and found the amount that students worked surprising – twice as much time on crops as American students. He departed, feeling thankful he had studied at Michigan. Latta was no casual observer; the next year he became first professor of agriculture at Purdue University, and he created Indiana's farmers' institutes.

### Agricultural Extension (1880s– )

With farmers and politicians also remaining sceptical about the value of the Guelph school, the college sought to improve relations by inviting inspection of the facilities and operations. Summer excursions to the college became increasingly popular: in 1879, 300 grangers came to visit, and then a group from the press. Commissioner Wood happily reported that American visitors (obviously not Latta) liked what they saw and thought Guelph better organized than their own schools: Professor Roberts had brought Cornell students to observe dairying, while the delegation from the Connecticut Board of Agriculture went home to organize its school along the lines of Ontario's.[54] Over time, tens of thousands of farmers from across the province arrived by train to visit and hear talks.

As well, the college was to use alumni to conduct experiments on their own farms. To this end, in 1880 Mills established the Ontario Agricultural and Experimental Union, in which college staff members and alumni ran field trials together and published their results. The college later coordinated this research with the Dominion Experimental Farms. These measures showcased the value of science to the farming community and probably worked as a recruiting tool. By the early 1890s, the Experimental Union's members were conducting nearly 6,000 experiments annually.

FARMERS' INSTITUTES

The college's most valuable organizational outreach was the farmers' institute. By the early 1880s, even with visits and the Experimental Union, Mills realized that enrolments remained low, along with farmers' respect. He sought more direct contact with farmers, something more sustained than Buckland's talks to agricultural societies in the 1860s or the events at the Michigan Agricultural College.[55] He looked south for inspiration.

Iowa State Agricultural College launched a farmers' institute during the winter of 1869–70 as a series of itinerant meetings with talks by college staff members. Other land-grant schools quickly picked up the idea.[56] Looking at Michigan's experience since 1876, Mills initiated the Ontario program in January 1885. He had earlier admitted to the agricultural commission that Ontario should follow Michigan's lead, but the college in East Lansing did not teach during the winter and expected instructors to serve in the extension program; Guelph had no winter break.

None the less Mills rearranged the academic schedule to extend the Christmas break three weeks into January to allow staff members to travel to rural locations. Farmers would organize local branches, the first in spring 1886, and raise funds. Additional money came from the province and counties. Unlike the township and county agricultural societies, most of which now directed only fairs and exhibitions, the farmers' institutes were truly educational. Typically, a college staff member and a successful local farmer such as a Fruit Growers' Association member would travel to a local club for a one-and-a-half-day meeting. Some institute meetings could attract hundreds of auditors. For its part, the Agricultural and Arts Association of Ontario was supportive. Its council noted that various groups in society had their own organizations, but not farmers: "The Grange organization was intended to do so; but there are certain things about it which have made it distasteful to many, and obnoxious to some. Hence it has not received the support of farmers generally, and cannot be said to represent more than a small section of the farming community"[57] The association regretted that the farmers' institutes lacked formal organization.

That deficiency soon evaporated when the province fostered formation of the Permanent Central Farmers' Institute of Ontario on 28 April 1887.[58] All institutes elected representatives to the provincial body, which met annually. Its first secretary was Thomas Shaw (1843–1918) of Hamilton. At its second annual meeting, delegates petitioned the government to appoint Shaw as Brown's replacement as professor of agriculture at Guelph; Shaw obtained the post and rapidly made improvements to the school's farm. While the movement already had seventy-one institutes with some 5,000 members across the province, its $1,000 annual grant was much less than the $2,500 its Wisconsin counterpart received from Madison. On broader education, C.F. Copeland of Hespeler argued that the public schools discriminated against farmers – "System is certainly calculated to educate the boys off the farm"[59] – and should teach agriculture, with teachers trained to handle it. A lively discussion led to no consensus. The Central Institute hoped for quick progress, now that a "real" farmer, Charles Drury, was minister of agriculture. By 1888, Mills could boast: "I venture to say that there is not another province or state on this continent that is holding so many successful meetings as our province, with so small an expenditure of public money."[60]

With Mills working hard to advance the institutes, their popularity increased. The additional work, however, was too much, so John Dryden, an MPP and member of the Central Institute, began to assist him in 1888. In 1894, when Mills asked Dryden, by then minister of agriculture, to relieve him of the administrative work, Dryden appointed F.W. Hodson superintendent of Farmers' Institutes. Hodson (born 1851) was an energetic organizer.[61] Growing up on a Whitby farm and having a common school education, he caught Weld's eye in 1880 and later worked two years for the *Farmers' Advocate* before returning to farming. The paper lured him back in 1887. A successful stock breeder, he helped organize the Dominion Sheep Breeders' Association (1889), the Dominion Swine

Breeders' Association (1889), and the Dominion Cattle Breeders' Association (1892) and acted as secretary to all three. After the collapse of the Agricultural and Arts Association of Ontario, the livestock societies focused on stock shows, and Hodson became a key figure in introducing winter shows in Ontario.

Hodson was tireless in promoting the institutes. In some cases, pre-existing organizations could easily convert themselves into farmers' institutes. For example, the Township of Puslinch Farmers' Club became the South Wellington Farmers' Institute in 1887. For this club, which had held wide-ranging discussions for a decade, the transition was easy. A few institutes added entertainment to their lectures and discussions, but headquarters frowned on this. Meetings were also strictly non-sectarian and non-political. By his third year as superintendent, Hodson noted that the program had grown from twelve meetings with 2,808 attendees in 1885 to 659 meetings with 125,177 attendees to hear 3,277 addresses in 1897.[62] The lectures were almost all practical and covered a wide range of topics such as drainage, fruit culture, gardening, grain storage, rotation, and stock matters. The annual reports of the Central Institute and, later, those of the superintendent included many of the talks.

Hodson was also keen to involve more women, both on the teaching side and in the audience. In 1897, of sixty-two speakers, four were women. Their topics were more within the emerging field of domestic science rather than agricultural science. Bessie Livingstone gave talks on the food value of milk and its derivatives; cooking of milk, cheese, and eggs; cookery for invalids; diet for children; cereal foods and breakfast dishes; cookery of vegetables; classes and combinations of foods; and hot supper dishes. Laura Rose, an assistant in the dairy department at Guelph and instructor with the travelling dairy, offered lectures on many subjects: the making of prize bread and butter; methods of cooking apples; a morning in an English dairy; a simple process of making cheese for home consumption; women's dress on the farm; and (a French proverb) "one eve in the fields, the other in town" – readings suitable for evening meetings. She went on to organize dairy instruction in Nova Scotia.

During the growth phase of the farmers'-institute movement, women's auxiliaries had formed in many of the clubs. The idea soon surfaced to organize separate institutes for women, in connection with the farmers' institute, which might deal with farm women's issues throughout the year. Hamiltonian Adelaide Hoodless (1858–1910), the key figure in introducing domestic science into Canadian schools and forming the national YWCA, spoke at the provincial farmers' institute meeting in

1896, pressing the claims of instruction for women. In the following year, she worked with a group of women in the Wentworth South Farmers' Institute to create their own society, the Saltfleet Women's Institute. While Hoodless organized the group and was its honorary president, the first elected president was Christina Smith, the wife of the prominent canner, E.D. Smith of Winona. According to its constitution, "The object of the Institute is to promote that knowledge of household science which shall lead to improvement in household architecture, with special attention to home sanitation, to a better understanding of the economic and hygienic value of foods and fuels, and to a more scientific care of children with a view of raising the general standard of the health of our people."[63]

The institute, with seventy-six members, held half a dozen meetings in its first year. Hodson commented that he hoped women's institutes would soon affiliate with most of the farmer's institutes: "The fact is now recognized that young women, as well as young men, require special training to fit them for life on the farm. Many thoughtful persons believe that a provincial school should be founded where farmers' daughters can receive a training suitable to their needs." The movement would expand internationally and help shape rural life in the twentieth century; but by 1900, only three women's institutes remained – in Saltfleet, North Grey, and Ontario South – and were not in good shape.[64]

Mills had seen the farmers' institutes as a means to teach farmers in their own locales and also to enhance their opinion of the agricultural college. Of the many visitors to Guelph each summer, increasing numbers were institute members. In June 1897, the college hosted 30,000 institute members coming to look over the field experiments and facilities. The pressure on staff to attend institute meetings became too great, and they dropped out of the program, leaving it in farmers' hands. In 1899, Hodson resigned to become livestock commissioner of Canada, and his replacement was George C. Creelman (1869–1929), one of Guelph's first degree holders and later Mills's successor. While the institute movement had spread wide in the United States, Creelman could also point to Ontario's success (see Table 5.1). The movement peaked just after the turn of the century, with almost 150,000 people attending institute sessions each year.[65]

THE COLLEGE GOES DAIRY

Even though dairying had become very widespread in Ontario and cheese and butter among the most profitable farm products, the

Table 5.1  Representative farmers' institutes, various jurisdictions (1899)

| Jurisdiction | State support ($) | Meetings | Attendance |
|---|---|---|---|
| Ontario | 9,900 | 677 | 119,402 |
| New York | 20,000 | 300 | 75,000 |
| Ohio | 16,300 | 274 | 98,210 |
| Minnesota | 13,500 | 59 | 22,600 |
| Pennsylvania | 12,500 | 308 | 59,000 |
| Wisconsin | 12,000 | 127 | 55,000 |

Source: Report of the Farmers' Institutes 1899–1900, Province of Ontario, Sessional Papers (1900), no. 24, 8.

college had been tardy in teaching it. Indeed, the lead had fallen to the two provincial dairymens' associations. However, in 1886 the college appointed James W. Robertson as dairy professor through the influence of Thomas Ballantyne. A Scottish immigrant, Robertson had worked in and managed cheese factories in the Ingersoll area. He rapidly built up the college's reputation and his own, becoming commissioner of agriculture and dairying of Canada in 1890. One of his pupils, Henry H. Dean (born 1865), graduated in 1890 and replaced him as dairy professor in 1891. Besides teaching, Dean toured the province with one of the college's three travelling dairies to teach farm people how to make butter at home, handing out his own *Hints on Butter Making* along the way. This was an initiative of Minister John Dryden's, imitating New York. Dean eventually decided to bring the students to Guelph and inaugurated a Dairy School in 1893. The attendees, many of them women, came for two-month, certificate "short courses" in making butter and cheese and managing dairy herds. By the late 1890s, the course was three months long and very popular, although not many students took the certificate. Dean later wrote the standard textbook, *Canadian Dairying* (1903).

Dairying was a locus of gender relations on the farm before industrialization, with women typically tending the cows and making the butter and cheese. With the arrival of creameries and cheese factories, they shifted to wage labour in the factories; as Derry notes, by the 1890s, men had taken over milking as well.[66] Dean's dairy school was, in a sense, a back-door way for women into the college, although he himself was dubious about women as students. At the turn of the century, the Ontario Agricultural College also operated a western dairy school in Strathroy and an eastern Ontario school in Kingston; the three schools together enrolled nearly 200 students annually.

*From Strength to Strength*

Guelph's Ontario Agricultural College went from strength to strength. The *University of Toronto Monthly* in 1903 labelled it one of the "best all-around equipped institutions of its kind in the world."[67] By that time, with a staff of twenty-two and more than 700 students, many from outside Ontario, it dominated the Canadian scene. Thirteen of its graduates became professors in US agricultural colleges, and it would also supply many to western Canadian schools soon to open as settlement expanded rapidly and the Dominion created Alberta and Saskatchewan as provinces in 1905.

In 1905, Wallace Buttrick, secretary of the United States General Education Board, toured agricultural schools in Minnesota, Wisconsin, Iowa, Ontario, and Quebec. Robertson's efforts at Macdonald College impressed him, and he found in Guelph "one of the most efficient and without doubt the most closely related to present farmers of any agricultural school on the continent."[68] The farmers' institutes of Mills and Creelman seemed to him especially noteworthy, radically different from US extension programs. Americans held occasional meetings, not always in connection with the local agricultural college or experimental station, but Guelph had direct links to farmers through the Experimental Union and local organizations. US Assistant Secretary of Agriculture William Hays had briefed him in advance on the differences, and after seeing for himself, Buttrick commented: "The very best agricultural extension work on the continent was being done in connection with the Agricultural College at Guelph. This judgement of Secretary Hays was confirmed and justified, not only by what I saw in Guelph, but also by my visits to the agricultural colleges of Minnesota, Wisconsin and Iowa."[69]

When Buttrick arrived in Ames, he learned that the Iowa Agricultural College had just begun to establish an experimental union under the direction of a Guelph graduate. The local farmers' institutes in the state provided farmers with valuable information, and "here again the Guelph idea has influenced the organization of the institutes." Buttrick's informants in the Midwest complained that their colleges were not turning out real farmers, but he attended one of Guelph's "excursions" for farmers and saw their number and enthusiasm, reporting that "scientific agriculture in Ontario has already gained the confidence of practical farmers who no longer speak slightingly of 'teacher-farmers.'"[70] One notable cross-border difference: US schools in the late 1890s began supplying graduates as "county agents," who made themselves available to local farmers for information and solving problems.[71] A similar system had already emerged in France. Ontario would follow suit when Creelman, knowing of the French scheme, argued in 1907 for appointment of "agricultural representatives."

It was not just Americans who recognized the advances made in Canada. The Scottish Commission on Agriculture, touring Canada in 1908, noted: "The rural prosperity of Canada, especially of the great Province of Ontario, is undoubtedly due in some degree to the foresight of the Dominion and Provincial Governments in providing Research Institutions and Agricultural Colleges. The agricultural education of Canada, from the rural school to the University, is rapidly assuming a homogeneity and co-ordination worthy of the closest study, and in a large measure worthy of imitation in less favoured countries."[72]

Still, some Canadians and Americans considered state support for agricultural colleges problematic. Even in 1915, Albert Leake, Ontario education inspector, noted that many observers still disparaged land-grant colleges for over-emphasis on engineering, too low admission standards, and lack of consensus among faculty members as to their role. While these objections were sometimes valid, generally they were not: "The mission of the college, however, is to train leaders, men who can control, direct, and inspire. Engaged in work of this kind, these men do much more to improve the condition of agriculture than if they returned directly to the farm. The colleges should not be judged by the numbers they return to the farm, but by the general improvement they have effected in agricultural practice and methods."[73] Indeed, looking at the Ontario Agricultural College's record, with nearly 2,000 graduates by 1915, Leake noted that only 20 per cent had returned to the farm.

### Eastern Competition?

By the 1890s, the possibility of competition for the Guelph school surfaced with a plan for an agricultural and engineering school affiliating with Queen's University in Kingston. A Presbyterian college since its founding in 1841, Queen's remained small and financially weak. Since the 1850s, governments, for political reasons, had denied financial aid to any sectarian college and directed all funds to the non-denominational University of Toronto. The University Act of 1887 allowed colleges to affiliate with Toronto, which the Methodists' Victoria University in Cobourg did in 1890. With Queen's University wishing to remain independent, however, Kingston city council sent a delegation to the provincial government to argue for a practical science school for Queen's. In the *Canada Educational Monthly* in 1887, Queen's chemistry professor William L. Goodwin (1856–1941) had argued that, while Toronto had its School of Practical Science and the Guelph college existed for agriculture, eastern Ontario had nothing. With interest growing in mining and technology, Queen's could emulate Toronto by employing its own science instructors in a specialized school for mining, engineering, and chemistry applied to industry "and generally on the applications of science to the mechanic arts, agriculture, navigation and other industries of the people."[74]

By 1893, the Kingston School of Mining and Agriculture was in operation, with Goodwin in charge, but there were no classes in agriculture, as city council would not approve the necessary $1,000; however, the city proposed to provide the school with the collegiate-institute site, worth $20,000. With eastern Ontario farmers having moved heavily into dairying, a school with a butter- and cheese-making program and milk-testing laboratory was relevant and would be beneficial. The dairy school, under John A. Ruddick (1862–1953), later dominion dairy commissioner, was in full operation by 1896, as was a veterinary school. The next year, Archibald Patterson Knight (1849–1935) became acting dean of veterinary medicine. Knight had taught science at the Kingston Collegiate Institute, written textbooks, and was registrar of the Kingston Womens' Medical College. Veterinary medicine proved less attractive than planners had expected, and he suggested the school's closure in 1898.

## AGRICULTURAL INSTRUCTION IN ONTARIO SCHOOLS

Beginning in the mid-1880s, the Ontario Agricultural College and the province's Department of Agriculture aimed their educational efforts at the college's students, alumni, and adult farmers and their families. Even more numerous were the students attending rural public elementary schools; teaching them had been a perennial discussion topic among leading agriculturists since the 1840s. Yet after Confederation the debate dragged on with almost no resolution. In 1869, the editor of *Canada Farmer* admitted that Ontario common schools were good, but, because they taught no agriculture, young men had to teach themselves. To that end, the editor provided a list of useful texts, both American and British.[75] Ryerson himself had long talked of making agriculture a subject for common schools but had done little to realize it. His 200-page *First Lessons on Agriculture; for Canadian Farmers and their Families* (1870) covered in catechism form the basics but offered little information on dairy farming. It would have been suitable for classroom instruction and a competitor to J.W. Dawson's text, had anyone used it. But a milestone in education came with compulsory primary education in 1871. Long a dream of Ryerson and his colleagues, even it would require attendance at school between the ages of only seven and twelve and for at least four months a year. This change made little difference in rural areas. Although farming families needed older children for farm work, attendance in common schools had increased rapidly between the 1840s and 1871 without compulsion.[76] Although John Carling, Ryerson, and others wanted agriculture in the curriculum, circumstances forbade this. First, by 1870 a majority of teachers were female, only a fraction of whom had studied at normal school; this was also true in the United States and Quebec. Thus most rural instructors would have no background to teach the subject. One can imagine, because of the attitudes of the time, that farmers might not want untutored women teaching their sons elementary agriculture, even though many of these teachers were rural in origin and had experience in farm work. Second, as Leake notes,[77] rural women teachers were often beginners; male Ontario urban instructors earned twice as much as their rural counterparts, allowing them to save for university and only increasing the number of female rural teachers. And third, local school trustees would have to agree, and many were reluctant to do so. Because of these complications, agriculture was in only the optional curriculum and almost never taught.

James Mills had testified to the agricultural commission of inquiry that in Britain the Royal Agricultural Society held examinations and awarded prizes in agriculture, as did the Science and Art Department, the latter doing a better job. Perhaps his message got through. In 1883, realizing that the Department of Education was not introducing agriculture in public schools, the Agricultural and Arts Association of Ontario decided to organize, in cooperation with the department, a scheme for young farmers: a course of home reading with a set list of texts on the basics of practical agriculture and examinations for students to coincide with the department's teacher exams. There would be certificates and cash prizes for successful candidates. Although the Ontario Agricultural College provided sound training, it reached too few people. As association president D.P. McKinnon stated, the scheme "is to induce the young men of the farming community to engage in a course of reading at their homes, by which they may obtain a knowledge of the laws of nature, and of the reasons of their operations in practical husbandry."[78] The association's report makes no mention of the origins of this idea.

Mills, in his college report for 1883,[79] observed that both the press and the government were now taking agricultural education more seriously. The association's scheme seemed sound, expecting candidates to master reputable texts for different levels of certificates.[80] In 1884, an association committee of Drury, Mills, and John Carnegie awarded the first prizes. But when only six candidates presented themselves in 1886 and all won prizes, the association admitted: "We have to express our regret that a larger number of farmers' sons do not take advantage of these examinations."[81] Nothing had changed two years later when seven wrote the examinations; five of the candidates had already attended Guelph. Association Secretary Henry Wade complained to the new minister, Drury: "It was very discouraging to the management to find that so little interest seemed to be taken in these examinations, which were designed to promote a desire for greater technical knowledge, and to foster the reading habit amongst farmers' sons. They had been told by means of thoughtful articles in the agricultural press, by addresses at Farmers' Institutes, and on the platform generally for years that if the farming community wished to keep up with the advance made in other industries, they must bring more technical knowledge to bear upon their labour, or they would soon find themselves, as a boy, eclipsed by the few leading spirits hardy enough to break loose from the worn out customs of their fathers, and awake before long to find that other countries had usurped their market."[82] Numbers did not improve, and by 1890 Wade reported that the scheme "was badly patronised and the council have decided to discontinue it."[83]

Thomas Shaw lectured in 1888 at the annual meeting of the Ontario Teachers' Association on "Agriculture in Our Rural Schools." He noted that most youngsters in elementary schools ignored agriculture, as it was optional; in 1887 it had attracted only 1,489 of nearly 490,000 students. Shaw wanted it obligatory in rural schools, and with a decent textbook.[84] In 1890, Mills and Shaw's school text, *The First Principles of Agriculture*, appeared.

Their publisher, J.E. Bryant, called on teachers at their 1890 convention in Niagara-on-the-Lake to resolve to put agriculture into rural schools. He argued that manufacturers needed skilled operators, some of whom, though few and urban, will receive scientific training to become directors of work. He reported that urban people have technical schools, or at least technical departments in high schools, but that rural people, 90 per cent of whom are farmers, have nothing. His was the old lament, but with a twist: instead of decrying state funding for lawyers' education, jealousy over working-class instruction. Farmers' children want "*not technical instruction* – for that they can get, sufficiently good for all practical purposes, at home, or from observation, reading, attendance at Farmers' Institutes, and the like – but the *scientific education* which will enable them to apply their home-acquired technical skills to the purposes of their after life with intelligence and effect."[85] What Ontario youths needed to know, he pointed out, was plants, scientific manuring, soils – of which many Ontario farmers knew little, unlike the French, whose education was better – along with crops, diseases, drainage, livestock, pests, tillage, and weeds. Rural teachers might know little about the subject, but they could learn.

Although agriculture eventually became compulsory in rural schools (and an option in urban schools) in August 1899, it was probably already too late. Yet the province was actually ahead of the times, as England's Board of Education was still exhorting its rural schools to introduce agriculture.[86] By the end of the century, nature study had made inroads into the Ontario curriculum, and school gardens were appearing. In fact, the Ontario Agricultural College was finally attracting many more students and having a real effect, even though few students or instructors had studied agriculture in elementary schools. Simply having an effective, province-wide elementary school system allowed Ontario's rural people to move ahead – probably like what Cochrane describes as the impact of the one-room schoolhouse: "That educational experience lifted farm people in the United States out of the class of peasants. It enabled some of them to become farm businessmen who could appraise accurately the options open to them. It enabled others to transfer to non-farm employment with relative ease. And it enabled most of them to become effective participants in the social and political processes of which they were a part ... That basic literacy emancipated American farmers from the dead hand of tradition."[87]

## CONCLUSION

When the new province of Ontario took over Canada West's agricultural administration, it left it largely intact, but with some name changes and minor tinkering, as in substituting the Agricultural and Arts Association of Ontario for the old Agricultural Association. For much of the rest of the century, the government kept its distance from the activities it funded. County and township agricultural societies continued, and more emerged; for them, with their annual grants, it was business as usual in running their local fairs and competitions. Governments, whether Conservative

(1867–71) or Liberal (1871–1905), acknowledged that the state's role was to provide financial stimulation – and some slight control – but to leave the actual planning and execution of activities to what were essentially private organizations. This was also true of the Ontario College of Agriculture, which had a distinct arm's-length relationship with the province. Still, agriculture was changing rapidly, and Ontario had to keep pace. Its models now were mostly American. With some of these – the agricultural college and farmers' institutes – over time, Ontario surpassed its mentors. Diversification of agriculture led to the emergence of specialist agricultural societies, which, together with agricultural journalists, displaced the agricultural societies as agents of informal education. By the 1890s, province-wide exhibitions and an umbrella association were obsolete, and Minister Dryden pulled the plug. Ontario's agricultural sector was far more complex at the end of the century, and its educational response was as good as any on the continent.

# 6

# Agricultural Education in Quebec

Because the nature of agriculture in Lower Canada/Canada East was different from that of Upper Canada/Canada West in terms of soils, climate, and technology, we would not expect the government's agricultural administration to respond in quite the same way after 1867. Complications for Quebec included its linguistic divide, the growing strength of the Roman Catholic church, and the frequent turnover of premiers – eleven up to 1900 – most of them Conservatives. The Liberals' control of Ontario for almost all of the last third of the century (Oliver Mowat was premier for 24 years) brought with it a continuity of vision. Economic drivers of agriculture were similar in both provinces, so we still find much in common in the thirty years after Confederation. One striking difference is the pivotal role in Quebec of an individual, Edouard-André Barnard (1835–1898), who was at the centre of many of the debates on changes to agricultural education.

This chapter's five parts consider in turn the organization of agriculture in Quebec; the agricultural societies (including specialist groups), exhibitions, and journals; the long and highly influential career of agricultural editor, educator, and promoter E.-A. Barnard, especially as the province's director of agriculture; the agricultural colleges and specialist schools; and agricultural education in the schools.

## AGRICULTURE AND ITS ORGANIZATION

### The State of Agriculture

While agriculture in Lower Canada/Canada East had lagged in the first half of the century, it began to turn the corner in the 1860s with US–Canadian reciprocity in trade (treaty of 1854), the Civil War, and the expansion of urban markets.[1] If agriculture in Quebec was "in crisis" before mid-century, according to Isbister,[2] it did not become more profitable in the second half. McCallum notes that lack of capital meant it could not diversify and compete with Ontario's agriculture; it had also missed the wheat boom of the 1850s and 1860s.[3] While Quebec's industry grew in the last quarter-century like – if a bit behind – Ontario's, its agriculture had few connections with its domestic industry, unlike its neighbour's. The transfer of youths from farm to city was similar in both provinces, and family sizes were approximately the same, but Ontario's farm families were more productive than Quebec's.

Historians of Canadian agriculture do not provide a consensus view of Quebec agriculture. McCallum argues that the province's agrarian society remained one of subsistence, a peasant society, until the twentieth century, unlike Ontario's more commercial outlook. Kerr and Smyth[4] have characterized Isbister's view as cultural stereotyping. They note that the soil and climate were bigger constraints for Quebec and that, in fact, its dairy industry was nearly as large as Ontario's by 1901, thus showing a commercial awareness. They also highlight French-Canadian entrepreneurial activity, to which Isbister agrees but suggests that, while population pressure should have driven many people to emigrate to obtain more land, most stayed put.

During the second half of the century, Quebec grew less and less wheat, but production of oats exploded, along with major increases in buckwheat, hay, peas, and rye. Late century, raising hogs became important, as they consumed waste skim milk from cheese-making and Britain offered a ready market for bacon. As in Ontario, dairy farming became a central feature of agriculture – a great boon, because it is less susceptible to poor soil or climate.[5] Cheese factories appeared very soon after those in Ontario: C.H. Hill's in Dunham (1865) and others' in Brome (1867 and 1868) and Beauce (1870), with the first commercial creamery in Missisquoi (1869); Jean-Charles Chapais, *père*, of St-Denis opened the first combined cheese factory and creamery in the province.[6] At Confederation, Ontario had more than ten times as many factories with eight times as much capacity as those in Quebec, which Hamelin and Roby attribute to a combination of factors, including better roads and rail, more export production, more capital, and more mechanization. Still, Quebec's industry grew from twenty-five creameries and cheese factories in 1871 to 1,991 in 1901. Until the early 1880s, American cheese dominated the British market, but the rapidly expanding US population soon was consuming most of it, clearing the way for Canadian exports. Commercial dairying required far more than having a cow or two for family consumption, and thus education would be essential for farmers to learn the techniques to become competitive.

The census also showed a major difference between the neighbouring provinces. Several manufacturers in Montreal and Quebec City produced threshing mills, and Quebec's farmers owned 15,476 of them, versus Ontario's farmers' 13,805. But the former group had 10,401 horse-drawn rakes, and the latter, 46,246! Quebec, Phillips explains, lacked a large-implement industry but had more farm labour. Drummond, in contrast, argues that Ontarians had more capital because their agriculture had expanded in the prosperous 1850s and 1860s, when their neighbours' had not. Still, Quebec mechanized more slowly. Both provinces took their cues from the Americans, who began exploiting machinery in the 1830s; Quebec farms started in the 1870s. Employing the 1871 census, Blouin finds that Ontario had nearly 50 per cent more farms, and its farmers owned five times more reapers and mowers, three times more horse rakes, and twice as many winnowing machines; only with threshers did Quebec farmers have an edge.[7] Like its neighbour, Quebec began producing farm machinery in the 1860s. Between 1861 and 1881, its implement manufacturers grew in number from eight to eighty-two, and its neighbour's, from thirty-eight to 141; however, its own were smaller, employing only 13 per cent as many hands, and they tended to serve more local markets.

### Overseeing Agriculture

Like Ontario, the new province of Quebec had to decide on how to oversee agriculture. This took some time. J.G. Ross, MLA for Compton, had introduced a reorganization bill in the assembly in January 1868, while Conservative Premier P.-J.-O. Chauveau introduced his own legislation to the legislative council (upper house). Ross tried again in January 1869, arguing that district agricultural societies' executives should consist of the presidents and vice-presidents of county societies, with the presidents and vice-presidents of district societies forming the Chambre d'agriculture/Board of Agriculture. His bill did not survive second reading, and Chauveau's, from the council, became law as An Act Respecting the Department of Agriculture and Public Works (32 Vict., cap. 15), with royal assent on 5 April 1869. As in Ontario, a commissioner would oversee a department, which would be in charge of agricultural, manufacturing, and mechanical interests. Thus the mechanics' institutes and other technical training activities would come within its purview, as in

Ontario, and the existing agricultural schools would receive public grants. The governor-in-council would appoint a new consultative Conseil d'agriculture/Council of Agriculture to replace the Board of Agriculture and the Agricultural Society of Lower Canada. On paper, the new council's activities appeared impressive:

- to organize exhibitions, found county agricultural societies, and run competitions
- to establish one or more model or experimental farms in connection with the classical colleges, schools, or universities
- to distribute grants for further agricultural education, if the legislature approved funds. However, the council would *not* be involved with the normal schools, should the latter desire to pursue agricultural instruction.
- to promote further agricultural instruction in any colleges or schools receiving public grants
- to offer bursaries for study in these schools
- to publish and distribute useful information
- to publish a journal of agriculture
- to support local agricultural societies, which should discuss new information, offer lectures, circulate agricultural papers, propose prize essays, hold exhibitions and competitions, and import animals and seed

Dr F.-X.-P. Larue (1824–1902), MLA for Portneuf, thought little of the list. On 20 January 1870, he attacked the government's lack of progress on the agricultural front. For him, the 1869 legislation was too complicated and would do little practical good. He argued, rather, for local agricultural *commissaires* who would work with district agricultural councils.[8] This was the idea of agricultural superintendents dating from the 1850 inquiry into agriculture. Other parts of the new legislation were also controversial. J.-H. Bellerose (1820–1899), MLA for Laval, claimed that Quebec had made great strides in agriculture over the past twenty years and was as good as Ontario and the neighbouring US states. He argued that it would be best to look to foreigners for good ideas, rather than to the local agricultural societies, which cost too much for the little good they did. As for the agricultural schools, "Les écoles d'agriculture ne sont pas non plus à la hauteur de leur tâche et ne rendent pas de grands services à ceux qu'elles sont appelées à instruire."[9] In response to these criticisms, Chauveau noted that the Hincks-Morin government

(1851–54) had appointed superintendents to lecture but that the MacNab-Taché ministry (1855–56) had ended the program.[10] The assembly's Standing Committee on Agriculture, Mining and Colonization would discuss Larue's ideas.

Louis Archambeault (1814–1890) became the first commissioner of agriculture and public works and remained in office until 1874. Archambeault, a legislative councillor, was a member of Cabinet but not a minister. He was strongly in favour of replacing the old system with tighter government control. Under the new act, he moved to appoint the first members of the Council of Agriculture, whose task would be to "encourager les expositions, les partis de labour, les concours des récoltes sur pied et des fermes les mieux cultivées: voilà l'impulsion la plus directe qu'il puisse donner à l'amélioration de notre système de culture."[11] The council met in Montreal for the first time on 12 October 1869. It had seventeen members in addition to Archambeault; of these eighteen, twelve were francophones. The abbé Pilote, head of the agricultural school at La Pocatiére, and T.-J.-Amédée Marsan (1844–1924), head of the school at L'Assomption, were both members. The council selected Henri-Gustave Joly, MLA for Lotbinière and leader of the opposition, as president; Matthew H. Cochrane, a Montrèal footware manufacturer and one of Canada's outstanding livestock breeders, as vice-president; and Georges Leclère as secretary. The council's first business was to keep the efforts of the old Chambre d'agriculture moving, but education was its primary focus.

## AGRICULTURAL SOCIETIES AND EXHIBITIONS

### Societies and Activities

The government's Council of Agriculture would organize provincial exhibitions and competitions and supervise county agricultural societies. The number of societies had expanded under the Union of 1841. Under the new provincial Agricultural Act of 1869, these societies still had the same objectives, including competitions and exhibitions, discussions, lectures, papers, and prizes for essays, and distributing seeds and importing livestock. Funding remained stable.

Out of the total appropriation for societies, 10 per cent went to the council's use and another 8 per cent for grants to agricultural schools, leaving typically about $40,000 each year for disbursements. The rather loose control under the Union became, at least in theory, tighter:

societies were to provide annual reports and to hold exhibitions or would lose part or all of their grants, although the council did not increase its scrutiny right away. By 1873, some seventy-nine counties had organized societies (some larger ones had two), although seven had not reported; twenty-six of them had English-speaking secretaries. The ensemble comprised 11,542 members, of whom 3,251 were anglophones.[12] Nearly 30 per cent were anglophones, when their proportion of the rural population in the 1871 census was a good deal less than 25 per cent.

A typical mid-century stimulus was prizes for the "best-kept farm"; such competitions were typical in both Canadas East and West. Early on, the Council of Agriculture set up rules for such competitions, with a first prize of $50 and five additional prizes across the province. Connections between societies barely existed, especially after abolition of the provincial society. Secretary Georges Leclère hoped for exchanges of information at agricultural congresses, which the best local agronomists could attend. The old board had organized such a congress in February 1852, under the presidency of Major Campbell, with some sixty people in attendance. Nothing came of Leclère's proposal. By 1879, Liberal Henri-Gustave Joly had crossed the floor to become premier (1878–79) and commissioner; he supported best-cultivated farm competitions and ploughing matches but noted that most societies ignored them: "I am thoroughly convinced that wherever such farm competitions shall be tried with good will and intelligence, farmers will derive from it great pleasure."[13] The council's president, L.H. Massue, was equally supportive. With some prodding, most societies had such events by the early 1880s, but the tide had turned; in the 1880 report, the president opined that societies, especially those losing members, should minimize such competitions and focus on produce and livestock exhibitions. Societies had long used some of their funds to provide seed to members, but the president believed that farmers should save their own seed and spend society funds instead on importing livestock and obtaining better machinery.

For decades, societies had failed to prepare annual reports. J.M. Browning, a well-known cattle breeder, began to crack down when he was president. In his 1875 annual report, he demanded proper accounting and the withholding of grants in its absence: "The instructions of the Council not having been enforced until this year, certain societies have imagined themselves hardly dealt with when required to conform, and have reluctantly complied, after in some cases appealing to the Honorable the Commissioner of Agriculture, who, I am happy to say, did not at all interfere with my action, after receiving the necessary explanations."[14]

Records of very few county societies survive. Records of the oldest such body – the County of Missisquoi Agricultural Society (originally the County of Bedford Agricultural Society, 1824, which emerged not long after the launch of the district societies) – provide us with a glimpse of how these organizations operated.[15] Its earliest minutes, from 1857, reveal a francophone president; almost all the other 126 members were anglophones. Its subscriptions were a little more than $4 a year. Apparently its only activities were two shows each year, in spring and in autumn. Almost all of its funds went to competition premiums, ranging from top prizes of $18 for the best-kept farm to $10 for stock; most categories of crops or stock had multiple prizes (e.g., $7, $6, $5, $4, $3, $2, $1). It spent a little more than $1,000 on prizes. During the 1860s, it added domestic manufactures to the competition, including cloth, coverlets, flannel, knit stockings, mittens, and quilts – and ploughs.

By 1874, little had changed; the Missisquoi society now counted 160 members – a handful of them francophone – and collected only $306 in subscriptions, many of them only $1 per annum; the provincial grant was $656; the balance of the $1,200 income came from entry fees and tickets at the exhibition in Bedford. Most of the society's disbursements went towards premiums, payment of judges, and $50 for the secretary-treasurer's annual salary. In that year, it spent $35 to hire a cornet band to entertain fairgoers. In 1892, exhibition entries fell into five categories: cattle; farm produce (butter, cheese, honey, maple sugar, etc.); horses; manufactures (now more implements and fewer domestic products); and swine, sheep, and poultry. Premiums were fewer and smaller. Income – the government grant, subscriptions (which now nearly matched the grant), and other revenue (from the fair and its "amusements") – went almost entirely to the exhibition. The minutes make no mention of discussions, distribution of books or newspapers, or model farms – not even the old "best-kept farm" competition.

Why did the Council of Agriculture spend all this public money on societies that had so many detractors? Was there a more cynical motive? Buying votes by "pork-barrelling" targeted constituents is as old as democracy itself. As farmers were the largest single occupational group in Canada, and those who joined societies literate, wealthier, and, most important, landowners who could vote, they were an obvious target group. Initially, grants to societies might have seemed a quid pro quo. Once the practice became institutionalized, however, the withdrawal of grants would have been dangerous for a government. Indeed, apart from a few attempts to increase the societies' accountability, the governments of both Ontario and Quebec never reduced grants but actually increased them over time.

### Agricultural Exhibitions

Provincial exhibitions had lapsed with the end of the Agricultural Society of Lower Canada in 1869. The Council of Agriculture was slow off the mark but worked with the Council of Arts and Manufactures to organize an exhibition of agriculture and industry. For that purpose, the two bodies dispatched a committee to visit the New York State Fair in Syracuse, the Missouri State Fair in St Louis, and the Ontario Provincial Exhibition to inquire into their operations. Many anglophone farmers were now breeding stock with the use of foreign imports, whereas many francophones maintained the "Canadian" line of cows; thus, because anglophones organized many of the exhibitions, imported breeds dominated the livestock competitions.

An ongoing problem of the provincial exhibition was one of infrastructure. In the Union period, the Board of Arts and Manufactures of Lower Canada had virtually bankrupted itself to build its Crystal Palace, and adequate space and buildings were still an issue in the 1870s. The Agricultural Act of 1869 required a provincial exhibition at least once every three years. There had been one in 1873, and the federal government proposed a Dominion Exhibition in Montreal for 1875, but the Council of Agriculture realized that it did not have an appropriate space. As Browning reported, the situation was a mess: in 1870, the council had purchased land at Mile End from the nuns of the Hôtel-Dieu to construct buildings for both agricultural and industrial exhibitions. It had to erect suitable structures, plant trees, and set out a public park. When it did not do so within the appropriate time, the sisters sued. Eventually, an out-of-court settlement returned the lands to the nuns. The council had also negotiated with Ottawa for the use of sixty acres of the Logan Farm on Mount Royal, the childhood home of Sir William Edmond Logan (1798–1875), founder and long-time director of the Geological Survey of Canada. However, the terms were for a provincial lease, and the council would have to put up and maintain the buildings. Thus, expecting an exhibition for 1876, the council was not only out of pocket several thousands of dollars, but it also had no exhibition grounds.

By 1877, the legislative assembly's Standing Committee on Agriculture was losing interest in the societies and their exhibitions because they involved few francophones. An 1877 revision of the Agricultural Act gave parish agricultural societies direct representation in county societies, but the standing committee found that 180 of 600 parishes had no members in an agricultural society, and another 100 parishes had six or fewer.[16] The Council of Agriculture expected county societies to hold exhibitions, but many did not bother. This may well have helped make the provincial exhibition shaky: there was no hierarchy of competition as in Ontario and the neighbouring US states. When a Dominion Exhibition took place in Ottawa in 1879, the council participated and cancelled its own. By the 1880s, however, Montreal began to host shows of fat cattle. For years, the Montreal Horticultural Society had organized an annual horticulture show. That society's precursor had emerged as early as 1811 but began to flourish only in the 1830s.[17] By the mid-1870s, it published fruit reports "for the guidance and information of those engaged in the culture of Fruit in this neighbourhood." Together with the local fruit growers, it held annual flower, fruit, and vegetable competitions.

*Specialist Societies*

Specialist societies like Ontario's also crystallized, but more slowly. In addition to the few horticultural societies, fruit growers formed local societies. One of the foremost, Jean-Charles Chapais, *fils*, at St-Denis, wrote on fruit-growing for his brother-in-law E.-A. Barnard's *Journal d'agriculture*. The Eastern Townships were ideal for cultivating fruit, and orchards had expanded during the second half of the century. By the 1890s, fruit-growers' associations were in operation in Abbotsford, Brome, Missisquoi, and Shefford and in the county of L'Islet. Apples were the chief crop, and their growers formed the Pomological Society of Quebec in 1893.

As in Ontario, forward-looking farmers in Quebec turned to dairying, but a province-wide organization came into being more than a decade after Ontario's. Barnard and his friend the abbé Théophile Montminy (1842–1899) had been promoting the activity since the late 1870s. By 1882, the Société d'Industrie Laitière de la Province de Québec/The Dairymen's Association of the Province of Quebec formed. One of its founders, St-Hyacinthe lawyer Pierre Boucher de la Bruère (1837–1917), was president from 1882 to 1889 and later the province's superintendent of public instruction. Another key figure was the abbé Montminy; keen for some years on agricultural matters, he organized the Club Saint-Isidore for farmers in his parish of St-Agapit. His interest in dairying brought him into the society in 1884; he would be its president from 1892 to 1896. As the general schools of agriculture appeared to downplay dairy practice, Thomas Chapais (1858–1946), Ultramontanist journalist and politician and Barnard's brother-in-law, opened a private dairy school in May 1881 at St-Denis. Under J.-M. Jocelyn, the institution – North America's first, according to J.-C. Chapais, *fils* – started with ten students. Barnard had for some time recognized the economic possibilities of dairying and how it was transforming agriculture in Ontario, just as it had in northern Europe. Western Quebec had 162 butter and cheese factories, but eastern Quebec had none. Technological advances – acid testing, maturation rooms, mechanical separators, and refrigerated storage and shipping – helped create the need for serious, systematic instruction.

The idea of technical training for the dairy industry grew quickly. A butter school appeared in Ste-Marie de Beauce in 1882; its head, S.-M. Barré, had been dispatched a year earlier to study the most modern techniques in Denmark. The centrifugal cream separator was state-of-the-art, and Barré obtained one for Ste-Marie. J.-C. Chapais, *fils*, considered it the first such device in a North American creamery. Barré wrote to the Standing Committee on Agriculture on 1 May 1882 on how to improve dairy practice in the province – for example, pay a travelling instructor to teach in various cheese factories and, possibly, inspect them and subsidize the new dairymen's association – and his own school. Funds for his school would create "an experimental establishment that would enable it to ascertain the best process of manufacture of Dairy products, to purchase apparatus, utensils and instruments of different kinds, to ascertain their real value and efficiency before introducing and recommending their use in new factories."[18] By 1885, Barré had moved to Guelph to become the first professor of dairying at the Ontario Agricultural College.

As in Ontario, the dairymen's organization in Quebec also moved directly into education by opening its own dairy school in St-Hyacinthe, the Ecole de laiterie, with Boucher de la Bruère's assistance, in 1892. While the Ontario dairymen's organizations bowed out in favour of the dairy department at Guelph, Quebec's agricultural schools had no real equivalent. The St-Hyacinthe school, which the provincial government funded, remained the key institution. By the mid-1890s, it enrolled between 200 and 300 students annually, primarily for the cheese-making course.[19]

*Agricultural Journals*

As literacy increased and agriculture became more specialized, the reach of agricultural journalism also expanded. Alongside the official provincial publication in Quebec, private-sector agricultural journals existed, as in Ontario.[20] The Montreal journal *La Minerve* published a separate weekly, *Le semaine agricole*, from 1857 until 1899. Hector Fabre (1834–1910), founder of the Quebec journal *L'événement* in 1867, added a weekly, *Le cultivateur*, in 1874; *Le Canadien* published it from 1881 to 1893. In eastern Quebec, the *Gazette des campagnes*, edited by Emile Dumais in 1861 and by J.-D. Schmouth 1871–5, survived until 1895. For anglophones, the *Montreal Star* launched the weekly *Family Herald* in 1870.

### E.-A. BARNARD AND THE AGRICULTURE DEPARTMENT

The most important figure to emerge in these years was the resourceful Edouard-André Barnard (1835–1898).[21] Descendant of an anglophone New England family, he grew up on a farm near Trois-Rivières where his father was a prothonotary (court clerk). His studies at Nicolet did not interest him, and he worked as a travelling salesman and read law. By the late 1850s, he was farming near Trois-Rivières while studying agriculture, experimenting, and taking an interest in dairying. After the *Trent* Affair in late 1861 involving Britain and the United States, Barnard joined the militia and then in 1867 helped organize devout young Catholics joining the Papal Zouaves in reaction to the Italian Risorgimento. When that effort failed, he returned home and, having taught himself the subject, began writing for J.-X. Perrault's *La revue agricole*. Over the next decade, as Perrault withdrew more and more from agricultural matters, Barnard emerged as the most prominent agronomist in the province, taking over the successor to *La revue agricole* and experimenting with his ideas for *causeries agricoles*.

### La semaine agricole *and* Causeries agricoles *(1869–72)*

In the last years of the Union, despite funding from the Board of Agriculture for Lower Canada, an agricultural newspaper under various names attracted few subscribers. The closing of *La revue agricole* at the end of 1868 and the board's demise created a vacuum. In the autumn of 1869, the Council of Agriculture began a $1,000 annual grant to a new, weekly journal, *La semaine agricole*, from Duvernay, Frères, in Montreal; its first issue appeared on 12 October 1869, promising sixteen pages weekly for a year for only $1. The publishers understood the difficulties facing agricultural papers:

> L'apathie générale de la campagne pour la lecture a découragé les hommes d'initiative et aujourd'hui, avec la certitude de ne réussir

que médiocrement auprès des abonnés, personne ne voudrait faire le risque d'un matériel d'imprimerie pour la publication d'un tel journal. Mais du moment que les circonstances nous permettent de fair[e] beaucoup plus qu'un éditeur spécial, nous n'hésitons pas à lancer ce nouveau journal auquel nous ne demandons qu'une chose: une recette suffisante pour nous empêcher d'y perdre de l'argent, nous réservant comme unique profit la satisfaction d'avoir fourni une voix, dans l'opinion publique, à cette classe importante, prépondérant, [dont] le travail est la base de la prospérité générale, la classe des cultivateurs.[22]

Of course, without the $1,000 yearly subvention, the paper would likely not have appeared at all. The directors of the new agricultural school in L'Assomption – but mostly its professor of agriculture, T.-J.-Amédée Marsan – provided the editorial work. Its finances were shaky – the council thought 25 cents a copy the maximum allowable price – and its budget could not allow it to reach the widest audience. There were also federal duties on agricultural papers, and rural people read little.[23] In 1869, Barnard became a correspondent of *La semaine agricole*, and a year later he was its editor.

Moving to Varennes to be closer to Montreal, Barnard, following George Buckland's lead in Canada West five years earlier, about 1872 began giving talks – *causeries agricoles* – to local groups, which would later become a valuable strategy for the department that emerged in 1869. In 1871, Commissioner Louis Archambeault dispatched Barnard as an immigration agent to Europe, where he visited agricultural societies and schools. He returned with the idea that Quebec farmers should grow sugar beets – a project that had some success – and acted as a colonization agent and lecturer for the department. Organization and publicity by local clergymen and newspapers helped sustain his continuing *causeries agricoles* to county societies. He estimated that his 115 talks over the years reached between 26,000 and 30,000 farmers; the groups he was dealing with had 11,542 members, about one-third of them anglophone.[24] In 1874, he married a daughter of J.-C. Chapais, *père*, former minister of agriculture in Ottawa. A year later, his talks appeared as *Une leçon d'agriculture: causeries agricoles*.

Barnard believed that the Council of Agriculture supported only those farmers requiring no assistance. He knew that the great mass of farmers, who were not members of county societies, had neither encouragement nor direction. To that end, Barnard, a firm Ultramontanist, would foster parish-level farm clubs (*cercles agricoles*) with the assistance of local priests. Such activity, however, would subvert the official machinery and increase the influence of the Catholic Church. By the early 1870s, Barnard approached bishops and priests to support his *cercles agricoles*. The bishop of Montreal, Mgr Ignace Bourget (1799–1885), sent a circular to his parish priests in 1870. *La semaine agricole* was in financial trouble by April 1872 and, when it merged with *La Minerve*'s weekly paper, dropped Barnard as editor. He had probably antagonized the Council of Agriculture with his efforts to create the *cercles agricoles* and his espousal of the "Canadian race" of cattle instead of imported breeds, which the wealthy farmers on the council strongly favoured.

### Director of Agriculture (1877–88)

Council members now lobbied hard for funds for an official agricultural paper. By February 1875, the legislature's Standing Committee on Agriculture supported them, recommending more money for a newspaper and brochures for farmers. In December, the committee requested double the funding for a newspaper (to $2,000), but the solicitor-general refused. Further pressure ensued, and by 1876 the government decided that the Department of Agriculture should manage and distribute its own agricultural paper, thereby removing it from the council's control. Barnard was on good terms with Conservative Charles Boucher de Boucherville (premier 1874–78), who made him editor of the new *Journal d'agriculture*, which began publication in 1877 with a distribution of 10,500 copies.[25] At the same time, Arthur N. Jenner Fust, a Cambridge graduate and professor of agriculture at the anglophone agricultural school in Richmond, edited an English-language version. The French version became the *Journal d'agriculture illustré* in 1879 (and *Journal d'agriculture et d'horticulture* in 1897). Barnard remained editor until 1890; his brother-in-law J.-C. Chapais, *fils*, spelled him during 1891; and then he continued alongside Jenner Fust until his own death in 1898.

When Barnard took up the reins of the official journal in 1877, he also started as director of agriculture within the Department of Agriculture and Public Works, answering to the deputy commissioner.

### Cercles agricoles (1876–1900)

During his time as director of agriculture, Barnard launched his greatest success, the *cercles agricoles*, which he had espoused since the early 1870s and which became venues for discussions on practical topics, but without competitions, premiums, or exhibitions. As an editor and speaker,

Barnard knew that many francophone farmers did not (or could not) read but could listen well and learn quickly – the motive for his own decades of *causeries agricoles*. He also knew that county agricultural societies attracted very few of them. Unlike Ontario, Quebec had not developed a layer of township-level societies, so Barnard focused on the parish; Quebec had nearly eighty county agricultural societies but more than 600 Catholic parishes. The movement had started slowly, with the first *cercle* on the Ile d'Orléans in 1862, but took off in the 1870s. In September 1875, delegates from twenty-five clubs met in convention – L'Union agricole nationale – in Montreal, together with members of the Council of Agriculture and agricultural teachers. By 1883, from a peak of forty-six *cercles*, forty were still operating, with 2,740 members.[26] As editor of the *Journal d'agriculture*, Barnard reported their activities to promote the idea among francophone readers. As the movement grew, Barnard's distaste for the traditional agricultural societies increased; in his 1884 departmental report, he declared "thirty-five thousand dollars, at least, are given by the Province to our agricultural societies! A dead loss, most of it."[27]

Like most of the traditional societies, the *cercles* also eschewed social events, politics, and religion, although most members were Catholic. Temperance and the disdain of luxury were also goals of the clubs. The movement was still young when Narcisse-Eutrope Dionne (1848–1917) reviewed it in 1881.[28] He opened with an apologia for rural life and the usual lament about emigration to the United States. He reflected that more agricultural colleges might have kept more farmers at home and that accordingly the *cercles* must become the farmers' schools. This idea was not new: Laval University chemistry professor Hubert La Rue had argued in 1867 that small parish libraries and associations would aid agriculture. The *Gazette des campagnes* also promoted the idea in December 1877, noting the value of such groups in Scotland and the United States. By 1887, the movement was sufficiently strong for Barnard to organize the first provincial congress of the *cercles*. It was to take place in Trois-Rivières, where he had moved back to his family farm in 1882 to carry on his demonstrations and dairy farming.

Barnard had worked to ensure firm church support for the *cercles*. In 1886, the bishops' meeting in Quebec recognized their work and provided them with a constitution, a name (Saint-Isidore the Worker), and a patron saint (Sacred Heart). Clerical support was evident at the Trois-Rivières congress, 19–21 January 1887: the honorary president was the Ultramontane bishop of Trois-Rivières, Mgr Louis-François Laflèche (1818–1898); the president, the abbé Samuel Garon; the vice-president, the abbé Montminy; and secretaries Barnard and his brother-in-law J.-C. Chapais, *fils*. Nearly 190 individuals appear on lists as attending, although the organizers claimed as many as a thousand, and many were priests. A few politicians, teachers, and bureaucrats added respectability: Conservative Louis-Olivier Taillon (1840–1923), premier for four days the next week; former premier de Boucherville; former Commissioner Archambeault; and Professors Marsan and La Rue.

Almost all the delegates were francophones. The issue of government support provoked lively discussion. Montminy, who due to illness could not attend, wrote to the abbé Garon lamenting that the Council of Agriculture had passed the following resolution: "Résolu: Que, tout en admettant que les cercles agricoles *peuvent* avoir une certaine influence locale dans chaque paroisse, ce conseil ne se croirait pas justifiable d'affecter une partie de l'octroi annuel aux sociétés d'agriculture en faveur des cercles agricoles, dont l'action combinée *devrait* plutôt *aider* les sociétés d'agriculture dans leurs louables efforts à favoriser les progrès agricoles, *au lieu de les paralyser* par une action indépendante et SECTIONNELLE."[29] This missive had surprised Montminy, who reported that council members had previously told him how much they appreciated the *cercles* and that Commissioner Louis Beaubien (1837–1915) supported financial aid.

Next for the delegates was a visit to E.-A. Barnard's experimental farm nearby. It is evident that Barnard and Chapais engineered the congress as a means to outmanoeuvre the Council of Agriculture, challenge the traditional agricultural societies, and foster Barnard's vision and career. The delegates struck a committee to present a memorial to the assembly's Standing Committee on Agriculture and to the Cabinet, but *not* to the Council of Agriculture. While the new committee's members came mainly from the congress organizers (Barnard, Chapais, Garon, and Montminy), they included Dr La Rue and journalist Jules-Paul Tardivel (1851–1905). La Rue represented educated professionals, while Tardivel was one of the most vociferous promoters of Ultramontanism. Barnard was a good friend and supporter of Tardivel's, who published Barnard's articles under the pseudonym "Agricola" in his newspaper *La vérité*.

The congress's memorial lauds the work of the *cercles*, although they received no support, but casts doubt on the agricultural societies: "Il est même reconnu qu'une partie notable de ces argents, octroyés chaque année, ne produit aucun bon résultat." The document suggests modest subventions of $50 a year to the *cercles* and that the department provide lecturers for their meetings. It proposes establishing an agricultural school for men and a school principally about domestic science for women, with clergymen and nuns, respectively, on the staff. Delegates had also expressed their astonishment that Barnard, who had done so much for agriculture in the province, was not a member of the Council of Agriculture.

Honoré Mercier's new Parti National government revamped Agriculture and Public Works as Agriculture and Colonization, with the notable colonization advocate the curé Antoine Labelle (1833–1891) as deputy minister. Barnard's long tenure as director of agriculture ended, and he moved to Quebec as secretary of the Council of Agriculture that he detested.

### The Cercles Continue

Of course, the Council of Agriculture opposed the *cercles agricoles*, but by 1893, because of their growth and sheer numbers, Taillon's second ministry officially recognized them and allowed grants to them. Barnard published in 1893 *Cercles agricoles: instructions pour l'organisation et la direction des cercles agricoles* and two years later a summary of his life's work as a practical farmer in the 500 pages of *Le livre des cercles agricoles: manuel d'agriculture*. The Department of Agriculture and Colonization distributed copies of both to members of clergy, legislators, agricultural societies, and *cercles*. The farmers'-institute model did not catch on in Quebec as it had in Ontario because the *cercles agricoles*, already thriving by the mid-1880s, played a similar role for the rural population, especially as there was no strong, central agricultural college to provide the knowledge and lecturers.

By century's end, with stable funding in place, membership in the *cercles* was impressive. According to Gigault, in 1896 some 509 *cercles* were in operation, with a total of 39,284 members. By comparison, in 1897, sixty-five county agricultural societies with 12,770 members were active, holding exhibitions biennially and competitions for the best-kept farms in alternate years.[30] As each *cercle* member and many agricultural-society adherents received the *Journal d'agriculture illustré*, informal education through the official departmental paper now had a wide reach. These activities cost the provincial treasury nearly $162,000 annually.[31]

### New Initiatives

During the 1890s, two other informal initiatives in agricultural education – lectures and agricultural missionaries – appeared. First, lectures to local audiences, which Barnard pioneered, resurfaced. The Department of Agriculture and Colonization hired T.-J.-Amédée Marsan in 1892 to circulate within the province as a lecturer. In 1895–96, he delivered fifty-seven lectures in fifty-four locations, attracting seventy-five to eighty auditors to each meeting. Now, however, the church was directly involved. The local priest would announce the forthcoming talk, and the meetings would normally take place in the church sacristy. Where Ontario's farmers' institutes organized at the grass roots, Quebec's itinerant lectures were from top down. Second, with increasing clerical support for agricultural instruction and the farming community, the church established a program of agricultural missionaries in 1894. Priests with some technical knowledge of agriculture circulated among the parishes giving talks; the abbé Montminy was the first of these men, whose talks engendered much enthusiasm and large audiences. Part of their role was to scout out talented local boys for the agricultural schools.

### Conclusion: A Shift from Above

All of this activity was very different from the staid operations of the county agricultural societies. Bruno Jean has argued that, in terms of the ideology of agricultural education, Quebec saw a shift from an elitist to a popular vision beginning in the 1880s.[32] The latter focused on self-help and mutual assistance through the *cercles*. A shift did take place, although the elitist tradition continued for some time, while it appears that popular vision was not so much a grass-roots movement as one that Barnard and his clerical allies engineered. A contest of visions was only part of a wider power struggle.

### AGRICULTURAL COLLEGES AND SPECIALIST SCHOOLS

While agricultural education came under the direction of the Department of Agriculture and Public Works, the future of agriculture as an industry in the province came briefly under the scrutiny of the Special Committee for Taking into Consideration the Best Means of Developing Industry in this Province, which the assembly struck in 1871. With Pierre-S. Gendron, MLA for Bagot, as chair, the committee held only a few meetings, including an interview with Emile Bonnemant, a celebrated French agriculturist and chevalier de la Légion d'honneur, who was visiting Quebec to help establish a sugar-beet industry. In 1872, Bonnemant addressed his pamphlet *Projet pour l'établissement d'une sucrerie de betteraves au Canada* to George A. Drummond, John Redpath's brother- and son-in-law and manager of his sugar refinery in Montreal.[33]

At the committee's request, Bonnemant provided a report on the creation of a "superior school of agriculture and industrial arts."[34] Well aware of continental European and British exemplars but particularly admiring Prussian and other German schools, he outlined a school to resemble Ste-Anne's at La Pocatière but with more science and industrial-related chairs for sylviculture and rural construction. He estimated $20,000 for a 100–150-acre farm and buildings and an annual outlay of $7,000–$9,000 for five teachers, a farm manager, a gardener, and three labourers. Contemporary American experience would suggest these figures were far too modest, as Ontario was discovering at Guelph. In the event, the committee made no formal recommendation, and, when the assembly later set up a standing committee on industry, it focused on manufacturing and mining, not agriculture.

### Collège de l'Assomption (1867–99)

At the time of Confederation, the short-lived agricultural schools at Rimouski and Ste-Thérèse had failed, leaving only the school at La Pocatière.[35] In 1867, the Collège de l'Assomption – in L'Assomption, a north-shore suburb of Montreal – decided to provide agricultural training, the only such instruction available in the Montreal region.[36] The local MLA, Louis Archambeault, and the county agricultural society had pressed for the school, and the legislature provided funds. For its agriculture professor, the directors chose T.-J. Amédée Marsan, a law student, who, on Archambeault's advice, enrolled at Ste-Anne's in La Pocatière to obtain his technical qualifications; the dying Board of Agriculture examined him and presented him his diploma in March 1868. The school, with a farm nestling in a loop of the Assomption River, opened on 5 November 1867 with few students. A two-year course catered to those who could read and write, and $50 bursaries enabled poorer students to attend. Inspection by a committee of the Council of Agriculture a decade later lamented the lack of progress and suggested the council revoke its annual $2,000 grant. But Marsan persevered, even when yearly grants to the agricultural schools dropped to $800 each, and the school slowly improved its operations and grew. Annual enrolment was between ten and twenty until the 1890s, when it rose to between thirty and fifty. Marsan was professor for the school's entire history, until it had to close in 1899.

## Agricultural Instruction

EN FRANÇAIS

The department did not directly concern itself with agricultural matters but left them to the Council of Agriculture. Very early in its proceedings, the council struck a committee on agricultural instruction. Its members, Joly among them, visited the two operating schools – La Pocatière and L'Assomption – and found both in good shape overall, although neither had many students. The committee realized that the schools supplemented their $800 yearly grant from the legislature by deducting 8 per cent from the agricultural societies' annual grants, which added $3,600, providing $5,200 for the two schools to share.

The committee wanted to apportion $1,450 to each school to pay three staff members plus one *chef de pratique*. The remaining funds would supply $60 bursaries for each of twenty students plus $25 prizes to graduates of the two-year program, but the committee wondered where the prospective students would come from. Rural parents, its members suspected, did not want their sons to leave the farm, did not like schools, and did not want their children to come into contact with other classes of society. Both schools had connections to *collèges classiques*, which tended to cater to the rural and small-town elite, so there may have been some truth to its suspicions.

In December 1875, the Standing Committee on Agriculture, Mining and Colonization reported on introducing agricultural instruction to the common schools and making obligatory Hubert La Rue's *Petit manuel d'agriculture à l'usage des écoles* (2nd ed., 1872). The committee also resolved that the province establish two model farms that would pay students for their work, to compensate farm families for the labour that they were losing. As the committee noted, the Michigan Agricultural College, which paid students for labour, had 150 attendees.[37]

IN ENGLISH

In the 1860s, anglophone farmers had remained relatively quiet on the educational front. The few calling for further efforts were an elite group. Typical was Sir Matthew Aylmer, 8th Baron Aylmer (1842–1923), who spoke on familiar themes at the Richmond County agricultural exhibition in 1868. Clearly, he argued, agricultural education for farming was necessary and generated wealth. The subject should be in the common schools, and teachers should pass an examination in the science of agriculture. "But," he added, "before any great change can take place in the present state of agriculture, several radical obstacles must be removed. The apathy of farmers must be overcome, the dignity of the pursuit must be felt by them. This great and fundamental cause of national wealth must receive encouragement from national legislation."[38]

In the mid-1870s, an anglophone group that hoped to open an agricultural school in Compton could reach no consensus on how to operate it. In its place, an anglophone school appeared in 1875, a project of St Francis College in Richmond. The school's principal, Rev. Charles Tanner, with the support of Lord Aylmer, began on a shoestring, hiring Arthur Jenner Fust as professor of agriculture. The Council of Agriculture withheld a grant because of its low enrolment (four students) and its lack of a proper farm. The school rarely had more than fifteen students a year, and by 1889 it closed. A second English-language agricultural school in Compton was marginally viable, operating from 1894 to 1904.

### Rethinking Agricultural Education (1873–90s)

By the early 1870s, Quebec had two nearby jurisdictions, Ontario and Michigan, with operating central agricultural colleges.[39] By the mid-1870s, Quebec possessed three small schools, two teaching in French (La Pocatière and L'Assomption) and one in English (St Francis), none of them under direct government control, but rather part of colleges with religious affiliations. Not surprising, several key figures in agricultural circles began to rethink the province's approach to formal agricultural education. Among them was Gédéon Ouimet, who had served as Conservative premier 1873–74 and also as minister of public instruction. When de Boucherville replaced him as premier, he suppressed the education ministry to appease the church hierarchy and reintroduced the non-Cabinet position of superintendent of public instruction, naming Ouimet to the post and also, ex officio, to the Council of Agriculture.

Another supporter of the single-school idea was Louis Beaubien, MLA, an energetic farmer in Outremont and member of the council. A critic of provincial schools as offering little practical education, he had visited both East Lansing and Guelph in 1877 and believed that a central school with paid labour was in the province's interest. He based his L'étude sur l'éducation agricole (1877) on his report to the council in March of that year. His criticism of the La Pocatière school stimulated its principal, abbé Narcisse Proulx, to defend the status quo in Les écoles d'agriculture de la Province de Québec vengées (1877).

The Council of Agriculture kept a close watch on the agricultural schools. In its June 1877 report, it had given La Pocatière a clean bill of health but had reservations about L'Assomption: it was not doing well, jeopardizing its subsidy. Councillors proposed a twice-yearly visit of inspection to monitor the situation. The St Francis school, however, seemed to be well organized, though with only four students – ten was the minimum for a grant.[40] In the event, it received a two-year subsidy of $1,200 in the following year. While the council had earlier doubts about whether it was a real school with a proper farm, Tanner's efforts to emulate the work at La Pocatière and L'Assomption impressed the council. By 1879, Joly was commissioner, and L.H. Massue succeeded him as president of the council. Ouimet, now chair of the council's agricultural schools committee, reported the committee's view that the province should have a single agricultural college under the council's direct control. The committee suggested incorporating the La Pocatière school as a separate entity and severing it from its college, Ste-Anne. In January 1880, council requested that Ouimet and Beaubien approach the assembly's Standing Committee of Agriculture to press the idea of making the existing schools independent or creating a provincial central school.

There was still no money to visit the out-of-province colleges, although council member J.M. Browning travelled to East Lansing. Finally in January 1883, the council dispatched President L.H. Massue, Vice-President Browning, and Secretary Leclère to Guelph and East Lansing. Reporting to the council and to the assembly in December, the group noted that it found much of interest in Michigan but saw Guelph as the more viable model, "sincèrement convaincu que cet enseignement est celui qui convient le plus à ce pays, et celui qui pourrait être introduit avec avantage dans la Province de Québec."[41] It came down squarely for a single, state-run, and well-financed school with competent, bilingual instructors.

They had no support, however, from Barnard or from his Ultramontane allies. In his 1884 report on agricultural schools to Commissioner John Jones Ross – by then Conservative premier (1884–87) – Barnard dismissed the idea of a central school like those in Ontario and Michigan. It seemed to him unjust to close down the existing schools as they provided for different linguistic and social groups. In Ontario, where many excellent farms already served as models to neighbours, a scientific and experimental college that would offer further knowledge made sense; in Quebec, however, where European scientific practices were lacking, practical farming instruction would be much more advantageous. Barnard also saw the need for farm schools in different parts of the province where differing soils, climates, and cultural practices prevailed. He worried, however, about the low enrolments in the existing schools. He could see that, while Marsan had done much good at L'Assomption, neither it nor La Pocatière attracted enough students. Barnard believed that those who were there were little more than children without the vocation of farmer and hypothesized that parents might be unwilling to send their sons to a school always in danger of closing.

At the time, he saw gleams of hope: a new francophone agricultural school proposed for Rougemont had garnered hundreds of applicants, while the St Francis School at Richmond attracted students from its region. As it turned out, the Rougemont school survived only one year. Barnard's editorial associate, Jenner Fust, who had established an experimental farm in connection with Lincoln College in Sorel that year, was making remarkable progress. Barnard made the report public the following year in his pamphlet: *Nos écoles d'agriculture* (1885).

In Barnard's mind, permanent funding and state control would allow the agricultural schools to thrive. He found three factors problematic: the lack of agriculturally knowledgeable priests to run the schools; the fact that students did not board and did little manual labour; and the schools' teaching of almost no dairy practice, despite its obvious and growing role.

AN AGRICULTURAL COMMISSION LOOKS TO GUELPH (1887–88)
Despite Barnard's opposition, council lobbying finally led in August 1887 to an agricultural commission to examine the educational question and to survey, once again, agricultural education in person.[42] Under Chair Nazaire Bernatchez (1838–1906), MLA for Montmagny and a farmer himself, commissioners heard from witnesses, such as Montminy and Perrault, and then went on the road. At La Pocatière, they liked the farm but noted that students did not do much practical work or handle most tools: "C'est un défaut grave et qui neutralise presque l'utilité de cette école." Only about ten students were in attendance, some from other parts of the province and others from elsewhere. L'Assomption displayed similar defects, including just ten students. Neither school taught butter- or cheese-making. From L'Assomption, in its first decade, only fifty-five of its eighty-eight students proceeded into farming, and in its second, only forty of eighty. The situation in Richmond was worse: M.F. Lyster had succeeded Tanner as head, but the school was in poor shape. Its accounts were not available, its managers were evasive, and it had only fourteen students – but it did produce butter.

At Guelph, President Mills showed the commissioners around, and they approved of what they observed. Facilities were superb and up to date, and some eighty-two students were in attendance. Mills admitted that Ontario farmers, initially cool to the college, were now enthusiastic. Students who returned home altered farming practice.

Reflecting on their own agricultural schools, the commissioners recognized a number of shortcomings. Although Quebec farmers had moved heavily into stock-raising and dairying, the schools taught little about animals or veterinary medicine; there were no museums; modern equipment was lacking; education suffered because the farms had to produce a profit; and students often lacked solid elementary education to absorb the lessons, with many attending irregularly while others dropped out before completion. The fact that the schools at both La Pocatière and L'Assomption were divisions of *collèges classiques* tended to inspire disdain for farming. Neither school taught dairying or undertook experimentation. Agricultural students' flight from farming after they left the schools made the actual cost per pupil much higher in Quebec than in Ontario.

In the end, the commissioners' report urged Quebec to mimic Guelph – that is, form a single agricultural school and hire competent professors to offer a full three-year program of studies. Such a college would require a complete farm, a dairy school, and a veterinary school. In an appendix, J.-X. Perrault, following up on his 1864 report, made suggestions about university training: with the Montreal branch of Laval University operating a veterinary school of thirty-five students, Laval could easily add a professorship of agriculture to complete the program.

### ALTERNATIVE MODELS (1887–88)

The commissioners inspected only the colleges in Lansing and Guelph, but not land-grant universities nearby, such as Iowa State, Ohio State, Purdue (in Indiana), and Wisconsin. However, they were aware of the politics of state support for universities and what they provided to the public. Land-grant universities were to be "agricultural and mechanical colleges" – that is, focusing on practical science and technology, not on the traditional arts, sciences, and professions of older universities – but by the late 1880s, many of them had added more traditional subjects. American critics were decrying their downplaying of agriculture in seeming neglect of their explicit mandate. Both East Lansing and Guelph were free-standing schools that, despite teaching a range of subjects as part of a general education, concentrated on agriculture.

In Quebec, the situation was more subtle. The schools in La Pocatière and L'Assomption were appendages of *collèges classiques* whose faculty and students had little interest in agriculture, rendering their status even more perilous than any in a land-grant university. While St Francis was free standing, it was too small to make any impact. A central, state-supported agricultural college à la Guelph or Lansing might have been viable, but several major issues provoked little serious discussion; the most crucial was language of instruction: bilingual or with separate facilities or campuses for anglophones and francophones. Other questions included location and source of clientele, which latter seemed to flummox existing schools. In Ontario, reasonably well-off farming families sent their sons to Guelph for agricultural education. In Quebec, would prosperous anglophone farmers turn to provincial schools? They clearly did not do so when a private school existed. Would the bulk of poor, rural francophone farmers do the same? Again, the answer appeared to be a resounding "no." Well-off francophones sent their sons to *collèges classiques*, and their anglophone counterparts sent theirs to English-language academies and then to university.

The only alternative to existing schools or to a stand-alone college would be to encourage the universities to create faculties of agriculture. Quebec had, by the late 1880s, only three universities: Laval, at the head of the system of francophone *collèges classiques*, and the English-language McGill and much smaller Bishop's in Lennoxville. McGill hosted Duncan McEachran's small veterinary school. Certainly, McGill's dynamic principal, J.W. Dawson, had been very supportive of teaching agriculture. Laval was another story. It was very aware of being the only French-language university in North America, building on a long French and local tradition of *collèges classiques*. The provincial government had pressed the university to create an engineering school, but Laval had refused, as it probably would have a similar proposal for agriculture, just as it had Perrault's in the 1860s. McGill, which by the 1880s did teach engineering, might have stepped in; but to have an anglophone university teaching agriculture with no francophone equivalent would have been politically unsupportable.

## BARNARD AND HIS ALLIES (LATE 1870S–90S)
Politics played a central role in the debate over agricultural schools. In general, Quebec's Conservatives favoured a decentralized group of schools, while Liberals were more likely to support a Guelph-style central

school. Barnard, a decentralizer, wanted an experimental-demonstration farm as a means to educate farmers by either direct visits or publication of results. His Varennes farm had served that purpose from 1869 to 1888; but, with no government support and a large family, he found the finances daunting. Because the dairy school he helped to set up in St-Denis was far from many of the province's farmers, Barnard persuaded Joseph-Adolphe Chapleau (Conservative premier 1878–82) to fund a school and dairy-demonstration operation on his own farm in Varennes; however, when Joseph-Alfred Mousseau became Conservative premier (1882–84), he insisted that the dairy operation and staff move to a new agricultural school in Rougemont in 1883 under the noted local cattle breeder George Whitfield, a member of the Missisquoi Agricultural Society. Barnard and his family, with herd and equipment in tow, trekked to the Eastern Townships. Whitfield's direction was less than stellar, students left, and by November the school closed.

In the meantime, Barnard had become seriously ill. He then had to re-establish himself and his family in the Quebec area to be closer to the department. After he appealed to Premier Ross in 1884, the latter allowed him to return to his farm in Trois-Rivières to resume his experiments with dairying and farm construction. When his and Chapais's congress of the *cercles agricoles* prodded the government to support a demonstration farm, Ross agreed to fund it, but Honoré Mercier's Parti National government soon took office. Thus when in 1888 the department removed Barnard as director of agriculture and forced him back to Quebec, his dream of a demonstration farm died.

Matters drifted. In 1889, Commissioner Col. William Rhodes admitted that he was unhappy with the schools. He had closed Richmond (which would re-open later) and felt the francophone schools needed greater independence from their colleges and a "good Scotch farmer" to teach practical agriculture. The council asked Barnard to visit each school four times a year. In 1891, with Mercier as premier and commissioner (and Joly still president of the council), the same refrain continued: the schools were poor; the defunct one at Richmond needed replacement; and the province needed a central school like Guelph's. It was clear, however, that little would change. The council's school committee, on which Ouimet and Joly sat, argued that the schools did not unite practice with theory: by the end of their program, students had not learned how to operate a profitable farm, plough, raise cattle and horses, or use modern implements. When it looked as if the Mercier government might finally create a single college, de Boucherville and the Conservatives returned to power, with Beaubien as commissioner.

Barnard and his clerical allies had mused about religious orders running agricultural schools for men and women. With the hierarchy's assistance, he helped to organize Le Syndicat des cultivateurs, modelling it on an existing French organization, as a means to ameliorate the state of Quebec farmers. Its patrons were Archbishop Taschereau and A.R. Angers (lieutenant-governor 1887–92). Mgr Bégin in 1892 took over most of the ill Taschereau's clerial duties and also became president. The Syndicat did not survive long, as Beaubien would not assist it financially; he supported instead a Montreal rival that his brother co-founded.

In 1893, Barnard corresponded with French agronomist the frère Abel, assistant director of the Institut des frères de l'instruction chrétienne in Ploermel, Brittany, to see if that order would provide monks to operate a practical agricultural school in Quebec, roughly half-way between the two existing institutions. He approached Beaubien, suggesting that a proper agricultural school was now within reach.

Barnard corresponded also with Mgr Bégin in hopes of enlisting his aid in the project. He had finally given up on the schools at La Pocatière and L'Assomption. As he intimated to Beaubien, both left much to desire. At La Pocatière, the dairy herd underperformed and the school was behind the times, having had only two professors in a quarter-century (Schmouth and Lippens), neither of whom had practical experience. At L'Assomption, Professor Marsan was a student of Schmouth's, and the best one could say of him was that he tried hard. In fact, in all the years that Barnard had been editing agricultural papers, he had never been able to print anything useful from the two colleges.

Changes, however, were on the horizon. In the late 1880s, when Barnard had to give up his farm, he visited the north on an inspection and lecture trip. Discussions with the Ursulines in Roberval led to their establishing a domestic science school for girls in 1882; a decade later, the province would start subsidizing it. In 1893, Barnard visited a similar institution that the Grey Sisters had just opened at St-Benoît, Deux-Montagnes, which featured domestic science relating to agriculture. At the same time, he dropped in on the Trappist order's new Ecole d'agriculture d'Oka. The monastery opened in 1881 in Notre-Dame du Lac, and its head from 1887 on was Dom Marie-Antoine Oger (1852–1913). As agricultural instruction formed part of the monastery's mission, Oger and Beaubien had worked to organize the school in 1893, but it was a private institution when Barnard visited. Already its operation was impressive, and Barnard reported to the commissioner that the Ecole, with provincial funding, would do far more than the existing schools. The three instructors all came from France. From 1896 to 1903, the professor of agriculture was Gustave Boron; Marsan replaced him in 1904.

## University Connections

The chronic weaknesses of the agricultural schools would persist. In 1896–97, the four operating schools (Compton, La Pocatière, L'Assomption, and Oka) had a combined enrolment of 130,[43] and the Ontario Agricultural College, 237. The Quebec schools remained a political football, with the Conservatives supporting multiple schools and the Liberals a single, provincial school. When the Liberals came back into power in 1897 under Félix-Gabriel Marchand (1832–1900), he lobbied Ottawa to fund a single agricultural school for Quebec, which would have been a constitutional anomaly. When that gambit failed, Marchand closed L'Assomption in 1899, even though it had the most students.[44] Oka affiliated with Laval's Succursale de Montreal in 1908. When the Montreal branch became autonomous as the Université de Montréal in 1920, the Oka school became, in essence, the faculty of agriculture. At La Pocatière, operations continued as usual. After St Francis had closed its doors in 1889, there was no provincial agricultural school for anglophones until the school in Compton, which survived for ten years.

Certainly, in comparison with Ontario, where Guelph increased student numbers and diversified programs, Quebec's situation was only marginally viable. It had no anglophone school between 1889 and 1894, and then Compton's sketchy existence for a decade. Although J.W. Dawson's earlier attempt to establish agriculture as an academic subject at McGill was a failure, Duncan McEachran's Montreal Veterinary College had carried on with a few students. His college's lack of training in French was a sore point; in 1877, a grant from the Council of Agriculture allowed him to open a francophone section, with two of his former students, Orphir Bruneau and J.-A. Couture, as instructors. Another student was Victor-Théodule Daubigny (1836–1908), a recent French immigrant (1872) and notarial clerk who, after graduating in 1879, took over the French section. In 1885, he and Bruneau formed a rival Ecole de médécine vétérinaire française de Montréal. This school affiliated with Victoria University in Cobourg, but when the two partners split Daubigny organized the Ecole vétérinaire française de Montréal and affiliated it with the Montreal branch of Laval, whose school of medicine provided science courses.[45] A McGill affiliate operating a parallel veterinary school in French seemed incongruous. Once two competing francophone institutions were in operation, McEachran dropped his French section. In 1889, his Montreal Veterinary College joined McGill as the Faculty of Comparative Medicine and Veterinary Science, with him as dean. At the same time, McGill instituted the doctor of veterinary science (DVS) degree.

By hiring from the sciences, the McGill veterinary faculty had nine instructors and nearly fifty students by 1890; by comparison, Daubigny's school had nine instructors (some from the university) and thirty-five students; Bruneau's, which affiliated with the Montreal School of Medicine and Surgery, had fourteen students; and the Laval school in Quebec counted eight.[46] The Department of Agriculture moved to simplify matters; by 1892, only the Laval-branch school operated for francophones in Montreal, and enrolment in Quebec had dropped to three. The 1890s were no kinder to McGill. With enrolments falling and no state funding, it pulled the plug on its veterinary faculty in 1903. Thus, by 1904, no English-language agricultural or veterinary training was available in the province.

### Macdonald College (1907)

The tobacco manufacturer Sir William Macdonald had already funded domestic science at Guelph and, a long-time friend of J.W. Dawson's, had been McGill's prodigious benefactor. With great interest in rural development and under the influence of his friend J.W. Robertson, he created the Macdonald Rural Schools Fund about 1902 to foster practical training in school gardens and workshops in Canada.[47] With specialized educational institutions for Quebec's rural anglophones disappearing, he turned to the idea of a college offering agriculture, domestic science, and teacher training. Dawson's successor at McGill, Sir William Peterson (1856–1921), persuaded him to locate the college in Ste-Anne-de-Bellevue at the western end of Montreal island and place it under McGill's control. The philanthropist built, equipped, and endowed Macdonald College, which opened in 1907. With Robertson as its first principal, the college counted thirty-seven staff members, and its enrolment immediately came close to Guelph's. The school quickly became one of the finest in Canada. The emergence of Macdonald College placed Quebec's small francophone institutions in stark contrast. The new facility undertook agricultural research from the beginning. It had taken the Guelph college some time to launch experimental work, as it had the American land-grant schools, but by the late 1880s teaching united with research became the Canadian and US norm for agricultural schools. This had not happened in the small Quebec agricultural schools.

Pressure built up in the nationalist press for the government to do more for agriculture, and in the end Lomer Gouin (Liberal premier 1905–20), who had supported Laval's move into forestry and surveying, enabled the university to absorb the Ste-Anne school at La Pocatière as its Ecole d'agriculture, essentially a faculty, in 1912. But, as Hamelin notes, "Les édifices sont neufs, mais les programmes, les laboratoires, les stages sont à organiser. Quel défi! L'Ecole d'agriculture n'a ni laboratoire ni matériel pédagogique adéquats; la bibliothèque est chichement dotée; le corps professoral est incompétent et les étudiants sont fort mal préparés."[48] The time for amateurs was over, and the university subsequently brought in Europeans to operate the school.

## AGRICULTURAL EDUCATION IN THE SCHOOLS

### Attempts in Schools and Normal Schools

The Department of Agriculture and Public Works was not the only player in Quebec agriculture. As a pre-Confederation superintendent of public instruction, Pierre-Joseph-Olivier Chauveau, like his predecessor Meilleur, had long hoped – and, like his counterpart, Egerton Ryerson in Toronto, failed – to insert agricultural instruction into the provincial schools. During 1867–68, Quebec retained Canada East's education office, and (Conservative) Premier Chauveau retained the education portfolio as minister. During 1867, when he toured Europe, Dublin impressed him as much as it had Ryerson decades earlier[49] – especially the city's Central Normal School, which required trainees to learn the elements of agriculture. Quebec's three normal schools – Jacques-Cartier and McGill in Montreal and Laval in Quebec – had taught little of the subject and anyway graduated only a minority of the province's teachers. Chauveau proposed to follow the Irish lead and attach model farms to the three normal schools but ran into opposition in Cabinet, particularly from Commissioner Archambeault, and dropped the idea.[50] In 1869, Chauveau sent the abbé J.-O. Godin, professor of agriculture at the failed school at Ste-Thérèse, to Europe, especially to Ireland, to gather information.

Although the abbé Hospice Verreau (1828–1901) was willing to increase agricultural instruction at his Ecole normale Jacques-Cartier, McGill principal J.W. Dawson noted that neither parents nor school commissioners supported the subject. Furthermore, even though teachers already had so much to handle, they would have to teach agriculture during vacation without pay. A further complication: most of the students at McGill Normal School were women. The best Chauveau could manage was to have the Council of Public Instruction strike a subcommittee on agriculture; council chair Mgr Jean Langevin, bishop of Rimouski, had written an agricultural catechism. When Gédéon Ouimet became Conservative premier and minister of public instruction in 1873, he authorized the use of Hubert La Rue's *Petit manuel d'agriculture à l'usage des écoles* (2nd ed., 1872) in elementary schools, expecting that teachers would introduce the subject.

For teachers open to the idea, the *Journal de l'Instruction publique*, which Chauveau edited until 1868, inserted notes on agricultural techniques and events. After Premier de Bourcherville closed the Department of Public Instruction in 1875, the *Journal* became simply an official bulletin and dropped the wide range of scientific and practical information. The economic arguments in favour of teaching agriculture were usually paramount in the press and in political discussions, but Chauveau added a moralistic argument. In a prize ceremony in 1868, he intoned:

Que de nombreux élèves accourent donc vers ces écoles fécondes de Ste. Anne Lapocatière et de l'Assomption où ils acquerront une science qui vaudra mieux qu'un patrimoine, la science de conserver, d'améliorer et de féconder le sein épuisé de la patrie. Ces institutions placées comme elles le sont sous la direction d'ecclésiastiques nous donnent lieu d'espérer que les réformes qu'elles sont appelées à opérer dans les campagnes s'étendront aussi bien aux mœurs, qu'aux intérêts purement matériels. Or les mœurs de nos cultivateurs sont généralement la principale cause de leur décadence et de leur ruine.[51]

For all the discussion on introducing agriculture into the elementary school curriculum, one major roadblock remained. As in Ontario, an increasing number of lay teachers in the province were female, many of whom would have neither received agricultural instruction nor worked on a farm or in a garden. Furthermore, had they taught agriculture, would farm boys have respected their authority on such matters? Or, more important, would their fathers have accepted such "correct" scientific knowledge without demur? It seems even more unlikely in Quebec than in Ontario.

A number of textbooks appeared over the next decades, beginning with the abbé Nazaire-A. Leclerc's ninety-page *Catechisme d'agriculture ou la science agricole mis à portée des enfants* (1868). The catechism format, with religious overtones, covered the basic ideas but ignored the emerging dairy sector. Ten years later, A.C.P.R. Landry, a graduate of Ste-Anne at La Pocatière, intended his *Traité populaire d'agriculture théorique et pratique* for both student and public use. The Council of Agriculture approved the book, which appeared in a new edition in 1886. Landry wrote at a time of marked change: "Notre agriculture, de l'aveu général, est dans une époque de transition. Ce grand essor que prend notre industrie naissante influera, nous le croyons, sur notre système de culture; la création d'industries nouvelles, intimément liées à la production agricole, peut changer du jour au lendemain les conditions de [cette] dernière. Attendons."[52]

In 1890, J.-C. Langelier's *Traité d'agriculture* in catechism form noted that a number of French-language agriculture manuals were available, but mostly from France. He claimed to have written his text from scratch. Landry, in contrast, had based his 1878 book on Girardin and Du Breuil's popular *Traité élémentaire d'agriculture* (1875) but left out important issues for Quebec, such as raising livestock. William Evans's *Treatise on the Theory and Practice of Agriculture* (1835) was still available in English, but long out of date. More modern was J.W. Dawson's *First Lessons in Scientific Agriculture for Schools and Private Instruction* (1864).

Norbert Thibault published a series of articles in *Le courrier du Canada* in December 1870 under the pseudonym "Agricola" and grouped them in *De l'agriculture et du rôle des instituteurs dans l'enseignement agricole* (1871) – a paean to the nobility of rural life and the pitfalls awaiting those who followed other paths. For him, the school curriculum was largely irrelevant to daily life: what students needed was agricultural instruction. He admitted that local and provincial exhibitions and agricultural journalism were informative but wanted universal teaching of agriculture. He agreed with La Rue that students in colleges and seminaries should know some agricultural chemistry and physics.

*A Professor of Agriculture*

Normal schools had, since 1862, made agriculture compulsory, but only at the time of Thibault's work (about 1870) had the Ecole normale Jacques-Cartier appointed a professor: abbé J.-O. Godin. While the three schools' principals favoured annexing model farms, Thibault echoed La Rue's views that working on a farm was a waste of time for teacher trainees. Once they arrived in elementary schools, they could cultivate a school garden with the children. What to read? Several manuals, some French, some Canadian, were available, but La Rue's recent *Petit manuel d'agriculture à l'usage des écoles* (2nd ed., 1872) was excellent, despite criticism by the *Gazette des campagnes* and *Semaine agricole.*

Frédéric Ossaye had taught agriculture part time at Jacques-Cartier in the 1860s. But activity increased after abbé Godin returned in 1869 from the schools at Grignon and Beauvais in France, Gembloux in Belgium, and Glasnevin, near Dublin. Godin taught agriculture at the normal school until 1883. By 1870, McGill Principal J.W. Dawson, who directed also the McGill Normal School, called for a professor of agriculture at all three normal schools, who might also inspect (non-existent) rural agricultural classes. The abbé Verreau spoke about attaching a farm to Jacques-Cartier, not just as an experimental plot but as a self-financing operation, like those at La Pocatière and Ste-Thérèse.[53]

## COMPARE AND CONTRAST

Agricultural education in Quebec in the later nineteenth century looked a bit like that of Ontario, largely because of the administrative heritage from the United Province. Agricultural societies and their exhibitions still carried on informal education, with minimal government intervention. Provincial exhibitions were of less importance than in Ontario. The rising specialist societies, which educated their members directly and through publications, were similar to those of Ontario and neighbouring US states. Ontario's farmers' institutes democratized local agricultural education, as did Quebec's *cercles agricoles.* In neither province was the educational bureaucracy, despite much talk, able to introduce agriculture into elementary schools. Where the differences appear had much to do with linguistic and confessional divisions in Quebec. The small and relatively ineffective agricultural schools were appendages of religious colleges; their staffs were small and had sketchy training; and their government funding was derisively small. Ontario, following the American states' leads of creating a single school with more resources, saw much better results, although it took many years. The dominant Roman Catholic Church played an increasing role in agricultural education in Quebec, something that could not happen in Ontario. Finally, Quebec's political landscape was less stable between 1867 and 1900, with eleven premiers (most of them Conservative), compared with Ontario's five (four of them Liberal, with Oliver Mowat in charge for twenty-four years).

# 7

# Technical Education in Ontario

With the segregation of powers between the federal and provincial governments in 1867, education became strictly a provincial responsibility. The two pre-Confederation offices of education – for Canada West and Canada East – had been, for all intents and purposes, independent of one another and effortlessly became provincial bureaucracies in Ontario and Quebec, respectively. In Toronto, Rev. Egerton Ryerson continued as superintendent. Despite his interest in scientific, technical, and artistic education, Ontario's education department did not initially expand into any of these areas and would not have any direct hand in technical instruction until 1880. Before 1867, the mechanics' institutes reported to the Department of Agriculture; under 32 Vict., cap. 32, they now reported to the commissioner of agriculture and public works, as if the legislature was not treating technical instruction as education in the usual sense and regarded industry and those who worked in it as low priorities. It was not until 1882 that the assembly set up a Bureau of Industry to gather statistics on industrial activity.

Commissioner of Agriculture and Public Works John Carling's modified agricultural bill, which received royal assent on 4 March 1868, placed industrial arts societies and institutions in the new Agriculture and Arts Association of Ontario (AAAO). The demise of the Board of Arts and Manufactures for Upper Canada early in 1868 created a gap in representation of the mechanics' institutes, which had only a small voice on the council of the new Agriculture and Arts Association of Ontario. George Buckland remained as secretary of the Bureau of Agriculture; there is no evidence that he was ill-disposed towards the institutes, but his life-long interest was in agriculture. Fortunately, the institutes had a friend at head office in William Edwards, erstwhile secretary of the Board of Arts and Manufactures for Upper Canada. Beginning in the early 1870s, the province's rapid industrialization raised the stakes for technical education, but, as we see below, there was little progress towards a concrete resolution.

In this chapter, we examine in turn workers, industry, and technical education in Ontario; the post-1867 resuscitation of the mechanics' institutes; class instruction in the institutes in the 1870s (under the Department of Agriculture) and the 1880s (under Education and Dr Samuel May); the life and times of small institutes, with Galt, Preston, and Caledon as examples; the institutes' winding down and conversion to public libraries; the working-class dream – the School of Practical Science – and its absorption into the University of Toronto; and the complex tale of the introduction of art education (Ryerson's vision): the emergence of the Ontario Society of Artists, the Ontario School of Art in Toronto, and art schools in other cities.

## WORKERS, INDUSTRY, AND TECHNICAL EDUCATION IN ONTARIO

### Industry and Labour

Canada West in the 1840s, at the time of the first, crude industrial census, was shifting from pioneer industries such as brewing, distilling, milling, and potash production to somewhat more complex technologies. The first Dominion census in 1871 took a much more detailed look at industry, revealing an Ontario starting to industrialize along the lines of its American neighbours.[1] Agriculture and forestry remained the core of primary industry right into the 1890s, while secondary industry grew to occupy approximately 20 per cent of the workforce, with a five-fold increase in numbers after 1851.[2] Agriculture provided more than one-third of Ontario's gross domestic product at Confederation but only one-quarter by 1900. Secondary and service industries made up much of the difference, with mining beginning to make a contribution.

Expansion of the railway network, which began in the late 1850s, was transforming the industrial landscape in the 1860s and 1870s.[3] Steel production, rolling mills, and manufacture and maintenance of railway locomotives and cars required larger facilities and workforces. The Great Western Railway operated its shops in Hamilton; the Grand Trunk had its car and locomotive shop in Brantford; the Northern centred on Toronto, where also the St Lawrence had its foundry, machine, and car

Table 7.1  Distribution of workers in industry, Ontario (1871)

|  | Rural (%) | Urban (%) | Hamilton (%) | Toronto (%) |
|---|---|---|---|---|
| NON-POWERED INDUSTRY (WORKERS) | | | | |
| Artisans (1–5) | 45.4 | 17.8 | 7.5 | 6.1 |
| Sweatshops (6–25) | 5.8 | 20.2 | 18.7 | 16.2 |
| Manufactories (26–50) | 0.3 | 4.8 | 6 | 6.6 |
| Manufactories (>51) | 0.5 | 5.5 | 7.9 | 15.3 |
| Totals | 52 | 48.3 | 40.1 | 44.2 |
| POWERED INDUSTRY (WORKERS) | | | | |
| Small (1–5) | 15.8 | 3.2 | 0.5 | 0.5 |
| Medium (6–25) | 19.6 | 13 | 6 | 5.4 |
| Factories (26–50) | 5.4 | 8.3 | 6.6 | 7.2 |
| Factories (>50) | 7.2 | 27.2 | 46.8 | 42.7 |
| Totals | 48 | 51.7 | 59.9 | 55.8 |

Source: Adapted from Bloomfield and Bloomfield, The Ontario Urban System, Table 11.

shop, which employed more than three thousand hands in 1871.[4] Many of these men would have been skilled labourers and mechanics, but their training would have occurred elsewhere or on the job.

Outside the province's central region (the Hamilton and Toronto areas), secondary industry typically related to the local primary industry. As Gilmour has shown, certain industries clustered in particular areas. Counties relying most on secondary industry were Wentworth and Simcoe, followed by York, Northumberland, Waterloo, and Lincoln. Production of agricultural implements concentrated in York, Ontario, Oxford, Perth, and Lincoln counties in 1871, with Brant joining in by 1891. Very skilled trades such as engraving and lithography were concentrated mostly in Hamilton and Toronto. Most notable during the last third of the century was the growth of consumer products. As Ontario farmers moved to dairying, production of cheese and butter grew, much of it in smaller centres. In the cities, the manufacture of baked goods, confections, and tobacco products increased, and services such as dry cleaners appeared. Across the province, skilled or semi-skilled labourers worked in shops producing carriages, furniture, and machinery. As the Bloomfields have shown, industry was an urban phenomenon by 1871: Ontario's 110 cities, towns, and villages accounted for only 24 per cent of the population but 32 per cent of industry, 45 per cent of steam power, 59 per cent of industrial labour, 64 per cent of the gross value of production, and 67 per cent of value-adding manufactures.[5] Table 7.1, adapted from Bloomfield and Bloomfield, The Ontario Urban System, provides a sense of the distribution of industrial labour in 1871.

Artisanal labour was clearly more likely in small centres. Very large manufacturing establishments, such as the Massey-Harris firm, would come later. Hamilton and Toronto performed much of the larger-scale manufacturing, such as iron and steel and general metal fabrication. While men made up three-quarters of the industrial labour force, women provided 15 per cent and children 9 per cent. Women were most numerous in clothing production. Smaller towns had a mix of trades. In Waterloo County, for example, one could find bakers, blacksmiths, carpenters, carriage and wagon makers, coopers, knitters, milliners, saddlers, shoemakers, tailors, tinsmiths, and weavers.[6] Obviously, the nature of labour was not static, and working people had to adapt constantly.[7]

*Technical Education?*

Perhaps not surprising, Ontario's nascent labour movement paid little attention to technical education, in the light of the much larger, immediate issues facing it. While there are few hints of its having any interest in mechanics' institutes or seeking specialized schools, Ontario's burgeoning secondary industry certainly did require skilled workers. English technological impresario Henry Cole's vision of the worker with scientific and artistic training improving industrial design had little scope in Ontario, where only manufactures such as cabinet- or carriage-making, furniture, and machines involved much design work. Ontario still imported design-heavy luxury items. Thus *what* skills to teach the working class was a serious question, as was the venue of such training.

The educational system was one possible venue. With industrialization and the accompanying greater complexity of Ontario society, the older system of common school plus grammar school required a new approach to educating the burgeoning population.[8] The expansion of secondary education in the 1880s and 1890s marks, for Ontario, a shift away from the British model to a more, but not quite, American model of public education beyond elementary training. Most working men and women in the United Kingdom, having little access to primary education before the 1860s, could not obtain a secondary education, but by the 1880s the Science and Art Department's science schools provided something not too different. Ontario's mechanics' institutes in theory offered similar education but were not even vaguely comparable to British science schools.

The shift from the old grammar school to the high school was already under way during Ryerson's last years in office in the early 1870s. Science increasingly entered the curriculum, which focused on university matriculation, as Ontario high schools had not yet moved to American-style mass education. Did working-class children avail themselves of high schools? J.A. Ketchum's study of four high schools shows that 12 per cent of students' fathers were semi-skilled workers or labourers, while 14 per cent were skilled workers. As Gidney and Millar argue: "In all, a quarter of those sending children to high school came from the lower half of the socio-economic order, thus lending credence to claims that the school system offered Ontarians equality of educational opportunity. And there undoubtedly was real upward mobility by means of the school system. Skilled and unskilled workingmen may have been substantially under represented in the extent to which they used the high schools, but they were not a token minority."[9]

This suggests that many working-class children had only marginal educations. While the province had made elementary education compulsory in 1871, twenty years after Massachusetts, many working-class youths attended irregularly and left school early to obtain work.[10] Where we do find working-class support for secondary education, as in the case of Hamilton's Central School, it may have been, according to Katz, because technology had eroded traditional skills; sons of working men could not follow their fathers into their trades and did not possess sufficient capital to establish their own businesses.[11] In mid-century Britain, science education was practically synonymous with technical education, but science was clearly an academic subject in the Ontario high school. While some commercial education took place, there was no curricular extension into trades-related skills such as occurred in many American high schools. Even with the confusion over what might constitute technical education for post-elementary schools, it is clear that neither the department nor the public at large was willing to expand secondary education to embrace the practical educational needs of the working class.

Gidney and Millar summarize the role of the Ontario high school: "Unlike the American high school, already beginning to move towards mass secondary education, the Ontario high school would remain the preserve of a minority of adolescents for decades to come. Its importance, in other words, did not lie in the sheer numbers it educated. Rather it lay in its role as gatekeeper for the occupational and social order. In this respect the Ontario high school operated more like a British or European than an American secondary school. Rather like the modern undergraduate arts program, the high school of the late nineteenth and early twentieth centuries controlled the key access points to nearly all the professions and prestigious white collar occupations."[12]

Technical education, then, was not available in the province's public schools. Immigrant artisans and mechanics might have had some before coming to Canada, but native-born people, having no schools and no systematic apprenticeship system, had to rely on on-the-job training. The only educational alternative for them was the mechanics' institute.

## RESUSCITATION OF THE MECHANICS' INSTITUTES (1868–)

The withdrawal of public grants to mechanics' institutes after 1858 dealt an almost fatal blow,[13] particularly because maintaining private institutions in Canada was difficult at the best of times. Providing a full array of educational functions – classes, lectures, library, and reading room – was an expensive proposition, one that most working-class members could not afford individually or corporately. Commissioner of Agriculture and Public Works John Carling understood this but stated: "These institutions, some fifty of which exist in the Province, are calculated to render important services to society; occupying, as they do, the position of 'People's Colleges,' or schools for instruction of youths and adult artizans and the industrial classes generally."[14] To sound out the possibility of wider interest, Carling distributed a circular to the existing institutes in April 1868. The Ontario legislature, now believing in the "intimate connection and mutual interests existing between the agriculturist and the mechanic," agreed to provide an annual grant of up to $200 to provide classes or a library to any institute matching these funds.

There was now a subtle shift: "A large proportion of these institutions are located in Rural Districts, where both the books and the classes may be made available for the agriculturist as well as the artizan, and should, therefore, have the countenance and support of all classes of the community." In other words, the mechanics' institutes would no longer be purely for the mechanic or artisan but also for farmers; indeed, the institutes in the villages of Ayr and Streetsville called themselves Mechanics' and Farmer's Institutes, although most retained the traditional name. Carling noted that people of the "industrial classes" had to leave school early to work but still required a wider range of knowledge. He believed that the experience of the Toronto institute had shown that the classroom approach was successful. While such an assertion was debatable, Carling seems to have missed the fact that institutes in rural districts had very few members of the industrial classes to serve. Table B3 in Appendix B indicates the long-lasting impact of the post-1868 expansion of institutes in the province – it appears that there is nothing like a government grant to stimulate local activity: institutes and membership mushroomed.

### Adapting to New Provincial Grants

Existing mechanics' institutes now had to reorganize themselves to fit into the new administrative structure. Accordingly, the Association of Mechanics' Institutes of Ontario held its first general meeting in Hamilton on 23 September 1868. The pre-Confederation leaders of the Board of Arts and Manufactures were back at the helm, with Dr John Beatty from Cobourg as president and William Edwards as secretary-treasurer. One of the key organizers was Galt newspaper editor and manufacturer James Young (1835–1913), also a new Liberal MP, who would later serve as president 1870–81. These men recognized what they had to do to bind together the disparate institutes, provide a list of books for libraries, and obtain wholesale prices for these volumes. The association would also need to foster the introduction of classes and a lecture series to increase attendance and membership. Allotment of the first year's grants made clear the weakness of the movement. Only three institutes (in Dundas, Peterborough, and Toronto) qualified for the full $200, while the ten others (Bowmanville, Chatham, Galt, Guelph, Hamilton, Oshawa, Paris, Strathroy, Streetsville, and Whitby) each obtained between $50 and $180. Even with matching funds, this was very little money to build up a creditable library or operate night classes. More encouraging were the applications for funding from nine new institutes in 1869. Total grant monies naturally grew with increases in grants and numbers of members. The grants were not a great drain on the provincial treasury: although the totals grew from $1,535 in 1869 to $22,885 in 1879 under the agriculture department, the latter amount was only about one-third of total grants to agricultural societies.

Apart from a slight dip in the late 1870s, the institutes' growth was steady if unspectacular. Toronto was by far the largest, with about 1,000 members throughout the decade. Hamilton doubled from 500 to 1,000, and London fluctuated between the high 300s and 500. For the rest, the average membership in 1879 was 116, ranging from more than 200 in larger centres (Belleville, Galt, Guelph, Kingston, Peterborough, St Catharines, Seaforth, and Woodstock) down to dozens in villages (Waterdown with twenty-six and Blyth with thirty-seven).

*Classroom Instruction*

Classroom instruction continued a sore spot. In his 1870–71 report for the Bureau of Agriculture, Buckland admitted: "It is to be regretted, however, that in so many of these institutions, class instruction in such subjects as are necessary to be understood by artisans of all classes has not, as yet, been introduced; and even where it has, the results in several instances have not been encouraging."[15] The document made it evident that a $200 annual grant was insufficient, and in 1870 an amendment to the Agriculture and Arts Act raised it to $400. While this certainly led to more institutes and libraries, Buckland wanted the institutes not to lose sight of what he considered their primary function:

> The general experience has hitherto been that to make these institutions popular and extensively useful, amusement must be combined with instruction; and to the absence of the former element in the earlier history of these organizations in England their comparative failure was attributed. The introduction of social gatherings, music, recreation, readings, &c., speedily effect a marked revival, and it is satisfactory to find in several of the Reports transmitted to the Department that the adoption of rational recreations has been attended by similar results in this Province. While, however, the introduction of recreations of a social and refining character in these institutions is desirable and useful, it should never be lost sight of in all attempts at improvement that their chief function consists in teaching in a popular manner the principles of those sciences, with their various applications, which appertain to the different industries of life.[16]

Buckland's 1874 report reiterated his hope that the institutes should do what they must for working-class men and not degenerate into reading rooms of "sensational literature." The Association of Mechanics' Institutes, in its report for the same year, was more optimistic: "Your committee are pleased to learn that in some of the Institutes the classes are open to both sexes, and it is to be hoped that hereafter the ladies will avail themselves more largely of this advantageous means of instruction and improvement."[17] This was not entirely novel: the Toronto institute had offered a women-only class in making wax flowers. Apparently instruction focusing on working-class men was not sustainable. To encourage local classes further, the association offered $10, $6, and $4 prizes to any institute operating a class on twenty-five separate nights for at least twelve working-class students – no one who was a student at a university or collegiate institute, a professional, a certified teacher, or a graduate. The subjects were a mixture of low-level technical instruction and basic education:

- arithmetic, geometry, and mensuration
- chemistry
- English grammar and composition
- freehand drawing
- geometry and decorative drawing
- penmanship and bookkeeping
- principles of practical mechanics

### Lectures

In the 1830s and 1840s, before class instruction became important, mechanics' institutes reached out largely through one-off lectures or courses of lectures, sometimes on scientific or technical topics. This had the advantage of uniting disparate social groups for a common intellectual cause. By the 1870s, however, lectures had faded in most institutes. Larger cities and towns, especially Toronto, had learned clergymen, professionals, professors, and teachers to draw on. Smaller centres would have far fewer resources, although one might expect a greater thirst for knowledge in outlying areas of the province.

In 1875–76, the fifty-five institutes reporting offered their members a total of eighty-six lectures. The Garden Island Mechanics' Institute, with seventeen, was perhaps the only truly working-class group in the province: although it was very close to Kingston, most of its members lived on the island and worked for the Calvin family's lumber, shipbuilding, and shipping operations. At large institutes as well, lectures had receded, with Toronto and London offering six apiece that year, and Hamilton only two. For most groups, one or two was the norm, and thirty hosted none at all. However, by the mid-1870s the reports speak increasingly of literary readings and musical evenings. Agricultural Commissioner Samuel Casey Wood recognized this in 1877: libraries were the real attraction of the growing number of institutes, while class instruction was difficult in smaller centres and lectures were in decline.

### Libraries

Libraries became the focus of almost all institutes by the late 1860s, but the absence of provincial funding had stunted the growth of libraries and reading rooms at the few surviving institutes. For 1867, twenty institutes reported total holdings of 25,000 volumes: Toronto's library, dating from the 1830s, was the largest, with 7,400, and most of the others had 1,000–1,200.

Although these collections formed the historic core of many Ontario municipal libraries of the twentieth century, other library facilities were available to Ontarians. Superintendent Egerton Ryerson had for many years supported public libraries connected with the schools and supplied material from the provincial Book Depository. Adam Crooks (1827–1885), a Liberal MLA who succeeded Ryerson in 1876, becoming the province's first minister of education, reported 1,450 free public libraries in Ontario containing 281,586 volumes, 2,532 Sunday school libraries with 387,757, and 159 other libraries with 142,954, for a total of 4,141 libraries with 812,297 books.[18]

The reintroduction of provincial grants, and their later increase, spurred growth of the institutes' libraries. By 1876, the reporting institutes had an aggregate of 80,000 volumes. New institutes with generous members and patrons could obtain a $400 matching grant – and provide more themselves if means allowed – to build up their collections. The association helped them obtain discounts for technical books – rarely more than a quarter of the holdings. New branches typically possessed 400–500 volumes; at least fifteen institutes had 2,000 or more, including Hamilton with 5,300 and Toronto with nearly 8,100. Unfortunately, the Hamilton and Gore Institute, the second largest, soon ran into financial difficulties. With neither the voters nor city council willing to rescue it, mortgagors foreclosed on it and auctioned off the library in 1882.

## CLASS INSTRUCTION IN THE INSTITUTES

### Under the Department of Agriculture (1870s)

#### EVENING CLASSES

Whatever other "rational" entertainments the institutes offered, and libraries and reading rooms were probably the most attractive of these, the provincial Department of Agriculture increasingly focused upon class instruction. The commissioners, the Agricultural and Arts Association of Ontario, Buckland, and the Association of Mechanics' Institutes of Ontario all encouraged class instruction in the institutes, which at least some of them were offering. A school inspector, reporting on a visit to the Thorold Mechanics' Institute in 1873, noted: "It may not perhaps be necessary to say more than that numbers of young men who were formerly found filling billiard rooms, are now seen frequenting the mechanics' institute; for when it is attended with results so noticeable we may, I think, feel sure that it exerts a wholesome influence throughout society."[19] However, in the equally industrial town of Berlin (later Kitchener), the school inspector, Mr Pearce, reported that "mechanics do not avail themselves of the advantages of this institution as they ought."[20] In 1871, Carling's successor as commissioner of agriculture, Archibald McKellar, worried that evening classes still needed development, although he wanted them to concentrate not on elementary education – the public schools' realm – but on mechanical and industrial training. Institutes spent too much of their efforts on literary and musical evenings and ought to revert to systematic courses of lectures.[21]

At the same time, the Association of Mechanics' Institutes of Ontario resurrected the course syllabus and examination scheme that had failed in the 1860s. The new syllabus,[22] which it passed on 25 September 1872, laid out five diploma classes:

- arithmetic, geometry, and mensuration
- chemistry and experimental philosophy (i.e., physics)
- English grammar and composition
- geometrical and decorative drawing and modelling
- practical mechanics

Institutes faced several challenges to providing evening courses. First, if classes were to be free, institutes would have to pay for the instructor, space, heat, lighting, and disposable materials, but they faced small annual grants and competing demands for books and periodicals and so on. Second, finding qualified teachers was always a problem, especially for drawing, although local clergymen, physicians, or teachers could often teach general subjects. Third, the teaching of art or mechanics required apparatuses or models, and in 1876 the association asked Secretary-Treasurer William Edwards to write to South Kensington to request examples.[23]

Directors of the institutes, though often sympathetic, worked on building up libraries and reading rooms, for these were what their members desired. At the time of Confederation, the annual subscription cost for most Ontario institutes was $1 or $2 per annum. For Toronto, with more than 1,100 members, local fees generated a considerable amount; but marginal institutes such as Cobourg (thirty members), L'Orignal

Table 7.2 Mechanics' institutes offering classes, Ontario (1869–70)

| | Dundas | Hamilton | Peterborough | Richmond Hill | Toronto | Woodstock |
|---|---|---|---|---|---|---|
| Drawing (mechanical) | 10 | | | | 37 | |
| Drawing (ornamental) | | | | | 37 | |
| Bookkeeping | | | 12 | | 107 | 30 |
| Arithmetic/mathematics | 15 | | | | 44 | 21 |
| Grammar/composition | 15 | | 12 | | 38 | 12 |
| Phonography | | 80 | | | | |
| Mutual instruction | | | | 20 | 24 | |
| French | | | | | 25 | |
| Chemistry | | | | | 12 | |
| Elocution | | | | | 25 | |
| Total | 40 | 80 | 24 | 20 | 349 | 63 |

Source: Province of Ontario, Sessional Papers (1870–71).

(twenty-eight), and Waterdown (twenty) had few books and no class instruction. In the late 1860s, Toronto, for example, charged $2 a course for members and $3 for non-members. In 1870, twenty-four institutes received provincial grants, and at least eight others were operating without grants; of these thirty-two institutes, only six offered classes in the 1869–70 session (see Table 7.2 for subjects and enrolments). Some of the subjects came from the syllabus: arithmetic and mathematics, chemistry, grammar and composition, mechanical and architectural drawing, ornamental drawing, and penmanship and bookkeeping. Others were of local value: elocution, French, mutual instruction, and phonography. The Paris institute had attempted to form classes but failed; this would occur in many of the institutes.

By 1870, the Ontario institutes together had more than 4,000 members, but enrolments in the table amount to only 576. Statistics suggest that quite a few people enrolled in more than one course, significantly reducing the actual number of students. Toronto's numbers were not particularly large for the size of the city, while the rest of the province accounted for little more than 200. Of course, the point of holding classes, following the lead of the South Kensington system, was to enhance the knowledge and skills of working men. The technical courses – chemistry, drawing, and mathematics – enrolled 176, or 31 per cent of the total. Most institutes offering classes must have recognized these as their raison d'être. Eventually, the departmental bureaucracy would begin to understand this.

These results were not a rousing start. The association increased matching aid, to a maximum of $400, hoping that institutes would do more. Buckland argued:

It should not, however, be lost sight of that among the objects sought to be promoted by the Mechanics' Institutes, class instruction specially adapted to the wants and circumstances of working men, occupies a prominent position. As these institutions increase in age and resources, it is hoped that but few will be found without the teaching functions being largely developed. It is true that as our public system of education improves and ramifies throughout the country, the necessity of evening classes for teaching adults the rudimental branches of learning will diminish. But it is the characteristic work of Mechanics' Institutes to teach the application of knowledge acquired in ordinary schools to the practical purposes of life, including such technical subjects as specially relate to the every day pursuits of the various classes of the working population.[24]

Larger grants certainly did stimulate the formation of more institutes across the province, although mostly in the western districts. By the time of the department's 1875–76 report – on the eve of Ontario's participation in the Centennial Exhibition in Philadelphia – classroom instruction in the institutes had expanded. While fifty-seven institutes sent in reports, at least another ten did not. For those reporting, aggregate membership had risen to 8,439. Of the nearly seventy institutes, only twenty-five (fifteen of them west of Toronto) had class instruction The subjects for that year's courses appear in Table 7.3, with the technical subjects first.

While memberships had only doubled, the 1,649 enrolments were nearly triple the total from 1870, although many were probably duplicates, reducing the total number of students closer to 1,200. Of the total enrolments, 753 were in technical subjects, which represented less than half of all subjects taught. Only Barrie, Clinton, Galt, Guelph, Hamilton, London, Peterborough, Sarnia, Seaforth, Stratford, and Whitby had more than half their enrolments in technical subjects. Toronto, always the leader in class instruction, had risen little from 1867–68, when it had 202 enrollees, with the proportion in technical subjects unchanged. Surprisingly, the long-established Hamilton and Gore Institute, second largest in the province with nearly 900 members, had fewer enrolments than did tiny Ayr.

Table 7.3 Subjects taught in mechanics' institutes, Ontario (1875–76)

| Subject | Enrolment |
|---|---|
| Architectural/mechanical drawing | 200 |
| Algebra | 8 |
| Arithmetic/mathematics | 402 |
| Geometry | 6 |
| Ornamental drawing | 115 |
| Telegraphy | 14 |
| Photography | 8 |
| Bookkeeping/penmanship | 442 |
| Elocution | 71 |
| German | 18 |
| Grammar/composition | 305 |
| Mutual instruction | 30 |
| Music | 10 |
| Phonography | 16 |
| Wax flowers | 4 |
| Total | 1,649 |

Source: Province of Ontario, Sessional Papers (1877).

## Under the Department of Education and S.P. May (1880s)

With the continuing emphasis on technical classes, the Bureau of Agriculture's oversight of the mechanics' institutes must have seemed increasingly anomalous. Accordingly, in 1880 a new education act (43 Vict., cap. 5) passed direction of the institutes to the Department of Education, with Dr Samuel Passmore May (1828–1908) as supervisor; he also directed the Educational Museum and library. May, born in Truro, Cornwall, immigrated to Canada in 1853 and, after working for the Literary and Historical Society of Quebec, moved to Canada West. Taking a medical degree from Victoria University in 1863 – the medical school was in Toronto – he taught and curated for the university. In the 1870s, he had joined Superintendent Ryerson's staff.[25]

The Education Act of 1880 empowered the department to make rules for evening classes, handle the grants to institutes, and inspect and audit them. To receive grants, institutes would have to match at least half the grant from their own resources and maintain a library, reading room, and/or evening classes. Adam Crooks, in his ministerial report, opined that municipalities should begin to help fund institutes. Like Carling, he believed that farmers' sons should also have access: "By extending, also, the subjects of Evening Classes, Mechanics' Institutes could meet a manifest want which exists throughout the Province, and supply as well the sons of farmers and others with opportunities for obtaining such practical knowledge of agriculture, chemistry and mechanics as would enable them to better understand the properties and capabilities of the soil and improved modes of cultivation, as well as such knowledge of mechanical arts as would materially assist in agricultural operations."[26] The era of benign neglect was over.

May was a consummate bureaucrat. His official writing suggests a dour personality. He railed against reading novels and thought that frivolous material filled most institute libraries and that grants to mechanics' institutes had been handled very sloppily over the past decade. Although a few institutes had, in fact, come under the scrutiny of public school inspectors, May felt it was time for a closer inspection.[27] With Crooks's permission, he checked out almost all of them. His findings – in *Special Report of the Minister of Education on the Mechanics' Institutes (Ontario)* of February 1881 – described each institute and his ideas for improvement. May had strong opinions on the use of public monies and felt that the institutes had not managed their grants well and did little to raise their own funds: "A serious question for consideration arises here, whether too much pecuniary assistance by the Government to these Institutes does not create an apathy and carelessness among the members and directors. I find that other literary societies which are self-supporting have sprung up and flourished in some places where Mechanics' Institutes have failed. In England these Institutes are almost wholly dependent upon local subscriptions, the only government assistance they receive being paid through the Committee of Council on Education and the Science and Art Department for evening Classes."[28]

Of the existing institutes, about fifty were either defunct or had lost many members over the previous few years ("This is certainly a very bad proof of their prosperity."). A few offered special fees for apprentices: Belleville, Dundas, Hamilton, Paris, Port Elgin, and Woodbridge charged half the regular rate, while Clinton provided free membership.

The libraries he inspected covered a wide range of subjects, but, appalling to him, most of the books in circulation were novels. Toronto's library had the largest circulation: in 1879–80, of 32,920 volumes issued, 25,209 were fiction. For May, this was unnecessary, as several successful American libraries for artisans contained mostly non-fiction. His cross-province journey, an eye-opener, showed him that several institutes – Belleville, Milton, Peterborough, and Toronto – were first class and had stable memberships, active operations, and financial solidity; some were moribund or looking to reorganize themselves – Bracebridge, Brockville,

Chatham, Kingston, Kincardine, Owen Sound, and St Thomas; and some had closed altogether – Aurora, Brampton, Dunnville, Merrickville, Oshawa, Pembroke, Renfrew, Schomberg, and Smiths Falls – the last being a particularly shocking case:

> This is one of the oldest Institutes in Ontario, but certainly is not the most popular. On my arrival at Smith's Falls, I experienced great difficulty in finding the Institute, and was informed by old inhabitants that they had never heard of any Mechanics' Institute being established in the town.
>
> The library is kept in a very small room over a store. When visited, there was no door to the room, and the shelves were rough boards, without even the edges being planed.
>
> The books were not numbered or labeled, and were scattered around the shelves, that it was impossible to find consecutive volumes of any series of books without considerable difficulty. The plan adopted for delivery of books is to allow members to go upstairs and help themselves to three books at a time.
>
> The Library is valued in assets at $3000. The books in Library when I visited this Institute were not worth more than about $500, but I am since informed that there are two additional boxes of books which were going to be sent to be bound.
>
> The Institute has never organized Evening Classes or established a Reading Room. It had more members ten years ago than it had at date of last Report. There is no record kept of the subjects of books issued.
>
> The treasurer was not at home when I visited this place, and I was unable to examine vouchers, etc.[29]

In all, 129 mechanics' institutes existed on paper, but only 119 were active. Aggregate membership was 13,058, with total library holdings of 140,684 volumes. It was now time for May to crack down.

May's recommendations covered financial and educational reforms for the institutes. First, he saw the maximum grant of $400 to be a failure, as "the education of the working classes has been neglected." He believed that Ontario was more liberal in financing institutes than was any other jurisdiction in the world; in England, the government expected municipalities to support local initiatives, and May felt that should also occur in Ontario. Facing the reality of the institutes, May thought it might be better to provide them with $100 annually just for book purchases, as "the majority of the so-called Mechanics' Institutes are only circulating libraries and that, too, for the dissemination of light literature." May saw at first hand many of the obstacles that institutes faced: there was no easy way to find proper books and purchase them at a discount; libraries had no systematic cataloguing; space for most institutes was quite inadequate; their financial affairs were casual and records sloppy, if they existed at all; and farmers were not participating. The greatest failure was in the provision of evening classes. The whole point of the institutes was technical education, a term that would now become central in the department: "It may be well to describe the meaning of technical education for the working classes. Davidson says: 'Technical instruction may be briefly defined as the application of the great questions of science to the various branches of industry; it gives, in fact, a knowledge of practical science and art adapted to the required purposes and to the conditions imposed by the nature of the materials employed; and it teaches the principles upon which the processes of working are based, of what nature soever the occupation of the workers may be.'"[30]

During the 1870s, evening classes had fallen into two categories, general and technical. May believed that institutes needed to focus on just the technical subjects: chemistry; free hand, architectural, geometrical, mechanical, and object drawing; geology and mineralogy; natural philosophy (theoretical and applied mechanics, hydrostatics, pneumatics and hydraulics, physics, heat, light, and electricity); statics and dynamics; and zoology and botany. Apart from drawing, very few institutes taught any of these other subjects. May's solution was to suggest paying grants specifically for evening classes rather than all-purpose grants. In a form of payment-on-results scheme, any class of forty students in elementary subjects could receive a grant of $56, while a class of forty in a technical subject would receive $80. Student fees would be low: 50 cents for an elementary course and $1 for a technical course. Any surplus funds would go towards the purchase of scientific apparatuses or stocking a museum. As to the procurement of teachers, May posited that "in every village, there are professional men quite capable of teaching Elementary Science. Clergymen, Physicians, Engineers, Architects, and others, are to be found in every locality, who would willingly assist in a public movement like this, which is for the benefit of the whole country."[31] Further, May thought that certificates of merit, which had been very popular in the Garden Island institute, would be much more appropriate than the association's prizes.

Several of May's suggestions, though quite constructive, were not likely to interest most institutes: museums of technology and science; reciprocal membership arrangements for visiting other institutes; annual conventions for institute executives; industrial exhibitions, as the English institutes had done; and more popular science lectures. He noted that a number of institutes were paying librarians too much: "It is suggested that women can be employed at a far less cost, and they make excellent librarians. Two or three of the best-regulated Institutes in Ontario are in charge of women."[32]

May's personal visit did make a difference in several towns, with local leaders resuscitating and reorganizing flagging institutes. The *Special Report* garnered approval from G. Mercer Adam, editor of the *Canada Educational Monthly*, who agreed there was too little supervision. It appalled Adam that the Pembroke institute could receive two $400 grants, then close down and sell off its books by auction, and that Berlin's received $400 but raised only $29 itself. For Adam, the solution was simple: "If municipal honesty were in better repute, we would rather see the Institutes drop their inappropriate title and become Public Libraries, supported by municipal assessment, and free to the people. Some day, when the public mind sickens of party politics, we may see this realized."[33]

The department's 1881 *Special Report* laid out the new rules for evening classes: "Each institute is hereby also authorized to conduct Evening Classes for those persons only who, in good faith, require technical instruction," but the subject list was shorter than that in the *Special Report*. Classes would now be given in drawing (machines, designs, objects, freehand, architectural and geometrical); chemistry (applied to manufactures and agriculture); and natural philosophy (elements, along with applied mechanics, pneumatics and hydrostatics). A sliding scale of Department of Education payments was more generous than that laid out in May's original recommendations: an institute with a technical class of forty could garner a grant of $90; together with fees, such a class could generate a revenue of $130. With such a high requirement for enrolment, however, few institutes would likely be able to attract so large a class. A few institutes roused themselves, but most did not.

The transition to the Education Department regime was also rocky for the Association of Mechanics' Institutes. Hearing that Dr May had been deputed to visit the institutes caused some consternation for the board. James Young, in his 1880 presidential address, hoped that such visits would be constructive rather than a sign that the department might restrict the individual institutes' freedom of movement. He felt that radical change for mechanics' institutes would be a grave mistake and reflected that agricultural societies were responsible for running their own activities without being tightly controlled by government. Young likely had a good sense of the way in which the department operated. After the inspection tour and May's report, the board of the association pressed the government, through Young, to make changes in the act that would unburden the association. The act was amended to cut the association loose from the AAAO and to end the vexing 5 per cent tax on institute grants to maintain the head office. After the change, the Mechanics' Institute Association would receive an operating grant directly from the treasury. In addition to this structural transition, there were also petty annoyances. In 1880, when Edwards was trying to assemble the statistics for the annual report, he noticed that few institutes had sent in their forms. Upon enquiring, he found that institutes had been directed by the Department of Education to send one copy to the department and to retain one; Edwards had to write to May to remind him of the act's requirement to provide the association with a copy as well.[34]

Late in 1883, the association decided to launch a subsidized lecture programme in which it would choose a few well-known lecturers and vet a series of topics, then suggest to the institutes that they request lecturers of their choice. It was hoped that at least one lecture could be provided to each of the 132 institutes during the year and that each institute would be required to provide some local funds to help cover expenses. May certainly favoured lectures, so the idea may well have come from him as he sat in on the association's board meetings. Edwards sounded out his contacts, Commander J. Cheyne of Uxbridge and Rev. R.C. Moffatt of Collingwood. The Preston institute recommended that Rev. Dr Reinhold von Pirch of Baden give lectures in the Waterloo area. Edwards had heard that von Pirch's recent lecture on Luther was very good but, as he told the association's president, Otto Klotz, von Pirch would have to be able to speak on other topics, for topics such as Luther "would not be in character to be delivered under the auspices of the association, the reasons will be evident to you."[35] This was because funds were available to pay lecturers $6 to $8 for every literary lecture or $20 for a scientific lecture. In time, the association hoped to become a provincial "lecture bureau." Once lecturers were lined up and Edwards had prepared a circular to be distributed to institutes, May was unable to see the minister, whose approval was required. The minister finally did see the proof of the circular but held it up to make changes, meaning distribution of the circular was stalled. As Edwards intimated to Klotz: "I have felt exceedingly troubled about this delay, as I consider that it has tended to defeat – or to render somewhat more doubtful – the object we are striving to attain."[36] None the less, the scheme did get off the ground, with May himself delivering nearly half the lectures.

### INSIDE THE SMALL MECHANICS' INSTITUTES

When one glances over the annual reports of Ontario mechanics' institutes from the third quarter of the century, their operations seem, on paper, to be very similar. Part of this is an artefact of the reporting system and the structure they were each supposed to emulate; however, each community's educational and working demographics resulted in operations of a much greater variety in reality. While the records of most institutes have disappeared, we do have those of the largest institute of all, in Toronto, and limited ones from a few small institutes. We will have a brief look at the operations of the institutes in Galt, Preston, and Caledon.

Galt was already a thriving industrial town in the 1860s. Its institute, founded in 1853, was one of the few to soldier on when provincial grants were withdrawn. In the surviving minutes[37] of January 1862, the directors speak of a crisis in the affairs of the institute: "In every other way save financially, the Institute has been completely successful during the year." This was true, of course, of almost all the institutes and voluntary organizations of the time. As the income and expenses were not much more than $200 a year, part of the financial crisis arose from the cost of the librarian's salary of $110, which left only $32 for books and newspapers. The Galt institute, with 148 members at the time, was one of the mid-sized institutes which, like most, saw its membership numbers bounce up and down; it surpassed 200 members by mid-decade, only to drop later by 25 per cent. The reintroduction of provincial grants had the salutary effect of increasing membership. The occasional public lecture brought in some money, and the institute sponsored an art exhibition in 1866. In its January 1871 report, the directors proudly proclaimed that "the Institute has never been in a more flourishing condition generally than during the past year and never were its prospects brighter than now." Membership stabilized during the 1870s in the 160–180 range, which represents approximately 5 per cent of the town's population.

As Galt was an industrial centre, was the mechanics' institute primarily there for the needs of mechanics and artisans? Its leadership certainly was dominated by non-tradesmen: in 1864, for example, the president was the ambitious James Young, then a twenty-seven-year old newspaper publisher and manufacturer; his vice-presidents were accountant Alexander McGregor, manufacturer Richard Blain, and bookkeeper David Brown; his secretary was John Brogan, a plasterer; and his treasurer Alexander Addison, a cabinet maker. Several of these men were active in the institute's direction for years. Lacking detailed membership lists, we can infer from the library collection and reading room subscriptions the memberships' reading interests. An inventory of the library's 933 volumes in July 1864 shows twenty-four volumes on natural history, botany, and gardening; seventeen on geology and mineralogy; twenty-six on chemistry and natural philosophy; and eighty volumes of periodical literature on science and arts, which formed about 16 per cent of the collection. The reading room was clearly devoted to a more general readership: some eighteen newspapers, mostly local, along with two each from Toronto and Montreal, one from Buffalo and the New York *Tribune*, were available. These were accompanied by key literary and political reviews of the day: *Harper's, Atlantic Monthly, Blackwood's, Scottish American Journal, Illustrated London News, North British Review, Westminster Review, British Messenger, Edinburgh Review, Chambers' Journal, Punch, Good Words*, and the *London Quarterly Review*. The only publication relating to science and art was *Scientific American*, although a copy of the *Journal of the Board of Arts and Manufactures* was on the table, as the Galt Institute adhered to that body. This list reflects clearly the middle-class orientation of the institute's readers. In 1868, when the possibility of a grant materialized, the directors suggested they would now be able to subscribe to both the *London Engineer* and the *London Builder*.

During the 1870s and 1880s, the Galt Institute focused mostly upon its library function. While it did not respond to the first pressure to hold evening classes, by 1875, classes in mechanical drawing for twenty students and penmanship-bookkeeping, also for twenty, were held; the students were likely the same in both classes. By the 1880s, membership climbed beyond 300 to nearly 400 as the library's collection grew to nearly 3,000 volumes. A short-lived scientific society seems to have existed in the 1880s. In April 1891, the Galt Scientific, Historical and Literary Society, in connection with the Galt Mechanics' Institute, formed, and its members agreed that "the object of the Society shall be the promotion of scientific and literary culture by discussions, original essays, historical research, and practical work done in the field and in class." This was a form of mutual adult education that was quite distant from the original intention to instruct the working class in science and art. Indeed, one of the first tasks of the new society was to enquire whether the University of Toronto was willing to create a university extension system similar to that recently launched in Britain.

The village of Preston, although perhaps only a half-hour carriage drive from Galt, had a different character. Not so industrial, it was a typical large Ontario village – with about 1,400 residents in the 1870s – with a range of commerce, small-scale manufacturing, and trades. It also had a sizeable German population – some recent immigrants and others descendants of the Pennsylvania Germans who had arrived earlier in the century – many of whom still spoke and read their native tongue.

The Preston Mechanics' Institute, from its organization in September 1871, obtained equal support from both language groups. Founder and chief visionary Otto Klotz (1817–1892) arrived in Preston from his native Kiel in 1837 and set up as a brewer and hotelier. An ardent supporter of public schools, he was active with the freemasons, the local agricultural society, the municipal government, and the volunteer fire department. He was president of the institute from 1872 until his death twenty years later.

The institute, founded "for the purpose of improving the mind by the promotion of useful knowledge among its members," came closer to that ideal than did most organizations of its day. Naturally, the reading room and library were central to the members, with German papers and books alongside the English, and, because of Klotz's interest in education, the institute offered evening classes in bookkeeping and penmanship as early as 1874, although few students appeared. In the following year, its classes in penmanship/bookkeeping attracted nineteen students, while its mathematics enrolled sixteen. In 1873, it sponsored a public entertainment – a common occurrence in institutes of the time. One of the musicians was Carl Klotz, one of Otto's sons and an institute member; the speaker was another, Otto Julius Klotz (1852–1923), then a young land surveyor and later dominion astronomer and director of the Dominion Observatory in Ottawa.

Although no membership rolls exist, the minutes record the election of members, apprentice members, and subscribers[38] – some ninety-one names in total between 1871 and 1892. Employing the 1871 and 1881 census records along with a contemporary directory,[39] we can identify occupations of thirty-nine members. These include baker, blacksmith, bookkeeper, butcher, two cabinet makers, two carpenters, dentist, dyer, excise officer, three farmers, two hops growers, three hotel keepers, iron founder, three labourers, manufacturer, three masons, three merchants, millwright, two moulders, notary public, physician, surveyor, tailor, tanner, three teachers, and wagon maker: in short, a microcosm of the village. Another fourteen members have the same surnames as members with known occupations and were probably relatives; 64 per cent of the members were of German or Swiss origin, and most of the others English speakers. Although members were never numerous, rarely topping eighty, they were serious about the library: by 1883, with only eighty members and twelve years of existence, the institute had nearly 3,400 volumes. Only ten of the province's 174 reporting institutes had more than that.

By the time the Department of Education replaced the Department of Agriculture supervising the mechanics' institutes, all sizeable towns in Ontario possessed one. During the 1890s, growth continued apace, with much smaller centres now forming their own – often cross-roads hamlets. Although their small libraries served rural populations, there was no pretence that they served mechanics, tradespeople, or even farmers in terms of technical education; they were simply local libraries and community centres. A great many small facilities were in western Ontario.

Table 7.4 shows the distribution in 1895 by county and district. Towns north of Orillia and in the vast northern regions the province had recently annexed formed their own institutes, eighteen in all. Eastern Ontario had always lagged behind. While more institutes popped up in small centres, counties east of York had eighty-one, and those to its west, 207, partly because of larger population, better land, and a somewhat milder climate. The northern reaches of many of the eastern counties, still largely bush, supported only tiny logging and milling communities. Table B3 in Appendix B shows the locations for institutes and free libraries in 1895.

An example of the small, rural institute in this period is that of Caledon[40] – one of a dozen in Peel County, with ten of them in Caledon Township. Some were older (Claude, 1877, Bolton, 1879) but the rest started in the 1880s and early 1890s: Alton, Belfountain, Caledon, Cheltenham, Forks of the Credit, Inglewood, Mono Mills, and Mono Road.

The Caledon Farmers' and Mechanics' Institute organized itself on 7 July 1883 in a schoolroom in Charleston (now Caledon village), which had about 250 people.[41] Not surprising, the first order of business was to obtain a provincial grant, after which members went to Toronto to purchase books. Donations augmented the library. While the institute was too small and impecunious to afford regular lectures, it tapped into the

Table 7.4 Geographical distribution of mechanics' institutes, Ontario (1895)

| County/district | Number of institutes |
| --- | --- |
| Algoma | 3 |
| Brant | 4 |
| Bruce | 21 |
| Carleton | 5 |
| Dufferin | 6 |
| Dundas | 5 |
| Durham | 2 |
| Elgin | 7 |
| Essex | 3 |
| Frontenac | 2 |
| Glengarry | 4 |
| Grenville | 7 |
| Grey | 14 |
| Haldimand | 8 |
| Halton | 5 |
| Hastings | 4 |
| Huron | 15 |
| Kent | 10 |
| Lambton | 13 |
| Lanark | 7 |
| Leeds | 3 |
| Lennox & Addington | 4 |
| Lincoln | 4 |
| Manitoulin | 3 |
| Middlesex | 12 |
| Muskoka (includes modern Parry Sound) | 9 |
| Norfolk | 4 |
| Northumberland | 9 |
| Ontario | 12 |
| Oxford | 6 |
| Peel | 12 |
| Perth | 8 |
| Peterborough | 4 |
| Prescott | 1 |
| Prince Edward | 1 |
| Rainy River (includes modern Kenora) | 2 |
| Renfrew | 6 |
| Russell | 1 |
| Simcoe | 13 |
| Stormont | 1 |
| Thunder Bay | 1 |
| Victoria | 9 |
| Waterloo | 8 |
| Welland | 7 |
| Wellington | 14 |
| Wentworth | 2 |
| York | 17 |

Source: Province of Ontario, Sessional Papers (1895).

association's lecture scheme and took up a collection to obtain the services of Rev. Moffat in 1886. In that year, the institute's directors included Samuel Harris, son of the local storekeeper; Samuel Stubbs, former deputy reeve of the township; and local farmers. In 1888, the institute elected as president Rev. Alexander McFaul, the local Presbyterian minister who had founded a congregation in nearby Orangeville. By 1888, its library had grown to 707 volumes, fifty-three of them about science and art, and by 1892 the collection nearly doubled.

Although the institute discussed evening classes in 1889, it limited itself to occasional lectures by local people and concerts. In 1883, there had been sixty-three founding subscribers, most contributing $1; by 1895, there were still sixty-two members, who now paid 50 cents annually. Officers typically came from the local clergy. These surviving records are a rarity for such a small institute, but one suspects that the story they tell unfolded much the same in dozens of other small centres across the province.

## TRANSFORMING THE MECHANICS' INSTITUTES (1885–95)

During the late 1880s and into the early 1890s, the Department of Education's supervisor of mechanics' institutes, Dr Samuel Passmore May, continued to tout their value in the delivery of technical education but shifted his focus to art education. Evening classes were stable, and, in its 1885 report, the Association of Mechanics' Institutes of Ontario remained sanguine: "Your committee rejoices in the success so far attained; but would fain see the system extended to embrace studies applicable to branches of the manufacturing arts other than the merely decorative."[42] Drawing classes accounted for nearly a quarter of all evening enrolments, and general subjects for all the rest. Hopes for a role for the new School of Practical Science in Toronto (see next section) did not materialize: "While our factories and industrial establishments are increasing in number and extent on every hand, we have no organized system of instruction provided on technical objects, except in the Ontario School of Science, in which but a very limited number of mechanics and artizans could possibly attend, even if the studies pursued were more suited to their special requirements."[43] It would be the association's last pronouncement on technical education: passage of a bill (49 Vict., cap. 35) ended the association on 30 September 1886 and Secretary-Treasurer William Edwards's nearly thirty years of labour on behalf of the mechanics' institutes.

The revised act fine-tuned the granting program, modified the syllabus for evening classes, and laid out four courses of instruction:
Commercial (arithmetic, bookkeeping, and writing); Drawing (preliminary, advanced, mechanical); English (composition, grammar, and
English and Canadian history); and Science (botany, physiology, and
sanitary science). The teaching of chemistry, mechanics, and physics
had been a complete bust, and the shift to biological science – in keeping with the provincial school curriculum – led to almost no classes.
Changes to grants pleased May, however. Directors were developing the
institutes, which was paying off socially: "I am told of several instances
where young men have forsaken bad habits, and become useful members of society, through the influence of reading rooms and evening
classes, and further some of the parents themselves have become better
citizens since their children became members of Mechanics' Institutes."[44]

By the 1890s, the system of mechanics' institutes was thriving, with
new branches each year and continually rising memberships. Yet almost
all the interest focused on the libraries and reading rooms, not on evening classes, which continued to decline. Throughout the period, about
a quarter of the enrolments were in drawing classes.

One of May's concerns was the lack of financial support from local
municipalities. As institute libraries and reading rooms could benefit
many people, he believed in local assistance. Consequently, the department introduced a bill to allow any institute to transfer its property to the
local municipality, which could then assess taxes to maintain the library.
Oliver Mowat (Liberal premier 1872–96) was enthusiastic, but, not surprising, backbencher James Young, new past president of the association, was not. As the *Globe* reported: "Mr YOUNG thought the Bill would
go a long way towards destroying the Mechanics' Institutes. He failed to
see the present necessity for the Bill."[45] But the Free Libraries Act, 1882
(45 Vict., cap. 22), passed. Whether individual institutes prized their
autonomy or municipalities avoided new responsibilities, few mechanics' institutes became free libraries.

Even though such libraries could obtain annual provincial grants of
$250, five years later only six of the more than ninety institutes in opera-
tion had moved to that status: Berlin, Brantford, Guelph, St Thomas,
Simcoe, and Toronto. For the last – the oldest, largest, and richest in the
province – the transition generated regret by some long-time members,
such as William Edwards and J.E. Pell, whom the institute's final meeting
essentially snubbed. Samuel Thompson, who had been a member since
the 1840s, provided a suitable epitaph: "During its fifty-three years of

existence, it had done a good work. Thousands of young men of this city, by its refining and educating influences, had their thoughts and resolves turned into channels of industry and usefulness, that might otherwise have run in directions far less beneficial to themselves and to society ... In Toronto, as elsewhere, the Mechanics' Institute has had its day. But times change, and the public taste changes with them."[46]

By the 1890s, even Dr May seems to have understood that institutes were not going to deliver technical education. In his reports, he stopped discussing evening classes and began to extol the virtues of public libraries. While he would have wished libraries leaned to scientific and technical material, he realized that that was not what people wanted to read. His contempt for novel-reading remained as strong as ever: "intellectual dram-drinking which ultimately emasculates both mind and character, and unfits man for the duties of active life. This is, no doubt, applicable to the reading of the ephemeral trash which is poured with such an unremitting stream into this country, in the shape of dime novels."[47] During his inspection tours, despite searching for offending books, "I am pleased to state that owing to the oversight of the directors and committees appointed to select the books, that I have not yet found one book which might be condemned as immoral."[48] He considered Ryerson's public libraries in Ontario schools, with supplies from the Book Depository, a failure. Because municipalities had not supported them, eventually the depository closed.

The libraries of mechanics' institutes and the few free libraries now constituted Ontario's public library system.[49] While the institutes did charge an annual fee, it was nominal. Comparison with US states with free library systems showed Ontario in quite a favourable light: in 1890, its institute and free libraries held 383,000 volumes, while US figures from 1886 showed Illinois and Ohio comparable and all other states well behind. Only Massachusetts, with more than 1.77 million, was significantly larger.

Under the Department of Education, beginning in 1880, total grants to institutes had continued to rise slowly, then contract as May tightened the rules. By the mid-1890s, with nearly 300 institutes in operation, total grants never reached $40,000; by 1900, when the institutes had disappeared, public libraries received $47,000, compared with $74,000 for agricultural societies.[50] Legislation had caught up with reality when the passage of the Free Libraries Act, 1895 (58 Vict., cap. 45), converted all the mechanics' institutes into public libraries. While some libraries retained their original institute names, and, although they could continue

Table 7.5 Growth of mechanics' institutes, Ontario (1883–95)

|                   | Mechanics' institutes (1883) | Free libraries (1895) |
| ----------------- | ---------------------------- | --------------------- |
| Number reporting  | 93                           | 300                   |
| Members           | 13,672                       | 98,428                |
| Evening classes   | 28                           | 36                    |
| Volumes           | 154,093                      | 604,719               |
| Circulation       | 251,920                      | 1,687,806             |

Source: Province of Ontario, Sessional Papers (1884, 1896).

to provide evening classes, they no longer made the pretense of providing technical education.

The transformation of mechanics' institutes into free libraries was a great success in terms of numbers. Table 7.5 shows the comparative statistics for 1883 and 1895: the number of institutions tripled, membership expanded seven-fold, holdings quadrupled, and circulation expanded seven-fold. The provincial population increased only about 10 per cent, so interest in reading grew by leaps and bounds.

Attendance at night courses did not follow that pattern. The writing had been on the wall – as it were – for many years: working people would or could not use institute evening courses to upgrade their skills.

## A SCHOOL OF TECHNOLOGY AND THE WORKING CLASS (1872–82)

Historical accounts have always presented the story of the School for Practical Science (SPS) as an evolution of the Faculty of Applied Science and Engineering of the University of Toronto.[51] But its creators intended it in part to serve working-class students better than did the mechanics' institutes. Agriculture Commissioner John Carling had been the key mover behind creation of Ontario Agricultural College in Guelph, but he had other ideas on education. In his 1870 report, he admitted that, while agriculture was crucial to the Ontario economy, manufactures and commerce were increasing their contribution. Being aware of the weakness of technological training in the mechanics' institutes, he mused on the concept of a free-standing school for technology:

In order, therefore, to promote more effectually the interests of manufactures, mining, and the useful and ornamental arts generally, the establishment of a Technical School of Arts, is much to be desired. This should embrace systematic instruction, with a constant application to practical purposes, in mining, civil engineering, architecture, chemistry, in its various applications to manufactures and arts, designing, modeling, mechanical drawing, &c. In such a school, our youth designed for any of these pursuits, would have an opportunity of going through a thorough course of instruction suited to their wants, and of acquiring the knowledge and habits requisite for performing those practical operations of analysis and construction, which are essential to success. The utility of such an institution will become apparent upon a careful consideration of the present state of our mineral and manufacturing industries, and the inadequacy of the means we at present possess of an educational character, of meeting this want.[52]

Such schools were common on the Continent and appearing in major US cities, while the science and art schools in the United Kingdom taught all classes of workers what they needed to maintain British industrial superiority. Following the modus operandi he employed for the Ontario Agricultural College, Carling dispatched John George Hodgins, Superintendent Egerton Ryerson's lieutenant, and Toronto physician Alex Machattie to visit US technical schools.

In January 1871, Hodgins and Machattie's *Report of an Inquiry in Regard to Schools of Technical Science in Certain Portions of the United States* provided data on students, faculty, buildings, equipment, and finances from several prominent eastern schools of science and engineering: the College of Chemistry, Physics, Mechanical Arts connected with Cornell; the Cooper Union of Science and Art in New York City; the Free Institute of Industrial Science in Worcester, Massachusetts; the Lawrence School at Harvard; the Massachusetts Institute of Technology (MIT); the School of Mines connected with Columbia; and the Sheffield School at Yale. Most were four-year, degree-granting schools.

According to Hodgins and Machattie, "The kind of instruction, and the method of giving it, should be as practical as possible"[53] – that is, applicable to industry, not the way University College, Toronto, taught it. The Massachusetts Institute of Technology and its interest in the working class much impressed them: "Provision might also be made for popular lectures and instruction in the evenings, at which Teachers, young men, mechanics and others employed during the day might attend. This we found to be an interesting feature in some of the institutions we visited. At the Massachusetts Institute of Technology at Boston, Mr. Lowell, with his usual munificence, had provided at a cost to himself, of $3,000 per annum, an evening course of lectures, which had been attended by an average number of 500 persons – chiefly Teachers, and persons engaged in manufacturing establishments."[54] Although well aware of technical education in Britain and Ireland, the authors argued strongly for adopting the American model – a free-standing school of science and technology to support Canada's burgeoning industrial sector.

Once the government had received the report, it acted. In the next departmental report, Buckland noted that the legislature had voted funds "for the commencement of such an institution for the Province of Ontario, in which operatives and others engaged in the various mechanical and manufacturing arts, and such also as are interested in mining pursuits, might receive the necessary instruction especially adapted to their wants, so as to fit them to prosecute their respective avocations with intelligence and success."[55] The government set aside $50,000 for the school. Edward Blake (1833–1912), Liberal leader and a warm friend of the University of Toronto, argued that a separate college would weaken the university and dilute funding for higher education; however, the government provided the start-up funds as cheaply and efficiently as possible. One form of savings was to purchase and renovate the Toronto Mechanics' Institute building on Church Street rather than erect a new building. The new college was to train civil, mechanical, and mining engineers, but also to instruct industrial workers in flax and woollen fibres, leather, and wood and to teach modellers and carvers in the decorative and industrial arts, and persons studying chemistry as it applies to various manufacturers.

The School of Technology opened in May 1872 under William Hodgson Ellis (1845–1921), a graduate of the University of Toronto and a physician and chemistry instructor in two Toronto medical schools. In essence, the school operated as an extension of the mechanics'-institute classes, holding the first series of lectures in the evenings from May to the end of July 1872, and an autumn term running from September to December. Ellis taught chemistry on Mondays and Wednesdays, while civil engineer, artist, and draughtsman William Armstrong (1822–1914) ran mechanical and architectural drawing on Tuesdays and Thursdays. On Friday evening, Ellis taught chemistry until mid-November, then James Loudon (1841–1916), physics lecturer at University College, lectured on natural philosophy.

Classes at the School of Technology were free, whereas the mechanics' institutes charged a small fee. For reference books, the old Board of Arts and Manufactures library, still in the Mechanics' Institute building, also

Table 7.6 Occupations of students, School of Technology (1872)

| | |
|---|---|
| Architect's pupils 2 | Moulders 6 |
| Bricklayers 5 | Organ builders 1 |
| Builders 3 | Plasterers 2 |
| Blacksmith 1 | Pattern makers 3 |
| Brassfinisher 1 | Painters 3 |
| Bobbin turner 1 | Plumbers 3 |
| Clerks 31 | Printers 3 |
| Compositors 3 | Physician 1 |
| Carpenters 23 | At school 10 |
| Cabinetmakers 4 | Students 7 |
| Druggists 9 | Silversmith 1 |
| Engravers 3 | Stair builder 1 |
| Engine turner 1 | Sewing machine merchant 1 |
| Fitters 3 | Stencil cutter 1 |
| Instrument maker 1 | Scale maker 1 |
| Jeweller 1 | Tinsmiths 5 |
| Joiners 2 | Typefounder 1 |
| Music seller 1 | Teachers 3 |
| Machinists 17 | Wood turners 5 |

Source: Province of Ontario, Sessional Papers (1873).

had more recent books. The school had no laboratories. In the autumn term of 1872, 181 students enrolled, including ninety-eight in drawing, ninety-one in chemistry, and fifty in natural philosophy. In Ellis's report, the occupations of 174 of the students (Table 7.6) show working-class men the primary users, making up some 60 per cent of the student body.

Politically, a "working-man's college" was not going to succeed, as Blake's Liberals won the December 1871 election. He and his successor as premier, Oliver Mowat, both friendly to the university, worked to integrate the two institutions. During the second year of operations, the school, now the School of Practical Science, had moved into the Toronto Mechanics' Institute, which retained the library, reading room, and board room for its own use. The Liberals' act of 29 March 1873 let the province allow students of the school to take classes at University College and vice versa. In that second year of operation, student numbers dropped slightly, to 129. Ellis noted[56] that many began the courses out of curiosity but, finding it hard to study and work, eventually dropped out. Several new occupations appear in the 1873 list, including bookbinder, coachbuilder, five dentists, engineer, mason, two reporters, shoemaker, and warehouseman. But, by 1876, a shift had become obvious. Of the 157 enrollees that year, Ellis found thirty-five students from the Veterinary College, twenty-one druggist's assistants, eighteen students, seven professional men, four teachers, and seven "others." Eighteen students hailed from various trades, alongside forty-seven mechanics. Working-class men dropped to 40 per cent of the student body.[57]

By 1879, the "revolution" for mechanics and artisans was largely over. The three-year diploma in engineering had attracted its first seven students. As a new building near University College (1859), the spectacular home of the University of Toronto's teaching arm, was not yet complete, only the engineering program was up and running. The departments of chemistry and of assaying and mining geology had yet to open. Apart from the regular students, "occasional students" could now take individual courses. These now numbered twenty-two men: six in chemistry and twelve in biology. Ellis recorded that most of these occasional students were from Toronto's two medical schools,[58] a fact that observers noticed. As Adam commented in the *Canada Educational Monthly*, "The Agricultural College is doing something for the farmer; and the Toronto School of Practical Science, if it were recruited from some preparatory schools of trade, would be of service to the end for which it was founded. In some of the industrial centres of the Province an experiment might be made in one of the schools to give instruction in manual arts, and, with the necessary equipment, to direct this to practical ends."[59] Of course, no such schools existed, and no such experiment immediately took place.

The university's integration of the School of Practical Science continued apace, although Ellis remembered in 1882 that the act had stated "instruction shall be given to artisans, mechanics, and workmen, by Evening Classes, in such subjects as may further their improvement in their different callings." The school then began introducing evening courses of lectures by members of the science faculty at University College: Ellis on inorganic chemistry, specifically the non-metallic elements; John Galbraith (1846–1914), the school's first engineering appointment, on applied mechanics – strains and strengths of materials; James Loudon on light and sound; William H. Pike (1851–1921) on the objects of chemistry as a science; Sir Daniel Wilson on ethnology; and zoologist Robert Ramsay Wright (1852–1933) on natural history – the minute structure of the human body.

Wilson, as president of the college, gave the opening lecture, *On the Practical Uses of Science in the Daily Business of Life: The Inaugural Lecture to the Evening Courses of Lectures for Working Men* (1881):

Thus, then, is this People's College; it remains to be seen how far those for whom such practical advantages are thus supplied will be found prepared to avail themselves of them, and so encourage us in giving permanence to a movement which, so far as the professors of University College are concerned, must involve a great addition to the amount of work already devolving on them ... [The school's aim] is to train intelligent workmen for all the ordinary applications of skilled labour. The course of evening lectures ... is to offer to the intelligent artisan and to all other practical students, the elementary knowledge requisite to start them on lines of enquiry leading to systematic research in every branch of technology specially adapted to useful handicrafts.[60]

Ellis compiled statistics on the attendees. In his own course, virtually all 193 were veterinary students or druggists. For Galbraith's course, of the fifty-five in attendance, ten were workingmen who obtained special tickets. Overall, the group included 110 veterinary students; fourteen engineers, machinists, blacksmiths, etc.; twenty-six architects, builders, carpenters, joiners, etc.; four brass moulders, glass-silverers, etc.; and thirty-nine druggists and clerks.[61] Clearly, the move to professionalization was edging out workingmen. Only two courses ran the following academic year: Galbraith's lectures on the theory of the steam engine, which attracted six auditors, and Ellis's lectures on the chemistry of metals, which brought in 139, mostly veterinary students. Ellis also noted that with the cost of operating evening lectures being high, more funds would be required. In the following year, the school had reduced its evening lectures to a single course in chemistry, for one term, for 113 students. Thus, in less than a decade, the middle class had essentially taken over the working-class school as an extension of university education. For all intents and purposes, the School of Practical Science became the University of Toronto's faculty of engineering.

## INTRODUCTION OF ART EDUCATION

Throughout much of the nineteenth century in Ontario, anyone wishing to further an interest in art had to either study with an individual artist or, for formal instruction, leave the province. This situation stands in sharp contrast to that in the United Kingdom. There, Henry Cole and Richard Redgrave built up the art school network.

In Ontario, mechanics' institutes had dabbled in art instruction. Several of their night schools had taught free-hand drawing, in effect as a skill to enable industrial, not aesthetic, pursuits. Superintendent

Egerton Ryerson, who set up the Educational Museum in Toronto in imitation of the South Kensington Museum, had long hoped for a school of art in association with it. The copies of busts, paintings, and statues that he had purchased in Europe were, like those in South Kensington, to provide models for art students. Students in the normal and model schools studied linear drawing so they could teach it to elementary students; however, drawing was not a priority in the Ontario curriculum before Ryerson's retirement in 1876.

### Ontario Society of Artists

In the event, artists themselves took the lead. On 25 June 1872, several Toronto artists met to discuss forming an organization, and on 2 July the Ontario Society of Artists adopted its constitution. Initially, it made no mention of art education, focusing on staging exhibitions and building up a "national" gallery.[62] A society prospectus of December 1875 proposed a gallery and a possible school of art "whenever practicable." Members soon visited the new minister of education, Adam Crooks, to ask for a $1,000 government grant. On 4 April 1876, the society struck a committee – society co-founder Thomas Mower Martin (1838–1934), Vice-President Lucius O'Brien (1832–1899), Vienna-born George T. Berthon (1806–1892), architect Frank Darling, and W.J. Lauder – to develop a proposal for a school of art. By October, their plan had gone forward to Crooks, who, though agreeable, deferred to the society's president, William H. Howland (1844–93), son of the province's first lieutenant-governor (the Queen's representative) and later himself mayor of Toronto. As the committee reported, "[Crooks] stated that it was in effect a copy of the system adopted in England in the Department of Science and Art." The drawing teachers would include Martin as director, Michael Hannaford (1832–1891), W.J. Lauder, Marmaduke Matthews (1839–1913), and William Revell (1830–1902). The government also agreed to allow the new school to use the busts in the Educational Museum.

It is no surprise that Ontario would ape the South Kensington model. Almost all the society's leading lights were English: Frederic M. Bell-Smith (1846–1923) trained in South Kensington; John Fraser (1838–1898), at the Royal Academy school in London; Matthews and Robert Ford Gagen (1847–1926), in England; and J.T. Rolph (1831–1916), at the School of Design in London's Somerset House. Martin had some lessons in England but was largely self-taught.

Only Lucius Richard O'Brien had grown up in Toronto: he had attended Upper Canada College when the drawing master was the

architect, engineer, and surveyor John G. Howard (1803–1890), a pro-
lific watercolourist and a founder in 1834 of the Toronto Society of
Artists. By the 1870s, O'Brien was one of the best-known landscape artists in Canada, his style similar to that of Fraser's. He went on to help
found the Royal Canadian Academy and served as its first president
1880–90.

## Ontario School of Art

With Crooks having placed a $1,000 grant in the provincial estimates,
the society opened the Ontario School of Art in October 1876 at a location on King Street, Toronto, with courses in elementary drawing.
Howland and O'Brien's report of 14 January 1878, on behalf of the committee of the society's council, noted: "The English Arts Schools centre-
ing [sic] at South Kensington, have been the means of reinstating English
manufactures in the fields, which for want of training they had previously lost, and the best workmanship has now no chance in the competition of nations, unless accompanied with elegance of design."[63] They
also noted that the Americans had followed the South Kensington model
in the public schools, particularly in Massachusetts, which had put in
place a costly program.

The following year, the society dispatched Bell-Smith and O'Brien to
Boston to examine the state's system. They concluded that Ontario
should emulate Massachusetts's free drawing lessons in the public
schools.[64] The head of that system was Walter Smith (1836–1886), himself a graduate of South Kensington and one of the few to have mastered
all stages of the curriculum. Smith had argued at a conference in
Washington, DC, for integrating art into the public-school curriculum.
He was particularly aware that working-class men had low status and little education and that US education must pay attention to artisans.
Smith noted French admiration for British advances through the South
Kensington system and hoped that Americans would soon follow suit. In
1870, his state's legislature enabled evening art classes in towns as part of
the regular school system. Classes commenced the following year, with
Smith directing the Boston schools. In 1873, the state opened a normal
school to train art teachers. O'Brien found all this activity surprising,
particularly as Massachusetts had 400,000 fewer residents than Ontario.

The founders of the Ontario School of Art believed in teaching art on
a solid basis, using classical models. Following the English lead, they
sought to have the province designate their facility the provincial central
school, which would provide annual exams and diplomas for the entire

system, with local schools in other towns affiliating with it. The founders admitted: "The above scheme differs in no essential particular, except economy, from that of the south Kensington system, and its details may be the same."[65] They wanted art schools to be part of the provincial education system, in keeping with the society's attitude about art training: "The elementary training of eye and hand would be most valuable, not only to artists and designers of every kind, but to every skilled mechanic, and we desire to put it within their reach ... For these artizans [i.e., ornamental workers in iron, stone, wood] it is evident that the classes must be held in the evening, and the terms must be low."[66] This was, of course, what the mechanics' institutes had hoped to do for decades, with little success; however, a school of art would be more likely to succeed.

London was not far behind Toronto. The Western Ontario School of Art and Design opened in 1878 in the local mechanics' institute building, with four instructors. By 1881, it offered three terms per year: the first term had forty-six day and sixty-six evening students; the second, thirty-one and fifty-two, respectively; and the third, forty-two and 100. Administrators reported primarily "ladies" and young people at the afternoon classes and working men and some fifteen public-school teachers in the evenings. A survey found those working men to be architects, book-binders, bricklayers, cabinet-makers, carpenters, carriage-makers, machinists, pattern-makers, carriage painters, lithographers, marble-cutters, photographers, printers, tinsmiths, and wood-carvers[67] – precisely the tradesmen the province had always hoped to support though part-time education. At the Ontario School of Art, however, in 1882, only forty-seven of 121 evening students were artisans and mechanics; the rest were clerks, students, and teachers. None of the eighty-one day students came from the working class.[68] Women dominated the day classes, men the evening, with women making up a little more than half the school's enrolment.

By the early 1880s, the Ontario School of Art taught antique and perspective drawing, design, elementary drawing, flat copy, oil painting, and watercolours. In 1881, the students came from box-making, engraving, glass staining, jewellery, lithography, machining, paper-hanging, photography, piano-stool manufacturing, sign-painting, tinsmithing, and wood carving. The students had a variety of motives for taking classes (see Table 7.7).

Only a handful of British students – including Walter Smith in Massachusetts – passed through more than a very few of the twenty-three stages of the South Kensington syllabus. Toronto offered the first seven

Table 7.7 Occupational intentions of students, OSA (1881)

DAY CLASSES

| Men – occupation | Men – intention | Women – occupation | Women – intention |
| --- | --- | --- | --- |
| Professional 1 | Architect | Teachers 3 | Teaching |
| Technical 1 | Artist | Art teachers 8 | Teaching |
| Clerical 2 | Varied | Art students 10 | Teaching |
| Students 9 | Varied | None 49 | Indefinite |

EVENING CLASSES

| Men – occupation | Men – intention | Women – occupation | Women – intention |
| --- | --- | --- | --- |
| Technical/trades 35 | Technical/indef | Teachers 5 | Prof. artists |
| Clerical, shop 12 | Technical/indef | Art students 3 | Prof. artists |
| Teacher trainee 1 | Professional | Designers 2 | Technical |
| None 15 | Varied | Photographer 1 | Technical |
|  |  | Telegraphist 1 | Professional |
|  |  | None 6 | Indeterminate |

Source: Province of Ontario, Sessional Papers (1882).

stages, and London, Ontario, the first eight, and both schools added a version of South Kensington's twenty-third stage. In Britain, the art world had long divided on teaching and its role – whether to train industrial or "real" artists, and whether to follow South Kensington or the Royal Academy, respectively. The same division was apparent in Canada. Richard Baigent (1830–1890), an influential member of the Ontario society, wrote that art in a liberal and general education was meant to produce artists but also to "place within the reach of all such an education in form and colour as shall enable any one to ascertain and unfold whatever capability he may possess of observation and imitation or of pictorial expression."[69]

In 1882, the Toronto school transferred to the Department of Education, with Dr May becoming the school's superintendent, and it physically relocated from King Street to the normal school, placing it close to the Educational Museum, which Dr May directed from 1879 on. May explained the relocation: "This has been done with an understanding that special instruction be imparted, embracing subjects of a practical character suitable to mechanics, and as bearing on their employments, in which the arts of drawing and design may be accessories, and of benefit in their respective occupations. Also, that classes be conducted for the training of Teachers who may hereafter conduct drawing-classes throughout this Province. It is considered that which will afford honourable and useful employment to women, and that many will avail themselves of these advantages, and particularly those to whom self-support may be necessary."[70]

The ageing collection now available to students had its detractors. In a January 1884 editorial, the *Toronto World* opined that art education would create occupational possibilities for women in art and industrial design but attacked the collection, which John George Hodgins of the Department of Education still claimed to be "admirable": "It is much better to get rid of the worthless collection with which good Dr. Ryerson in his inexperience of art, has saddled the normal school museum, and to buy a very few good and original pictures, one of which would teach the student more than acres of chromos and copies that look like chromos."[71]

After his initial collecting spree in Europe between 1855 and 1867, Ryerson had added little to the museum collection.[72] During the 1870s, new art from members of the Ontario Society of Artists joined the copies of old masters, but soon the museum's days as an adjunct to art education were near their end. During the 1880s, the Canadian Institute developed a scientific museum with collections in archaeology, mineralogy, and ornithology.[73] David Boyle (1842–1911), its curator, was a self-taught archaeologist who undertook field-work on Ontario native sites with the support of the Liberal minister of education, George W. Ross, and funds from his department. In 1896, Ross moved to expand the provincial museum at the normal school by adding one storey and transferring the Canadian Institute's collection to it. Boyle was curator of archaeology, but stepped up to the superintendency in 1901. After his death in 1911, the museum became part of the Royal Ontario Museum under the control of the University of Toronto. Its change in focus led to the dispersal of Ryerson's art collection, most of it to other provincial normal schools.

In 1883, May acknowledged the system of art instruction in Massachusetts and the night schools in Quebec, but claimed: "At the present time, Ontario has equal if not superior advantages to any other country for Art education, as we have over one hundred Mechanics' Institutes liberally assisted by the Legislature and encouraged to establish classes for technical education."[74] With enrolments of about 1,500 in the mechanics' institutes, and few of those in drawing, it seems an overestimation. May had strong opinions: "Art in this country has long been considered as an amusement or a luxury; it, however, stands in the foremost ranks of practical subjects; it is valuable to every person and concerns the advancement of the rich as well as the poor; it exercises an influence for culture and refinement, and when applied to the commonest product of labor, it increases its value ... It is one of the necessities of the workingman's education, and there is no department of science and art, or industry, where it is not called into requisition."[75]

And what was valuable for the individual was also key to national prosperity. Sounding like Henry Cole, May noted: "The value of this technical education to the manufacturers of this Province must be very great, as those countries which encourage education in the Arts and Sciences become the most prosperous and wealthy. The principal factor in the value of a manufactured article is the design and artistic skill employed in its manufacture. Technical education also effects a saving of labor. Experts state that a knowledge of drawing, which is the fundamental principle of technical education, saves at least one-third of the labor in large manufactories."[76]

Members at the Ontario Society of Artists soon tired of May's strong opinions as the department's representative on the school's board. When O'Brien resigned as the society's representative on the board in 1884, the society withdrew from the school's control. While the minister, George Ross, understood the tensions, he left May in place. These events did not impress Archibald MacMurchy (1832–1912), new editor of the *Canada Educational Monthly*. Why had the society backed out of running the school? Where was the evidence that teaching drawing would aid industry? MacMurchy himself followed Baigent's (and John Ruskin's) lead in seeing a broader calling for art teaching: "Art education would look beyond mere training of the young artisan in simple elementary industrial form and design – it would aim at a general advancement of the public taste by such a course of instruction as would have for its principle the dissemination of art knowledge as a formative power. The artificer in artistic embellishment has to depend on the public taste, and the higher or purer taste cannot be secured if the public be too ignorant to appreciate, or be unable to decide on the true merits of the production."[77]

In 1890, the society resumed management of the school and renamed it the Central Ontario School of Art and Design. In its subsequent history, it relocated several times, building up a solid reputation in art instruction; it survives as the Ontario College of Art and Design University.

### Other Art Schools

Despite the problems at the central school, art education expanded throughout the province in individual art schools, rather than in the integrated manner of Massachusetts, with institutions appearing in Ottawa (1879), Kingston (1884), and Hamilton (1886), and also in

Brockville and St Thomas. (Most survived until the turn of the century, when either they closed or local schools absorbed them.) Each affiliated with the Toronto school during this period. In 1885, the Department of Education received authority to establish regulations and administration for local schools of art, with all following the same curriculum and examinations for provincial certificates.[78] The system worked well. Between 1882 and 1895, the department awarded 43,576 elementary art certificates and 2,600 advanced, including 327 in ornamental design. Between 1883 and 1895, certificates in mechanical drawing numbered 1,005; certificates in extra subjects for 1885–95 totalled 954.

The earliest form of drawing that mechanics' institutes taught was linear drawing, as the basis for mechanical or architectural drawing, not as an aesthetic exercise. Drawing classes moved in a step-wise fashion, so that students would master one technical skill before practising another. Before there were enough trained art teachers, elementary and high school teachers worked with drawing books, which provided examples for both mechanical drawing and freehand copying. Between 1882 and 1886, Ontario schools employed Walter Smith's drawing books, already in use in Massachusetts and Quebec; a Montreal printing of Smith's *Technical Education and Industrial Drawing in Public Schools* appeared in 1883. In 1886, the homegrown *Dominion Drawing Books* replaced them. By 1890, the Toronto *Globe* exulted in the progress: while art training originally emerged for the trades and to produce teachers for mechanics' institutes, it was now providing Ontarians with a better aesthetic vision.[79] Still, some artistic quarters disparaged the South Kensington approach to drawing. English artist and critic John Ruskin (1819–1900) opposed it vehemently and believed that Henry Cole had destroyed English art instruction. There was clearly tension between the members of the Ontario Society of Artists and the bureaucrats who controlled art training in the province. Charles D. Gaitskell, in his 1948 report to the Department of Education, *Art Education in the Province of Ontario*, commented on the South Kensington system of art training: "The methodology was based upon an extreme form of authoritarianism. The series of drawing books tended to keep the programme uniform and rigid throughout the schools ... This type of drawing cannot be said to be art since the personal factor of expression is largely, if not entirely, eliminated."[80]

Of course, Gaitskell was writing in a post–John Dewey educational world and from the point of view of a professional artist. The South Kensington system came into being to train working men in a technical skill, one that they could use to improve industrial design. Cole and his associates believed that such training could improve a person's aesthetic sense as a by-product of the training. In a sense, both Ruskin and Gaitskell were wrong, as many successful artists in the United Kingdom, Canada, and the United States commenced their formal tuition in this "uniform and rigid" system.

## CONCLUSION

During the last third of the nineteenth century, the yawning divide between Ontario's industrial needs and what its bureaucracy could or would provide is very evident. Mechanics' institutes, an idea of the 1830s, were hopelessly out of date in the 1870s and beyond. Institutes were too small, too poor, and too unconnected to provide technical instruction for the rapidly changing industrial segment of Ontario's workers. Despite carrots and sticks from the Departments of Agriculture and Education, the institutes' evening classes never coped with technical education; indeed, they were marginal even with adult general education. In the end, they could not compete with the provincial educational system. While Samuel May retained his faith in providing technical instruction first through evening classes and then through art instruction following the South Kensington lead, it could not succeed. Ontario simply was not England. Ontarians wanted libraries, and in the end that is what they obtained. When it seemed that a special institution, the School of Practical Science, might provide the working class with trades training, the professionalizing university quickly absorbed it for its own purposes. Over time, art instruction drifted from artisanal orientation to aesthetics. By the end of the century, technical education for the working class was almost nowhere in Ontario.

# 8

# Technical Education in Quebec

For Quebec, as in Ontario, provincial administration of agriculture and education took some time to become workable. The single greatest difference in how the two provinces evolved was in the machinery for technical instruction. While the Board of Arts and Manufactures disappeared in Ontario, its analogue carried on with only cosmetic changes in Quebec. Because of the decline of mechanics' institutes in Quebec, activities of that province's board affected technical instruction more directly, because there were no intermediaries analogous to the Agriculture and Arts Association of Ontario and the Association of Mechanics' Institutes of Ontario. Confessional and linguistic divisions also made the story more complex than Ontario's, but in the end neither jurisdiction had much to show for thirty more years of discussion and activity.

The six parts of this chapter examine technical education in Quebec: the context (workers, industry, and education); the decline of the mechanics' institutes after Confederation; the night schools of the Council of Arts and Manufactures; art education and technical instruction; the history of engineering education; and the relations between technical education and adult education.

## WORKERS, INDUSTRY, AND EDUCATION

### Workers and Industry

Quebec industrialized at the same time as Ontario but in a somewhat different way.[1] Ontario's population outstripped Quebec's in the second half of the century, although neither grew spectacularly fast, and both bled emigrants to the US Midwest and New England. However, Ontario's industry grew much faster: Quebec's industrial workers were nearly 70 per cent as numerous as Ontario's in 1871, but only 58 per cent of Ontario's in 1891.[2] Ontario urbanized more rapidly – in 1891, it had Toronto and ten other cities with 10,000 or more people, while Quebec had only five: Hull, Montreal, Quebec, Sherbrooke, and Valleyfield. These cities were the loci of secondary and service industries.

Montreal, being so large, dominated the economic landscape.[3] Although the provincial capital was in Quebec, a city that was essentially its equal in population and industry early in the century, it began to slip economically as its traditional industries – the square-timber trade and shipbuilding – faded. Montreal vaulted forward in the 1850s and 1860s, thanks to being a railway hub and through the development of industry along the Lachine Canal. By the 1860s, its port, with both ocean-going and Great Lakes shipping, was one of the busiest in North America. Already the commercial and financial capital of Canada, its increasing industrial strength made it the national metropolis into the twentieth century. By 1901, it had one and one-half times the population of Toronto, its only serious rival.

Secondary industry grew up in direct connection with primary industry: flour milling and sugar refining, along with the production of building and metal products from the factories and foundries along the Lachine. By the 1880s, production for consumers was expanding – food processing, shoe and boot manufacturing, textiles and clothing, and tobacco products – while the Grand Trunk Railway's Pointe-St-Charles shops turned out railway rolling stock. Outside the city, industrial growth was most evident in the small towns of the Eastern Townships and in the towns close to Montreal, such as Joliette, St-Hyacinthe, and Sorel. Most industry by this time was in the cities and towns, and the last three decades of the century saw a real shift away from pioneer industries. Table 8.1 compares some Quebec industries with 500 or more establishments in 1870 and 1890. Clearly, traditional ones stagnated, consolidated, or grew slowly, while those that added value grew more rapidly – most notably, men's and women's ready-made wear and the dairy industry. Much of the clothing, food (except butter and cheese production), footware, and textile industries concentrated in Montreal.

The growth of new industry in search of cheap labour led to the hiring of many women and children in Montreal, as it did in Toronto and Hamilton.[4] The rise of factory production had already displaced rural women in the dairy industry. Displaced rural people and immigrants made up much of the urban working class, most of which held down

Table 8.1  Changes in numbers of industrial establishments, Quebec (1870–90)

|  | 1870 | 1890 | Increase/decrease (%) |
|---|---|---|---|
| Sawmills | 2,104 | 1,027 | -51 |
| Flour mills | 810 | 871 | +8 |
| Forges | 2,129 | 2,726 | +28 |
| Shoes/boot manufacturers | 1,419 | 1,905 | +34 |
| Carriage builders | 841 | 1,136 | +35 |
| Bakeries | 471 | 687 | +46 |
| Men's clothing | 359 | 1,052 | +193 |
| Women's clothing | 333 | 1,883 | +465 |
| Creameries/cheese factories | 25 | 728 | +2,812 |

Source: Adapted from Angers and Parenteau, Statistiques manufacturières du Québec, Table 24.

low-paying work requiring few skills. Probably many of these workers had eluded elementary school or were illiterate; for those of marginal literacy, adult instruction would be the only means of furthering their education. Mechanics' institutes and similar organizations would assist only those on the upper rungs of labour, those with very skilled trades. When labour organization grew up in Canada, skilled tradesmen led it. As we saw above with the life memberships of the Mechanics' Institute of Montreal, the list consists of skilled tradesmen, not factory operatives or labourers. With the latter's preponderance over skilled labour in Quebec, the need for education was great, but opportunities for it were few if any.

Apprenticeship had been withering for decades. By 1888, a survey of apprenticeships for a dozen major trades showed none available for teasers and spinners of wool and cotton; the older apprentice system for joiners and coopers dead; a partial or brief apprenticeship available to coach builders, millers, shoemakers, tailors, tanners, and typographers; and the only legal apprenticeships on offer to cigar-makers and marble-cutters.[5]

## Education, Religion, and Language

The transition of Canada East's system of education after Confederation was difficult. Pierre-Joseph-Olivier Chauveau led the Conservatives to victory in the first provincial election in 1867. Having been superintendent of public instruction since 1855, he naturally retained that post, now as minister, when the legislature created the Department of Public Instruction in 1868. Superintendent Egerton Ryerson, in Toronto, could direct a unified educational system, in which the Roman Catholic separate schools' curriculum was firmly under his control. After 1876, under succeeding ministers, Ontario's Department of Education became more dominant and bureaucratic as the century wore on. Chauveau, in contrast, faced powerful rivals for control of public education: the Roman Catholic hierarchy and its lay allies pressed for greater power while anglophone Protestants fiercely defended their educational rights.

A complicating factor in Quebec was the lack of unanimity in the Roman Catholic Church itself. For decades, Montreal, with the most people, and Quebec, the seat of the archbishop, had struggled with each other. Ultramontanism, with its rejection of liberalism of any kind and its complete fealty to the pope, had emerged in church circles after the French revolution. First establishing itself in Canada in the 1820s, its greatest promoter was Bishop Ignace Bourget. The Canadian Ultramontanes, for whom the state was subordinate to the church, naturally strongly opposed both *rouge* politicians and the Institut canadien movement, both fostering liberal and democratic ideals. Ultramontane church leaders forged alliances with conservative politicians to ensure control; as Fahmy-Eid remarks, "[Les rouges] qui constituèrent, durant deux décennies au moins, la faction radicale de la petite-bourgeoisie, étaient alors identifiés comme les ennemis communs des deux groupes, considérés comme représentant une menace sérieuse à l'exercice du pouvoir hégémonique auquel visait, chacun de son côté, le clergé autant que la faction conservatrice (majoritaire) de la petite bourgeoisie."[6]

This alliance of conservatives and the clergy thwarted the liberalization of education in Quebec from the mid-1870s onward. Despite the Ultramontanes' strong opposition to liberal ideas of any kind, they undertook surprisingly little debate on the place of science in society.[7] Apart from the ravings of Jules-Paul Tardivel, who saw conspiracies of the *francs-maçons* (freemasons) everywhere, Quebec intellectuals had little issue with science. Even the seminaries and *collèges classiques*, many of whose staff members were Ultramontanes, continued to teach science.

The Province of Canada created the Council of Public Instruction for Lower Canada in 1856 to support the superintendent. The council consisted of ten Catholics and four Protestants, most of them lay people. After intense lobbying and threats by Protestant councillors and members of the assembly, Chauveau had to grant virtual autonomy to the Protestant schools in the Educational Act of 1869. Although the council remained in place, it effectively split into two autonomous confessional committees with greater clerical membership. Chauveau's Conservative successor as premier and minister, Gédéon Ouimet, had attempted to follow Ryerson's lead by introducing a book depository and to mandate textbooks for schools; the hierarchy and allies forced him to back down on both counts. In 1875, Conservative Premier de Boucherville closed down the ministry, to the satisfaction of the Catholic hierarchy; educational direction now reverted to its pre-Confederation form, but with parallel systems in place. Thus a powerful educational bureaucracy could not emerge in Quebec as it had in Ontario, where the Protestant majority divided along sectarian lines, and the mutual distrust among them allowed Ryerson and his successors to maintain a "secular" system with little organized opposition.

Behind these machinations in Quebec lay a larger-scale debate about the church's role in education and the nature of that education. Anglophones supported a number of academies, the equivalent of the grammar schools of Upper Canada. For francophones, the church-run *collèges classiques* held an almost total monopoly over secondary education to well into the twentieth century. Their roots date back to the Jesuit Collège de Québec, founded in 1635. During the nineteenth century, twenty-seven colleges or seminaries were in operation, although some failed after a few years. These were all church-run private schools for boys, with almost all teachers being clergymen. Following the French model, the classical curriculum built on elementary studies with a little mathematics and, for the few students who remained to the end of the program, some science, often reasonably up to date. As Galarneau notes, most students were heading for the priesthood, law, or medicine.[8] Convent schools for girls focused on general education and domestic skills. Although middle-class women were more literate than men, and even though they attended school for far less time, most had only two career options besides homemaking: teaching or roles in the church. The former was poorly paid and low in status.[9] Working-class girls were certainly not going to receive technical instruction in schools run by nuns, so for many of them work in the factories in industrial towns was their only occupational choice.

An overlapping set of private Catholic schools consisted of the so-called *collèges industriels*, which offered a more practical curriculum. A dozen such schools for Catholics and one for Protestants existed by 1870, with a total enrolment of a little more than 2,000, but, as Charland observes, they were really commercial or commercial-academic schools.[10] In time, most were converted into *collèges classiques*. They seem to have covered technical subjects not even at the most elementary level, but perhaps agriculture in a few of them. J.-X. Perrault, whom we met several times above, taught agriculture briefly at the industrial college in Varennes after his own agricultural school failed.

In Ontario, where the high school replaced the grammar school towards the end of the century, curricular changes slowly responded to social and economic change. Commercial courses, science, and, in time, manual training and domestic science were an admission that not all students were preparing for university and the professions. In Quebec, however, the *collèges classiques* had not evolved in the same way, even though, by century's end, anglophone high schools more closely resembled their Ontario neighbours.

Although some graduates of francophone schools entered the world of commerce or industry, most would never become engineers or tradesmen. Many members of the francophone political and social elite of Quebec were products of this system. Yet those with a more liberal outlook did understand the need for educating students for occupations in commerce and industry. Conservative Premiers Chauveau and Ouimet and Liberal Henri-Gustave Joly (premier 1878–79) all commented on the dangers of too much classical education when more practical training was essential. A few other lonely voices spoke out: the ardently anticlerical journalist Arthur Buies (1840–1901), long an advocate of secular public education, wanted more science in the schools; his contemporary, journalist L.-O. David (1840–1926), argued that classical education would not serve Quebec and that, without practical education, francophones would never be able to obtain good positions like the anglophones had.

It may seem surprising that Quebec educationists did not champion French models as opposed to British ideas. Many of them visited France and followed its educational evolution. In fact, France concentrated technical training at the higher end – its grands écoles, such as the Ecole centrale des arts et manufactures, the Ecole des mines, the Ecole des ponts et chaussées, and the Ecole polytechnique all emerged before the revolution of 1830 and educated the technical elite, not the common worker. The Conservatoire national des arts et métiers had offered lectures on science applied to art as early as 1819, but, according to Prost, "Ces cours demandaient une assiduité et un niveau de connaissances qui en écartaient la plupart des ourvriers."[11] By 1868, private organizations provided more than 400 night classes, and trade unions also offered classes, as apprenticeship was practically dead in France. Jules Ferry's Education Law of 1867 called for the teaching of manual work and use of tools, along with drawing and modelling. But neither that law nor industrial training acts in the 1880s brought about immediate technical instruction.[12] Observers in Quebec concluded that their system could learn more from the Americans.

## DECLINE OF THE MECHANICS' INSTITUTES

The mechanics'-institute movement was not as extensive in Quebec as in Ontario before Confederation, and those institutes that did exist probably had anglophone directors. In the 1840s, the francophone middle class had begun to migrate to the Institut canadien or to similar church-related literary or library organizations. With the loss of government funding after 1858, most mechanics' institutes had disappeared, leaving almost no trace. The Mechanics' Institute of Montreal remained an anglophone, Protestant bastion. The francophone elite and middle class had several organizations of their own, but there was nothing for the burgeoning working class until 1865, when the Institut des artisans canadiens de Montréal formed; it incorporated the following year. Editor J.-X. Perrault applauded this in the pages of his *Revue agricole*, adding that the Institut had already enrolled 600 men and could easily reach 1,000 if it offered night classes, a library, and a collection of models – in short, a *conservatoire des arts et metiers*. This was, of course, what the Board of Arts and Manufactures for Lower Canada was to have developed nearly a decade earlier. In its philosophy, the Institut differed in no major way from a mechanics' institute: "Le but de cet Institut est d'offrir à ses membres des moyens d'instruction dans les principes des arts et dans les différentes branches de la science et de leur donner les connaissances qui peuvent leur être utiles, nécessaires ou avantageuses, par le moyen d'une bibliothèque, d'une salle de lecture, d'un musée, de lecture et de classes."[13]

Fees were $2 annually for master artisans, merchants, and bourgeois and $1 for labourers, apprentices, and clerks. Lawyer and publisher L.-O. David carried news of the Institut in the pages of his *L'opinion publique*, which he edited in the early 1870s. He saluted the prime mover, industrialist J.-B. Rolland (1815–1888). Rolland, president in 1869, had resuscitated the Institut canadien-français and would later serve on the Council of Arts and Manufactures. David himself would address the Institut in October 1871, sparring with Gédéon Ouimet. The artist Napoléon Bourassa (1827–1916), who taught at the Institut, was president in 1870. Another prominent director was Dominique Boudrias, who would later teach at the Ecole normale Jacques-Cartier. Other officers were clearly middle class, so the Institut effectively was no different from the Mechanics' Institute of Montreal except in its language of operation.

The Institut's directors, however, did have a grievance. The president in 1871 emphasized the Institut's gaining representation on the Board of Arts and Manufactures, where French Canadians had hitherto had so little influence. Perrault shared that opinion, claiming that the Institut emerged partly because the board had ignored French Canadians and that, while every county had agricultural societies, workers in the towns did not organize themselves accordingly. The reason was, according to Perrault, because the board kept all the funds for itself, while the Institut, for example, received not one penny.[14] This was a bit disingenuous: the agricultural societies received much more funding than the board's paltry $2,000, which would not have stretched very far if it went to mechanics' institutes. However, Perrault knew the law; groups with at least twenty members could have a representative on the board.

There is no record of when evening classes first became an important function of the Institut, but they were in operation in 1870, possibly earlier. An advertisement in *L'opinion publique* announced three school locations, with classes in arithmetic, bookkeeping, elementary and advanced French and English, French and English grammar, French-English and English-French translation, and linear drawing and mensuration.[15] This was the same form of adult education available in Ontario, with the addition of French. Attendance must have been low: "Ouvriers, profitez donc des avantages que vous offrent ces Classes du Soir, et commencez à les fréquenter des à présent." Troubles must have accumulated, as the Institut appears in *Lovell's Directory* for 1877–78 and then seems to have disappeared.

As the provincial educational system focused on children, semi-literate young adults, many of whom had left school early to work, had few resources. Philanthropy provided little assistance, although, to help, in December 1869 the Société St Vincent de Paul in Quebec opened a free night school for young men, mostly from rural areas, who worked in factories or shops or as apprentices. Some 500 applicants appeared, suggesting a real need; the directors decided to accept only young men between fifteen and twenty-five. Classes were from 7 to 9 p.m., with an "interesting lecture" following until 10 p.m., and books and newspapers were available. The school, in quarters provided by the Christian Brothers, had five instructors, two of whom taught at the Ecole normale Laval. Within the four classes that encompassed arithmetic, bookkeeping, calligraphy, commercial education, English, and French, the emphasis was on language.[16] The province offered little else for working-class people. The only viable mechanics' institute was Montreal's; it no longer ran its own evening classes, as the Board of Arts and Manufactures had usurped them in the late 1850s and continued to operate them. The institute's Mechanics' Hall continued to be the venue of concerts and occasional lectures, but the institute itself eschewed social activities. Its library and reading room, which were essentially the remaining original components, exist to this day as the Atwater Library.

## NIGHT SCHOOLS OF THE COUNCIL OF ARTS AND MANUFACTURES

### A School of Art and Design (1867–73)

When the provincial government came into being in 1867, improbably it left in place the Board of Arts and Manufactures/Chambre des arts et manufactures. Considering how little the board had accomplished in its decade of existence, even in comparison with Canada West's, why did the Cabinet not look for an alternative or forget it altogether, as Ontario had done? Perhaps Conservative Premier Pierre-Joseph-Olivier Chauveau protected the board, on which he had sat ex officio as education super-intendent. Also, the anglophone Montreal elite that had dominated the old board would probably have lobbied to retain its form and function. Its Toronto counterpart had never developed equivalent political fire-power. In his report for 1868, Secretary Col. A.A. Stevenson reported that the premier had yet to affirm its continuing existence but believed the government would invite it to serve industrial youths.[17] Most of the board's energy had gone of late into the Paris Exposition of 1867. The never-ending saga of the Exhibition Building, on rue Ste-Catherine between University and Cathcart, continued with the militia now occupy-ing it. Drawing classes at the Mechanics' Institute and elementary classes at the Institut des artisans had gone well.

Although the board was far too large to be efficient – including as it did ex officio members, officers of the Geological Survey of Canada, profes-sors of physical science, and at least twenty representatives each from the Art Association, the Institut des artisans, and the Montreal Mechanics' Institute – its operation was in the hands of a subcommittee, seven of whose nine members in 1867–68 were anglophones. Henry Bulmer was president, George A. Drummond of the Art Association (and Redpath's) vice-president, Col. Stevenson from the Mechanic's Institute secretary, and Norton Corse from the Institut des artisans treasurer.

While the Montreal Mechanics' Institute had a history of offering drawing courses in the evening, the board now wanted to pursue its old dream of creating its own school of art and design. In the spring of 1868, partly due to prodding by the Art Association, the board began planning for such a school, because "the establishment of schools of art and design by this Board is of the utmost importance and absolutely essential to the advancement of the mechanical and manufacturing interests of this Province";[18] its design would facilitate a "technical education to the Artizans of this Province." Within a year, the board forwarded a scheme for the school in a petition to the governor general. Classes would be available in architectural construction; architectural drawing; design and modelling for manufactures; mechanical drawing; painting; practical geometry; and physics and chemistry applied to arts and manufactures – an ambitious and expensive program. The board estimated nearly $3,900 for preparing the space, and each year $1,800 for five teachers (three at $400 and two at $300) and other expenses of $2,250, for a total annual outlay of $4,050. By the summer of 1869, the school had located space on an upper floor of Molson's Bank, but funds did not allow for the full curriculum. The school opened in October 1869.[19]

Still, the board's overall impact must have been slight, as no report from it appeared in the legislature's sessional papers again until 1874. The 1871 public accounts list a grant of $2,500 to "schools of sciences applied to arts," and the education report notes a school of arts and manufactures with six teachers and forty students, presumably in Montreal. By 1873, a sum of $500 was granted for a "school of design" in Quebec; this was the first such expansion outside the metropolis. A subtle shift occurred at the same time. After Confederation, the old Board of Agriculture/ Chambre d'agriculture for Lower Canada became the Council of Agriculture/Conseil d'agriculture, but the original nomenclature survived for arts and manufactures. In 1873, the board became the Council of Arts and Manufactures for the Province of Quebec/Conseil des arts et manufactures de la Province de Québec (CAMPQ) and held its first meeting under its new name in August.[20] Samuel Cottingham Stevenson (1848–1898), Col. Stevenson's son, became secretary and remained so until his death. By the mid-1870s, he would also act as inspector of the council's schools, for which he received $500 per year.

Advocates had long touted evening classes for teaching technical matters to the working class, although the experience of the mechanics' institutes in both Canada East and Canada West had shown that classes in general elementary subjects were more popular. In a time when many people had little primary education, providing in effect elementary adult education made sense. In Ontario, the demand fell over the century, as more students became sufficiently literate and capable, thanks to public education.

For Quebec, however, several factors slowed progress, which in turn made evening classes more necessary. The participation rate in public schools was less than that of Ontario, with many students leaving school at an early age. Many of the female teachers replacing men in the last third of the century had less training, which suggests that the teaching of science and mathematics would have suffered. Also, increasing numbers of teachers were clerical; whether that would have discouraged a more scientific and technical outlook is difficult to determine. In any case, the 1891 census showed more illiterate residents twenty and older in Quebec than in Ontario.[21]

## Expansion (1873–79)

During 1873–74, the Council of Arts and Manufactures expanded its operations from Montreal and Quebec to local schools in Lévis, Sherbrooke, Sorel, and Trois-Rivières. An annual grant of only $3,000 was a severe constraint. The schools in Montreal and Quebec absorbed $1,000 and $750, respectively, primarily for teachers' salaries, and the others $200 apiece, leaving $450 for other activities, including operating the free reference library. Numbers were small: Montreal had 138 students, and the others 130, for a total of 268. Classes included architectural, linear, mechanical, and ornamental drawing, along with geometry and modelling. Secretary Samuel Stevenson admitted that the council lacked funds to encourage the teaching of science and art beyond that level.[22] In the summer of 1875, when two more schools opened in New Liverpool and St-Hyacinthe, he enthused: "An increasing desire has been manifested on the part of the working classes to avail themselves of the technical education offered to them, and we feel assured that a superior taste and finish will soon be noticeable in many of our leading lines of manufacture."[23]

Chemistry, mensuration, and watercolour painting joined the curriculum. In most cases, the council tried to have one of its members residing in the school location to act as a local supervisor. Obtaining competent drawing teachers was a continuing problem: schools opened, operated for a year or two, and then closed until a new teacher surfaced. In St-Hyacinthe, which had several manufacturing establishments, lawyer Pierre Boucher de La Bruère fostered the school, although its creation "was not without its difficulties, seeing that the pupils had no idea whatever of drawing and very few understood its usefulness."[24] Although funding had not increased, the council still dreamed of an industrial museum, maintaining its reference library, and establishing "schools of practical science and design." In fact, it struck a committee in August 1874 to work towards a normal school of art and design like that in South Kensington.

With the run-up to the Centennial Exhibition in Philadelphia in 1876, the council redoubled its efforts to press art education (see next section). Ouimet, now superintendent of public instruction, was sympathetic: his departmental report mentioned the lessons of the London exhibition of 1851 and recent efforts in France and Massachusetts, quoting sections of the council's report on its visit to art schools in Boston and New York. He believed the province required a school of art and design "from which the working class must derive the greatest benefit.[25] Taking heart, perhaps, the council now asked for an increase in its annual budget to $10,000. New classes opened in Granby, Hochelaga, Huntingdon, and St-Henri. The former board and the new council had always operated classes for men only. The council had tentatively discussed an art school for women in 1876 – these were quite common in England under the Science and Art Department – after which it opened a ladies' class in the Montreal school in 1877. Council would have liked to open a female art school like those in Boston, New York, and Philadelphia but had to concentrate on the male "artisan class" of society.

Over time, the long-serving elite members who made up the Council of Art and Manufactures gave way to new men. The council's complexion in 1877–78 represented better the interests of technical instruction: seven manufacturers, two architects, two builders, along with an artisan, an artist, a banker, a merchant, a priest, and a printer. Half were francophones, half anglophones. Napoléon Bourassa represented the art interest, and the inventor and clockmaker Cyrille Duquet (1841–1922), the artisans; however, the pro-Conservative newspaper *La Minerve* believed that the twenty-month ministry of Henri-Gustave Joly in 1878 and 1879 had stacked the council with liberals: "Cette illustre aéropage occupe assez peu d'art et ne manufacture que de la politique. Voulant récompenser M. Joly de l'inquieté de leur propre nomination, ils s'ingénient à faire des misères à leur sécretaire, dont le seul tort est d'être conservateur."[26] The council now turned the direction of schools over to local management committees. Enrolments were encouraging: at the end of 1879, 1,482 students, 152 more than the previous year, although Stevenson cautioned: "We must not forget that this work of Industrial

Education is only commencing in this Province, and we must not be dissatisfied if the results fall short of what we anticipate."[27] He also echoed the refrain so common in Ontario: "It is a matter of regret that our manufacturers do not give to our Schools the encouragement and support they deserve; the object of Schools is to educate the working classes and improve the taste. If our manufacturers are to be successful, and if they are to hold their own against foreign competitors, our workmen must have intelligence and skill, because, in the end, the cheapest of all labor is skilled labor."[28]

The council's mandate included organizing the industrial section of provincial and international exhibitions in cooperation with the Council of Agriculture. In 1879, it corresponded with the Agricultural and Arts Association of Ontario to develop plans for the first Dominion Exhibition. After nearly twenty years of debts, law suits, and squabbling, the province finally took over the Crystal Palace on rue Ste-Catherine and relocated it to the new exhibition grounds at Mile End, where the council had hoped to locate its Montreal school and offices. By 1879, it removed the free library of reference from the Montreal Mechanics' Institute and sent the older books to the parliamentary library in Quebec. Many of the dozen schools staged annual exhibitions of student works, and in 1880 the new Royal Canadian Academy invited several teachers to join it.

### Adding Technical Education (1880–1900 and Beyond)

Until the 1880s, almost all school instruction focused on drawing, but Stevenson suggested moving into technical education more generally and examining American schools such as the Massachusetts Institute of Technology, the New York trade schools, the Stevens Institute of Technology in New Jersey, and the Worcester Polytechnic Institute in Massachusetts; he also visited C.M. Woodward's Manual Training School in St Louis, Missouri. In Quebec, only the council's Montreal school had developed technical training beyond drawing, with classes in chemistry, lithography, wood carving, and wood engraving. Despite a slash in its yearly budget from $10,000 to $3,000, it ran schools sporadically in Fraserville, Iberville, Ste-Cunégone, St-Jean, St-Jérôme, and Sillery. Still canvassing for ideas, Henry Bulmer travelled to London in 1886 to look around South Kensington. Stevenson followed later that year, accompanying Ouimet in a fact-finding tour that also took them to Paris to see technical and evening schools and the Ecole polytechnique. In his report to the council later, Stevenson noted that English teachers, despite good training, made their evening program too advanced for Canadian needs, although council-supported schools sometimes did as well as corresponding English schools.[29] With his interest in trades training, Stevenson particularly esteemed the City and Guilds of London Institute, which had offered classes to artisans since 1880. Perhaps in response to these visits, the council introduced practical work, in addition to mere copying, in drawing and trades classes. Montreal added pattern-making for shoemakers, plumbing, and stair-building; Farnham, carpentry; and Sorel, stair-building.

The number of schools had remained fairly stable at a dozen, as did enrolments, typically about 1,200 each year. Despite the introduction of trades and manual training, however, problems still remained. The council's president, publisher Samuel Dawson (1833–1916), noted in his 1888–89 report that the average attendance was only about half the initial enrolment: "At Montreal the committee had always been embarrassed by the fact that on the opening of the classes, a large number put down their names, attended for two or three evenings, and then stayed away. These idlers might have been endured if they had not blocked the reception of more earnest students."[30] A possible solution was to charge a one-dollar deposit on enrolment and return it on successful completion. With only eleven schools in operation, the council found local authorities apathetic and unwilling to raise funds for schools. A wider issue for the council was labour's lack of dignity. Council members, believing that society needed to deflate the value of professionals and those who distribute goods, reasoned that a central day school for practical manual training might help improve society's view of industrial labour. This American idea was causing increasing debate and had some traction in Ontario.

During the 1890s, total enrolments reached a plateau of about 1,000. Table 8.2 indicates the schools' curriculum in 1891–92. The language of instruction depended on the locale: in 1893, the Montreal school had nine francophone and five anglophone instructors (with some duplication of courses in both languages); Quebec, five francophones and one anglophone; Granby, two francophone monks; Huntingdon, two anglophones; Iberville, one francophone monk; Lévis, four francophones; New Liverpool, one of each language; St-Hyacinthe, one francophone; and Sorel, one francophone.

An 1894 list of former students at Montreal suggests that the council's schools were, in fact, reaching and training artisans.[31] In the mechanical class, the twenty-nine former students, mostly anglophones, represented several trades, including draughtsmen, engineers, foremen, and machinists; eleven had left the province or the country altogether. The eighteen

Table 8.2 Subjects taught in evening schools, CAMPQ (1891–92)

| | Number of students | Freehand drawing | Mechanical drawing | Architectural drawing | Geometry | Linear | Mensuration | Specialized |
|---|---|---|---|---|---|---|---|---|
| Montreal | 261 | • | • | • | | | | modelling and sculpture lithography decorative painting stair construction plumbing shoemaking |
| Quebec | 249 | • | • | • | | | | modelling decorative painting stair construction plumbing shoemaking |
| Lévis | 284 | • | • | • | | | | technical drawing steam engines |
| Sherbrooke | 104 | • | • | • | • | | | |
| Huntingdon | 81 | • | • | | | | | |
| New Liverpool | 62 | • | • | | | | | |
| St-Hyacinthe | 33 | • | | | | | | industry |
| Sorel | 33 | | | | | • | | industry |
| St-Jérôme | 21 | | | | | | • | |
| Totals | 1128 | | | | | | | |

Source: Province of Quebec, Sessional Papers, 1892.

former architecture students, a few of them francophone, had become architects, carpenters, clerks, contractors, and moulders. The fifty-eight alumni of decorative painting, half of whom were francophone, were almost all active as decorators. The twenty-four in lithography, about one-third of them francophone, were mostly engravers and lithographers; two had left for France and two for the United States. The stair-building class of sixteen, about half francophone, worked as contractors, foremen, or stair builders. Of the thirty-one students of the boot and shoe-pattern class, almost all were francophones working in the local shoe industry. Finally, forty-nine veterans of modelling-wood carving, mostly francophones, had employment as architects, carvers, cutters, modellers, and painters; three had moved to Paris, but the rest worked in the province.

For a large city, these numbers are small and statistically insignificant, yet in this sample it appears that francophone students gravitated towards the traditional and decorative trades and to the city's largest industry – shoe and boot manufacturing. Indeed, the council had hopes of forming a specialized school of shoemaking.

After 1895, the school network under the aegis of the Council of Arts and Manufactures shrank to just seven branches – Montreal, Quebec, Lévis, St-Hyacinthe, Sherbrooke, Sorel, and Trois-Rivières – but continued, with between 850 and 1,000 students. After twenty years, the issue of female classes again arose when the Montreal Women's Club petitioned the council for female classes. The response was cautious: "There is some doubt as to whether the act constituting the Council provides for classes for women, but in any way great care will be required in dealing with the subject."[32] Council discussed the matter over the next year and planned to offer classes in cooking, millinery, and needlework. Dress-cutting might be possible too, not for commercial purposes, however, being "specially useful in the homes of the middle classes."[33] In 1895–96, Mme E.L. Ethier taught dress-cutting to a dozen women.

The Montreal school rented quarters. In the mid-1890s, J.C. Wilson, a member of the council, offered $5,000 towards a permanent home if the city and province matched the funds; nothing came of the proposal. Technical education was simply not on the provincial government's agenda. Boucher de la Bruère was now superintendent of public instruction. Although a friend of technical education, active both in art education and in the dairy industry, he was also a staunchly conservative Catholic and could not countenance the state's running the system. In 1897, however, the council's president, L.-I. Boivin, and secretary,

Stevenson, wrote directly to the premier suggesting that the province follow Britain's lead on technical education. There, in 1889, the Technical Instruction Act had authorized the new county councils to levy rates to fund local technical schools, to which the government added the residue of duties from alcohol sales, the so-called whiskey money. Boivin and Stevenson suggested that Quebec adopt a similar scheme. If it levied a tax of just 5 per cent on alcohol sales by innkeepers and liquor sellers in Montreal, it could collect some $140,000 – sufficient to build a fine technical school – in five years.[34] Nothing came of this proposal, either. Whereas the ineffective technical instruction of the mechanics' institutes in Ontario was finally shutting down, the marginally successful schools that the Council of Arts and Manufactures for the Province of Quebec operated survived into the 1920s.

### ART EDUCATION AND TECHNICAL INSTRUCTION

The place of art education in Canadian society was deeply ambiguous. Instruction in drawing, the core of the evening schools of Quebec's Council of Arts and Manufactures, was a means to an end: the first step towards better industrial design. However, as in Ontario, most artists in Quebec pursuing fine art in itself or as a commercial pursuit did not think of themselves as having anything to offer to technical education, but some artists, to earn a living, worked in both realms.

### The Art Association of Montreal

Although Montreal, as Canada's metropolis, had the population and wealth to support and develop the arts, progress was slow and often halting. The short-lived Montreal Society of Artists, which successful artists such as Cornelius Krieghoff (1815–1872) and James Duncan (1806–1881) founded in 1847, exhibited its members' works. Its successor was the Society of Canadian Artists, which formed in 1867 and incorporated in 1870, although Robert Harris notes that internal strife weakened it in time.[35] Individual artists took on students, but no systematic art education, as in Britain and France, existed. Art lovers and collectors had organized the Art Association of Montreal in February 1860. A project of the anglophone social elite, the association naturally reached out to South Kensington for guidance as well as financial assistance; Henry Cole responded by providing literature on the South Kensington Museum and its collections.[36] In 1868, the association had petitioned the Board of Arts and Manufactures for Lower Canada to establish a drawing school.

Exhibitions formed the association's primary activity until 1879, when the estate of Benaiah Gibb (d. 1877) gave it a collection of paintings, a site in Philips Square, and funds to erect a gallery. Although Gibb had directed the merchant-tailor firm his father founded, he, like fellow association members, had risen above the artisan class. Art classes commenced in 1880, but results were below expectations. In 1883, it brought in South Kensington trainee Robert Harris (1849–1919) to direct the classes, which continued for only three years; his friend landscape painter William Brymner (1855–1925) succeeded him and directed the school until his death. Brymner's initial art training came from the abbé Chabert in Montreal, and his mature studies were in Paris. Under both Harris and Brymner, fine art, not drawing for technical training, was the focus of the school.

### Art Education: Napoléon Bourassa and Joseph Chabert

Drawing as a form of technical education was an activity of the Montreal Mechanics' Institute and the Board of Arts and Manufactures in pre-Confederation days. By the late 1860s, the need to expand the teaching of drawing was becoming acute. On his educational tour to Europe in 1866–67, P.-J.-O. Chauveau had observed the strides in technical education, especially in Belgium and Prussia, but concluded that Quebec lagged most in art education;[37] however, other actors were in motion, including Napoléon Bourassa, the abbé Joseph Chabert, and Edmond-Marie Templé.

Napoléon Bourassa, after studies at the Petit Séminaire de Montréal, had articled with a lawyer, soon discovered a love for art, worked with the Quebec painter Théophile Hamel, and then spent three years in Europe.[38] After drawing entered the curriculum of Montreal's Ecole normale Jacques-Cartier, Bourassa taught there 1861–63 and at the Collège Sainte-Marie and in the Institut des artisans' night school in 1867. That year, he gave a public lecture, "De l'utilité des cours publics [sic] de dessin." Though very much part of the fine-art tradition, he favoured more practical teaching than the Art Association or the Institut des artisans and in 1868 argued, in his own *Revue canadienne*, for a more practically oriented school.

The abbé Joseph Chabert (1831–1894) was a curious figure in the annals of Canadian art.[39] Born in France, he was a novice of the Pères de Sainte-Croix but left them in 1864. He seems to have studied for three years at the Ecole des beaux-arts in Paris. After he came to Canada in 1865 as a member of an evangelical mission to the north, illness diverted him to Canada East, where he found a position teaching drawing at the Séminaire de Ste-Thérèse; another post followed at the Séminaire de Terrebonne. Chabert later moved to Ottawa, where he opened an art school in 1866. In a lecture before the Institut canadien d'Ottawa in 1867, he argued for educating the working class in art, as his school's name emphasized: Institution nationale des Beaux Arts, appliqués à l'industrie.

Chabert's interest in Bourassa's work and views on the teaching of drawing perhaps attracted him to Montreal, where he sought a post at the Ecole normale Jacques-Cartier by lobbying the principal, the abbé Hospice Verreau, but Premier Chauveau blocked his appointment. So in January 1870 he set up l'Institut national des beaux-arts, science, arts et metiers et industrie; wealthy leather merchant J.-B. Prat (or John Pratt, 1812–1876) provided it space on the rue St-Jacques.

At first, Chabert's school went well, with the blessing of Bishop Bourget. Chabert was able to obtain artistic materials from the French government and broadened his program to include mathematics and mechanics as well as architecture, drawing, engraving, painting, sculpture, and technical drawing. In 1875, he incorporated the institute and obtained a $1,000 grant from the provincial government. That same year, he launched a short-lived journal for the working class, *L'ouvrier et le propriétaire*. Then, Chabert's life began to unravel: he faced a charge of assault; patron Prat died; and the Council of Arts and Manufactures delayed his grant. While his Institut moved quarters and carried on as best it could, Chabert left for a two-year stay in Europe. On his return in 1879, finding that the school had been vandalized, he closed it. He tried to revive it in the mid-1880s but faced three further charges, and in 1887 a fire destroyed his possessions. The shattered Chabert was committed to a mental institution in January 1888 and remained there for the rest of his life.

Chabert's institute had an uneasy relationship with the Council of Arts and Manufactures, through which it received its grant. It was next door to the council's Montreal school on rue St-Gabriel, and the council believed that it poached students, who would return to the council school later in the term, disrupting it. By the summer of 1883, authorities seized and sold Chabert's defunct school, allowing the council to take over the building.[40]

Chauveau, when premier (1867–73), had hoped to make drawing part of the regular elementary-school curriculum, but there weren't enough trained teachers. When de Boucherville served as premier (1874–78), he first asked Brother Alphraates, superior of the Christian Brothers in

Quebec, to add the subject in the order's schools. As a result, the brother travelled to Europe to seek teachers and purchase equipment. About the same time, de Boucherville dispatched Bourassa to Europe to survey methods of art training and collect pedagogical materials. Meanwhile, the council, also wanting properly trained teachers, sent Henry Bulmer to the National Art Training School in South Kensington in 1873 to encourage its graduates to emigrate to Canada; he collected letters from several interested students, but in the end no one followed through.

Yet the council remained adamant about doing something:

> In view of the valuable results which have been achieved by Great Britain, France, the United States and other countries in the cultivation of Art, as necessary to all communities engaged in manufacturing enterprises, it is deemed a matter of the highest importance that this Council should adopt such measures as may be found available for the cultivation of Art, by the employment of one or more persons trained in Great Britain or other foreign schools whose services may be availed of in the instruction of school teachers, and also of such other pupils it may be found convenient and desirable to instruct and also by the employment of all necessary means and appliances, which such foreign schools shall or may afford.[41]

### Drawing Manuals: Smith v. Templé

In 1875, the Council of Arts and Manufactures appointed a committee to investigate art teaching in Boston, New York, and Philadelphia. The group learned that US art schools aimed as much at keeping domestic industry competitive with its European rivals as at expanding general education: "The material prosperity of the State depends chiefly upon the profits of its manufactories. That these profits might be immensely augmented by the application of a higher artistic skill, is no longer doubted by any well informed person."[42] Canadians had better heed this message if they wished to remain an industrial nation, and "a grand effort should be made to place our Schools of Art and general Technical education on such a footing as to spread such education widely amongst the masses."[43] During the committee members' visit to Boston, Walter Smith's achievements and methods much impressed them, and the following year Montreal observers at the Centennial Exhibition in Philadelphia viewed the classwork from Massachusetts. Smith had based a series of drawing manuals on the South Kensington system, and the council decided to adopt them for its own schools, where they remained in use until 1891.

Smith's manuals entered both Protestant and Catholic schools in 1877, but progress in teaching drawing was slow. To stimulate discussion, the council brought Smith to Montreal in April and May 1882 to give a public lecture and to meet with teachers. He spoke first on industrial drawing; like Cole, he believed anyone could learn to draw, but industrial drawing specifically "would assist the artisan in the workshops to be a more economical workman, to use his material to better advantage, to produce a more tasteful object, and would, therefore, make him of more value to himself as a laborer, more profitable to his employer and a better and a more productive individual to society"[44] – an axiom in Britain since the 1840s. Smith's own experience in England and Massachusetts showed the need for state intervention: "We are assembled in Mechanics' Hall, and mechanics' institutes, young men's institutes, evening drawing schools and some technical classes have long existed in the several provinces of this Dominion, and have doubtless here, as elsewhere, done great good. But permit me as one who has watched this great question in another country similarly circumstanced to this, to say to you with all frankness and good intent, that these private or semi-public organizations will not provide a national remedy for a national deficiency. The question is too great, the matter at stake is too important to trust it to the efforts, usually feeble and often intermittent, of the few."[45] These remarks by Smith appeared the next year in the Montreal printing of *Technical Education and Industrial Drawing in Public Schools.*

Unfortunately, the attendance at Smith's Montreal lectures had not met the council's hopes, and the normal schools were doing nothing about drawing.[46] In fact, many drawing instructors in both countries disliked Smith's system, and Brymner had stopped using it at the Art Association's school. Even the council found it too comprehensive for night school.[47]

Some competition further muddied the picture. Edmond-Marie Templé (c. 1851–1895) had arrived from France after the Franco–Prussian War and later became a drawing master at both the Académie commerciale de Montréal and at Jacques-Cartier.[48] By 1886, Templé was producing his own set of drawing manuals, *Méthode nationale de dessin: cours préparatoire,* not very different in method from Smith's, and badgered education officials to adopt them. In 1887, the Catholic schools replaced Smith's manuals with Templé's, but the Council of Arts and Manufactures had serious reservations. The journalist and education bureaucrat Oscar Dunn (1845–1885) had translated Smith's manuals into French, and, even though both he and Smith were now dead, the council thought it would be a great inconvenience to replace the old manuals. Besides, a committee that had looked over Templé's work saw no reason to adopt it.[49] But in 1891, both the Protestant schools and the council's evening schools went with Templé. Templé's connections with the Liberals garnered him the directorship of Montreal's adult night schools, which he held 1889–91 (see below), and he was about to become provincial director of art instruction – a position much like Smith's in Massachusetts – when the Conservatives replaced Honoré Mercier's Parti National in power. Templé ended up as a travelling salesman.

## ENGINEERING EDUCATION IN QUEBEC

### McGill v. Laval (1867–71)

Despite abortive attempts in the 1850s to establish engineering instruction at the University of Toronto and McGill, by the 1870s it was increasingly evident that engineering had to become part of Canadian higher education. J.W. Dawson's lecture *The Duties of Educated Young Men in British America* (1863), which he delivered just as McGill's engineering program collapsed, was sanguine: "We have not in British America sufficient number of schools of art and practical science, which could bear directly on the fine and useful arts, and on the growth of our manufactures ... We [at McGill] have met with some success, though we have found that in some respects this country is still below the point at which the want of such training is felt. But this infant state of our society is passing away, and the time may come sooner than we expect when British America may have not merely schools of Law and Medicine, and Engineering and Normal schools, but Military, Mining, Agricultural and Technological schools, and schools of fine art and ornamental design."[50]

In Ontario, between 1872 and 1882, the working men's School of Technology quietly evolved into the School of Practical Science and then the engineering faculty of the University of Toronto, jettisoning mechanics and tradesmen on the way. The confessional and linguistic divides in Quebec complicated the evolution of engineering education in the province. Once more, Dawson took the lead. Seeing the plans in Ontario, on his return from England in 1870 he began looking for funds. He knew from the engineering schools at Yale, the Royal College of Chemistry in London, and Owens College in Manchester that local philanthropy was crucial, so he began to canvass Montreal's anglophones for funds for an engineering school and received $1,800 from the Molson and Redpath families. In 1870, he obtained $1,000 for his School of Science Applied to Arts and Manufactures from funds the province had set aside from the Jesuit Estates for superior education.[51] Instruction in mining commenced in 1871, with Bernard J. Harrington (1848–1907), the first Canadian PhD in science from Yale, who later married Dawson's daughter, as professor. Mining soon expanded into a Department of Applied Science, employing science professors in the Faculty of Arts for the non-engineering side of tuition, much in the way University College, Toronto, supported the School of Practical Science. By the 1880s, engineering was now on firm footing as a fully professional subject at McGill.

If francophones were to train in engineering, there were two options: a free-standing school or a university faculty. In the early 1870s, the province's only francophone university was Laval. During the 1860s and 1870s, it had two distinguished science teachers, geologist Thomas Sterry Hunt (1826–1892) of the Geological Survey of Canada and chemist Hubert La Rue, on staff. La Rue had already contributed to agricultural education and was key to fostering training for engineers at Laval. In the event, it was the government, not the university, that pressed for change. As Hamelin notes, the city of Quebec had certain disabilities, being a city of church, politics, and services but still proto-industrial, while "l'horizon de l'Université est davantage de relever le niveau de l'enseignement des sciences dans les collèges, de diffuser les connaissances nouvelle dans le grand public que d'en faire un outil de développement économique."[52]

For economic, educational, and political reasons, Conservative Premier Chauveau wanted engineering at Laval to counterbalance the emerging school at McGill; to that end, in October 1870 he offered the rector, Elzéar-Alexandre Taschereau (1820–1898), $2,137 to start up and an annual $1,200 to create a program in applying science to the arts.[53] Despite strong internal support from La Rue (who sketched out a three-year program), Thomas-Etienne Hamel, the professor of physics, and law professor François Langelier (1838–1915), Taschereau hesitated. The funds on offer were small, and the premier attached strings. Laval drew up a possible curriculum, and a report to the Faculty of Arts, with input from La Rue, was positive but ambiguous about the program's goal. La Rue's approach involved courses for local capitalists and educated townspeople, along with Laval students who would eventually become physicians, priests, and teachers. This vision, reflecting the region's minimal industrial development, did not imply evening courses for the working class. Although Hamel and La Rue taught courses in physics and industrial chemistry, respectively, nothing more happened during the next year.

In 1871, with Taschereau's having become archbishop of Quebec, Hamel became rector and, although supportive of engineering, was not happy with the conditions. Muddying the waters further, Langelier attacked Chauveau publicly. By Christmas 1871, Hamel decided definitively to turn down the government's offer and returned the first instalment of funds. It would not be until 1907 that the university would take the first steps towards engineering education, setting up the Ecole centrale de préparation et d'arpentage. As a result, a few francophone students sought professional engineering training in English at McGill.

### The Ecole polytechnique (Montreal)

With the first option for engineering training for francophones dead in Quebec by 1871, the second emerged in Montreal. There, in 1860, Urgel-Eugène Archambeault (1834–1904) had opened the Académie commerciale catholique de Montréal. Archambeault, one of the first students at the city's Ecole normale Jacques-Cartier, was one of the few prominent Catholic lay teachers of the period.[54] Although the so-called industrial colleges, which specialized in general and commercial education, had thrived earlier as a system parallel to the *collèges classiques*, by the 1870s many had metamorphosed into *collèges classiques*, which still focused on preparing boys for the priesthood or the professions.

None the less the Académie commerciale catholique de Montréal thrived. Thanks to Archambeault's leadership, a handsome new building – the "Académie du Plateau," on the eastern shoulder of Mount Royal – opened in 1872. Support for more practical education came from liberal francophones Arthur Buies and L.-O. David and articles in *La Minerve, Le national,* and *L'opinion publique.* The editor of the last was ecstatic: "Les choses ont été faites princièrement; on n'a rien épargner pour que tout soit complet, aussi parfait que possible, pour donner à l'enseignement industriel et commercial toute l'efficacité désirable. On a compris dans ce cas l'importance de bien traiter et payer les professeurs suivant leur mérite, et les services qu'ils rendent et la position qu'ils occupent dans la société. Plaise au ciel que cet exemple porte ses fruits dans tout le pays!"[55]

Archambeault was already thinking about the industrial side and during 1873 undertook the organization of an Ecole scientifique et industrielle as a division of his academy.[56] As the plan for applied science at Laval had fallen through, the superintendent of public instruction, Gédéon Ouimet, was happy to support Archambeault's idea. With financial assistance from Montreal's Catholic education commissioners, Archambeault was able to open the school in January 1874, and two years later it became the Ecole polytechnique de Montréal.

Despite its name, the Ecole polytechnique occupied an educational no-man's-land: it had links to a secondary school and no affiliation to a university, offered no degrees, and was not specifically for the working class. Despite securing some competent teachers and a reasonable amount of equipment, the school was no magnet for students. Gagnon identified fifty-two students from 1877 to 1889, twenty-one of them from *collèges classiques*, fifteen from the academy, twelve from unknown backgrounds, three from the normal school, and one from an independent college.[57] Gagnon has also discerned the father's occupation for 106 students attending between 1873 and 1885: twenty-seven small merchants, twenty-six farmers, twenty workers, fourteen liberal professionals, ten white-collar workers, six engineers/architects/surveyors, two industrialists, and one teacher.[58] Thus about half the students hailed from the agricultural and labour social groups.

In 1887, the Ecole polytechnique affiliated with Laval's Succursale de Montréal. When the university branch gained autonomy in 1920 as the Université de Montréal, the Ecole polytechnique became, in effect, its engineering faculty. The Ecole's early history resembled that of Toronto's School of Technology: little funding, not enough staff members, inadequate equipment, and no clear purpose. Like its Toronto counterpart, it later evolved into a university's engineering faculty, but the delay was longer, partly because of the bitter "*querelle universitaire*" between church and university leaders in Montreal and Quebec. Moves to ground professional engineering training in the universities in the 1850s were obviously premature and ended in failure in both Quebec and Ontario; but by the mid-1870s rapid industrialization and urbanization and growing technological demands led to success at Toronto and McGill and, a little later, at the Ecole polytechnique. The days in which a person could train with an engineer and learn on the job had passed. Engineering was now a profession with roots in the university and no longer part of technical education for the working class.

## TECHNICAL EDUCATION OR ADULT EDUCATION?

By the 1870s, the schools that Quebec's Council of Arts and Manufactures operated were focusing on technical instruction, especially drawing. Most night classes in Ontario's mechanics' institutes offered general education – reading, writing, mathematics, bookkeeping – closer to today's adult education. As Hamelin notes, one needed little education in Quebec to find work, although that work provided a very precarious life.[59] The Catholic school commissioners in Montreal created commercial night schools in the early 1870s, but these were neither technical nor broad-based adult schools. From the church's perspective, adult night schools would be useful for social control: the abbé Léon Provancher (1820–1892) opined in 1873 that their teaching of science and drawing would rein in immorality and drunkenness and allow local priests to keep tabs on wayward youths,[60] but little other activity or discussion occurred until the 1880s. Heap has prepared a detailed study of the most important, but short-lived, attempt to provide adult education to the working class.[61]

### Libraries and Books for Workers

In Ontario, the growing labour movement had exhibited little interest in educational matters, but in Montreal the Knights of Labour pressed the provincial government in 1885 to create night schools and public libraries for workers. The province of Quebec had no public libraries – only the libraries of private organizations, such as the Institut canadien de Québec, or parish libraries. As early as 1841, Charles Mondelet had argued for creation of school libraries following the lead of New York's superintendent of common schools, but nothing came of the idea. Premier Chauveau was a proponent of parish libraries; while superintendent, he had tried to create a book depository like Ontario's to supply local libraries. He was blocked, but his successor, Ouimet, in his 1873 education report, argued that local libraries with works on agriculture, arts, horticulture, and manufactures, among other subjects, would be valuable and that he would approach the assembly the following year for funds.[62] In the event, the book depository was not in operation until 1877; the assembly voted to suppress it in 1879, but the legislative council rejected the bill. Ouimet noted that the facility had not cost a cent and did good work.[63] By that time, with a coalition of Conservatives and Ultramontane prelates and clergymen working to block any educational efforts by the state that were not under church control, the book depository did not survive; public libraries would thus not appear in the province until the mid-twentieth century.

If libraries were rare, what about books for purchase? While taking evidence in Montreal in 1888, the Royal Commission on the Relations of Labor and Capital asked bookseller John Redmond whether books useful for working people were available. Redmond replied that mechanics and working men did purchase books but favoured the novels of Charles Dickens, Sir Walter Scott, and William Makepeace Thackeray. While they might have purchased technical books, the dominion duty on imports inhibited them: "There are no publications in Canada to speak of on the Mechanical Arts. Books of the Mechanical Arts are not published in Canada and they have all to be imported."[64] This had been an issue for mechanics' institutes as well when they were in existence.

### Growth, Expansion, and Collapse (1888–92)

After Louis-Olivier Taillon's Conservative government fell in 1887, the Parti National's Honoré Mercier became premier. Although he believed in sectarian education and sought Ultramontane support, he recognized the need for technical and professional education and increased the annual grant to the province's Council of Arts and Manufactures from $3,000 to $9,500. In the next year, the Montreal labour leader and Independent Conservative MP Alphonse-Télésphore Lépine (1855–1943) persuaded his friends Liberal MLA L.-O. David and civic politician James McShane (1833–1918) to support evening schools for the working class. McShane was also briefly commissioner of agriculture and public works and would have been familiar with the Council of Arts and Manufactures schools. A key ally was J.-D. Rolland, chair of the finance committee on city council. By October 1888, Rolland told the council that the Mercier government would provide $3,000 to pay teachers in night schools. Local labour leaders then met with the premier, and an outline of the schools' curriculum emerged. With classes in arithmetic, bookkeeping, English, French, geography, history, industrial drawing, and reading, these night schools were thus more like the Ontario mechanics' institute classes than those of the council.

Mercier was fully supportive. In a speech to the Club National, he pledged his government's support to "faire pénétrer la lumière de l'instruction dans toutes les classes, surtout dans les classes les plus pauvres et les plus humbles ... Le peuple demande que nous lui versions l'instruction à pleines mains et nous allons la lui verser ... Nous ne reculerons point devant la tâche."[65] The government appointed Edmond Templé (of the drawing manuals, above) as director-general. The proposed schools aroused great interest in the metropolis, with 5,000 men signing up for classes in 1889. When it became apparent that workers in the provincial capital also wanted night schools, a funding scheme emerged: Quebec city council would provide paper and books; local school commissions the venue, heating, and lighting; and the provincial government teachers' salaries. The curriculum was more limited than Montreal's, with only arithmetic, English, French, reading, and writing. Lépine and his associates knew that many working-class men had left school early and that evening classes would give them a sound footing for life.

With the success of the Montreal and Quebec schools, Mercier wanted to expand the network into smaller towns and rural areas. After his government won the 1890 election, schools opened in Farnham, Joliette, Richmond, St-Hyacinthe, St-Jérôme, Sherbrooke, Sorel, and Valleyfield, and a number also in villages. All was not well, however, with the new system. Templé was unpopular for his autocratic ways, and there was a whiff of corruption when Mercier's brother obtained a position. Attacks by *La presse* and in the assembly increased, with legislative councillor Pierre Boucher de La Bruère leading the charge, claiming that Mercier was planning a state-controlled system. The province, facing financial difficulties, cut teachers' salaries twice. In the 1892 election, Charles Boucher de Boucherville and the Conservatives returned to office; on the pretext of financial strain, he cut back evening classes. In his first premiership (1874–78), he had suppressed the Department of Public Instruction; he now turned the evening schools over to the Council of Public Instruction and reduced the public grant from $50,000 to $10,000. In Montreal, eight evening schools, no longer free, enrolled 800 men, but typically only 200 attended. Fees helped reduce enrolments, but Heap explains that most workers, after long hours of labour, had no energy for study. By the end of 1892, de Boucherville resigned and Taillon became premier. One of his first acts was to dismantle the night schools completely, after only four years. From then on, the working class had to be content with the night schools of the Council of Arts and Manufactures.

## CONCLUSION

Although Quebec lagged behind Ontario in population and industrialization towards the end of the century, the differences were mostly of scale. Montreal, unquestionably the nation's metropolis, maintained a wide variety of industries with a considerable working class. The educational system, with its confessional and linguistic divisions and political wrangling – all much more intense than Ontario's – adapted more slowly to the new industrial landscape. The Ontario-style high school was not available to francophone youths; those hoping to enter the professions, commerce, or the church attended *collèges classiques* or, while they lasted, *collèges industriels*. For those heading for farming or factory labour, elementary schooling was the only option. Because no trade or technical schools emerged during the nineteenth century, anyone entering the trades had to learn skills on the job. As most mechanics' institutes had disappeared, the only evening classes available for the working class were those of the Council of Arts and Manufactures. By the late 1880s, these schools had moved beyond elementary drawing classes and taught real skills. Still, their number was small and total enrolment never large. While the council's schools profoundly affected hundreds of working peoples' lives, they were never even close to sufficient. Montreal's Ecole polytechnique made engineering careers possible, for a handful of francophones; middle-class anglophones could become professionals through McGill's engineering program. By the end of the century, political division and Ultramontane horror at the possibility of a secular school system conspired to deny most working-class students technical instruction and, except very briefly, even adult education at night.

# Conclusion

When Robert Stamp refers to the "campaign for technical education" that the Canadian Manufacturers' Association and others began in the late 1870s, what are we to think about the prior half-century of efforts by private individuals, institutions, and governments to secure technical instruction for farmers and the working class? Were they only a "*préhistoire interminable*" (Charland's phrase), or did they also form a campaign for technical education? In a way, they were both. The first phase encompassed the wide variety of attempts to educate farmers, mechanics, and artisans by adapting ideas from elsewhere, mostly from Britain, but also from the United States, France, and Ireland. Some ideas succeeded, but many failed, often because of insufficient support and/or the use of an inappropriate model for Canadian society and its economy.

Here we examine two conclusions to this study. First, formal agricultural education in Victorian Canada was perhaps the right idea at the wrong time, while informal instruction in both Canadas became a notable and variegated success. Second, British-style technical education – including in the mechanics' institutes – became in Canada partly general education for a small group of workers, while the formative influences in engineering education seem to have flowed from the United States, and those in art education from south of the border, with origins in South Kensington.

## AGRICULTURAL EDUCATION: RIGHT IDEA, WRONG TIME?

### *Formal Instruction: A New Idea*

By the time of Confederation, Canadians had for almost eighty years been trying, in one way or another, to disseminate knowledge of new agricultural techniques. Agricultural journalists, educational writers, and administrators had been agitating for formal education on the subject for nearly forty years. By 1867, there were a few small schools, but proponents were painfully aware that farmers were not really keen on enrolling their sons. Was this reluctance simply conservatism? As late as 1915, Albert Leake claimed: "The farmer is strongly conservative, owing largely to his individualistic training, and it is no small task to overcome his strong attachment to old and well-established practices. The first, and sometimes the hardest, of the educational problems is to lead him to see that the education of his children is at least as important as the fattening of his hogs."[1] He noted Sir Horace Plunkett's (1854–1932) great difficulty in persuading Irish farmers to band together to form cooperative creameries when countries pursuing cooperation such as Denmark and, increasingly, Canada and the United States were advancing economically.

No doubt individual conservatism was at least one factor. Certainly, American farmers early on resisted land-grant colleges for their sons, despite their general embrace of new agricultural technologies. Perhaps those who did embrace change and prosper without specialized education would have seen no need for it. By the 1860s, the expanding group of well-off farmers in the Province of Canada may well have felt the same. Yet the many public calls for more education came from a relatively small group of men. And Canada East's *habitants* faced additional burdens: illiteracy, population pressure on arable land, and a social cohesion resistant to British ideas.

A brief comparison with other countries refutes the hypothesis that Canadians lacked the good sense to embrace a form of education that would enrich them eventually. Even by the 1860s, agricultural education was hardly a raging success in the United States, where rural and economic conditions most closely resembled Canada's. Agricultural courses were rare, with a few colleges offering the subject but with desultory results. In three northern-tier states bordering Canada – New York, Ohio, and Michigan – pre-1861 attempts at educating the farmer in the art and science of agriculture were little in advance of those in Canada. Indeed, many farmers in western New York had close ties with the more forward-looking farmers of Canada West. Canadian agricultural journals filled with reprints of articles from their US counterparts, which in turn reported on Canadian conditions. So both were aware of each other's experiences. Apart from a short-lived agricultural college that started near Cincinnati in 1833, there were no US agricultural colleges until 1855. The Morrill Act, which spurred emergence of a nation-wide system of agricultural and mechanical colleges, came into force only in 1862, after a false start. Even with the great dislocation of the Civil War, the act's fruits were not evident until well into the 1870s, by which time the Ontario Agricultural College had already begun to come fully into its own. In terms of government organization of agriculture, proto-federal Canada was ahead of the United States and of many individual states such as New York, Ohio, and Michigan.

A major roadblock to formal agricultural education – university courses or programs leading to diplomas – was the occupation's lower social status, no matter how progressive or wealthy the farmer. The agricultural press was often defensive, as in its many references to the nobility of agricultural pursuits. Even the urban, middle-class educationists who advocated agricultural education sometimes sounded patronizing, as if – even though this advance would increase the country's wealth – they considered it really a matter for the "agricultural classes."

Another roadblock that French Canada had long lamented was the "engorgement des professions libéraux." Early in the century, francophones wanting to leave the farm, and unable to pursue military and high civil-service careers, turned to the liberal professions: medicine, law (as lawyers, clerks, or notaries), and the church or – less estimable, but easier of access – journalism. The step to politics from any of these professions was a short one. Although social mobility and a profession were easier for anglophones in Lower or Upper Canada, many still found professional careers attractive. Only a small fraction of professionals became wealthy; in Lower Canada, particularly, that status and penury were often synonymous. Even gifted and well-connected men such as P.-J.-O. Chauveau had to scramble for a living at various stages.

With the legislative assemblies of Upper and Lower Canada, and later of the United Province, naturally attracting politicians from the professions, what interest in agricultural issues would politicians who were liberal professionals have? After all, with many of them having escaped rural life through education, they were not likely to be empathetic. There were many complaints in agricultural journals about how much government was willing to spend on classical education and how little on educating the farming population. The few enquiries and minimal parliamentary debate on agricultural organization and education before Confederation speak eloquently of the politicians' priorities.

In a way, the very spokesmen for agricultural education – Ryerson, Evans, Edmundson, McDougall, Buckland, Pilote, Taché, Chapais, Fergusson, Chauveau, Meilleur, and the others, none of them ordinary farmers – were very similar to the politicians. They were civil servants, lawyers, merchants, politicians, priests, and professional journalists. When William Evans declared that his long struggle was in vain, perhaps it was because the message could not easily reach the audience that he intended. While middle-class proselytizers could preach to the converts – well-off "improving agriculturists" – who would listen, the great bulk of the farming population was out of reach. The success of more grass-roots methods in Quebec after Confederation suggests some truth to this.

### Informal Education: Improving on US Models

The other side of the coin was the message itself. The emphasis through-out the first half of the century was on *scientific* agriculture – that farmers should learn about agricultural chemistry. But how many farmers were capable of learning agricultural chemistry, even assuming they were liter-ate? And would it, in fact, have made much difference to practical farm-ing? The tepid reception for books and courses proffering scientific theory of agriculture indicates the indifference of many intelligent, edu-cated farmers. To argue that farmers were notoriously conservative in their practice is not sufficient; even the French-Canadian practitioner, whom historians usually depict as the most backward in nineteenth-century Canada, embraced new techniques later in the century. While Canadian agriculture required considerable improvement during the first half of the century, the movement for education provided few work-able solutions. And, although science would eventually become an essen-tial element in progressive agriculture, in pre-Confederation Canada it was a case of the right idea at the wrong time.

Despite Canadian educational writers and politicians' almost-slavish obeisance to Britain's Science and Art Department regarding technical education for the working class, English agricultural instruction pro-vided no useful models. Instead, men such as Ryerson, Buckland, and Chauveau admired the efforts of Ireland's National School Board to train peasant farmers in new techniques. Ireland was still profoundly agricultural, and its farming practices were still way behind England and Scotland's. But the Irish model (like that of France), an expensive one, boasting many schools with attached farms, in the end Canada rejected, as eventually did Ireland.

Thus, by default, Canadians looked to neighbouring Americans, par-ticularly those at the Michigan Agricultural College. Ontario directly and

Quebec indirectly adopted post–Civil War ideas such as agricultural extension and farmers' institutes. By the 1890s, one could argue that Ontario Agricultural College was as good as and possibly superior to every American land-grant school, while Ontario's extension program and farmers and womens' institutes became pre-eminent in North America.

In Quebec, however, although many people understood the great advantages of having a single provincial or state agricultural college such as New York, Michigan, or Ontario's fine exemplars, the constant tug-of-war for the control of education ensured that the Ste-Anne college at La Pocatière would never develop fully, nor would the other small, ephemeral colleges contribute much to educating farmers. In the absence of a strong, central college, Barnard's *cercles agricoles* proved to be a good approximation of the farmers' institutes in other jurisdictions. They were also acceptable to the Roman Catholic Church. Late-century state–church relations made a non-denominational agricultural college with government support and an extension program very unlikely.

When more modern colleges did emerge after 1900 – McGill's Macdonald College, the Université Laval's absorption of the school in La Pocatière, and the Université de Montréal's of the Oka school – they remained within the almost-watertight Protestant and Catholic systems. Thus in Quebec, formal agricultural education reached very few people in the last forty years of the century, and in Ontario, by the late 1880s, enrolment at Guelph was little more than 100.

Formal agricultural education may have been weak in central Canada, but informal approaches proved useful. Agricultural societies, despite their rhetoric, appear to have achieved more through their social functions and by attracting government resources to rural areas. Society exhibitions and, later, provincial and national ones may well have spurred some farmers to adopt new methods or breeds. Agricultural journalism spread new ideas better, with Canadian journals regularly reporting advances and experiments from Britain, continental Europe, and the United States. Papers in Canada West had greater circulations than those in Canada East, but even the latter's French-language official journal reached an impressive number of farmers by 1900. By the late 1880s, farmers' institutes in Ontario and *cercles agricoles* in Quebec had brought some discipline into informal education, and by the early twentieth century formal agricultural instruction in colleges and specialized schools began to have traction. The most likely reason for this was the groundwork that informal education had laid in the preceding decades:

only when a critical mass of farmers knew and cared about scientific and technical progress could agricultural colleges and schools succeed. This was just as true in England and the United States.

### TECHNICAL EDUCATION: US MODELS FROM SOUTH KENSINGTON

*British-style Technical Education for the Middle Class*

Throughout the nineteenth century, there was no unanimity on the content of technical education, its target, and how to teach it. When mechanics' institutes began to appear in Canada in the 1830s, there was a disconnect between the model and the reality. The early promoters of technical education in Canada, most of them middle-class men who came directly from the United Kingdom, thought of technical education in British terms: the popular science lectures, the classes in the burgeoning mechanics' institutes and philosophical societies, and the cheap encyclopaedias of universal knowledge for sale in bookstalls. They spoke of the "industrial," "labouring," and "working" classes, and they thought of the workers in the British collieries, engineering firms, engine plants, iron works, potteries, railway shops, shipbuilding yards, textile mills, and tool firms. But in the mid-1830s, central Canada did not have these activities, but rather the pioneer industries of gristmills, potasheries, sawmills, and tanneries; the "mechanics" were blacksmiths, millwrights, and shipwrights, while the "artizans" laboured in small shops alone or with a few others.

Yet in Montreal and Toronto's mechanics' institutes, whose directors spoke blithely of the need to educate these mechanics and artisans in science and design, the British model was all they knew. They based the models they adopted – or, more typically, adapted – not on hoary institutions and long-time practices of the old country but on institutions and practices that were still evolving rapidly back home. The provincial art schools, evening science schools, South Kensington Museum, and Science and Art Department all date from the after-shock of the poor British showing at the 1851 Exhibition. The French and Irish ideas that Canadians admired were, as well, equally recent.

By the late 1850s, when growing pressure finally prodded the government of the Province of Canada into doing more than making occasional and desultory grants to institutions, a working-class population of some size did exist. Central Canada was on the verge of the railway age, and the attendant industries that a maturing colony required were coming into existence. Both halves of the province had thousands of operatives and highly skilled workers, but many of them – both immigrants and native-born – lacked elementary education. The sketchy figures on literacy prevent firm generalization, but we can imagine that a large percentage were, though perhaps not outright illiterate, certainly not able to study the chemistry or physics that the promoters of mechanics' institutes thought they needed.

The surviving records of the early mechanics' institutes reveal the working man's perception of their value: in virtually all such organizations in Upper and Lower Canada, mechanics and artisans shunned their activities. The reasons are evident. The middle class firmly controlled such institutions, whether in Montreal or Belleville; the directors were local clergymen, factory owners, lawyers, merchants, or tradesmen of some substance; and the condescension in their programs was not subtle: it was blatant. The directors did not whisper about workers' lack of culture; they spelled it out on handbills and preached in their institutes' public lectures about the need for mechanics to pull themselves up in society through education. But their actual audiences were largely the same as the directors.

It is not surprising that working men and women generally ignored the call. No doubt some spent time in taverns and billiard halls, but most, after working ten hours for $1 a day, went exhausted to their families, for whom they worked all their lives. And if the opportunity for 50 cents more an hour was available in Michigan or Massachusetts, they went, just as thousands of Canadian farmers left for Missouri or Iowa. Contemporary accounts leave little doubt that the vast majority were God-fearing, responsible citizens. Before the state educational system began its homogenization process, the group for which technical education was intended resisted absorption into the middle-class social order, with its often-stern Protestant, pro-temperance attitudes.

### Evening Classes for General Education

But there is another major reason for the irrelevance of the British model in central Canada: the subject matter. Canadian manufacturers and artisans complained, even before mid-century, that it was difficult to obtain workers who knew their jobs. As the old European apprenticeship system had not migrated to North America, it was only through direct on-the-job experience that a young worker could learn a new trade. This was rarely systematic or satisfactory. If, for example, a Montreal steam-engine builder required a man to operate a cylinder-boring machine, could he send him to the mechanics' institute for a course? No: the workman could learn drawing or chemistry or mineralogy there. The British view, which many other nations shared – that scientific knowledge led to better technology – was a late eighteenth-century notion that was axiomatic in the United Kingdom by the mid-nineteenth century. A mechanic or artisan who understood the scientific principles of his trade would be a better workman and, possibly, become an innovator. Of course, no one had actually demonstrated this to be true; in fact, many of the great inventors of the Industrial Revolution did remarkable things with little or no scientific training.

The Canadian government became an active participant in the promotion of technical education, albeit reluctantly and timidly, only in 1857. This seems to be an outcome of the first great international industrial exhibitions of London in 1851 and Paris in 1855, both of which offered Canadians their first real opportunity to display their raw materials and to show their nascent manufacturing talents. In Britain, from Prince Albert on down, industrial and educational leaders decried the eclipse of British manufactures and saw in technical education, especially in scientific and artistic instruction, their salvation. The Science and Art Department, the South Kensington Museum, and the science and art schools appeared in rapid succession once politicians agreed that these were the solution to the problem. Naturally, Canadians (and Americans) responded in the same way, even though their manufacturing sector emerged out of a recent pioneer economic past. Thus, just as they earlier imported notions of what to teach as technical education from an entirely different context, so did they borrow the imagined boost to manufacturing competitiveness, although Canadian manufactures were scarcely competing anywhere in the world.

One of the central tenets of the South Kensington model of technical instruction was that a worker with more education could be more efficient or design better in the shop or factory, which would make the firm more competitive. But why would a worker want to? Would he receive preferment or financial reward? When Britain's Society of Arts introduced its system of examinations and the Science and Art Department then adopted it, promoters quickly realized that they had to offer monetary rewards – factory owners ignored mere certificates. Indeed, when the Board of Arts and Manufactures for Upper Canada introduced examinations, detractors noted that Canadian manufacturers or merchants were no more likely than their British counterparts to recognize such efforts.

In the end, the evening classes that were popular in mechanics' institutes tended to offer general education, and the typical student was more likely to be a young shop clerk – who could aspire more easily to the ranks of the middle class – than a mechanic or artisan. And many joined the classes because they had fallen through the cracks of the British or Canadian school systems. They were not illiterate, but they had little education. Many may have been English immigrants who had some rudimentary schooling before state-supported schools for the general population started in the 1860s. We know that many of the immigrants to Canada from the old country during that period were labourers.

By the time the Ontario government gave evening classes higher priority in the 1880s and 1890s, they were already largely irrelevant, thanks to basic schooling in the province since the 1840s. Supporters of evening classes for scientific and technical training often cited the many working-men in Britain attending the Science and Art Department's evening classes. Commentators seemed never to understand, or at least state, that a typical working-class English lad wanting to "get ahead" had to take Science and Art classes. Unlike the situation in the United Kingdom, in Ontario and Quebec public high schools, academies, and *collèges classiques* educated a far larger proportion of the school-age population. Such widespread public and private secondary schooling made the old-style evening classes unnecessary for much of the population.

### Technical Education: US Models

The structure for technical education that the Canadian state began to erect in the late 1850s, which changed very little in the successor Quebec and Ontario, was quite distinct from that for regular education. Had it been otherwise, the results would likely have been the same, for the men in charge of the Boards of Arts and Manufactures, the agricultural bureaux, mechanics' institutes, art schools, and night schools shared the overall social vision of leaders such as Egerton Ryerson, J.-B. Meilleur, and Pierre Chauveau. Their goals were as much social control and social homogenization as education. Even before 1867, the francophone experience differed from the anglophone, but the result was much the same. French Canadians had shunned the anglophone-dominated mechanics' institutes and participated little in the Board of Arts and Manufactures for Lower Canada, and their own literary and political institutes tended to be socially conservative and as middle class as the anglophone institutes. The confessional division of the province's education, although sharply different from Ontario's in some ways, reacted to technical education in the same way. Both the Protestant (anglophone) and Catholic (francophone) educational councils, like their Ontario departments, spoke of agricultural and mechanical training at the elementary level but did little to promote it.

As the nation industrialized during the second half of the century, the need for trained engineers grew acute. An expanding country always required civil engineers to build bridges, canals, dams, roads, and, above all, railways. The earliest engineers, who came from the old country, brought with them practices not necessarily suitable for local conditions. British railway construction was very different from Canadian, which followed the American lead. As immigrant engineers adapted, they trained their successors in a quasi-apprentice way, much as lawyers and physicians did before the advent of medical and law schools. By the 1870s, civil, mechanical, and mining engineers were essential, and, within a decade, electrical and chemical engineers as well. Here, too, American models were much more likely to succeed than British or continental ideas. McGill and Toronto's engineering programs looked very much like their opposite numbers in the United States. While the founders intended the schools to provide technical training to the working class, they very quickly became centres for professional training. Despite its tenuous beginnings, the francophone Ecole polytechnique in Montreal moved as quickly as it could to start purveying the same kind of education. In the process, all three schools became preserves of the middle class, while the dream of providing practical instruction rather than theoretical ideas faded.

### Art Education: From South Kensington via Massachusetts

Finally, the framework for thinking about art education in both Ontario and Quebec, from the late 1840s on, had been contemporary British practice. Canadians thoroughly adopted the ideology of South Kensington that art instruction for the working class – drawing particularly – was essential for industrial progress. Many schemes surfaced in Canada from the late 1840s onward to provide such instruction, but, as we saw above, there was scarcely any manufacturing industry that could secure any value from employees who so trained; this was a discourse with no basis in reality. Whether the very few students of drawing at the Montreal, Toronto, and a few other mechanics' institutes actually used the skills they learned – and if most of them took only a single class, these skills would have been very narrow indeed – we will never know. Both Quebec and Ontario adopted the South Kensington system of art training, although the practice of Massachusetts more directly infected both in the 1880s. At the turn of the century, authorities still saw art education, which had spread to the school systems of both provinces, as a form of technical education. In fact, it became more a form of low-level aesthetic training.

Ideas about the value of technical education, how to deliver it, and to whom embraced a wide range of attitudes: those of hard-headedness, idealism, paternalism, philanthropy, and utopianism. Yet almost never did anyone ask a very obvious question: how do you know that teaching science or art will translate into industrial advancement? And if it does, how does one measure its success in any direct way? Henry Cole and his allies knew that Britain's industrial goods in 1851 were generally inferior to continental, particularly French, manufactures. By 1862, after a decade of "science and art," Britain had regained the lead – because of technical education. This seems overwhelmingly a case of *post hoc, ergo propter hoc* thinking. It may well be that British manufacturers, reacting to their humiliation at the Crystal Palace, simply sought the few innovative artisans that they could find. Were they products of the South Kensington system? We may never know for certain. But it was this kind of faith and self-interest that propelled schemes of technical education. Introducing Liebig's artificial fertilizers would revolutionize agriculture, so Canadian farmers needed to learn agricultural chemistry. Had it revolutionized German agriculture? Certainly not when proponents were touting it in Canada in the 1840s. Would a class in mechanical drawing make an iron founder a better artisan? Perhaps. It might simply have given him more confidence in his abilities, which might have been more valuable to society in the long run, but promoters of technical education focused more on the immediate product.

It is easy to discount educational programs because they cannot demonstrate outcomes. Our contemporary educational ideas are in no way superior; we are forever re-inventing the educational wheel, which never turns out to be round. Just as some British and French generals in 1939 were planning to fight the Great War again, so our means of teaching science and technical subjects seem always to be appropriate to last year's or last decade's technical demands. Certainly, since the 1860s, the world of industry, science, and technology has moved much faster than the social order and its institutions, especially education, could adjust. In terms of technical education, Canadians in the nineteenth century always lagged behind the needs of industry, but then so did everyone else.

# Epilogue: Towards the Twentieth Century

By the end of the nineteenth century, central Canadians had attempted a variety of approaches to technical and agricultural education, formal and informal, public and private. Despite the expenditure of hundreds of thousands of dollars, almost none achieved positive, lasting results. By today's standards, these outlays of public funds seem minuscule, but for the budgets of the time they were substantial, although insufficient, investments in education outside the public systems. Surveying the landscape of educational opportunities for the farmer and worker in the 1890s, the lack of vision and the absence of both a clear notion of direction and any demonstrable measure of success could depress the observer. Yet after 1900 both Ontario and Quebec began moving into new educational ventures that did appear to respond to the needs of the new industrial reality.

Here we look briefly at the changes then that laid the foundation of twentieth-century technical education. They started, for the most part, from scratch, not building on the work of the preceding century. Indeed, the transition from the first phase of technical education – attempts and failures borrowing from British models that the South Kensington bureaucracy worked out – to the second, more successful phase – which derived largely from American models – took place between approximately 1885 and 1910. The debate over what to teach, whom to teach, and why to teach was multifaceted and somewhat disjointed. Below I sample the voices of the time and sketch how technical education evolved after 1900 in three sections: about the increasing role of American models, especially in manual training and in separating the teaching of mechanical and of decorative drawing; about the Canadian debate on technical education; and about replacing the South Kensington vision with domestic answers – for example, the Toronto Technical School (1892), the Montreal Technical Institute (1906), and a number of initiatives in manual training and domestic science.

For the working class, agricultural education was much less problematic than technical education. In the former, Ontario's era of experimentation had largely finished by the 1890s. Any notion of emulating the English, French, or Irish gave way to an essentially American solution: the single agricultural school with government support. With Ontario Agricultural College in Guelph operating at full strength, the agricultural extension program expanding, and the agricultural societies humming along with little state supervision, the pattern of agricultural education had mostly fallen into place for the early twentieth century. If one were to somewhat discount Ontarians' pride at claiming the best agricultural school on the continent, it certainly was performing well and supplying the province's farmers with experimental evidence, information, and graduates. Apart from its absorption of the veterinary college, it was doing business as usual. On the informal front, the farmers' institutes faded away soon after 1900, but agricultural journalism, trained local agronomists, and plentiful scientific and technical literature from Guelph more than made up the difference.

In Quebec, maintaining several small, financially weak schools continued to hamper agricultural education. Only in the 1910s, in response to the success of Sir William's Macdonald College, did the francophone universities build up true faculties of agriculture. In time, these institutions would graduate enough agronomists to provide extension services to the countryside and, in 1937, a professional organization of agronomists, l'Ordre des agronomes du Québec.[1]

Where the farmers'-institute movement in Ontario was both democratic and reasonably free of class conflict, in Quebec, the francophone *cercles agricoles*, with their church support, were in conflict with the older county societies, which attracted anglophones and wealthier francophone farmers. It is likely, although difficult to establish, that the *cercles*, like the farmers' institutes, conveyed new ideas to tradition-bound farmers. At least, it seems plausible that they were more effective as purveyors of informal education than were the agricultural societies and their exhibitions. To the extent that agricultural education was successful in both provinces in the early twentieth century, it did that by adapting American ideas to a Canadian context. This would also be the case for technical education.

## LOOKING SOUTH OF THE BORDER

That senior bureaucrats such as Ryerson and May, volunteers such as Edwards and Stevenson, and politicians such as Chauveau and McGee would look to South Kensington for ideas is not at all surprising. Because Canadians thought of themselves as British, its concepts did not seem foreign to them in any sense. Yet, no matter what they attempted along those lines, they achieved little. Canadian legislatures were unwilling to invest enough to support fully South Kensington–type programs, and, whatever their private feelings about US institutions and ideas, they could not help but see the great strides they were making, as was all too evident at Philadelphia's Centennial Exhibition in 1876. Ryerson, although ever a British loyalist, was also an unabashed admirer of Horace Mann and his achievements in Massachusetts and, keenly watching events in neighbouring states, reported on them regularly. No reader of his *Journal of Education* or, for that matter, of its Quebec counterpart could be ignorant of American educational trends. And, as Americans had moved to industrialize more quickly than had Canadians, they needed technical education sooner. They had not warmed up to the mechanics'-institute movement, so they needed alternatives.[2]

We saw above that Americans attempted to provide knowledge, particularly scientific, to working people through lyceums and other institutions, but as public education grew apace, this form of informal education faded and had little impact by the time of the Civil War. The Chautauqua movement, which emerged in New York State in the 1870s, had a similar appeal but focused more on cultural activities. In formal schooling, the major shift in American practice was from manual-labour schools to manual-training schools. The former, following the lead of Fellenberg, instructed the poor and was more likely to have philanthropic support, and social control was always just below the surface. As William Ellery Channing (1780–1842) argued, manual labour, together with education, might help an individual to improve him or her self inwardly and maintain his or her station in life. The creators of the science schools of Harvard, Yale, and Rensselaer, for example, aimed not for technical education for the working class but to form the basis of middle-class professional education, especially in engineering. Toronto and McGill would follow the same path twenty years later. During the Civil War, Congress mandated the land-grant colleges to supply technical education, but they too quickly succumbed to middle-class professionalism.

Public education there, as in Canada, had provided basic literacy to the mass of the population. Unless he or she were a skilled immigrant, an American working person seeking a trade or the skills to be a factory operative had to obtain this knowledge on the job. Rapid industrialization, however, spurred on the debate over how to train workers for the new tasks. One locus was high schools, which had emerged as central to the democratic ideal of universal education. They were, as Barlow suggests, the Americans' "people's colleges," but much more comprehensively than how Ontarians spoke of their mechanics' institutes. Manual training – the training of hand and eye through direct application in a classroom or workshop – was the key to post–Civil War US technical education. This was not new in Europe, where Froebel's influence had led to manual training – the *sloyd* system – in Sweden and Finland in the 1860s. In Russia, Viktor Della-Vos (1829–1890), director of the Imperial Technical Academy in Moscow, developed a program of manual training using graded exercises with a variety of tools.

Massachusetts had first tried workshop-oriented teaching on a small scale in the 1870s; the issue would become whether to incorporate manual training in a high-school curriculum or teach it in a stand-alone school. Professor Calvin M. Woodward (1837–1915) of Washington University in St Louis, Missouri, pioneered the second approach in setting up the city's manual-training school in 1879. The exhibit of the Russian Imperial Technical Academy at the Centennial Exhibition in Philadelphia in 1876 intrigued him. Woodward's version taught boys to work with tools, not to prepare them to produce goods but to coordinate eye and hand. His idea caught the attention of educators in larger cities, and similar schools soon opened in Chicago, Philadelphia, St Paul, Minnesota, and Toledo. Although manual-training schools became increasingly popular in the 1890s, other school systems simply integrated manual training into regular high schools. By the turn of the century, more than 100 American cities operated such high schools.

Introducing manual training generated significant controversy. Some observers considered it something to teach in reformatories, not in mainstream schooling. Many educators believed that manual and trades instruction had no place alongside literary and scientific studies. Debates on the nature of secondary education began in earnest in the 1870s; by the 1880s, opposition to Woodward's ideas was surfacing in the meetings and proceedings of the National Education Association (NEA). His most notable opponent was William T. Harris (1835–1909), US commissioner of education from 1889 to 1900 and an influential figure in the National Education Association. Harris, a Hegelian philosopher, had directed and greatly improved St Louis's public schools until 1880. Some saw Woodward's approach as pointless if one wished to train boys for real occupations. Opponents of manual training also had strong views of the stratification of society: if the working class were to move upwards, it could do so only through the education of the intellect, especially by studying science; otherwise it would fall in the social order. The European approach – trades training and manual training – did not answer the needs of Americans. Vocational training might be useful, but only after "real" education. Specialized post-secondary technical schools, such as the Massachusetts Institute of Technology and the Stevens Institute, did exist and were models for Ontario's School of Practical Science. Art education, too, was part of the educational debates in the National Education Association during the 1880s. Massachusetts had been at the forefront in this realm, but educational leaders faced the same dichotomy that the British and Canadians had faced: should art be taught as the basis for technical education or to elevate taste and aesthetic feeling?

In the twentieth century, the solution was to segregate the goals of art education by placing mechanical drawing in trades training and decorative drawing in the regular school curriculum. While manual training was for boys, domestic science (US home economics) was for girls. By the beginning of the new century, both were entrenching themselves in American high schools. The next steps, already under way, would be to develop more post-secondary specialist trade schools and to push manual training further down into elementary schools.

## THE CANADIAN DEBATE ON TECHNICAL EDUCATION

In the period just before and after Ontario's Department of Education took control of the finances and organization of mechanics' institutes, several voices registered their concerns about the institutes' role in technical education. The institutes had no dearth of both supporters and detractors. The provincial government thought them sufficiently valuable to support them financially, and councillors and officers of the Association of Mechanics' Institutes of Ontario publicly supported the system. In 1877, the association sponsored an essay contest on the value of institutes. Two prizewinners, both from the Toronto Mechanics' Institute but neither of them mechanics, trotted out the usual arguments.

Thomas Davison argued that institutes, while ostensibly for the working class, should not neglect other social groups and that night classes were essential for those with little education, as the government provided nothing for them. Davison's priorities were arithmetic, drawing, grammar, phonography, spelling, telegraphy, and writing. The prize essay by Richard Lewis received more notice: he argued in favour of British-style science and arts instruction; however, as Ontario had no central school such as that in South Kensington but did have an industrial population, he understood that the mechanics' institutes would have to carry the load. Their members' uneven educational backgrounds necessitated preparatory training. Lewis closed with his belief that it was the government's duty to support the institutes financially, as they were really "Colleges for the Industrial Classes."

In the spring of 1876, Montreal architect Frederick Nepheau Boxer (c. 1822–1910), editor of the *Canadian Mechanics' Magazine*, lamented the lack of technical schools in Canada. He wanted every town to build one, partly from public funds, because "it is extraordinary the lethargy into which the Mechanics of Canada have fallen and what little interest they take in objects which would tend to their advancement. It is high time that the artizans in the various branches of the building trade and mechanical industries, begin to arouse themselves and seek to raise the standard of workingmen in this country; there is a most lamentable deficiency of technical education, and as a consequence, of mechanical skill."[3] A year later, he reiterated the value of reference libraries and the active teaching of science and mechanics but doubted that the mechanics' institutes could work in Canada, as too often the wrong people ended up managing them; the best substitute would be more government assistance and a national association.[4]

When his journal became *Scientific Canadian*, he inaugurated a series of articles and reprints – mostly American – on technical instruction. In February 1880, Boxer stated that there was no system of technical education in Canada and that "so far the establishment of Mechanics' Institutes in this country has been a complete failure, and the Government grant of $400 per annum to each may be said to be entirely thrown away."[5] He wanted the grants to end and go instead to real technical education. In March, he continued his attack, saying that, since the Montreal Mechanics' Institute in particular was not operated by or for mechanics at all, mechanics in that city should organize an institute of their own. Even worse to him, many grant-receiving institutes did not even subscribe to *Scientific Canadian*. Boxer, on receiving a letter from a Manitoba mechanic, again argued for a national organization. In May, he penned "An Address to the Mechanics of the Dominion," providing his bona fides: that he had been in Canada for thirty years and in the United States for five and had visited many manufacturers' establishments; that the Americans impressed him – they had more institutions and technical education than did Canadians; that mechanics' institutes and the Board of Arts and Manufactures (Quebec's) were useless; and that the board was silently working good, "very silently, assuredly." He reiterated his proposal to form a national society.[6]

Boxer next criticized the Ontario institutes, which, he believed, were for the middle class, not for mechanics, the opinion also of future minister of education George Ross. His further articles attacked the waste in the Canadian system compared with the American. He felt that mechanics' institutes should become popular schools of technical education, giving free, public, and interesting lectures on elementary science, which, when speakers demonstrated them with apparatuses, would inculcate a taste for science and technology. They should cease offering classes in bookkeeping, grammar, and mathematics, which belonged in public schools, and concentrate instead on practical subjects such as drawing and design. Boxer was not, however, keen on the British system of awarding prizes, and, ironically, what he envisaged for Canada the British already considered passé. His stepping down as editor of *Scientific Canadian* in December 1880 essentially ended the discussion, and no national organization came into being. In case no one in charge of Ontario institutes was reading his articles, Boxer wrote an essay and sent it to the Association of Mechanics' Institutes of Ontario. The article reiterated the need to have mechanics in charge of institutes, to have only technical books in the libraries, and to teach trades-related and scientific subjects. In its 1880 annual report, the association's directors demurred: "Whilst welcoming all mechanics, and hoping they may largely increase the membership, your Committee are of the opinion that neither membership nor management of the Institutes should be confined to any particular class of the community."[7]

After *Special Report of the Minister of Education on the Mechanics' Institutes (Ontario)* of 1881 (which S.P. May wrote) criticized their management, their champion Otto Klotz prepared a rejoinder. Klotz – whom we met above, in chapter 7 – was president of the Preston Mechanics' Institute as well as of the Association of Mechanics' Institutes that year. He had two major issues with the department's vision. First, May argued that the institutes' primary function – and the main purpose of their grants of public money – was to provide evening classes in technical education. But, as Klotz reminded the reader, "throughout the whole 'Report' there is abundant, incontrovertible and plain evidence that from the origin of Mechanics' Institutes in this Province (1835) to the present time (1881), all attempts to make Evening Class instruction in Mechanics' Institutes if not universal at least general, have proved a failure, and a grand failure."[8] The old Board of Arts and Manufactures had managed to create no interest in evening classes, nor had it created its own school of design. Exertions of the Association of Mechanics' Institutes had done little better. In Klotz's reading of May's report, there was no evidence to support May's conviction that changing the rules would bring success. The idea of employing local teachers seemed unlikely, as they needed leisure time and had to perform domestic duties, study, and prepare for lessons for their day-time employment. But the absence of students would be worse. While May might argue that evening classes for young, working-class men might be successful in London, Edinburgh, or Manchester, in Ontario "the fact is that the population is too small in our small towns and villages, that it is too heterogeneous and of too roving or moving a nature. Experience has amply demonstrated that the almost constant moving from one place to another of men employed in factories or other places, the artizans, mechanics, and other factory hands, is one of the chief causes why those very men for whom the Evening Classes are intended do not as a rule become members of Mechanics' Institutes."[9]

Klotz's second issue was the department's imminent takeover of institutes. The institutes had always been independent, and, where they thrived, their directors were men of stature in the community. If the department ran the institutes like it did its school system, it would demote any director to "a mere machine or menial servant," who thus naturally would not volunteer in the first place. Schools were throughout the province, but not mechanics' institutes, which relied on local community support. Klotz's real fear was that institutes would lose their ability to govern themselves, which would doom his association. Klotz, in fact, understood the actual role of the mechanics' institute in Ontario far more clearly than did May.

An alternative venue was the public-school system. In the year (1876) Ryerson retired from the Department of Education, his long-time lieutenant, John George Hodgins, participated in Philadelphia's Centennial Exhibition. His experience there strengthened his view, earlier Ryerson's, that public schools needed technical instruction. In an address that he gave around the province, "A Plea for Elementary Science and Industrial

Training in Our Schools," he argued for teaching drawing, mechanics, natural history, and science in public and high schools: "There are few schools in which there are not boys possessing talent – scientific, inventive, or industrial talent – or constructive genius, which is never evoked, much less aroused or stimulated."[10] He was obviously clinging to the South Kensington vision of industrial education; but, with Ryerson out of the picture, Hodgins's view would remain only a plea.

By the 1890s, Ontario's Department of Education finally recognized that the institutes were middle-class lending libraries, not technical schools. With the institutes' metamorphosis having ended the teaching of technical drawing, the provincial art schools took on that role; but by the late 1890s fine art was nudging out technical training. As mechanics' institutes had died earlier in Quebec, only the evening schools of that province's Council of Arts and Manufactures could supply the kind of technical training it thought necessary for industry. These schools were small, with poor equipment and minimal finances, yet survived almost three decades into the twentieth century. When engineering training in both provinces began to professionalize in the 1870s, it could no longer offer technical training to the working class.

Discussion now shifted to the recent American experience. In Kingston, A.P. Knight of the Kingston Collegiate Institute and later biology professor at Queen's argued for four types of high schools in Canada: one to prepare students for university; one to train teachers; one to train farmers; and technical high schools to train boys for the trades. One could then abolish the mechanics' institutes: "As Institutions for imparting technical education they have been, and are, complete failures, and the public grant now frittered away in eking out their struggling existence, might far better be spent establishing a new class of High Schools to do the work which these Institutes have never done, and never will do."[11] S.C. Stevenson, long-time secretary of Quebec's Council of Arts and Manufactures and director of its evening schools, made a visit to C.M. Woodward's manual-training school in St Louis, Missouri, in 1885 and declared: "I was very much impressed by my visit and I am convinced that if popular education is to supply the needs of the day it must, while not neglecting, or even subordinating mental culture, include in its scope this practical character, which will better enable the coming generation to deal with the material forces and the active work of life."[12] Stevenson believed that Canada must follow suit but left open the question of who should create similar schools; however, his own report for his council make it clear that he wanted it to take the lead. He probably would have agreed with Quebec Liberal MP Sydney Fisher (1850–1921),

Laurier's minister of agriculture, who told his province's teachers' association that "something has been done in Montreal in technical education, yet a system which needs such a night school deserves nothing but condemnation."[13]

W.S. Ellis, principal of Kingston Collegiate Institute and later head of the Kingston School of Mining and Agriculture, understood that major social changes due to industrialization called for new forms of education. In his 1901 *Report on Elementary Technical Education for Ontario*, he argued for manual training in the American fashion rather than in European-style trades training and for making it available in the early years of schooling.

By the late 1890s, Ontario's Department of Education began to take notice and dispatched Deputy Minister John Millar (1842–1905) to Boston; on his return in 1899 he published his *Technical Education: Report of a Visit to the Schools of Massachusetts, and Opinions on the Subject of Technical Education*. He found that the state mandated all towns with more than 20,000 people to provide manual training at the high-school level and that about half had complied. Boston, always a leader in educational reform, maintained twenty-seven manual-training schools that taught cooking, sewing, and woodworking and also a manual-training high school similar to one in Brooklyn. Millar believed in introducing the subject at a young age because the correlation of hand and brain offers a moral as well as an intellectual advantage and thought that some of its elements were easier to teach younger children. Another reason: in Massachusetts, many students left school before they had any exposure to it. According to Millar, "There is an erroneous impression held by some persons that manual training schools are schools for teaching trades and these are not in the interest of skilled mechanics. In the United States the laboring classes and the mechanics are, I was told, the most ardent friends of technical education. It is a mistake to infer that the masses need only a good elementary education."[14] Millar also clearly understood an important difference in Ontario: it designed high schools to produce graduates for university matriculation. This was also true of Quebec's anglophone high schools and *collèges classiques*.

Two years later, Millar's *Education for the Twentieth Century* (1901) again made the case for manual training and domestic science, not just for the working class but for all students. In his view, education must be democratic and not a form of policing or a means to increase productivity. Ontario's school system was failing a substantial portion of the population: "It is a serious drawback to the young person who becomes a farmer, a mechanic, or a merchant, to find that several years of his student life were wasted in a fruitless acquisition of what mainly concerns the lawyer, the doctor, or the teacher."[15] Throughout this period, the main educational periodicals, such as the *Canada Educational Monthly*, the *Educational Journal*, and the *Educational Record of the Province of Quebec*, featured articles and excerpts on manual training and technical education.

In Toronto, there were other influential voices for technical education. One of the first Ontario educationists to interest himself in American ideas was James L. Hughes. He found particularly attractive Froebel's concepts, much in vogue in the United States at the time. It was Hughes who introduced kindergarten to Toronto schools in 1883. Manual training, through the lenses of Fellenberg, Froebel, and Pestalozzi's ideas, as Hughes and others saw it, was not so much technical instruction for the working class as excellent life training for all classes of society. Another ally in the movement was Albert Leake, who had trained as an art instructor at the City and Guilds Institute in London, England. His travels had acquainted him with the Swedish *sloyd* approach to handicraft training, which had some influence on American schools. By 1901, he was inspector of technical education for Toronto schools.

Organized labour had participated little in the debate. The Knights of Labour were active longer in Quebec than in Ontario and, as we saw above, brought their influence to bear on the short-lived evening adult schools. For the Trades and Labour Congress, which emerged only in 1886, technical education was a low priority. Vocational education was an occasional item in the Hamilton paper *Palladium of Labour*. Mindful that apprenticeship was virtually defunct, delegates to annual meetings of the Trades and Labour Congress who pressed for further efforts for technical instruction strongly opposed manual training. They believed, not without reason, that partially trained young men from manual-training schools could become scab labour. In the event, officialdom proceeded with caution. In 1899, when the provincial Department of Education mandated agricultural instruction in rural schools, it also laid down regulations for schools wishing to teach domestic science and manual training. As both would require substantial capital investments and specialized teachers, there was no rush to add either to the curriculum of most school boards.

## REPLACING THE SOUTH KENSINGTON VISION

By the 1880s and 1890s, the British began to shift their approach to technical instruction, especially in the schools with connections to the Science and Art Department and in the examinations of the department and the Society of Arts. Science and art schools had never provided truly technological and trades-related training; with departmental prodding, the City and Guilds Institute, which Philip Magnus (1842–1933) founded in 1878, took over the Society of Art's technological examinations and then established a school of its own, Finsbury Technical College, in 1881. At the same time, the Royal Commission on Technical Instruction (1882–84) called for more technical schools and the teaching of more drawing, mathematics, and science in regular schools. Many parliamentarians thought technical instruction a task not for local school boards but for municipal councils, which should raise tax monies to fund classes; the Local Government Act of 1888 and the Technical Instruction Act of 1889 effected that change. That second act, however, specifically forbade new county authorities to offer trades or industry-related training, and the Science and Art Department's vision remained in place. A way around this blockade was to bring in manual training, which began in London and spread to provincial cities through the 1890s. By 1899, Parliament created a new Board of Education for England and Wales to run science and art training, supplanting the half-century-old Science and Art Department, although the South Kensington museums and schools remained. Although Canadian observers watched all this activity with interest, by the 1890s their ideas about technical education had already begun to swing towards US solutions.

Despite all the Canadian talk of manual training and American technical schools, two new educational ventures in the period of transition continued to follow the well-worn path. In Toronto, where the mechanics' institute had disappeared and evening classes for mechanics had ceased at the School of Practical Science, several local politicians and stationary engineer A.M. Wickens organized the Toronto Technical School in January 1892, while local boards of education stood aloof. With financial support from the city and a board of city councillors, trade unionists, and technical men, the school offered free evening classes in chemistry, drawing, geology, mathematics, mineralogy, and physics. Drafting had a practical bent, focusing on architectural and machine drawing, industrial design, lettering, machine construction, and shading. This was not a manual-training school but a realization of the mechanics' institutes' ideal: "The design of the school is to aid those who have not had the advantages of an education in the boyhood period of life. It is especially intended for artizans, tradesmen, mechanics, laborers, etc., and those who follow the usual occupations of an industrial community."[16] Organized labour presumably supported the school because it would enhance the technical abilities of men already in the workforce. Day classes commenced in 1901, but evening classes dwarfed them, enrolling well over 1,000 students. The Toronto School Board eventually took over the school and in 1905 dispatched Albert Leake to consider US models for a new building. Having visited sixteen schools in Boston, New York, and Philadelphia, he prepared *Education and Industrial Efficiency* for the minister of education in 1905.

In Quebec, although some anglophones had seen the need for trades-related schooling in the late nineteenth century, the first specialist school, the Montreal Technical Institute, did not come into being until 1906. It was a joint venture of the Canadian Manufacturers' Association, the Montreal Mechanics' Institute, and the Protestant committee of the Council of Public Instruction. It was really a reorganization and expansion of the Council of Arts and Manufactures' Montreal night school. By 1910, the Montreal Technical Institute was offering forty-five courses to 843 students in subjects like those of the council's school, including applied mechanics, chemistry, dress-making and millinery work, mathematics, and technical drawing. However, instructors also taught technical, occupational subjects, such as building construction, culinary arts, electricity, and metal work. The preparatory course, culinary arts, and practical mathematics attracted the most students, suggesting that many had little elementary education. Fully one-third of enrollees in 1910 worked in business, probably as clerks. While the format of teaching in the Montreal Technical Institute and its Toronto counterpart was not innovative, the creation of these two schools ended the marginalization of technical instruction.

Two schools in Canada's two largest cities were wholly inadequate to the need, and the movement for technical education demanded much more. As Stamp recounts, a number of allies came together during the late 1890s and the first decade of the twentieth century to press for more technical education. The Canadian Manufacturers' Association lobbied and published articles in its journal *Industrial Canada*. By 1899, the Trades and Labour Congress and boards of trade were allies. Adelaide Hoodless, working through the YWCA and womens' institutes, pressed for domestic science in the schools. In Quebec, nuns had long taught domestic skills to girls; a few specialized schools such as the one in Roberval were in operation at the turn of the century. In 1900, Hoodless had established the Normal School of Domestic Science and Art in Hamilton.

Montreal's Sir William Macdonald was, as we saw above, a firm supporter of domestic science, manual training, and rural education. In 1899, working with James W. Robertson, he established the Manual Training

Fund to provide support for elementary schools for boys only, and, as Axelrod notes, these had an element of social control to them.[17] Under Albert Leake, a manual-training school opened in Brockville in 1899, and schools in Ottawa and Toronto followed the next year. In Quebec, schools in Bedford, Knowlton, Waterloo, and Westmount added manual training with Macdonald funding. As Robertson and Leake noted, these schools were not trade schools in the European sense nor were they apprenticeship programs; further, "It is not technical education, although it gives, during the period of general education, the necessary preparation whereby anyone may derive the full measure of benefit from technical instruction at a later age."[18] Robertson reported that the work of the City and Guilds Institute in London during the late 1880s had introduced manual training into English elementary schools after 1890. In fact, Macdonald and Robertson's focus was on rural and elementary schools, not secondary education, because Macdonald sought above all to improve education for rural anglophones in his own province. He extended his largesse to domestic science in 1903 by the creation of the Macdonald Institute of Home Economics, which absorbed Hoodless's normal school, at Ontario Agricultural College in Guelph. Another of his philanthropic ventures, the Macdonald Rural Schools Fund, financed workshops and gardens in elementary schools in the countryside.

Officials in Ontario's Department of Education were well aware of the discussion on technical education, in which John Seath (1844–1919) would play a key role.[19] Already interested in manual training while principal of the St Catharines Collegiate Institute in the 1870s and early 1880s, he became a high-school inspector and vocal champion for highly centralizing the school system. His visits to New England in 1889 and 1890 to study methods of manual training resulted in his 1901 report, *Manual Training and High School Courses of Study*. Seath was also very supportive of domestic science and commercial education in high schools. With the Conservatives in power in Ontario after a third of a century in opposition, Premier James P. Whitney appointed Seath superintendent of education in 1906, giving him greater leverage to usher in technical instruction. Further study of European and American practices led to his *Education for Industrial Purposes: A Report* (1911), his blueprint for bringing manual training and domestic science to Ontario secondary schools. With solid government support, Seath was able to draft the Industrial Education Act for that year, which allowed municipalities to create technical schools and to insert manual training and domestic science into existing elementary and high schools.[20] It was a true balancing act for Seath, who faced opposition from universities, entrenched teachers, and organized labour, but had support from the Canadian Manufacturers' Association and the vocal lobby for technical education. In the short run, however, progress in the form of new or enhanced schools was slow.

In Quebec, technical instruction for the working class had expanded little since the 1880s. This changed when Lomer Gouin's Liberals came to power in 1905.[21] Like the Conservative James P. Whitney in Ontario, Gouin understood how industrialization was changing the country; and, like his father-in-law, former premier Honoré Mercier, he was keen to improve education. With more federal transfer payments available, Gouin's government was able to fund the new Montreal Technical Institute and to increase the annual subsidy to the Council of Arts and Manufactures' evening schools after prodding by the Montreal Board of Trade. State-supported technical schools like those in the United States and Britain came next, with the opening of the Ecole technique de Montréal in 1907, under the direction of a corporation with board members from the Board of Trade, the Chambre de commerce, and city council and provincial appointments. At the same time, Quebec gained a similar school. These technical schools targeted students who had left elementary school and were heading for industry; in effect, with their three-year programs, they were a form of secondary education for those not enrolling in *collèges classiques* or anglophone high schools. In addition to science and mathematics, students would study the technical details, in a shop environment, of carpentry, drawing and modelling, electricity, forging, and metal work. Gouin's fifteen years in power led to technical schools in Beauceville, Hull, St-Hyacinthe, Shawinigan, Sherbrooke, and Trois-Rivières.

The federal government's involvement was slight until this time on constitutional grounds. In 1887, the Royal Commission on the Relations of Labor and Capital in Canada had taken evidence on education for the working class and heard testimony on the value of manual training.[22] Although the commissioners advocated special classes for technical instruction and technological colleges for the working class, educational issues disappeared beneath the everyday problems facing industrial labour; the commission's report had no real impact on education.

Ottawa's appointment of the Royal Commission on Industrial Training and Technical Education in 1910 allowed for the widest-ranging collection of information on technical instruction ever in Canada. With James Robertson as chair and his relationship with Sir William Macdonald, the final report in 1913 featured manual training and domestic science, along with the teaching of drawing and science. Of course, Ottawa could not prescribe how the provinces would organize agricultural and technical education, but it could stimulate their efforts with funding. Thus in 1913 the Agricultural Instruction Act offered $10 million to the provinces over a ten-year period. After the delay of the First World War, technical instruction had its turn with the Technical Instruction Act of 1919, which provided the same amount over the same period. By the 1920s, technical and agricultural education was well under way but no longer resembled the forms of instruction of a half-century earlier.

# Appendices

# County Agricultural Societies
# (1864–1865)

## TABLE A1 COUNTY AGRICULTURAL SOCIETIES
## IN CANADA EAST (1865)

The pre-Union governments of Lower and Upper Canada provided grants to agricultural societies but not in a systematic way. According to statistics in *Journals of the Legislative Assembly of United Canada* (1847), Appendix k.k.k., between 1802 and 1840 Lower Canada granted a total of £19,834 for agricultural societies; during the 1820s and 1830s, the annual amounts were approximately £1,000, although variations occurred.

Table A1 lists the seventy-three county agricultural societies of Canada East and the number of members in 1865. Aggregate membership was just above 10,300; note that few societies were very large, and, in general, larger societies were in the earliest-settled regions.

| | | | |
|---|---|---|---|
| Argenteuil | 99 | Chambly | 160 |
| Arthabaska | 150 | Chateauguay | 200 |
| Bagot | 800 | Chicoutimi et | |
| Beauharnois | 220 | Saguenay | 40 |
| Beauce | 40 | Compton | 40 |
| Bellechasse | 40 | Two Mountains | 40 |
| Berthier | 161 | Dorchester | 120 |
| Bonaventure No. 1 | 66 | Drummond No. 1 | (not operating) |
| Bonaventure No. 2 | 58 | Drummond No. 2 | 72 |
| Brome | 75 | Gaspé No. 1 | 56 |
| Charlevoix No. 1 | 144 | Gaspé No. 2 | 41 |
| Charlevoix No. 2 | 177 | Hochelaga | 215 |
| Champlain | 288 | Huntingdon | 260 |
| | | Iberville | 267 |

| | | | |
|---|---|---|---|
| Jacques Cartier | 175 | Portneuf | 267 |
| Joliette | 340 | Quebec (city) | 62 |
| Kamouraska | 40 | Quebec (county) | 101 |
| Laprairie | 199 | Richelieu | 178 |
| L'Assomption | 279 | Richmond | 195 |
| Laval | 90 | Rimouski | 40 |
| Lévis | 40 | Rouville | 40 |
| L'Islet | 40 | Shefford | 130 |
| Lotbinière No. 1 | 52 | Sherbrooke | 100 |
| Lotbinière No. 2 | 40 | Soulanges | 224 |
| Maskinongé | 40 | Stanstead | 228 |
| Mégantic No. 1 | 74 | St-Hyacinthe | 643 |
| Mégantic No. 2 | 38 | St Johns | 40 |
| Missisquoi | 157 | St-Maurice | 171 |
| Montmagny | 53 | Terrebonne | 40 |
| Montmorency | 102 | Témiscouata | 40 |
| Montcalm | 84 | Three Rivers | 70 |
| Montreal | 215 | Vaudreuil No. 1 | 55 |
| Napierville | 167 | Vaudreuil No. 2 | 40 |
| Nicolet No. 1 | 161 | Verchères No. 1 | 296 |
| Nicolet No. 2 | 81 | Verchères No. 2 | 372 |
| Ottawa No. 1 | 58 | Wolfe | 150 |
| Ottawa No. 2 | 49 | Yamaska | 165 |
| Pontiac | 267 | | |

Source: Province of Canada, *Sessional Papers* (1866), No. 5.

## TABLE A2  COUNTY/ELECTORAL-DIVISION AGRICULTURAL SOCIETIES IN CANADA WEST (1864)

The pre-Union governments of Upper and Lower Canada gave ad hoc grants to agricultural societies. Upper Canada started doing so in 1830 and gave a total of £9,280 by 1840, with annual outlays in that decade somewhat larger than those in Lower Canada.

Table A2 lists Canada West's sixty-three county or electoral-district societies in operation in 1864; it omits the 236 township or branch societies (which Canada East did not have). Total members' subscriptions were $32,000 and provincial grants $51,000.

| | | |
|---|---|---|
| Addington | Huron | Peel |
| Brant East | Kent | Perth |
| Brant West | Kingston | Peterborough |
| Brockville | Lambton | Prescott |
| Bruce | Lanark North | Prince Edward |
| Carleton | Lanark South | Renfrew |
| Dundas | Leeds and Grenville | Russell |
| Durham East | North | Simcoe North |
| Durham West | Leeds South | Simcoe South |
| Elgin East | Lennox | Stormont |
| Elgin West | Lincoln | Toronto |
| Essex | Middlesex East | Victoria |
| Frontenac | Middlesex West | Waterloo North |
| Glengary | Niagara | Waterloo South |
| Grenville South | Norfolk | Wentworth North |
| Grey | Northumberland East | Wentworth South |
| Haldimand | Northumberland West | York East |
| Halton | Ontario North | York North |
| Hamilton | Ontario South | York West |
| Hastings North | Oxford North | |
| Hastings South | Oxford South | |

*Source:* Province of Canada, *Sessional Papers* (1866), No. 5.

# Mechanics' Institutes after 1850

## TABLE B1 MECHANICS' INSTITUTES IN CANADA WEST (1850s)

The centres in Canada West with mechanics' institutes appear in this table with their first and last dates of grants, although some antedate the granting system. Where we know their date of formation (or incorporation), that appears in square brackets. Some had obtained individual grants from the legislature before regular funding began in 1851. Of the seventy-one receiving grants, at least twenty-five were already in operation by 1854, showing Canada West's openness to the movement.

Aurora (1856/1857)
Aylmer (1856/1858)
Ayr (1856/1858)
Baltimore (1858)
Barrie (1855/1858)
Belleville (1851/1858)
Berlin (1855/1858)
Bowmanville (1855/1858)
Brampton (1854/1858)
Brantford (1853/1858)
Brockville (1851/1858) [1851]
Cayuga (1857/1858)
Chatham (1853/1858)
Cobourg (1856/1858)
Collingwood (1856/1858)
Drummondville (1857/1858)
Dundas (1855/1858) [1841]
Dunnville (1856/1858)
Elora (1858)

Fergus (1857/1858)
Flamboro (1855)
Fonthill (1855/1858)
Galt (1853/1858)
Goderich (1853/1858)
Guelph (1851/1858)
Hamilton (1851/1858) [1849]
Kingston (1847/1858) [1835]
Lindsay (1858)
London (1849/1858)
L'Orignal (1856/1858)
Merrickville (1857/1858)
Metcalfe (1856/1858)
Milton (1853/1858)
Mitchell (1855/1858) [1849]
Napanee (1857/1858)
Newcastle (1858)
Newmarket (1857/
Niagara (1851/1858) [1848]

| | |
|---|---|
| Norval (1858) | St Thomas (1853/1858) |
| Oakville (1855/1858) | Sarnia (1853/1858) |
| N. Ontario (1858) | Simcoe (1851/1858) |
| Owen Sound (1856/1858) | Smiths Falls (1855/1858) |
| Ottawa (1853/1858) | Stratford (1854/1858) [1846] |
| Paris (1855/1858) | Streetsville (1857/1858) |
| Perth (1851/1857) | Thorold (1858) |
| Peterborough (1855/1858) | Toronto (1847/1858) [1830] |
| Picton (1851/1858) | Vankleek Hill (1858) |
| Port Hope (1853/1858) | Vienna (1857/1858) |
| Prescott (1855/1858) | Waterdown (1855/1858) |
| Ramsay (1857/1858) | Wellington N. (1856/1858) |
| Renfrew (1855/1858) | Weston (1858) |
| Richmond (1857) | Whitby (1853/1858) [1849] |
| St Catharines (1853/1858) [1849] | Windsor (1857/1858) |
| St George (1857/1858) | Woodstock (1852/1858) |
| St Marys (1856/1858) | |

*Sources:* Province of Canada, *Journals of the Legislative Assembly of United Canada* (1852–59); Province of Ontario, *Sessional Papers*.

## TABLE B2 MECHANICS' INSTITUTES IN CANADA EAST (1850s)

Apart from a handful of stable organizations, the mechanics'-institutes movement in Canada East was much more ephemeral than Canada West's. The increase in funding in the early 1850s soon led to many more mechanics' and literary institutes, but there is little trace of most of them after funding ended in 1859. This table lists all the mechanics' institutes that received provincial grants and the years of the first and last grants, which will approximately date their creation and demise. Only the Montreal and Quebec institutes were much older; almost all the others date from the 1850s. A glance at the list of sixty-one institutes shows that the majority (thirty-nine) obtained their first grants only in 1857 or 1858, at the end of the granting program.

Bagotville (1857/1858)
Barnston (1857/1858)
Bécancour (1857/1858)
Berthier (1854/1857)
Chambly (1855/1857)
Chatham (1857/1858)
Chicoutimi (1857/1858)
Cookshire (1858)
Danville (1857/1858)
Drummondville (1857/1858)
Dumontville (1856/1858)
Eaton (1858)
Fraserville (1858)
Hemmingford (1855/1858)
Huntingdon (1855/1858)
Iberville (1854/1857)
Industrie (1856/1858)
Lachine (1858)
Lachute (1855/1858)
Lanoraie (1855/1858)
Laprairie (1858)
L'Assomption (1857)
L'Avenir (1857/1858)
Magog (1857)
Mégantic (1858)
Montmagny (1857/1858)
Montreal (1851/1857)
Napierville (1857/1858)
New Ireland (1857)
Quebec (1851/1858)
Ramsay (1857/1858)

Richmond (1857/1858)
Rimouski (1856/1857)
Rivière du Loup (1857/1858)
St-Alexandre – Iberville (1858)
St-Ambroise de Kildare (1857/1858)
St Andrews (1856/1858)
St-Antoine de la Baie (1857/1858)
St-Césaire (1856/1858)
St-Charles (1858)
St-Eustache (1857/1858)
St-Félix de Valois (1857/1858)
St George (1857/1858)
St-Hyacinthe (1854/1858)
St-Jean Port Joli (1858)
St John's (1858)
St-Joseph de Maskinongé (1857/1858)
St-Léon (1856/1858)
St Michael Lachine (1857).
St-Michel de Bellechasse (1858)
St-Ours (1857/1858)
Ste-Rose de Lima (1857/1858)
St-Scholastique (1857/1858)
St-Vincent de Paul (1854/1857)
Sherbrooke (1854/1857)
Sherbrooke County (1853/1857)
Sorel (1854/1858)
Stanstead (1856/1858)
Three Rivers (1852/1858)
Varennes (1858)
Yamachiche (1857/1858)

*Sources*: Province of Canada, *Journals of the Legislative Assembly of United Canada* (1852–59). Yvan Lamonde, "Liste alphabétique de noms de lieux où existèrent des associations 'littéraires' au Québec (1840–1900)," presents thirty-two mechanics' institutes or *instituts d'artisans*; of these, nine do not appear in the assembly journals as having received grants: Aylmer, Baie du Febvre, Charleston, Melbourne, Notre-Dame de la Victoire, Plessisville, St-Christophe d'Arthabaska, Ste-Elizabeth, and Terrebonne. Thus seventy institutes may have existed, at least briefly, in Lower Canada.

## TABLE B3 MECHANICS' INSTITUTES/LIBRARIES IN ONTARIO (1890s), BY COUNTY/DISTRICT

With Ontario's re-introduction of grants after Confederation, the number of institutes began to increase, almost explosively by the late 1880s and early 1890s. Table B3 lists the 331 mechanics' institutes and free libraries by county and district in the 1890s. Those in italics were former institutes that became free libraries after the 1882 act. In 1895, all were converted into free libraries. Note how many institutes formed in very small centres and the concentration of institutes in the west of the province.

ALGOMA DISTRICT (3)
Chapleau
Sault Ste Marie
Thessalon

BRANT (5)
*Brantford*
Burford
Glenmorris
Paris
St George

BRUCE (21)
Bervie
Cargill
Chesley
Hanover
Holyrood
Kincardine
Lion's Head
Lucknow
Mildmay
Paisley
Port Elgin
Ripley
Riversdale
Southampton
Tara
Teeswater
Tiverton
Underwood
Walkerton
Westford
Wiarton

CARLETON (5)
Kars
Manotick
Metcalfe
North Gower
Ottawa

DUFFERIN (6)
Grand Valley
Lucille
Mono Centre
Orangeville
Shelburn
Violet Hill

DUNDAS (5)
Chesterville
Iroquois
Morewood
Morrisburg
W. Winchester

DURHAM (2)
Bowmanville
Orono

ELGIN (8)
Aylmer
Duart
Dutton
Rodney
*St Thomas*
Shedden
Sparta
Springfield

ESSEX (3)
Essex Centre
Kingsville
Leamington

FRONTENAC (2)
Garden Island
Kingston

GLENGARRY (4)
Alexandria
Lancaster
Maxville
Williamstown

GRENVILLE (7)
Algonquin
Cardinal
Kemptville
Merrickville
Oxford Mills
Prescott
Spencerville

GREY (14)
Bognor
Chatsworth
Clarksburg
Dundalk
Durham
Flesherton
Holland Centre
Lake Charles
Markdale
Meaford

Owen Sound
St Vincent
Thornbury
Walter's Fall

HALDIMAND (8)
Caledonia
Cheapside
Dufferin
(Clanbrassil P.O.)
Dunnville
Hagersville
Jarvis
Nanticoke
Victoria (Caledonia)

HALTON (5)
Burlington
Georgetown
Milton
Oakville
Waterdown

HASTINGS (4)
Belleville
Deseronto
Trenton
Tweed

HURON (15)
Blyth
Brussels
Clinton
Dungannon
Ethel
Exeter
Fordwich
Goderich
Gorrie
Hensall
Molesworth
St Helens
Seaforth
Wingham
Wroxeter

KENT (11)
Blenheim
Bothwell
*Chatham*

Dresden
Highgate
Ridgetown
Romney
Thamesville
Tilbury Centre
Tilbury E. (Valetta)
Wheatley

LAMBTON (13)
Aberarder
Alvinson
Arkona
Copleston
Courtright
Forest
Mayflower
Oil Springs
Petrolia
Point Edward
Sarnia
Watford
Wyoming

LANARK (7)
Allans Mills
Almonte
Carleton Place
Dalhousie
(McDonald's Corners)
Pakenham
Perth
Smiths Falls

LEEDS (3)
Athens
Brockville
Gananoque

LENNOX &
ADDINGTON (4)
Camden East
Enterprise
Napanee
Newburgh

LINCOLN (5)
Beamsville
Grimsby
Merriton

Niagara
*St Catharines*

MANITOULIN (3)
Gore Bay
Little Current
Manitowaning

MIDDLESEX (13)
Ailsa Craig
Belmont
Coldstream
Delaware
Dorchester Station
Glencoe
*London*
Lucan
Melbourne
Parkhill
Strathroy
Thorndale
Wardsville

MUSKOKA DISTRICT (8)
Bracebridge
Burk's Falls
Emsdale
Gravenhurst
Huntsville
Port Carling
Sundridge
Windermere

NORFOLK (5)
Delhi
Port Rowan
*Simcoe*
Vittoria
Waterford

NORTHUMBERLAND (9)
Brighton
Campbellford
Cobourg
Colborne
Cold Springs
Fenella
Hastings
Port Hope
Warkworth

ONTARIO (12)
Beaverton
Brougham
Cannington
Claremont
Columbus
Greenwood
Oshawa
Pickering
Port Perry
Sunderland
Uxbridge
Whitby

OXFORD (7)
Embro
*Ingersoll*
Norwich
Plattsville
Thamesford
Tilsonburg
Woodstock

PARRY SOUND
  DISTRICT (1)
Parry Sound

PEEL (12)
Alton
Belfountain
Bolton
Brampton
Caledon
Cheltenham
Claude
Forks of the Credit
Inglewood
Mono Mills
Mono Road
Streetsville

PERTH (8)
Atwood
Listowel
Logan (Mitchell P.O.)
Milverton
Mitchell
St Marys
Stratford
Tavistock

PETERBOROUGH (4)
Lakefield
Millbrook
Norwood
Peterborough

PRESCOTT (1)
L'Orignal

PRINCE EDWARD (1)
Picton

RAINY RIVER
  DISTRICT (2)
Keewatin
Rat Portage

RENFREW (6)
Admaston
Arnprior
Calabogie
Douglas
Pembroke
Renfrew

RUSSELL (1)
Russell

SIMCOE (13)
Allandale
Alliston
Barrie
Beeton
Bradford
Collingwood
Creemore
Elmvale
Midland
Orillia
Penetanguishene
Stayner
Tottenham

STORMONT (1)
Cornwall

THUNDER BAY
  DISTRICT (2)
Port Arthur
Schreiber

VICTORIA (9)

Bobcaygeon
Coboconk
Fenelon Falls
Lindsay
Little Britain
Kirkfield
Manilla
Omemee
Woodville

WATERLOO (10)
Ayr
Baden
*Berlin*
Elmira
Floradale
Galt
Hespeler
New Hamburg
Preston
*Waterloo*

WELLAND (7)
Fonthill
Fort Erie
Niagara Falls
Niagara Falls south
Port Colborne
Thorold
Welland

WELLINGTON (15)
Arthur
Belwood
Clifford
Drayton
Elora
Enottville
Erin
Fergus
Glen Allan
*Guelph*
Harriston
Hillsburg
Morriston
Mount Forest
Palmerston

WENTWORTH (3)
Dundas

*Hamilton*  
Saltfleet

YORK (18)  
Aurora  
Highland Creek  
Islington  
King

Maple  
Markham  
Newmarket  
Parkdale  
Queensville  
Richmond Hill  
Scarborough

Schomberg  
Stouffville  
*Toronto*  
Vandorf  
W. Toronto Junction  
Weston  
Woodbridge

*Source:* Province of Ontario, *Sessional Papers.*

# Notes

### INTRODUCTION

1 The report, in four volumes, appeared in 1913 as Canada, *Royal Commission on Industrial Training and Technical Education: Report of the Commissioners.*
2 John Seath presented a document to the Department of Education, which published it as *Education for Industrial Purposes* (1911).
3 Robert Stamp, "The Campaign for Technical Education."
4 A limited literature exists for the Atlantic provinces and the west, but much research still needs doing. For Nova Scotia, see Macleod,"Practicality Ascendant"; Guildford, "Coping with De-Industrialization"; Keane, "A Study in Early Problems and Policies"; and Jarrell, "Science and the State." For New Brunswick, Hewitt has discussed the Saint John Mechanics' Institute in "Science, Popular Culture, and the Producer Alliance" and in "Science as Spectacle." For Prince Edward Island, see Hewitt, "The Mechanics' Institutes." For Saskatchewan, consult "The Grenfell Mechanics' and Literary Institute" and Blenkinsop, "A History of Adult Education." For Manitoba, see Taylor, "Professionalism."
5 A good example is the dating of the creation of the Council of Arts and Manufactures of the Province of Quebec/Conseil des arts et manufactures de la Province de Québec. Several authors claim 1872 or 1875. Charland, *Histoire de l'enseignement technique et professionel,* gives 1869. In fact, the United Province created it in 1857 as a board/chambre. Stirling, "Postsecondary Arts Education," has the correct date but refers to the Conseil throughout the period, although its name did not change until 1872–73.
6 See Millard, *The Master Spirit.*
7 McKay, "The Liberal Order Framework." See also Roy, *Progrès, harmonie, liberté,* and Fecteau, *Un nouvel ordre.*

8   Constant and Ducharme, eds., *Liberalism and Hegemony*, 11.
9   Curtis, *The Politics of Population*. For a representative sample of state-
    formation analyses of aspects of nineteenth-century Canadian society,
    see Greer and Radforth, eds., *Colonial Leviathan*.
10  McKay and others describe the actions of these groups in Gramscian
    terms: creating and enforcing hegemony but willing to compromise when
    necessary. Whether one follows Gramsci – I remain agnostic – surely social
    groups will do what they can to be dominant rather than subordinate.
11  The term "middle class" is remarkably fluid. For central Canada in our
    period, that group came largely from the business community and edu-
    cated members of society. The key to understanding them is the time they
    spent in voluntary associations, churches, and other organizations and
    their sense of duty to society. See Holman, *A Sense of Their Duty*, and Marks,
    *Revivals and Roller Rinks*. The most detailed account is Ferry, *Uniting*. This
    was not just a central Canadian story: Samson in *The Spirit of Industry*
    describes a similar trajectory for Nova Scotia. However, Sandwell in "The
    Limits of Liberalism" reminds us about the largely invisible, marginal
    people who do not fit comfortably within the story, as we can see from the
    apparent indifference of many of them to the educational proselytizers.
12  Charland, *Histoire de l'enseignement*, 31.

## CHAPTER ONE

1   Leake, *The Means and Methods*, xvi.
2   For a review of this history, see McInnis, "A Reconsideration." For the eco-
    nomic history of agriculture, see Hamelin and Roby, *Histoire économique*.
    The backwardess theme is central to Jones, "French-Canadian
    Agriculture," and Séguin, *La 'nation canadienne'*; see also Séguin, ed.,
    *Agriculture et colonisation*. The key proponent of the *crise* explanation is
    Ouellet, *Histoire économiqu* and *Le Bas-Canada*. But Macallum, *Unequal
    Beginnings*, raises a number of objections.
3   Jean-Charles Chapais, *fils* (1850–1926), writing on the eve of the First
    World War, claimed that the habitants "possessed, however, no knowledge
    of progressive farming, and their ideas of agriculture were no more
    advanced in 1850 than they had been before the Conquest"; "Three
    Centuries of Agriculture," 518. However, the story is much more complex.
    See, for example, Beutler, "L'outillage agricole," and Courville, "Le mar-
    ché des 'subsistences'" and "Villages and Agriculture." On the interpreta-
    tion of data, see McInnis, "Some Pitfalls."

4  Early Upper Canadian farmers faced different problems but had their own struggles. See Wood, *Making Ontario*; McCalla, *Planting the Province*; and McInnis, *Perspectives*.

5  McInnis suggests that farmers in the two halves of the province at mid-century differed little in output. According to Darroch, more than half of Canada West's farm families had "middling" or substantial farms, which were cleared and productive. There were few poor farmers, and even new entrants were doing well as part of the rural middle class. Darroch, "Scanty Fortunes."

6  A variety of local and state societies emerged in the 1790s, including the New York Society for the Promotion of Agriculture, Arts and Manufactures in 1791 (renamed the Society for the Promotion of Useful Arts in 1804).

7  The committee's report is in *Journals of the House of Assembly of the Province of Lower Canada* (1816), appendix E. The idea for a board of agriculture came from David Anderson, a contributor to the committee's hearings.

8  Savard, "William Sheppard"; *Société d'agriculture de Québec*.

9  Lessard, "Louis Gugy." Report of the Agricultural Society established in the District of Three-Rivers, *Journals of the House of Assembly, Lower Canada*, vol. 28, Appendix D. Act of 1821 (1 Geo. IV, cap. 5), Act of 1829 (10/11 Geo. IV, cap. 25), and Act of 1834 (4 Will. IV, cap 7). The last act required county societies to raise at least half as much as the legislature's annual grant – a maximum of £80. As the annual sub-scription to a society was 5 shillings, only a society with 160 members could receive the full amount, although wealthy members subscribed larger sums.

10  See Talman, "Agricultural Societies." More general works include Jones, *History*, and Reaman, *A History*.

11  Osborne, "Trading on the Frontier."

12  The most complete study of exhibitions in Canada is Heaman, *The Inglorious Arts*. For her, a fair is an occasional event for the sale of goods, while an exhibition has prizes for the best exhibits.

13  See Fair, "Gentlemen." Irwin, "Government Funding," looks at these organizations later in the century.

14  For the social outlook of rural organizations, see Ferry, *Uniting*, chaps. 5–6.

15  Lachlan, *Address of the Directing President*, 13.

16  An Act to Encourage the Establishment of Agricultural Societies in the Several Districts of this Province, 11 Geo. IV, cap. 10.

17  For the growth of agricultural societies in Canada West, see Table A2 in Appendix A.

18  New Hampshire had a state board from 1820 to 1822; Ohio started fund-
    ing local societies in 1839 and formed a board in 1846; and Massachusetts
    created a board in 1852. For details, see True, *A History*. Canada formed
    an embryonic department of agriculture as early as 1852, but New York
    did not reorganize its dairy commission into a true department of agricul-
    ture until 1893.

19  Brown, *Views of Canada*, 408.

20  Fergusson was a wealthy magistrate from Perthshire and a director of the
    Highland and Agricultural Society who brought his family to Upper
    Canada in 1833, settled near Waterdown, and helped found the town of
    Fergus. See Jones, "Adam Fergusson."

21  See Fergusson's comments in *Journal and Transactions of the Board of
    Agriculture for Upper Canada* I (1856), 18.

22  *Constitution of the Provincial Agricultural Association and Board of Agriculture
    for Canada West*, item 7. *Journal and Transactions of the Board of Agriculture for
    Upper Canada* I (1856), 23–4.

23  *Journal and Transactions of the Board of Agriculture for Upper Canada* I (1856),
    31.

24  Johnston, *Notes on North America*, 266.

25  Ibid., 272.

26  Col. Edward W. Thomson was a prosperous York County farmer, con-
    tractor, and MLA. He was founder and first president of the Home District
    Agricultural Society (1830) and president of the county agricultural society
    in 1850. He also served as a Canadian representative to the London exhib-
    itions in 1851 and 1862. See MacKenzie, "Edward William Thomson."

27  Henry Ruttan had served in the Upper Canadian legislature and was sher-
    iff of Newcastle District and the United Counties of Northumberland and
    Durham (1827–57). A member of the Board of Agriculture, prominent in
    the Cobourg Mechanics' Institute, he also invented a system for ventilat-
    ing railway carriages. See Ritchie, "Henry Ruttan." Between 1846 and
    1849, he published the *Newcastle Farmer*, which supported the expansion
    of township societies.

28  At the provincial exhibition (London, 1854), the president, Sheriff
    Charles P. Treadwell (1802–1873), of L'Orignal, mentioned the Society of
    Arts' collection of speeches on the lessons of 1851, particularly Sir Henry
    de la Beche on industrial education; Professor Solley on professional edu-
    cation for the practical man; and Professor Wilson on agricultural imple-
    ments. See *Journal and Transactions of the Board of Agriculture of Upper
    Canada* I (1856), 422.

29  *Canadian Agriculturist* 2 (Oct. 1850), 218.

30  A comparative list of entries for the Kingston shows in 1849 and 1859 reveals the four-fold increase in exhibits, from 1,321 to 5,676. *Canadian Agriculturist* 13 (Nov. 1861), 644.

31  *Journal and Transactions of the Board of Agriculture of Upper Canada* I (1856), 133.

32  Jarrell, "Justin de Courtenay."

33  For the history of agriculture in Québec, see Letourneau, *Histoire de l'agriculture*. Several useful papers appear in Séguin, ed., *Agriculture et colonisation*. A good survey of the background is Linteau, Durocher, and Robert, *Histoire*.

34  *Journal d'agriculture et procédés de la Société d'agriculture du Bas-Canada* 1 (May 1848), 144. While more than 60% of members were anglophone, the anglophone farming population made up a considerably smaller proportion in the province.

35  *British American Cultivator* 1 (1 Jan. 1845), 5–7; and *Newcastle Farmer* 1 (1 Aug. 1846), 3.

36  *Canada Farmer* 1 (1 June 1864), 152.

37  An overview on the improver movement is Fussell, "The Agricultural Revolution, 1600–1750." Fussell has published a number of books on agricultural tools and techniques in the period. Two articles give a good sense of the improvers' work: Brown, "Reassessing the Influence," and Wykes, "Robert Bakewell."

38  Writing in 1869 of the farmers of his youth, physician William Canniff (1830–1910) paints a picture of ignorance: "The old men satisfied with the abundance of to-day, and drawing a contrast between the present and the past, when starvation was at the door, and in the cupboard, were quite content with the primitive system of agriculture, which his soldier father had adopted. He saw no other mode of tilling the soil, and with no reason sought not a change, so no innovations by scientific agriculturalists disturbed the quiet repose of many of the steady going plodders. Their sons rarely went abroad to learn the ways of others; and often what did come to their ears was regarded with great suspicion. They wanted no new-fangled notions." Canniff, *History*, 591, offers a nice counterpoise to the traditional view of the ignorant *habitant* farmer.

39  For biographical details, see Gundy, "Hugh Christopher Thomson."

40  "There cannot be a more delightful employment than that of a scientific agriculturist. Gentlemen of intelligence and leisure may amuse themselves, whilst they subserve the public welfare by collecting and publishing the results of practical experiments, made by themselves and others. The newspapers read in the district, are open to such publications, and they

will be perused with more interest, than speculations on similar subjects made in other countries." *The Prompter*, 54.

41  See Kelly, "The Transfer."

42  Johnston, *Notes*, 265, 294.

43  See Jarrell, "Rise and Decline"; also Chartrand, Duchesne, and Gingras, *Histoire*, chap. 3.

44  For Girod, see Bernard, "Amury Girod."

45  Gagnon, "Napoléon Aubin,"

46  Aubin, *La chimie agricole*, introduction (translation).

47  For more details, consult Rossiter, *The Emergence of Agricultural Science*, chap. 1.

48  See Hurt, *American Agriculture*. Many farmers were still too isolated, poor, or illiterate to gain value from the press.

49  Robert, "William Evans."

50  Evans, *A Treatise*, x.

51  Evans, *Agricultural Improvement*.

52  See *Debates* LAUC 4 (1844–45), 752ff.

53  Ibid., 564, 712.

54  The history of Evans's periodical and its successors is very complex. Beaulieu and Hamelin, *Le presse québécoise*, vol.1, provides details. The journal was *Canadian Agriculturist* from its launch in January 1843 until December 1847. Lack of subscribers closed a French-language version, *Revue agricole*, in 1845. From January 1848 on, the English version was the *Agricultural Journal and Transactions of the Lower Canada Agricultural Society*, and the French version, *Journal d'agriculture et Transactions de la société d'agriculture du Bas-Canada*. In May 1853, when it became the official organ of the Board of Agriculture, its names changed to *Farmer's Journal and Transactions of the Lower Canada Board of Agriculture* and *Journal du Cultivateur et Procédés de la Chambre d'agriculture du Bas-Canada*. From 1861 on, the English version was *Lower Canada Agriculturist*, reverting to *Canadian Agriculturist* for 1867–68. The French was the *Journal d'agriculture et des Travaux de la Chambre d'agriculture du Bas-Canada* 1857–58, *L'Agriculteur, Journal officiel de la Chambre d'agriculture du Bas-Canada* 1858–61, and *Revue agricole* (1861–). Evans was editor of the English version until 1850, then R. Abraham, 1850–53, H. Ramsay, 1853–57, and James Anderson 1857–68. J.-X. Perrault edited the French version 1857–68.

55  Evans, *Agriculture in Lower Canada*.

56  Séguin, *La 'nation canadienne,'* 138.

57  For details, see Landon, "The Agricultural Journals," 167–75.

58  MacKenzie, "William Graham Edmundson."

59  *British American Cultivator* 1 (Jan. 1842), 1.

60 MacKenzie, "George Buckland."

61 In 1850, Evans's paper had a circulation of 3,500, which sounds respectable, although probably many readers were urbanites, not farmers.

62 Goddard, "The Development."

63 See Orwin and Whetham, *History*, and Russell, *A History*.

64 There are at least two reasons for such a tardy response to agriculture. First, British governments before the 1860s tended to be non-interventionist, representing various shades of Tory paternalism or laissez-faire liberalism, and, second, Britain was not a developing country, having neither a frontier to subdue nor an industrial economy to establish.

65 *Agricultural Journal and Transactions of the Lower Canada Agricultural Society* (July 1850), 209.

66 Report of the Special Committee on the State of Agriculture in Lower Canada, *Journals of the Legislative Assembly of United Canada (Journals LAUC)* (1850), Appendix T.T.

67 Compare Jarrell, for example, on Nova Scotia, "Science and the State in 19th-Century Canada," and on Michigan, "Science and the State in Ontario."

68 On the evolution of the administrative departments, see Hodgetts, *Pioneer Public Service.*

69 An act to provide for the establishment of a Bureau of Agriculture, and to amend and consolidate the laws relating to agriculture, 16 Vict., cap. 11. There was also a personal element in the bureau's creation. Hincks, as premier, had attempted to include Cameron in the cabinet as president of the council, but the latter refused to take on a sinecure. As Hincks recalled, "as the chief difficulty was that Mr. Cameron wanted more work for the same salary, it was determined to take the opportunity of establishing a Bureau of Agriculture, and to attach it to the Presidency of the Council. This simple expedient proved satisfactory and Mr. Cameron accepted office." Hincks, *Reminiscences*, 256.

70 Second annual report, Upper Canada Board of Agriculture; first annual report, Lower Canada Board of Agriculture, *Journals LAUC* (1854–55), appendix I.I.

71 *Agricultural Journal and Transaction Lower Canada Agricultural Society* 4 (Feb. 1851), 37–8.

72 Hind, *Eighty Years' Progress*, 38.

73 *Journals LAUC* (1852–3), Appendix S.

74 *Debates LAUC* (1852), 280, 334.

75 *Journals LAUC* (1854–5), Appendix I.I.

76 Ibid.

77 *Journals LAUC* (1857), Appendix 54.

78 Boyce, *Hutton.*

79 LAC, RG 1, E7, Vol. 41, Submissions to the Executive Council, Province of Canada, 668–72.

80 Documents submitted by the Bureau of Agriculture (1855), *Journals LAUC* (1854–55), Appendix I.I.

81 An Act to make better provision for the encouragement of Agriculture, and also to provide for the promotion of Mechanical Science, 20 Vict., cap. 32.

82 *Canadian Agriculturist* 9 (June 1857), 170.

83 See *Transactions of the Board of Agriculture and of the Agricultural Association of Upper Canada*, vol. 5.

84 Jean-Charles Chapais, *père*, MLA for Kamouraska, had a certain influence. Macdonald appointed him a senator at Confederation, minister of agriculture (1867–69), and receiver-general (1869–73). See Désilets, "Jean-Charles Chapais [*père*]."

85 See Jones, *History*.

86 *Transactions of the Board of Agriculture and of the Agricultural Association of Upper Canada*, vol. 3.

87 *Journal of Education for Upper Canada* (*JEUC*) (Oct. 1861), 147–8.

88 *Transactions of the Board of Agriculture for Upper Canada*, vol. 5, 456ff.

89 Province of Canada, *Sessional Papers* (1863), No. 4.

90 Ibid. (1865), No. 6, 4.

## CHAPTER TWO

1 For the Irish background, see O'Sullivan and Jarrell, "Agricultural Education." The broader educational picture is available in Akenson, *The Irish Educational Experiment*.

2 *Albert Agricultural College. Centennial Souvenir, 1838–1938*, 11.

3 The system reached its peak in the late 1850s, when the board supported some forty-two model agricultural schools with farms, sixty-four work-house farms, and forty-seven ordinary national schools with agricultural instruction. British government opposition to state support for agricultural education then whittled away at the system, forcing the board to jettison schools until, by the late 1870s, only two remained.

4 The most detailed account of Quebec agricultural schools is J.-C. Chapais, *fils, Notes historiques*; also see his *Réminiscences*.

5 See Jolois, *Joseph-François Perrault*.

6 Doctor Charles Duncombe's Report upon the Subject of Education, *Journal of the House of Assembly of Upper Canada* (1836), appendix 35, 86.

7 *Debates LAUC*, 8 (1849), 111, 252, 306. At the same time, the St-Hyacinthe municipal council asked for model farms.

8 *Journals LAUC* (1850), Appendix T.T. On Taché, see Nadeau, "Joseph-Charles Taché." The committee had independent support for its doubts: J.F.W. Johnston'a recent report on New Brunswick agriculture had suggested teaching agriculture only in elementary schools and on two school farms. Johnston, *Report on the Agricultural Capabilities.*

9 *Journals LAUC* (1851), Appendix J.

10 This may have been an echo of Lord Clarendon's "practical instructor" scheme in Ireland.

11 *Journals LAUC* (1851), Appendix J.

12 Chapais, *fils, Notes historiques.*

13 Perron, "Frédéric-M.-F. Ossaye." According to Perron, there is no trace of Ossaye after the early 1860s. However, a Frederic Ossaye, a farmer aged 64, his wife, and two adult children arrived in New York in July 1886 as immigrants. This is approximately the right age for Ossaye; he may have returned to France. Immigrant Ships Transcribers Guild, www.immigrant-ships.net/v7/1800v7/pennland1889070501.html

14 At the same time, William Ruthven, of St-Louis de Lotbinière, asked for assistance to promote his simplified textbook on agricultural chemistry, as did Ossaye for his compilation *Les veillées canadiennes*. The legislature's library committee said no: "No proof has been adduced of their special merit or value, so as to enable the Committee to decide whether they are deserving of aid from the public funds; and it is not thought advisable to encourage indiscriminate applications of this nature, or to make appropriations on their behalf, unless in the case of works of special excellence or utility." *Debates LAUC* 11 (1852), 2650. The assembly concurred. For petitions, see pp. 173, 237, 806, 867, 1085, 1185. The committee noted that Ruthven had already received a grant of £12 6s in 1849 for the same book.

15 While normal schools go back to the eighteenth century in Germany and France, becoming key institutions in France when François Guizot (1787–1874) was minister of education in the 1830s, they were still a novel institution in North America. Massachusetts, whose education system influenced Upper Canada's, opened two in 1839; New York followed suit in 1844. *JEUC* (April 1856), 49. Lower Canada had attempted to organize normal schools in the mid-1830s, which would have made them the first on the continent, but a number of factors militated against their creation.

16 *Journals LAUC* (1846), Appendix P.

17 Report of the Superintendent of Public Instruction for Lower Canada, Province of Canada, *Sessional Papers* (1861), No. 17. See also Hudon, *L'action agronomique.*

18 *L'agriculteur* (Oct. 1860), 139.

19 Apart from his autobiography, *The Story of My Life*, edited by J.G. Hodgins, the standard biography is Sissons, *Egerton Ryerson*.

20 On Ryerson's views on the place of science in education, see Zeller, *Inventing Canada*, 146–7. For a revisionist approach to Ryerson's educational program, see Curtis, *Building the Educational State*.

21 For French technical education, see Artz, *The Development*, 220ff. The first notable school did not appear until 1822 and followed the model of Fellenberg's school at Hofwyl. Although the Conservatoire des arts et métiers widened its activities to include agriculture during the 1830s, state activity was not significant until after the Revolution of 1848. Farm schools were organized for each *département*, then district schools for farm managers, and finally a national school in Versailles for teachers. The system resembled that of Ireland's and was initially successful: by the end of 1851, some seventy-one local schools had 1,500 students. The central school did not fare so well; open briefly from 1849 to 1852, it did not re-emerge until 1876. Only in the 1880s did agriculture as a subject become part of the curriculum at all levels of the French educational system.

22 An Act for the better establishment and maintenance of Common Schools in Upper Canada, 9 Vict., cap. 20.

23 Hodgins, *The Establishment*, vol. III, 314.

24 See Morton, *Henry Youle Hind*, and Jarrell, "Henry Youle Hind."

25 *JEUC* (April 1848), 103–7; (June 1848), 166–72; (July 1848), 198–202; (Aug. 1848), 225–8.

26 Ryerson, *Report on a System*, 141.

27 *JEUC* (Nov. 1848), 331–2.

28 The examiners included the normal school's headmaster, Thomas Jaffray Robertson (1805–1866), who had been chief inspector of the National Schools of Ireland before coming to Toronto; King's College chemistry professor Henry Holmes Croft (1820–1883); the new professor of agriculture at King's, George Buckland; and E.W. Thomson and F. Neale, president and vice-president, respectively, of the Home District Agricultural Society. *JEUC* (Jan. 1849), 8; (April 1849), 58.

29 Ibid. (April 1850), 49–50.

30 Ibid. (Nov. 1853), 170.

31 See Richards, "Agricultural Science."

32 For the Belfast chair, consult Adelman "The Agriculture Diploma"; on the background, see Jarrell, "Some Aspects."

33 The *Agricultural Journal and Transactions of the Lower Canada Agricultural Society* (July 1850) duly noted the opening of the Belfast institution.

34 For contemporary American activities, see Cochrane, *The Development*, and Dunbar, *The Michigan Record*.

35  See Madill, *A History*, chap. 4.

36  *Debates LAUC* 4 (1844–45), 629. In the spring of 1846, James Wickens, president of the Simcoe Agricultural Society, argued for endowing a professorship at King's. Soon thereafter, the president and secretary of the Talbot District society requested a chair in agricultural chemistry and a model farm. They were ignored. *Debates LAUC* 5 (1846), 211, 259–60, 864.

37  *Agriculturist and Canadian Journal* (1848), 50.

38  Jarrell, "The Influence."

39  Report of the University of Toronto, Province of Canada, *Sessional Papers* (1861), No. 17.

40  First Annual Report of the Board of Agriculture of Upper Canada, *Journals LAUC* (1852–53), Appendix S. See also Friedland, *The University of Toronto*, 52. The farm was in the area where the university's Hart House now stands.

41  *Canadian Agriculturist* 9, no. 8 (Aug. 1858), 170–3.

42  Typical questions included:
   • Question 1: Define agriculture as a *science* and an *art*. How can a knowledge of its *Theory* and *Practice* best be acquired?
   • Question 2: Mention those branches of physical science which have relations to agriculture – with illustrations.
   • Question 4: How is matter divided? Define and illustrate *elementary, compound, organic* and *inorganic* substances. What are soil, plants and animals composed of?
   • Question 5: State the composition and uses of *atmospheric air* and *water,* and their relations to vegetable and animal life.

43  On Dawson's career, see Sheets-Pyenson, *John William Dawson*, and Frost, *McGill University ... 1801–1895*.

44  This second, revised edition appeared in Halifax in 1856, after Dawson had left Nova Scotia; at least two other versions had slight variants in title.

45  One of the four King's professors, William Brydone Jack, pushed for practical education. He helped to introduce the first civil engineering course in British North America in 1854. See Jarrell, "Science Education at the University of New Brunswick."

46  Report of the Commission appointed under the Act of Assembly relating to King's College, Fredericton, *Journals of the House of Assembly of the Province of New Brunswick*, 1854, appendix, clxxxv.

47  Dawson, *On the Course*, 23.

48  Ibid., 24.

49  The only other university treatments of agriculture in Canada were Dawson's botany courses at McGill, and those at Queen's College in Kingston by George Lawson (1827–1895). These courses followed the

Edinburgh University tradition, as both men had studied there. Although Queen's had a botanical garden, it was not designed for agricultural instruction.

50 Perrault to Taschereau, 9 March 1864, Archives du Séminaire de Québec (ASQ), Univ. 103, no. 43.

51 Taschereau to Perrault, 11 March 1864 (no. 45) and 21 March 1864 (no. 49); Perrault to Taschereau, 23 March 1864 (no. 50); Taschereau to Perrault, 11 May 1864 (no. 58); and Perrault to Taschereau, 11 May 1864 (no. 59). The abbé Pilote wrote from Ste-Anne-de-la-Pocatière to warn the rector that it was all a question of politics, but that he ought to respond: 23 May 1864 (no. 63), 1 June 1864 (no. 66). ASQ, Univ. 103.

52 The Irish were the first to establish schools on Fellenberg's principles: between 1821 and 1826, the Anglican clergyman and agricultural writer William Hickey (1787–1875), writing as "Martin Doyle," operated a Hofwyl-style school at Bannow, County Wexford. He taught the three Rs and agricultural theory, while a Scottish farmer taught practice. The boys provided the labour. Despite some assistance from agricultural societies, the school failed financially. In the year it closed, another opened at Templemoyle, County Derry. There, theory was minimal and practice foremost; it survived until 1866. Twenty to thirty students was a typical year's enrolment at both schools. See O'Sullivan and Jarrell, "Agricultural Education." In England, the Royal Agricultural College at Cirencester, Gloucestershire, opened in 1845, supported by wealthy landowners. Although it obtained a royal charter, it was a private institution – the first agricultural college in the English-speaking world. J.-X. Perrault was one of its earliest students.

53 Three of the best known were the Gardiner Lyceum in Maine (1821–32), the Cream Hill Agricultural School in Connecticut (1845–69), and the Farmers' College near Cincinnati, Ohio, founded in 1846, but which did not survive the Civil War. Although these and other ephemeral schools did not lay the foundations of agricultural colleges after the Civil War, they did practise the ideal of US schools with manual labour that did survive. See True, A History. See also Bidwell and Falconer, History.

54 For more detail, see Marti, "The Purposes"; True, A History; and Hedrick, A History.

55 The New York State Agricultural College had no financial resources, but the Ovid Academy adopted it. Several years passed before the academy opened the agricultural school in 1861; it survived one year and closed when its headmaster took a commission in the Union army. The People's College, organized by a citizen group in Lockport and warmly endorsed

by Horace Greeley (1811–1872), editor of the influential *New York Tribune*, combined education with manual labour. Although it obtained one of the first grants under the Morrill Act, its funds were insufficient, and it never opened.

56 The act passed just after a Republican administration and legislative majority had come to power; the Republican Party was organized in Michigan in 1854 and had widespread support among farmers. See Dunbar and May, *Michigan*. For the college's early history, see Kuhn, *Michigan State*. A valuable survey of the movement is Dabney, *Agricultural Education*.

57 *Transactions of the Board of Agriculture of Upper Canada*, vol. 4, 102.

58 Ibid., vol 5. During this period, the Science and Art Department funded courses of lectures in Irish towns for similar purposes.

59 *Canada Farmer* 2, no. 5 (1 March 1865), 74.

60 See Gattinger, *A Century*.

61 Goulet and Jean, "Duncan McNab McEachran."

62 Ibid.

63 Province of Canada, *Sessional Papers* (1866), No. 5, 192.

64 *Canada Farmer* 2, no. 22 (15 Nov. 1865), 346.

65 Province of Canada, *Sessional Papers* (1865), No. 5, 191.

66 A telling official item in the *Journal of Education* in 1866 relates a local superintendent's request to the Education Office for permission to organize an agriculture class in a common school using the only English-language textbook available, that of McGill's J.W. Dawson. He said he understood that teaching agriculture in the common schools was unlawful and not approved by the department. The department replied that it was indeed lawful and a commendable pursuit. *JEUC* (March 1866), 43–4.

67 J.-C. Chapais, *fils*, claimed this to be the second agricultural college in North America; it was certainly the second oldest to survive into the twentieth century. For details, see Chapais, *fils*, "Three Centuries"; for more detail, see his *Notes historiques*. The Michigan Agricultural College opened two years before Ste-Anne at La Pocatière. Two earlier American colleges had closed after short existences. The early history of the Ste-Anne school is in *Le cinquantenaire*.

68 See Têtu and Gagnon, *Mandements, lettres pastorales et circulaires des évêques du Québec*, vol. IV (1888).

69 For Pilote, see Gagnon, "François Pilote"; for the college, Lebon, *Histoire*. For its scientific impact, see Hatvany, *Marshlands*.

70 Report on the School of Agriculture at St. Anne, Province of Canada, *Sessional Papers* (1866), No. 5.

71 Extracted in "Agricultural College at St. Anne's, Kamouraska," *Journal of Education for Lower Canada* (Jan. 1866), 12.

72 A typical day (with seasonal variations) encompassed the following routine:

| | | | |
|---|---|---|---|
| 5.00 a.m. | Rise | 1.00 p.m. | Lecture |
| 5.20 a.m. | Prayers | 2.00 p.m. | Study |
| 5.30 a.m. | Lecture | 4.00 p.m. | Recreation |
| 6.20 a.m. | Breakfast | 6.30 p.m. | Supper |
| 7.00 a.m. | Study – stables | 7.00 p.m. | Practical horticulture |
| 9.00 a.m. | Recreation | 8.00 p.m. | Prayers |
| 9.30 a.m. | Study – workshop | 8.15 p.m. | Lecture |
| 11.30 a.m. | Dinner | 9.00 p.m. | Bed |

Half the students laboured on the farm during study periods while the other half studied.

73 Province of Canada, *Sessional Papers* (1864), No. 32.

74 Ibid.

75 Report of the Special Committee on Agricultural Instruction, *Journals LAUC* (1864), Appendix A.

76 Ibid., 44.

77 Province of Canada, *Sessional Papers* (1863), No. 4.

78 Ibid. (1867), No. 3, 73.

79 *Farmer's Advocate* 6 (7 Feb. 1871), 36.

80 Report of the Special Committee on Agricultural Instruction, 38 and 22.

## CHAPTER THREE

1 Consult Layton, *Science*, on the structure of British science in the nineteenth century; see Cardwell, *The Organisation*.

2 Hinton ("Popular Science") argues that in the 1830s the urban working class and the lower segment of the middle class, such as shop assistants, possessed very little leisure time for reading, and agricultural workers virtually none. The cheap books from Henry, Lord Brougham's (1778–1868), Society for the Diffusion of Useful Knowledge, the Chambers brothers, and Dionysius Lardner (1793–1859), among others, were often out of reach. Lardner's volumes sold for sixpence a volume, while those of the Library of Useful Knowledge, broken into thirty-two-page pamphlets, sold at sixpence a unit. Popular books on technical matters, such as the society's, which sought to unite the "rules" of trades with scientific knowledge – a fundamental ideal in the mechanics'-institute movement and technical education generally – probably reached few workers. One additional

barrier to further diffusion among the lower middle and working classes
was vocabulary: the language of science in public lectures or popular
books was, indeed, both difficult and unfamiliar to them.

3 Vincent finds that in a sample of upwardly mobile sons of working-class
fathers between 1837 and 1914, most (66 per cent) chose occupations
requiring little or no science: clerks, farmers, and shopkeepers. Vincent,
*Literacy.*

4 Lee, "George Birkbeck."

5 For adult education generally, see Kelly, *A History;* for mechanics' institutes, Tylecote, *The Mechanics' Institutes.*

6 With the Chartist threat still fresh in their minds, no doubt many institute
directors saw their organizations as safer channels for directing working-
class energies. Some historians, such as Shapin and Barnes ("Science"),
argue that the institute movement, in its early years, was a straightforward
exercise in social control. Proponents felt that the burgeoning and unruly
urban working class of early Victorian England required some form of
control to ensure industrial productivity and civic peace. Thus science,
particularly physical science purveyed as facts and laws, might work where
religion and moralizing had failed.

7 Garner and Jenkins, "The English Mechanics' Institutes."

8 In many localities, because of the paucity of secondary education and the
absence of public libraries, the middle class dominated institutions ready-
made to provide for their wants. This was quite evident in Canada

9 Royle, "Mechanics' Institutes." One can only speculate whether or not the
institutes accommodated the needs of the more "respectable" members
of the working class who arrived in the thousands for the one-shilling days
at the 1851 Exhibition at Hyde Park.

10 "Lyceum," *Wikipedia.* Accessed 12 Jan. 2015. As Fisher notes, "Even the
lyceums, however, ultimately missed the bulk of American artisans";
*Industrial Education,* 23. Visiting lecturers were central to their operation,
but "artisans and operatives found little of interest in the lectures, and
returned to their benches to await the next crusade" (24).

11 The majority of institutes in Ontario became public libraries. It may be
that minute and account books, at least, survive for some; there is no census of them. Modern published studies have appeared only for the institutes in London, Kingston, Montreal, and Napanee. The Archives of
Ontario includes four notable fonds:

- F1203: the Mechanics' Institutes Collection, which includes annual
reports, constitutions, and library catalogues for institutes in Belleville,
Bowmanville, Clarksburg, Cobourg, Dundas, Dunnville, Elora, Garden

Island, Hamilton, Montreal, Niagara, Oakville, Peterborough, Port
Hope, Sarnia, Scarborough, Streetsville, and Woodstock

- F2101: a miscellany of printed materials in the Association of
Mechanics' Institutes of Ontario fonds
- F2102: records of the Niagara Mechanics' Institute
- F2103: records of the Caledon Mechanics' Institute

12  See Jarrell, "The Social Functions." Numerous examples of the role of
societies' social activities appear in the works of Ferry, Holman, and Marks
(see Bibliography), for example, but mostly from later in the century.

13  The surviving documents of the Toronto Mechanics' Institute are in the
Baldwin Room of the Toronto Reference Library. For background information, consult Scadding, *Toronto of Old*, and Robertson, *Landmarks*, especially 398–9 and 756–60. Additional material is in the Archives of Ontario
(see note 11 above).

14  A copy of the society's constitution is in the Baldwin Room.

15  Dunlop, *An Address delivered to the York Mechanics' Institute March, 1832*.

16  From a broadside of 14 April 1835, Baldwin Room.

17  Thompson, *Reminiscences*. On Fothergill, see Romney, "Charles Fothergill."

18  See note 11 above.

19  Broadside in Baldwin Room.

20  Robertson, *Landmarks*, 756.

21  Although fewer than half concerned scientific or technical topics, the lecturers, such as Superintendent of Public Instruction Egerton Ryerson,
architect Kivas Tully (1820–1905), chemistry professor Henry Holmes
Croft, and Normal School lecturer Henry Youle Hind, were the best available locally.

22  *JEUC* 2 (Feb. 1849), 23.

23  *Toronto Mechanics' Institute Catalogue of Books in the Library*, copy in Baldwin
Room.

24  The exhibition included 208 oil paintings; about 150 curiosities (old
books, military items, and artisanal items); more than 100 bronzes, statu-
ettes, and manufactures; 95 watercolours and lithographs; 50-odd natural
historical and geological specimens; and 16 engravings, drawings, and
photos. *Hamilton & Gore Mechanics' Institute. Exhibition of Fine Arts,
Manufactures, Curiosities, etc.*

25  Eales, *Lecture*.

26  See Cohoe, "Kingston Mechanics' Institute, 1834–1850," and "Kingston
Mechanics' Institute to Free Library."

27  Preamble to the institute's act of incorporation, printed in the *By-laws and
Catalogue of the Hamilton and Gore Mechanics' Institute*.

28  Heron, *Working in Steel*, 64–5.

29  Ardagh, *An Address*, 18. For further details on the Barrie institute and its art program, see Chalmers, "Learning to Draw."

30  Friels, *Inaugural Address*. Ottawa Mechanics' Institute (pamphlet 1855).

31  *Journals LAUC* (1858), Appendix 45. Forty-one of the fifty-eight institutes in Canada West, with a total of 5,228 members, reported; the largest were in Toronto, with 780 members; Hamilton, 630; and Ottawa, 279. Only ten had libraries of 1,000 volumes or more.

32  For Esson, see McDougall, "Henry Esson," and McGuire, "Portrait of the Pastor."

33  For the early history, see Robins, "The Montreal Mechanics' Institute" and "'Useful Education.'" The minute books from 1828 are in Montreal's Atwater Library; these have been digitized and are available on the library's website. Several annual reports are in the Archives of Ontario (see note 11 above).

34  For contemporary accounts, see Lebrun, *Tableau statistique*, 249, and *The Quebec Guide*, 132.

35  *The Quebec Guide*, 131.

36  For example, the institute's 1853–54 lecture program included: Rev. W. Bond, "The Pleasure and Profit of Science"; B. Chamberlin, "Our Country and Our Duty to It"; Rev. John Cornder, "The Social Position and Rights of Women"; Rev. D. Inglis, "The True Patriot"; Rev. A. Lillie, "Robert Burns"; D.C. McCallum, MD, "The New Theory of the Relations of Forces"; T.C. Keefer, "The Ottawa"; W. Milln, "Causes and Prevention of Steam Boiler Explosions" and "The Steam Engine"; A.N. Rennie, "Poetry – Its Relation to History"; and Rev. W. Taylor, "Spirit Rappings." It is evident that the topics of "science and art" were not very visible in the lecture series.

37  Atwater Library, *Catalogue of Books in the Library of the Mechanics' Institute of Montreal*.

38  Ibid., Mechanics' Institute of Montreal, Minute Book 1847–52, reports of the annual meetings.

39  *Report of the General Committee of the Mechanics' Institute of Montreal (1854)*, 13.

40  Atwater Library, Mechanics' Institute of Montreal, Minute Book 1853–56, report of the annual meeting, 6 Nov. 1854.

41  Ibid., Record of Life Members 1841–1898; I have selected only those to 1880, when the institute narrowed its focus to the library.

42  Responses appear in tabular form in Province of Canada, *Sessional Papers* (1858), appendix 46. The Montreal institute, with 994 members, and that in Quebec, with ninety-four, dominated the scene, each maintaining a library of more than 2,000 volumes. The average membership of the other

fourteen institutes was fifty, a little more than half that of small-centre
institutes in Canada West, and the average library consisted of 500 books.

43 Lamonde, "Liste alphabétique"; see also Vernon, "The Development," 336.

44 Poirier, *Institut Canadien-français.*

45 Bruchési, "L'Institut canadien."

46 As its 1873 regulations note, its aims were to unite French Canadians and
"de promouvoir, par toutes les voix légales et légitimes, les intérêts natio-
naux, scientifiques, industriels, et sociaux." *Statuts de la Société St-Jean-
Baptiste de la Cité de Québec* (1873), 4.

47 Boisseau, *Catalogue.*

48 They siphoned away members from mechanics' institutes: in 1858,
Canada East's mechanics' institutes had an aggregate of 1,671 members,
while Montreal and Quebec's instituts plus the more conservative, church-
supported Institut canadien-français de Montréal (founded in 1858)
totalled 1.575.

49 Ménard, "L'institut des artisans."

50 Lamonde, "Le membership."

51 Of eighty-two members analysed, 46 were blacksmiths, butchers, conduct-
ors, engineers, farmers, joiners, labourers, and shoemakers, and 24.7 per
cent were boat captains, "bourgeois," businessmen, doctors, and lawyers.

52 10th Annual Report, Minutes of the Montreal Mechanics' Institute,
4 Nov. 1850.

53 Montreal *Gazette*, 20 Oct. 1855; the first part of the article appeared
8 October. In retrospect, it is surprising that Perry would be selected a
commissioner, given his role in the 1849 riots, in which he set the parliament building on fire and assaulted Lord Elgin.

54 Atwater Library, Mechanics' Institute of Montreal, Minute Book 1855–59,
11 Aug. 1856.

55 Province of Canada, *Journal of the Legislative Council* (1857), 25.

56 On Head's interests, see Kerr, *Sir Edmund Head.*

57 Province of Canada, *Journal of the Legislative Council* (1857), 34.

58 Atwater Library, Mechanics' Institute of Montreal, 3, 4, and 9 March 1857;
Letterbook 1841–58, Stephenson to Secretary, Toronto Mechanics'
Institute, 4 March 1857.

59 *The Mirror of Parliament*, Wed. 27 May 1857.

60 Annual Report of the Minister of Agriculture for 1856, *Journals LAUC*
(1857), Appendix 54.

61 18th Annual Report, in Atwater Library, Montreal Mechanics' Institute,
Minute Book 1855–59, 18 Nov. 1857.

62 Sabourin, in "La chambre," posits the Conservatoire as the model for the boards.

63 On the evolution of the British art schools, see Frayling, *Royal College of Art.*

64 See Wood, *A History.*

65 Cole's partial autobiography and excerpts from his articles and speeches appear in Cole and Cole, eds., *Fifty Years.* The best biography is Burton and Bonython, *The Great Exhibitor.* His remarkable diary is in the Victoria and Albert Museum in London.

66 For Redgrave, see Casteras and Parkinson, eds., *Richard Redgrave.*

67 For Playfair's role, consult Reid, ed., *Memoirs.*

68 For details, see Layton, *Science.*

69 On Cole's role in building the South Kensington Museum, see Alexander, *Museum Masters,* chap. 6.

70 Statistics Canada, E-Stat, Census of Upper Canada 1842; Census of Lower Canada 1844.

71 All small-scale enterprises, they included food and beverage makers (bakers, brewers, confectioners, distillers); clothing and accessory makers (boot and shoe makers, brush makers, comb manufacturers, dressmakers, furriers, hatters, jewellers, milliners, shirt makers, silk and woolen dyers, tailors, tanners, watchmakers, and wigmakers). We do not know what "mechanics not specified" might include; I have placed that group with industrial workers. "Engineers" may have referred to civil engineers, but more probably stationary engineers, although Canadian industry did not much use steam power in the 1860s. Apart from these groups, less than 20 per cent of immigrants had a trade or industrial skill (which again suggests that other peoples did not yet view Canada as an industrial nation): household-goods producers and the building trades (cabinet-makers, carpenters, carvers, chair-makers, clock-makers, gilders, hardware manufacturers, joiners, mirror manufacturers, musical instrument–makers, organ and piano–makers, plumbers, stove manufacturers, and upholsterers); general manufacturing (brass, copper, cordage, guns, iron sheet, nails, oil cloth, paint, printing presses, tallow, and tin plate); printing (bookbinders, engravers, lithographers, printers); printing (bookbinders, engravers, lithographers, printers); and transportation (coach and carriage builders, harness makers, and saddlers).

72 Province of Canada, *Sessional Papers* (1865), No. 6, 101–2, lists these occupations alphabetically, with columns for numbers of British and foreign immigrants; the list accounts for more than 7,800 immigrants, 81 per cent of them British. My Table 3.3 groups the occupations and orders them by numbers of immigrants in each sector.

## CHAPTER FOUR

1  An Act to repeal a certain Act therein mentioned, and make better provision for the encouragement of Agriculture, and also to provide for the promotion of Mechanical Science, *Statutes of the Province of Canada* (1857), 20 Vict., cap. 32, sec. 27.

2  Thus it was perfectly legitimate to suppose that a Toronto manufacturer and his shop foreman could visit the board's model room, obtain the details of a new American machine already possessing a US patent, manufacture the identical device, and patent it in Canada, all the while protecting himself and owing the American originator nothing. For the patent system of the period, see Naylor, *The History*, and Jarrell, "Governmental Response."

3  *Annual Report of the Toronto Mechanics' Institute* (1858), 7.

4  Memorandum, W. Edwards to J.-C. Taché, 17 Feb. 1865, Board of Arts and Manufactures for Upper Canada (BAMUC) Letterbooks III, Archives of Ontario (AO), F1189.

5  Memorandum, Minister of Agriculture to Governor General, 5 Jan. 1858. LAC, RG 17 A1.2, 117–18.

6  *Report and Proceedings of the Annual Meeting of the Board of Arts and Manufactures for Upper Canada, January 15, 1859* (copy in LAC, MG 24, D16, Buchanan Papers, vol. 105, 69309). These included Aurora, Ayr, Belleville, Dundas, Fonthill, Galt, Hamilton, Kingston, Mitchell, Napanee, Niagara Falls, Oakville, Paris, Port Hope, Smith's Falls, Toronto, Vienna, Waterdown, and Whitby.

7  For a review of the mechanics'-institute movement and statistics for Ontario, see Report of the Minister of Education, Province of Ontario, *Sessional Papers* (1910), No. 16, part 5, 485–7.

8  Province of Canada, *Sessional Papers* (1862), No. 32.

9  In a letter from Upper Canada to Lower Canada Board, 1 March 1859, reported in Montreal *Gazette*, 4 May 1859.

10  The manufacturers in the institutes had concerns about the Canadian patent laws, and the provincial secretaries' correspondences contain many appeals from the two boards concerning patent reform, which the government ignored.

11  Royal Society of Arts, Minutes of the Society of Arts, 15 April 1857.

12  He wrote to Peter LeNeve Foster (1809–1879), the society's secretary, requesting a list of published lectures that would be useful to mechanics. As he later reported to Hind, all he received was a copy of a list of books in the "Department of Science and Art, South Kensington Museum," which

was of little use. W. Edwards to LeNeve Foster, 14 June 1860; W. Edwards to H.Y. Hind, 8 Aug. 1860, BAMUC Letterbook III, AO, F1189. Obtaining inexpensive books was even more difficult for the Toronto Mechanics' Institute. When George Longman told Edwards in 1863 that the institute's affiliation with the society had been no end of trouble, Edwards concluded "that there are no advantages derivable to Colonial Institutions through affiliation to the Society of Arts." Longman to W. Edwards, 28 April 1863; Edwards memorandum, 30 April 1863, AO, F775, Miscellaneous Collection, 1863, No. 4.

13 For libraries and publications, see Wiseman, "Silent Companions"; for literary societies, Murray, *Come, Bright Improvement!*

14 For the origin and later evolution of the Book Depository, see Parvin, *Authorization.*

15 Hind, *Narrative.*

16 Ryerson's journal was not really a competitor, for Ryerson was an ex officio member of the board, though rarely active; but, as we see below, his promotion of technical education was not always in harmony with the board's. His *Journal* concentrated on items more directly relating to the needs of his constituency. The *Canadian Agriculturist* was not competitive, as it focused almost solely on agriculture. Although the Canadian Institute was in some ways a rival to mechanics' institutes, it saw itself as a more academic and scientific organization. There was substantial overlap in scientific content between the *Canadian Journal* and the board's journal, which is not surprising, because of Hind's experience as editor of the former.

17 Report of BAMUC, Province of Canada, *Sessional Papers* (1865), No. 6.

18 Taché to Edwards, 9 Jan. 1865, LAC, RG 17 A1.2.

19 *Journal BAMUC* (July 1867), 172.

20 Report of the Sub-Committee for January 1866, ibid., (June 1866), 35.

21 Ibid. (March 1866), 113–15.

22 Ibid. (July 1867), 169–73. More American and British examples ("Technical Education," 199–202) followed in the next month.

23 Letter to the editor, ibid. (Aug. 1867), 205–6.

24 Letter, ibid. (Sept. 1867), 236.

25 Ibid. (Oct. 1867), 259–60.

26 For the articles, see ibid., Nov. and Dec. 1867 and Jan. and Feb. 1868.

27 On the British examination movement, see Macleod, ed., *Days of Judgement.*

28 Chester published a series of articles in the *Journal of the Society of Arts* during the 1850s to push for examinations. He was also instrumental in forging a union of English mechanics' institutes.

29  BAMUC, Report of July 1861, AO, F1189, vol. 1.

30  *Canadian Agriculturist* 13 (1 Jan. 1861), 31.

31  BAMUC, Report of the Sub-Committee, 14 Jan. 1862, AO, F1189.

32  LAC, RG 17 A.1.1, vol. 3, file 74. The scheme depended on local committees. First, a candidate needed to pass an examination at the local institute, which forwarded it to the board. The board sketched syllabi and listed relevant books. Course and examination subjects included:
   • art subjects: geometrical/decorative drawing/modelling, ornamental and landscape drawing
   • general subjects: bookkeeping, French, German, geography, grammar, history, music, penmanship, political and social economics
   • mathematical subjects: algebra, arithmetic, conic sections, geometry, mensuration, trigonometry
   • scientific subjects: animal physiology and zoology, botany, chemistry, experimental philosophy, geology, mineralogy
   • technical subjects: agriculture and horticulture, practical mechanics, principles of mechanics

33  Report of the Board of Arts and Manufactures of Upper Canada, Province of Canada, *Sessional Papers* (1865), No. 6.

34  The 1859 list includes McGill professors Dawson, Hamilton, Johnson, Smallwood, Sutherland; Laval's Brunet, Hamel, and Sterry Hunt; and Bishop's Miles. The francophone contingent came from the colleges, with professors Boisvert and Michaud (Joliette); Laporte (L'Assomption); Bertram and Hermengilde (Lévis); F. Désaulniers and Gouin (Nicolet); Audet, Belleau, and Dion (Québec); Michaud (Rigaud); Pilote (Ste-Anne); Carrez and Haveque (Ste-Marie); Gauthier (Ste-Marie de Monnoir); M. Dagenais (Ste-Thérèse); and I. Désaulniers, Dumesnils, and Gigault (St-Hyacinthe). The lone anglophone was Cleveland of St Francis College.

35  Report, Board of Arts and Manufactures of Lower Canada, 1859.

36  Province of Canada, *Journals LAUC* (1858), appendix 45. Sixty-one institutes from the two Canadas received grants; the total membership was 8,780. The aggregate libraries contained some 53,000 volumes, and some 5,800 members used their libraries.

37  Published in Montreal in 1859; a copy of this rare pamphlet is in LAC.

38  A copy of the announcement that the Prince of Wales would be present is in LAC, MG 24, D16, Buchanan Papers, vol. 105, 069311.

39  *Journal BAMUC* (March 1861), 70–2.

40  Ibid. (April 1861), 103–5.

41  Report BAMLC, Province of Canada, *Sessional Papers* (1865), No. 6.

42  *Journal BAMUC* (Feb. 1866), 93–4.

43  Province of Canada, *Sessional Papers* (1866), No. 5.

44  *Journal* BAMUC (Jan. 1867), 36ff.

45  Province de Québec, *Doc. Sess.* (1869), No. 2.

46  LAC, RG 4, C1, Provincial Secretary (Canada East) Correspondence Files.

47  BAMUC, Minutes, 11 July 1867, AO, F1189, vol. 2.

48  Cambie to W. Edwards, 20 July 1867, LAC, RG 17 A1.2.

49  W. Edwards to John Carling, 25 July 1867, BAMUC, Letterbook IV, AO, F1189.

50  BAMUC, Minutes, vol. 2, 8 Jan. 1868, AO, F1189.

51  In 1858, the two Boards of Arts and Manufactures received a total of $4,000, the mechanics' institutes $36,500, and the agricultural societies more than $70,000. In the following year, grants to the mechanics' institutes ceased altogether. By the last full fiscal year before Confederation (1866), agricultural societies and agricultural education accounted for $102,000 and the arts and manufactures for $4,000.

52  Many Canadians were aware of the central role of art instruction in British technical education, which was largely a result of Henry Cole's vision and drive. This vision was evident not just in the metropolitan and provincial art schools but also in the South Kensington Museum, in which industrial art was paramount.

53  *Debates* LAUC 8, no. 1 (1849), 390.

54  Hind, "Schools," 38–40.

55  Annual Report, 1855, *Journals* LAUC (1857), Appendix 58.

56  Ibid., Appendix G, Educational Museum for Upper Canada.

57  Ryerson to J.G. Hodgins, 4 Sept. and 30 Oct. 1857, United Church Archives, Toronto (UCA), Ryerson Papers, box 4; Victoria and Albert Museum, Henry Cole Diaries, 4 Sept. and 29 Oct. 1857.

58  JEUC (Dec. 1857), 177–9.

59  BAMUC, Minutes of Jan. 1859, AO, F1189.

60  Ibid., Minutes of 5 Jan. and 6 April 1858; Circular of 10 Feb. 1858, AO, F1189. In the meantime, William Edwards had written to the Society of Arts to enquire whether it would make art books that it sold to British schools available to a school of art and design in Canada, "as the Board contemplates the establishment of such a department as soon as possible." W. Edwards to LeNeve Foster, 14 June 1860. Letterbook III, AO, F1189.

61  JEUC (Feb. 1861), 28.

62  Toronto *Globe*, 3 Dec. 1863.

63  BAMUC, Minute of 28 July 1864 and Report of 27 Oct. 1864, AO, F1189, vol. 2.

64  The school would have three divisions: the first would cover chemistry and natural philosophy; the second, design, drawing, and modelling; and the third, practical mathematics. In the first, students would cover material

relating to the board's exams in these subjects. The professor would teach these subjects four nights a week from October to May and provide one public lecture weekly. In addition, he would lecture at the Mechanics' Institute, edit the science sections of the board's *Journal*, and work part time as a chemical analyst. A second, half-time professor would teach drawing and mathematics. The total outlay would be $2,000 annually – $800 for the professor, $400 for his half-time colleague, and $800 for other expenses. The courses would be open to everyone (both sexes) and free to those "who may be able to furnish evidence of worthiness to participate in its benefaction."

65　Ryerson to Hodgins, 15 Dec. 1866, UCA, Ryerson Papers, box 5, file 147.
66　Province of Canada, *Journals LAUC* (1843), vol. 3, appendix Z. Lortie, "Jean-Baptiste Meilleur."
67　Province of Canada, *Journals LAUC* (1844–45), vol. 4, appendix Z.
68　See especially Galarneau, *Les collèges classiques*.
69　The most important college was the Petit Séminaire de Québec; see Baillargeon, *Le Séminaire de Québec*. ASQ holds a number of notebooks on science and mathematics, dating from the late eighteenth century until the early twentieth. These make it clear that courses were for general education, not scientific training as such.
70　T.-E. Hamel, rector of Laval, lamented this in his presidential address to the Royal Society of Canada in 1887. *Proceedings and Transactions of the Royal Society of Canada* 5 (1887), xv–xxii.
71　This was true especially in the teaching of Brunet, Casault, Demers, Horan, and others at Quebec and of the Désaulnier brothers at Nicolet and St-Hyacinthe. The textbooks, sometimes based on those current in France but almost always by Quebec teachers, were as up to date as any elementary texts in Canada West. But they did not have a practical bent: they cultivated the intellect. On science in Quebec generally, see Chartrand, Duchesne, and Gingras, *Histoire*. See also Jarrell, "The Rise and Decline."
72　With some government aid, Rev. Jean-Baptiste St-Germain (1788–1863), the curé of St-Laurent, was operating an Académie industrielle by 1850. With two priests and two laymen, St-Germain taught 160 children, farmed 170 *arpents*, and maintained two workshops, one for locksmithing and one for making shoes. The school proved to be a success, and in the next six years the government provided financial assistance to industrial schools in Alexandria, Pointe-aux-Trembles, Pointe-Claire, St-Eustache, St-Laurent, St-Martin, and Varennes. A total of 540 pupils received instruction, and the schools together maintained four workshops, with the addition of baking and carpentry.

73  See Chauveau's 1858 report in Province of Canada, *Journals LAUC* (1858), Appendix 43.

74  Thomas Coltrin Keefer (1821–1915), who worked on canals, harbours, and waterworks, trained with engineers on the Erie Canal. Sanford Fleming (1827–1915), notable railway engineer, studied privately under a Scottish engineer and with Toronto-area surveyor John Stoughton Dennis (1820–1885). Lower Canada's celebrated architect and engineer Charles Baillargé (1826–1906) apprenticed with a cousin.

75  For details, see Young, *Early Engineering Education.*

76  Friedland, *The University of Toronto*, 53.

77  Dawson, *On the Course*, 7.

78  Ibid., 23.

79  Frost, *McGill University, 1801–1895*, 188.

CHAPTER FIVE

1  Dean, *Canadian Dairying*, 5th ed. See also Innis, ed., *The Dairy Industry.*

2  Factory-made butter from local creameries did not travel well, and the domestic market consumed most of it until late in the century, when better quality and refrigeration allowed for increased trade to Britain. See Ankli and Millar, "Ontario Agriculture in Transition."

3  On the implement industry, see McCalla, *Planting*; Phillips, *The Agricultural Implement Industry*; and Pomfret, *The Economic Development.*

4  See Dembski, "Sir John Carling."

5  Report of the Commissioner of Agriculture and Arts for 1868, Province of Ontario, *Sessional Papers* (1868–69); for the structure and function of the Department of Agriculture, see Hodgetts, *From Arm's Length.*

6  "Its contents consisted of 17 ploughs, not one of which was as good as the worst plough exhibited at the Mosa Exhibition, an old fashioned cultivator and sewing machine, an old badly stuffed white cow's head, a straw cutter, 2 iron garden seats, an old cradle, a new horse hayfork, some flax and grain in the straw, a pile of old bones, 2 old wire cages, 2 empty barrels and some old crockery were the contents." *Farmers' Advocate* 2 (Jan. 1867), 3.

7  For 1877 figures, Province of Ontario. *Sessional Papers* (1878), No. 1.

8  Report of the Commissioner of Agriculture and Public Works for 1869, Province of Ontario, *Sessional Papers* (1869), 2.

9  Ibid.

10  Report of the AAAO for 1873, Province of Ontario, *Sessional Papers* (1874), No. 1, Appendix B.

11  Ibid., x.

12   Report of the Commissioner of Agriculture and Arts for 1869, Province of Ontario, *Sessional Papers* (1869), xi.

13   See Wood, *A History*, and Leake, *The Means and Methods*, 194–7.

14   Annual Report of the Commission of Agriculture and Arts for 1876, Province of Ontario, *Sessional Papers* (1877), No. 4, Appendix B, 189.

15   Marcus, *Agricultural Science*, 38.

16   For later developments, see Hann, *Farmers Confront Industrialism.*

17   Records of the club, including minute books, cash book, and membership lists, are in AO, Township of Puslinch Farmers' Club fonds, F1262.

18   Early, practical issues up for discussion included turnip culture in Canada and Britain; whether allowing animals to run at large is a public nuisance; whether mixed farming is the most profitable; the best mode for feeding cattle; dairy farming; breeding agricultural horses and the advisability of the club's purchasing a stallion.

19   LAC, MG 28 I 27, Minute Books of the City of Ottawa Agricultural Society.

20   A financial statement for 1876 shows that the society's income came from members' subscriptions ($515.50), its annual provincial grant ($350), and a municipal grant ($1,700); and exhibition income from gate receipts and a refreshment booth made up the remainder. While prizes were a large part of the expenses, the City of Ottawa Agricultural Society, possibly like many others, had indebted itself to the tune of $20,000 for buildings.

21   See Monod, "Thomas Ballantyne."

22   On cattle breeding, see Derry, *Ontario's Cattle Kingdom;* for beef cattle, see Derry's "The Development"; and for horses, Derry's *Horses in Society*. On the specialist societies, of which there were twenty by the 1890s, see Irwin, "Government Funding."

23   Annual Report of the Commission of Agriculture and Arts for 1877, Province of Ontario, *Sessional Papers* (1878), No. 1, x.

24   Annual Report of the Commission of Agriculture and Arts for 1879, ibid. (1880), No. 3, Appendix B.

25   Ibid., No. 3, ix.

26   Annual Report of the Commission of Agriculture and Arts for 1881, ibid. (1882), No. 3.

27   Ibid., No. 3, xiii.

28   Report of AAAO for 1882, Province of Ontario, *Sessional Papers* (1882–83), No. 3, Appendix B, 23.

29   Report of the Council of AAAO for 1889, ibid. (1890), No. 8, 23–33.

30   Mills, "Agricultural Education."

31   Campbell, "William Fletcher Clarke."

32   Cochrane, *The Development;* see also Marcus, *Agricultural Science.*

33 For an overview of Ontario developments, see Lawr, "Agricultural Education." An older survey is Madill, *A History.*

34 *Canada Farmer* 3 (1 Dec. 1866), 362.

35 Report of the Commissioner of Agriculture and Arts, Province of Ontario, *Sessional Papers* (1869), Clarke's Report, 375.

36 *Farmer's Advocate* 2 (Oct. 1867), 81.

37 Report of the Secretary of the Bureau of Agriculture, Province of Ontario, *Sessional Papers* (1871–72), No. 5.

38 For a comprehensive account of the college, see Ross and Crowley. *The College.*

39 Report of the Ontario School of Agriculture and Experimental Farm for 1875, Province of Ontario, *Sessional Papers* (1875–76), No. 13, Appendix B (Circular for the School for 1875).

40 Ontario Agricultural Commission, *Canadian Farming: An Encylopaedia of Agriculture being the Report of the Ontario Agricultural Commission,* 13.

41 AO, RG 18-18, Report of the Ontario School of Agriculture and Experimental Farm for 1875, appendix.

42 Ontario Agricultural Commission, *Canadian Farming,* 8.

43 Ibid., 11.

44 Ibid., 15.

45 Ibid., 49.

46 Goulet and Jean, "Duncan McNab McEachran."

47 For background, see Rossiter, *The Emergence.* On the establishment of research stations, see Hurt, *American Agriculture.*

48 Saunders, *Report,* found that the former then had 180 students, about one-quarter of whom graduated, while Guelph had eighty-one. Numbers were little different in England, with the Royal Agricultural College at Cirencester having about seventy students.

49 Ibid., 289.

50 Ibid.

51 On the federal department's research programs, see Anstey, *A Hundred Harvests.*

52 Hurt, *American Agriculture.*

53 University of Guelph Archives (UGA), XA1, MS A011. Latta was born in Indiana and took a BS from Michigan Agricultural College in 1877 and an MS in 1882.

54 Annual Report of the Commissioner of Agriculture and Arts, Province of Ontario, *Sessional Papers* (1879), No. 3; Annual Report, School of Agriculture of Ontario, ibid. (1882), No. 16; and Annual Report of the Commissioner of Agriculture and Arts for 1881, ibid., No. 3.

55 When complaining to Provincial Secretary Peter Gow about the proposed
   Mimico site of the college, William Clarke had presciently suggested that
   the future college hold county agricultural conventions similar to those of
   the Education Department. If the college's president addressed such gatherings, it could only help to popularize the institution. Clarke to Gow,
   12 Jan. 1872, in Return to an address of the Legislative Assembly to His
   Excellency ... All Correspondence on the Agricultural Farm, etc, 29 Feb.
   1872, ibid. (1871–72), No. 55.

56 Bailey, *Farmers' Institutes.* Bailey does note that New York had itinerant lecturers in the early 1840s. Alfred True, in *A History,* also mentions lectures
   that the Ohio State Board of Agriculture provided in the 1840s and lectures at Oberlin College and in Cleveland in the 1850s. Massachusetts
   operated something like farmers' institutes in the 1850s. True claims the
   first farmers' institute opened in Kansas in November 1868. In any case,
   the idea was not new and, with peace after the Civil War, spread quickly.

57 Report of the Council AAAO 1886, Province of Ontario, *Sessional Papers*
   (1887), No. 5, 18–19.

58 *Report of the Proceedings of the Second Annual Meeting of the Permanent Central
   Farmers' Institute of Ontario.*

59 Ibid., 18.

60 Fourteenth Annual Report of the OAC, Province of Ontario, *Sessional
   Papers* (1889), No. 21, 15.

61 Reports of Live Stock Breeders' Associations for 1899–1900, ibid. (1900),
   No. 23, 18.

62 Third Annual Report of the Superintendent of Farmers' Institutes for
   1896–97, ibid. (1897), No. 23.

63 Ibid., xl.

64 Ambrose and Kechnie. "Social Control or Social Feminism?"; for the later
   development of the movement, see Kechnie, *Organizing.*

65 Soon afterwards, with farmers' knowledge so much better than before, the
   institutes died, giving way, after 1905, to government-fostered farmers'
   clubs.

66 Derry, "Gender Conflicts"; see also Cohen, "The Decline," and Crowley,
   "Experience."

67 Friedland, *The University of Toronto,* 147.

68 UGA, XA1, MS A007, "Agricultural Schools and Agricultural Extension.
   Itinerary of Secretary Buttrick, June 1905," 9.

69 Ibid., 16.

70 Ibid.

71 See Baker, *The County Agent,* on American developments in local extension.

72 Scottish Commission on Agriculture, *Report*, 63.

73 Leake, *The Means and Methods*, 153.

74 Goodwin, "A School of Science," 88.

75 *Canada Farmer* 1 (15 Jan. 1869), 22–3.

76 See Axelrod, *The Promise*.

77 Leake, *The Means and Methods*.

78 Report of AAAO for 1883, Province of Ontario, *Sessional Papers* (1884), No. 11, 30.

79 Annual Report of the OAC, 1883, ibid., No. 13, 41.

80 There were third- and second-class certificates (the latter more advanced). For third class, students mastered well-known texts such as J.F.W. Johnston's *Elements of Agricultural Chemistry and Geology* (1842), Sir J.B. Lawes's *Soil of the Farm* (1883), Henry Tanner's *First Principles of Agriculture* (1878), Charles E. Whitcombe's *Canadian Farmer's Manual of Agriculture* (1879), and John Wrightson's *Agricultural Textbook, Embracing Soils, Manures, Rotation of Crops, and Live Stock, Adapted to the Requirements of the Syllabus of the Science and Art Department, South Kensington. Illustrated* (London, 1877) and *The Principles of Agricultural Practice as an Instructional Subject. Illustrated* (London, 1888). Candidates preparing for second class read a wider list of texts. There was no first-class certificate, and marks would depend on whether an examinee had studied in an agricultural college or not.

81 Report of Council of AAAO for 1886, Province of Ontario, *Sessional Papers* (1887), No. 5, 27.

82 Report of Council of AAAO for 1888, ibid. (1889), No. 8, 27.

83 Report of Council of AAAO for 1890, ibid. (1891), No. 8, 4.

84 Guillet, *In the Cause*, 130.

85 Bryant, *Agriculture*, 15.

86 James, *The Teaching*. Charles Canniff James (1863–1916) studied at Victoria College, taught chemistry at the Ontario Agricultural College from 1886 to 1891, and then became deputy minister of agriculture.

87 Cochrane, *The Development*, 239–40.

## CHAPTER SIX

1 A good collection of articles on agriculture is Séguin, ed., *Agriculture*. For the general context, see Linteau, Durocher, and Robert, *Histoire*.

2 Isbister, "Agriculture."

3 McCallum, *Unequal Beginnings*.

4 Kerr and Smyth, "Agriculture," and Isbister's reply, "Agriculture."

5 On dairying, consult Perron, "Genèse."

6  For the economic details of agriculture, see Hamelin and Roby, *Histoire économique.*

7  Blouin, "La mécanisation de l'agriculture," 98.

8  *Débats de l'Assemblée législative du Québec* (20 Jan. 1870), 150–1.

9  Ibid., 151.

10  The recommendation to appoint two superintendents appeared in a report to the assembly. One man would cover the Quebec, Trois-Rivières, and Gaspé districts, the other would handle the Montreal and St Francis districts; they would stimulate and supervise society activities, give lectures in each county, be present at exhibitions, and ensure placing of agricultural treatises in every school. While an act to that effect passed, I have seen no evidence of any appointment. "Report of the Special Committee to whom were referred the Report of the Lower Canada Agricultural Society and the Special Report of the Agricultural Society of the County of Beauharnois," *Journals LAUC* (1851), appendix J.

11  Report of the Commission of Agriculture and Public Works, Province de Québec, *Doc. Sess.* (1869), 4.

12  Province de Québec, *Doc. Sess.* (1873), No. 4.

13  Report of the Commission of Agriculture and Public Works, Province of Quebec, *Sessional Papers* (1878), No. 2, 3.

14  Province of Quebec, *Sessional Papers* (1875), No. 4, 23.

15  Minute Books of the Missisquoi County Agricultural Society, LAC, MG 28-I227.

16  Report of the Standing Committee on Agriculture, *Débats de l'Assemblée législative du Québec* (1877–78), 171–2.

17  Martin, *A History,* 92.

18  Province of Quebec, *Journals of the Legislative Assembly* (26 Feb. 1883), 132.

19  Report of the Commissioner of Agriculture, Province of Quebec, *Doc. Sess.* (1893), No. 2.

20  Details appear in Beaulieu and Hamelin, *La presse,* vols. 2 and 3.

21  On Barnard, see Perron, *Un grand éducateur agricole,* and Jean, "Edouard-André Barnard." He was baptized Edward but gallicized his name on his marriage in 1874. See also biographical notes in the fonds E.-A. Barnard at the Centre de recherche en civilisation Canadienne-Française, Université d'Ottawa.

22  *La semaine agricole* (12 Oct. 1869), 1.

23  Province of Quebec, *Doc. Sess.* (1871–72), appendix 1.

24  Ibid. (1873), No. 4.

25  Beaulieu and Hamelin, *La presse,* vol. 1, 250–1.

26  Province of Quebec, *Doc. Sess.* (1882–83), No. 2.

27  Ibid. (1884), No. 2, 106.

28 Dionne, *Les cercles agricoles.*

29 *Premier congrès des cercles agricole Saint-Isidore, Laboreur,* 14.

30 Gigault, "Agriculture," 50.

31 Ibid.

32 See Jean, *Les idéologies.*

33 Bonnemant, who was naturalized in 1872, appears to have resided in Maskinongé in early 1874; according to *L'opinion publique* (4 June 1874), he was setting up a cheese factory. He also proposed creating a national stud.

34 *Journaux de l'Assemblée législative de la Province de Québec* (1871), Appendix 3, 234–8.

35 On the history of agricultural schools, see Chapais, *fils*, "Three Centuries."

36 Chapais, *fils, Notes historiques.*

37 *Débats de l'Assemblée législative du Québec* (1875–78), 22 Dec. 1875, 280–1.

38 "Agricultural Education," *Journal of Education* 12, no. 10 (Oct. 1868), 153.

39 The third neighbour, the agricultural school at Cornell University in New York, did not become a college until 1888, although it existed as the university's agricultural department in 1874.

40 Province of Quebec, *Doc. Sess.* (1877–78), No. 4.

41 *Rapport du comité chargé par le Conseil d'Agriculture,* 24.

42 The commission's report appeared in print the following year: Province du Québec, *Rapport préliminaire de la commission agricole.*

43 Gigault, "Agriculture," 48.

44 Perron, *Un grand éducateur agricole,* 54–5.

45 On McEachran and his competing schools, see Goulet and Jean,"Duncan McNab McEachran."

46 General Report of the Commissioner of Agriculture for 1889, Province of Quebec, *Doc. Sess.* (1890), No. 2b.

47 On Macdonald, see Frost and Michel, "Sir William Christopher Macdonald."

48 Hamelin, *L'Histoire,* 128.

49 Chauveau presented his observations in his *L'instruction publique au Canada.*

50 Audet, *Histoire,* vol. 2, 131. See Chauveau's superintendent's report for 1867: Province de Québec, *Doc. Sess.* (1869), No. 1.

51 *Journal de l'Instruction publique* (July–Aug. 1868), 94.

52 Landry, *Traité,* iv.

53 *Journal of Education for Ontario* (Nov. 1870), 165.

CHAPTER SEVEN

1 Studies of the Canadian economy are numerous. Valuable overviews include: Ian Drummond, *Progress without Planning*; Easterbrook and

Aitken, *Canadian Economic History*; Norrie, Owram, and Emery, *A History*; Pomfret, *The Economic Development*; and Rea, *A Guide*. Economic statistics are available in Leacy, Urquhart, and Buckley, eds., *Historical Statistics*.

2 Gilmour, *Spatial Evolution*, 27.

3 See McCalla, "Railways."

4 Norrie, Owram, and Emery, *A History*, 167.

5 Bloomfield and Bloomfield, *The Ontario Urban System*, 6.

6 A county-by-county survey of industry appears in Bloomfield and Bloomfield, *Industry*.

7 In the extensive literature on Canadian labour in the nineteenth century, useful works include Cross, *The Workingman*; Kealey, *Canada*; and Palmer, *A Culture* and *Working-Class Experience*.

8 For an overview of the issues, see Axelrod, *The Promise*; Brewin,"The Establishment"; Rafferty, "Apprenticeship's Legacy"; and Zeller, "Roads not Taken."

9 Gidney and Millar, *Inventing Secondary Education*, 279.

10 See Katz, Doucet, and Stern, *The Social Organization*.

11 Katz, *The People of Hamilton*, 171.

12 Gidney and Millar, *Inventing Secondary Education*, 316.

13 For Ontario's mechanics' institutes in the later nineteenth century, see Blanchard, "Anatomy of a Failure" and "A Bibliography"; Wells, "Mechanics' Institutes"; and Wiseman, "Phoenix in Flight" and "Silent Companions."

14 Report of the Commissioner of Agriculture and Arts for 1868, Province of Ontario, *Sessional Papers* (1868–69), No. 4.

15 Province of Ontario, ibid., (1870–71), No. 5, vii.

16 Report of Secretary of Bureau of Agriculture, ibid. (1871–72), No. 5, xi.

17 Annual Report Association of Mechanics' Institutes of Ontario, ibid. (1874), No. 1, 215.

18 Education Report for 1876, ibid. (1878), No. 5, 9.

19 Province of Ontario, ibid. (1874), No. 1, 350.

20 Ibid., 339.

21 Ibid. (1872–73), No. 1, ix–x.

22 Ibid., 219–22.

23 W. Edwards to Secretary, Department of Science and Art, 21 April 1876, AO, F1189, Letterbook IV.

24 Buckland's Report, Province of Ontario, *Sessional Papers* (1871–72), No. 5, xi. Changes to Agriculture and Arts statute raised grants to $400.

25 "Samuel Passmore May."

26 Education Report, Feb. 1881, Province of Ontario, *Sessional Papers* (1881), No. 46, xii. The document appeared in print separately as *Special Report of the Minister of Education on the Mechanics' Institutes (Ontario)*.

27  On the nature of school inspection at the time, see Curtis, *True Government?*
28  *Special Report*, 140.
29  Ibid., 117.
30  Ibid., 66.
31  Ibid., 67. May adopted payment-on-results possibly because the department used it in the late 1870s to make grants to high schools depending on results of the intermediate examinations. It proved very unpopular, and the department eventually ended the practice. See Squair, *John Seath*, 40–1.
32  *Special Report*, 75.
33  *Canada Educational Monthly* 3 (April 1881), 190.
34  Edwards to May, 8 Sept. 1880.
35  Edwards to Klotz, 3 Dec. 1883.
36  Edwards to Klotz, 3 Jan. 1884.
37  City of Cambridge Archives.
38  City of Cambridge Archives, Mechanics' Institute and Preston Library.
39  McEvoy, ed., *The Province of Ontario Gazetteer and Directory*.
40  Caledon Mechanics' Institute fonds, AO, F2103.
41  Minutes of 7 July 1883, Minute Book of the Caledon Mechanics' Institute, ibid.
42  Report on Mechanics' Institutes, Free Libraries and Art Schools for 1884–85, Province of Ontario, *Sessional Papers* (1886), No. 3, 187.
43  Ibid., 187–8.
44  Education Report, Province of Ontario, *Sessional Papers* (1889), No. 6, 149.
45  Toronto *Globe*, 1 March 1881.
46  Thompson, *Reminiscences*, 382, 388.
47  Province of Ontario, *Sessional Papers* (1890), No. 6, 219.
48  Ibid., 220.
49  For further information on the emergence of the public library system, see Wiseman, "Phoenix in Flight," and Bruce, *Free Books*.
50  Public Accounts to 31 December 1900, Province of Ontario, *Sessional Papers* (1901), No. 1.
51  The most recent study is White, *The Skule Story*; earlier works include Harris and Montagnes, eds., *Cold Steel*, and Young, *Early Engineering Education*.
52  Agriculture Report, Province of Ontario, *Sessional Papers* (1870–71), No. 5, xiii.
53  Hodgins and Machattie, *Report of an Inquiry*, 9.
54  Ibid.
55  Buckland's Report, Province of Ontario, *Sessional Papers* (1871–72), No. 5, xv.

56 Report of the School of Practical Science (SPS) ending 31 December 1873, ibid. (1874), No. 12.
57 Report of SPS for 1876, ibid. (1877), No. 13.
58 Report of SPS of 13 January 1879, ibid. (1879), No. 23.
59 *Canada Educational Monthly* 3 (March 1881), 141.
60 Wilson, *On the Practical Uses*, 17.
61 Report of SPS for 1882, No. 5.
62 Surviving papers of the society are in the Ontario Society of Artists fonds, AO, F1140.
63 Province of Ontario, *Sessional Papers* (1878), No. 25, 1.
64 Ibid. (1882–83), No. 5, 244.
65 Ibid. (1878), No. 25, 3.
66 Ibid., 2.
67 Ibid. (1882), No. 5, 262.
68 Ibid. (1882–83), No. 5, 247–8.
69 Baigent, "Art Education," 60.
70 Report of Dr S.P. May, Superintendent of the OSA, Province of Ontario, *Sessional Papers* (1882–83), No. 5, 243.
71 *Toronto World*, 6 Jan, 1884.
72 On the museum's last decades, see Johnson, "The Fate."
73 On Boyle, see Killan, *David Boyle*.
74 Education Report, Part IV – Technical Education, Province of Ontario, *Sessional Papers* (1884), No. 14, 174.
75 Education Report, ibid. (1885), No. 5, 232–3.
76 Education Report , ibid. (1889), No. 6, 149.
77 *Canada Educational Monthly* 7 (1885), 143.
78 See Hodgins, *The Establishment*, vol. 3.
79 Toronto *Globe*, 21 June 1890.
80 Gaitskell, *Art Education*, 2–3.

## CHAPTER EIGHT

1 For overviews of the Quebec economy in the later nineteenth century, see Angers and Parenteau, *Statistiques*; Easterbrook and Aitken, *Canadian Economic History*; Hamelin and Roby, *Histoire économique*; Linteau, Durocher, and Robert, *Histoire*; Norrie, Owram, and Emery, *A History*; and Rea, *A Guide*.
2 Angers and Parenteau, *Statistiques*, Table 1.
3 On Montreal, useful overviews include Cooper, *Montreal*; Linteau, *Histoire*; and Rumilly, *Histoire*.

4 On labour, consult Bradbury, "The Family Economy"; Hamelin, ed., *Les travailleurs*; and Kealey, *Canada Investigates Industrialism.*

5 Harvey, *Révolution*, 116.

6 Fahmy-Eid, "Ultramontanisme," 65–6.

7 On Ultramontanism and science, see Jarrell, "L'Ultramontanisme et la science."

8 See Galarneau, *Les collèges classiques.*

9 For female education, consult Dumont, *Girls' Schooling.*

10 Charland, *Histoire.*

11 Prost, *Histoire*, 311. See also Male, *Education.*

12 For French technical education, consult Mayeur, *Histoire générale*, tome III, and Artz, *The Development.*

13 *Revue agricole* (Jan, 1866), 123.

14 Ibid. (Dec. 1866), 90.

15 *L'opinion publique* (16 Oct. 1873), 506.

16 *Journal de l'Instruction publique* 13 (Feb.–March 1869), 29–30.

17 Report of the Commissioner of Agriculture and Public Works, Province de Québec, *Doc. Sess.* (1869), No. 4.

18 BAMLC, Minutes of 6 March 1868. Copies of minutes of BAMLC and the Conseil des arts et manufactures are in the Bibliothèque et archives nationales du Québec and in LAC, Buchanan Papers.

19 "School of Art and Design, Montreal," *Journal of Education for the Province of Quebec* 14, no. 4 (April 1870), 60.

20 Commissioner Archambeault introduced a bill in the legislative council on 10 Dec. 1872 to effect the change; it passed on 19 Dec. *Journaux du Conseil Législatif du Québec* 6 (1872), 71, 103.

21 See Greer, "The Patterns."

22 Report of CAMPQ for the year ending 30 June 1874, Province de Québec, *Doc. Sess.* (1874), No. 4.

23 Report of CAMPQ, ibid. (1875), No. 4, 229.

24 Ibid., 232.

25 Report of Superintendent of Public Instruction for 1875–76, Province de Québec, *Doc. Sess.* (1876), No. 16.

26 Montreal, *La Minerve*, 31 July 1879.

27 CAMPQ Secretary's Report, May 12, 1879, Province de Québec, *Doc. Sess.* (1878), Appendix 3, 89.

28 Ibid., 93.

29 CAMPQ Report for 1879–81, Province de Québec, *Doc. Sess.* (1885–86), No. 2, Appendix II, 79–81.

30 CAMPQ Report for 1889, ibid. (1890), No. 2, Appendix III, 106.

31 CAMPQ Report, ibid. (1894), No. 2, 482–6.

32 CAMPQ Report for 1895, ibid. (1895), No. 3, 350.

33 Ibid., 341.

34 CAMPQ Report for 1896–7, Province de Québec, *Doc. Sess.* (1897), No. 3.

35 See Harris, "Art."

36 The best account of art education for this period is Stirling, "Post-secondary Arts Education."

37 Audet, "P.-J.-O. Chauveau," 178.

38 For details, see Vézina, "Napoléon Bourassa."

39 On Chabert, see Mulaire, "Joseph Chabert," and Larivière-Derome, "Un professeur."

40 CAMPQ Report for 1883–4, Province de Québec, *Doc. Sess.* (1883–84), No. 2, Appendix V.

41 Minutes of CAMPQ, 4 Nov. 1873.

42 Report of the Committee, Minutes of CAMPQ, 16 Feb. 1876.

43 Ibid.

44 Smith, *Technical Education*, 8.

45 Ibid., 15.

46 Annual Report of CAMPQ, Province de Québec, *Doc. Sess.* (1881–82), Appendix V.

47 Annual Report of the Secretary, CAMPQ, ibid. (1873), Appendix 3.

48 *Journal de l'Instruction publique* (April 1895), 341.

49 Report of CAMPQ for 1887, Province de Québec, *Doc. Sess.* (1887–88), Appendix V.

50 Dawson, *The Duties*, 13.

51 Maheux, "P.-J.-O. Chauveau."

52 Hamelin, *L'Histoire*, 61.

53 Maheux, "P.-J.-O. Chauveau."

54 See Gagnon, "Urgel-Eugène Archambeault (Archambault)."

55 *L'opinion publique* (27 June 1872), 302.

56 On the founding of the Ecole polytechnique, consult Gagnon, *Histoire*, and Audet, *La fondation*; on the background debate, see Gagnon, "Les discours."

57 Gagnon, *Histoire*, 70.

58 Ibid., 76.

59 See Hamelin, ed., *Les travailleurs*.

60 Provancher, "Les écoles d'adultes."

61 Heap, "Un chapitre."

62 Province de Québec, *Doc. Sess.* (1873), No. 3.

63 Ibid. (1878–79), No. 5.

64 Cited by Kealey, *Canada Investigates Industrialism.*
65 Heap, "Un chapitre," 604.

### CONCLUSION

1 Leake, *The Means and Methods.*

### EPILOGUE

1 On the history of l'Ordre des agronomes du Québec, see Hudon, *L'Action.*
2 Useful studies of nineteenth-century American technical education
   include Barlow, *History*; Bennett, *History of Manual and Industrial Education
   up to 1870* and *History of Manual and Industrial Education 1870–1917*;
   Bolles, *Industrial History*; Clarke, *Art and Industrial Education*; and Fisher,
   *Industrial Education.*
3 *Canadian Mechanics' Magazine* 4 (April 1876), 114.
4 "On the Importance of Mechanics' Institutes," ibid. 5 (Feb. 1877), 33–4.
5 *Scientific Canadian* 8 (Feb. 1880), 32.
6 Ibid. 8 (May 1880), 131–2.
7 12th Annual Report of the Association of Mechanics' Institutes of Ontario
   (1880), AO, F2101.
8 Klotz, *A Review of the Special Report*, 5.
9 Ibid., 7.
10 Hodgins, *The Establishment*, vol. 3, 354.
11 *Canada Educational Monthly* 6 (July–Aug. 1884), 285.
12 *The Educational Record of the Province of Quebec* 5 (March 1885), 71.
13 Ibid. 8 (Nov. 1888), 279.
14 Millar, *Technical Education*, 6.
15 Millar, *Education for the Twentieth Century*, 3.
16 *Canadian Engineer* 3 (Nov. 1895), 171. The school survives to this day as
   the Central Technical School; by the 1930s, its clientele was high school–
   age youths.
17 See Axelrod, *The Promise of Schooling*, chap. 6.
18 Robertson and Leake, *Macdonald*, 8.
19 On Seath, see Dowbiggin, "John Seath"; on the background, consult
   Brewin, "The Establishment."
20 Seath's Act described three forms of technical education: "industrial education" in day or evening schools for working people; "technical education" for foremen/women and managers in the trades; and "manual
   training and domestic science" for school-age children, preparatory for

the other two forms. These last subjects were cultural or practical subjects, not technical instruction per se. See Canada, *Report of the Commissioners. Royal Commission on Industrial Training and Technical Education*, vol. 4, 2000.

21 For technical instruction in Quebec after 1900, see Charland, *Histoire*, chaps. 2 and 3.

22 On the commission's work, see Kealey, *Canada Investigates Industrialism*, and Harvey, *Révolution industrielle*; evidence taken in Ontario and Quebec on the issue appears in *Report of the Royal Commission on the Relations of Labor and Capital in Canada*, vol. 5 (Evidence: Quebec) and vol. 6 (Evidence: Ontario).

# Bibliography

## ARCHIVAL SOURCES

### Archives du Séminaire de Québec (ASQ), Québec

Fonds Université Laval (Univ)

### Archives of Ontario (AO), Toronto

F1140. Ontario Society of Artists (OSA) fonds
Biographical Information – Ontario Society of Artists, Series I-3
    Ontario Society of Artists, Minute Books, Series III
F1189. Board of Arts and Manufactures for Upper Canada (BAMUC) fonds
    Vol. 1. Minute Book (1857–67)
    Vol. 2. General Committee Minute Book (1857–68)
    Vol. 3. Letterbook
    Vol. 4. Letterbook
F1203. Mechanics Institutes Collection
F1258. Darlington Township Agricultural Society fonds
F1259. Agricultural Society of the County of Addington fonds
F1262. Township of Puslinch Farmers' Club fonds
F2101. Association of Mechanics' Institutes of Ontario fonds
F2102. Niagara Mechanics' Institute fonds
F2103. Caledon Mechanics' Institute fonds
F2104. Toronto Mechanics' Institute fonds
MU 2115. Miscellaneous Collection
RG 2. Department of Education Collection

Series C-GC, F-2, F-3-A. Reports and correspondence of William Hutton
    C-l. Ryerson correspondence with Hutton
RG 18-18. Records of the Ontario Agricultural Commission 1881

*Atwater Library, Montreal*

Records of the Montreal Mechanics' Institute
    Minute Books of the Montreal Mechanics' Institute, 1828–

*Bibliothèque et Archives nationales Québec – Centre d'archives Québec*

Fonds Ecole normale Laval

*Bibliothèque et Archives nationales Québec – Grande bibliothèque*

197404 CON. Report of the Sub-committee of the Board of Arts and Manufactures for
    Lower Canada, 4 January 1859

*Centre de recherche en civilisation Canadienne-Française, Université d'Ottawa*

Fonds E.-A. Barnard

*City of Cambridge Archives*

Minute Book. Galt Scientific, Historical and Literary Society in connection with the
    Mechanics' Institute
Minute Book of the Galt Mechanics' Institute, 1862–77
Minutes, Mechanics' Institute and Preston Library, 1871–1921

*Library and Archives Canada (LAC)*

MG 24, D16. Buchanan Family Papers
MG 24, K63. Extracts from the Minutes of the Commissioners of National Education,
    Ireland (1831–70)
MG 28, I27. Ottawa Agricultural Society 1868–82
MG 28, I227. Missisquoi County Agricultural Society
RG 1, E7, vol. 41. Submissions to Executive Council, Province of Canada
RG 4, C1. Provincial Secretary (Canada East) Correspondence Files
RG 17, A1. Records of the Department of Agriculture
    1. Minister correspondence

2. General letterbooks

3. Unnumbered correspondence 1851–66

*Royal Society of Arts (RSA), London, England*

Minute Books of the Society

*Toronto Reference Library, Baldwin Room*

Papers of the Toronto Mechanics Institute

*United Church Archives (UCA), Victoria College, Toronto*

John George Hodgins fonds

Egerton Ryerson fonds

*University of Guelph Archives (UGA)*

XA1 MS A007. Description of Tour of Agricultural Schools

XA1 MS A011. Report of Trip by Professor Latta

*Victoria and Albert Museum, London, England*

Diaries of Henry Cole

### PUBLISHED WORKS

Adelman, Juliana. "The Agriculture Diploma in Queen's College, Belfast, 1845–1863, and Science Education in Nineteenth Century Ireland." *Irish Economic and Social History* 35 (2009), 51–67.

Akenson, Donald. *The Irish Educational Experiment: The National System of Education in the Nineteenth Century.* London: Routledge and K. Paul, 1970.

*Albert Agricultural College. Centennial Souvenir, 1838–1938.* Dublin: Albert Agricultural College, 1938.

Alexander, Edward P. *Museum Masters: Their Museums and Their Influence.* Nashville, TN: American Association of State and Local History, 1983.

Ambrose, Linda M., and Margaret Kechnie. "Social Control or Social Feminism? Two Views of the Ontario Women's Institutes." *Agricultural History* 73 (spring 1999), 222–37.

Angers, François-Albert, and Roland Parenteau. *Statistiques manufacturières du Québec 1665–1948.* Montreal: Ecole des hautes études commerciales, 1966.

Ankli, Robert E., and Wendy Millar. "Ontario Agriculture in Transition: The Switch from Wheat to Cheese." *Journal of Economic History* 42, no.1 (March 1982), 207–15.

Anstey, T.H. *One Hundred Harvests: Research Branch, Agriculture Canada, 1886–1986.* Ottawa: Research Branch, Agriculture Canada, 1986.

Ardagh, John. *An Address Delivered before the County of Simcoe Mechanics' Institute, Barrie, at the Close of the Session, May 21st, 1858.* Barrie, ON: J.H. Jones and J.F. Davies, 1858.

Artz, Frederick B. *The Development of Technical Education in France, 1500–1850.* Cleveland, OH: Society for the History of Technology, 1966.

Aubin, Napoléon. *La chimie agricole mise à portée de tout le monde.* Quebec: W. Ruthven, 1847.

Audet, Louis-Phillipe. *Histoire de l'enseignement au Québec.* Tome 2. Montreal: Holt, Rinehart and Winston, 1971.

– "La fondation de l'Ecole polytechnique de Montréal." *Cahiers des dix* 30 (1965), 149–91.

– "Le premier ministère de l'Instruction publique au Québec, 1867–1876." *Revue d'histoire de l'Amérique française* 22, no. 2 (1968), 171–222.

– "P.-J.-O. Chauveau, ministre de l'Instruction publique, 1867–73." *Mémoires de la Société royale du Canada* 5, 4th series (1967), 171–84.

Axelrod, Paul. *The Promise of Schooling: Education in Canada 1800–1914.* Toronto: University of Toronto Press, 1997.

Baigent, Richard. "Art Education." *Canada Educational Monthly* (Feb. 1881), 59–61.

Bailey, L.H. *Farmers' Institutes: History and Status in the United States and Canada.* Washington, DC: U.S. Government Printing Office, 1900.

Baillargeon, Noël. *Le Séminaire de Québec de 1800 à 1850.* Quebec: Les Presses de l'Université Laval, 1994.

Baker, Gladys. *The County Agent.* Chicago: University of Chicago Press, 1939.

Bannister, Jerry. "Canada as Counter-Revolution: The Loyalist Order Framework in Canadian History, 1750–1840." In Jean-François Constant and Michel Ducharme, eds., *Liberalism and Hegemony: Debating the Canadian Liberal Revolution.* Toronto: University of Toronto Press, 2009, 98–146.

Barlow, Melvin L. *History of Industrial Education in the United States.* Peoria, IL: Charles A. Bennett, 1967.

Barnard, Edouard-André. *Cercles agricoles: instructions pour l'organisation et la direction des cercles agricoles.* 1893.

– *Le livre des cercles agricoles: manuel d'agriculture.* 1895.

– *Nos écoles d'agriculture.* Quebec: s.n., 1885.

– *Une leçon d'agriculture: causeries agricoles.* Montreal: Compagnie Lith. Burland-Desbarats, 1875.

Beadle, D.W. *Canadian Fruit, Flower, and Kitchen Gardener.* Toronto: James Campbell & Son, 1872.

Beaubien, Louis. *L'étude sur l'éducation agricole.* 1877.

Beaulieu, André, and Jean Hamelin. *La presse québécoise des origines à nos jours. Tome premier 1764–1859.* Quebec: Les Presses de l'Université Laval, 1973.

– *La presse québécoise des origines à nos jours. Tome deuxième 1860–1879.* Quebec: Les Presses de l'Université Laval, 1975.

– *La presse québécoise des origines à nos jours. Tome troisième 1880–1895.* Quebec: Les Presses de l'Université Laval, 1977.

Bennett, Charles A. *History of Manual and Industrial Education up to 1870.* Peoria, IL: Charles A. Bennett, 1926.

– *History of Manual and Industrial Education 1870–1917.* Peoria, IL: Charles A. Bennett, 1937.

Berger, Carl. *Sense of Power: Studies in the Ideas of Canadian Imperialism, 1867–1914.* Toronto: University of Toronto Press, 1971.

Bernard, Philippe. "Amury Girod ou l'intellectuel militant." *Bulletin d'histoire politique* 12, no. 1 (2003), 90–6.

Bernier, Bernard. "La pénétration du capitalisme dans l'agriculture." In Normand Séguin, ed., *Agriculture et colonisation au Québec. Aspects historiques.* Montreal: Boréal Express, 1980, 73–91.

Bertrand, Réal. *L'Ecole normale Laval. Un siècle d'histoire (1857–1957).* Quebec: Société historique de Québec, 1957.

Beutler, Corinne. "L'outillage agricole dans les inventaires paysans de la région de Montréal reflète-t-il une transformation de l'agriculture entre 1792 et 1835?" In François Lebrun and Normand Séguin, eds., *Sociétés villageoises et rapports villes-campagnes au Québec et dans la France de l'ouest, XVIIe–Xxe siècles.* Trois-Rivières: Université du Québec à Trois-Rivières, 1987, 121–30.

Bidwell, P.W., and J.I. Falconer. *History of Agriculture in the Northern United States 1620–1860.* New York: P. Smith, 1941.

Bischoff, Peter C. "'Barrer la voie au syndicalisme': les manoeuvres de l'État québécois contre la Société bienveillante des journaliers de navires de Québec et les autres sociétés de secours mutuel, 1869–1899." *Labour/Le travail* 40 (1997), 21–73.

– "D'un atelier de moulage à un autre: les migrations des mouleurs originaires des Forges du Saint-Maurice et segmentation du marché du travail nord-américain, 1851–1884." *Labour/Le travail* 40 (autumn 1997), 21–74.

– "La Société de bienfaisance des journaliers de navires à Québec, 1855 à 1878." *Canadian Historical Review* 84 (2003), 321–53.

Blanchard, Jim. "A Bibliography on Mechanics' Institutes, with Particular Reference to Ontario." In Peter F. McNally, ed., *Readings in Canadian Library History.* Ottawa: Canadian Library Association, 1986, 3–18.

– "Anatomy of a Failure: Ontario Mechanics' Institutes, 1835–1895." *Canadian Library Journal* 38, no. 6 (Dec. 1981), 393–8.

Bleasdale, Ruth. "Class Conflict on the Canals of Upper Canada in the 1840s." *Labour/ Le Travailleur* 7 (1981), 9–39.

Blenkinsop, Padraig. "A History of Adult Education in the Prairies: Learning to Live in Agrarian Saskatchewan, 1870–1944." PhD thesis, University of Toronto, 1979.

Bloomfield, Elizabeth, and G.T. Bloomfield. *The Ontario Urban System at the Onset of the Industrial Era.* Guelph: Department of Geography, University of Guelph, 1989.

Bloomfield, G.T., and Elizabeth Bloomfield. *Industry in Ontario Counties, 1871 – A Preliminary Atlas.* Guelph: Department of Geography, University of Guelph, 1992.

Blouin, Claude. "La mécanisation de l'agriculture entre 1830 et 1890." In Normand Séguin, ed., *Agriculture et colonisation au Québec. Aspects historiques.* Montreal: Boréal Express, 1980, 93–111.

Boisseau, A. *Catalogue des livres de la bibliothèque de l'Institut canadien.* Montreal: Alphonse Doutre, 1870.

Bolles, Albert. *Industrial History of the United States, from the Earliest Settlements to the Present Time.* Norwich, CT: H. Bell, 1881.

Bonnemant, Emile. *Projet pour l'établissement d'une sucrerie de betteraves au Canada.* Montreal, Oct. 1872.

Bonython, Elizabeth, and Anthony Burton. *The Great Exhibitor: The Life and Work of Henry Cole.* London: Victoria and Albert Publications, 2003.

Bouchard, Gérard. *Quelques arpents d'Amérique. Population, économie, famille au Saguenay 1838–1971.* Montreal: Boréal, 1996.

Boyce, Gerald E. *Hutton of Hastings: The Life and Letters of William Hutton, 1801–61.* Belleville, ON: Hastings County Council, 1972.

Bradbury, Bettina. "The Family Economy and Work in an Industrializing City: Montreal in the 1870s." In J.M. Bumsted, ed., *Interpreting Canada's Past, Vol. 2: After Confederation.* Toronto: Oxford University Press, 1986, 92–115.

Brewin, Margaret J. "The Establishment of an Industrial Education System in Ontario." MA thesis, University of Toronto, 1967.

Brown, David. "Reassessing the Influence of the Aristocratic Improver: The Example of the Fifth Duke of Bedford (1765–1802)." *Agricultural History Review* 42, no. 2 (1999), 182–95.

Brown, James B. *Views of Canada and the Colonists Embracing the Experience of Eight Years' Residence.* Edinburgh: A. and C. Black, 1851.

Bruce, Lorne. *Free Books for All: The Public Library Movement in Ontario, 1850–1930.* Toronto: Dundurn Press, 1994.

Bruchési, Jean. "L'Institut canadien de Québec." *Cahiers des dix* 12 (1947), 93–114.

Bryant, John Ebenezer. *Agriculture in the Public Schools (An Address to the Ontario Teachers' Association, Niagara-on-the-Lake, August 1890).* Toronto: Warwick and Sons, 1891.

Buckner, Phillip. "The Long Goodbye: English Canadians and the British World." In Phillip Buckner and R. Douglas Francis, eds., *Rediscovering the British World.* Calgary: University of Calgary Press, 2005, 181–207.

Buckner, Phillip, and R.D. Francis, eds. *Rediscovering the British World.* Calgary: University of Calgary Press, 2005.

Buckner, Phillip, ed. *Canada and the End of Empire.* Vancouver: UBC Press, 2005.

Burr, Christina. *Spreading the Light: Work and Labour Reform in Late-Nineteenth-Century Toronto.* Toronto: University of Toronto Press, 1999.

*By-laws and Catalogue of the Hamilton and Gore Mechanics' Institute.* Hamilton, 1854.

Caird, James. *English Agriculture in 1850–51.* London: Longman, Brown, 1852.

Canada. *Report of the Royal Commission on the Relations of Labor and Capital in Canada.* Ottawa: A. Senecal, 1889.

Canada. *Royal Commission on Industrial Training and Technical Education: Report of the Commissioners.* 4 vols. Ottawa: C.H. Parmalee, 1913.

Canniff, William. *History of the Settlement of Upper Canada (Ontario: With Special Reference to the Bay of Quinté).* Toronto: Dudley and Burns, 1869.

Carbert, Robert W. "Agricultural and Horticultural Societies and Fairs in the Niagara Peninsula." In J. Burtniak and W.B. Turner, eds., *Agriculture and Farm Life in the Niagara Peninsula.* St Catharines, ON: Brock University, 1983, 47–62.

Cardwell, D.S.L. *The Organisation of Science in England.* Rev. ed. London: Heinemann, 1972.

Carle, Paul, and Jean-Claude Guédon. "Vulgarisation et développement des sciences et des techniques: le cas du Québec (1850–1950)." In D. Jacobi and B. Schiele, eds., *Vulgariser la science: le procès de l'ignorance.* Seyssel, France: Champ Vallon, 1988, 192–219.

Carter, John. "The Education of the Ontario Farmer." *Ontario History* 96, no. 1 (2004), 62–84.

Castéran, Nicole. "Les stratégies agricoles du paysan canadien-français de l'est ontarien (1870)." *Revue d'histoire de l'Amérique française* 41 (summer 1987), 23–51.

Casteras, Susan P., and Ronald Parkinson, eds. *Richard Redgrave 1804–1888.* New Haven, CT: Yale University Press, 1988.

Chalmers, F. Graeme. "Learning to Draw at the Barrie Mechanics' Institute." In Harold Pearse, ed., *From Drawing to Visual Culture: A History of Art Education in Canada.* Montreal: McGill-Queen's University Press, 2006, 31–46.

Chamberlin, Brown. *Report upon the Institutions in London, Dublin, Edinburgh and Paris for the Promotion of Industrial Education.* Montreal: s.n., 1859.

Chapais, Jean-Charles, *fils. Notes historiques sur les écoles d'agriculture dans Québec.* Montreal: s.n., 1916.

– *Réminiscences et revendications.* Quebec: s.n., 1910.

– "Three Centuries of Agriculture." In A. Shortt and A. Doughty, eds., *Canada and Its Provinces,* vol. 16. Toronto: Publishers Association of Canada, 1914, 505–27.

Charland, Jean-Pierre. *Histoire de l'enseignement technique et professionel: l'enseignement spécialisé au Québec 1867 à 1982.* Québec: Institut québécois de recherche sur la culture, 1982.

– *L'entreprise éducative au Québec, 1840–1900*. Québec: Les Presses de l'Université Laval, 2000.

Charland, Jean-Pierre, and Nicole Thivièrge. *Bibliographie de l'enseignement professionel, 1850–1980*. Québec: Institut québécoises de recherche sur la culture, 1981.

Chartrand, Luc, Raymond Duchesne, and Yves Gingras. *Histoire des sciences au Québec*. Montreal: Boréal, 1987.

Chatillon, Colette. *L'histoire de l'agriculture au Québec*. Montreal: Editions l'Etincelle, 1976.

Chauveau, Pierre-J.-O. *L'instruction publique au Canada*. Quebec: A. Coté, 1876.

Christie, Nancy, ed. *Transatlantic Subjects: Ideas, Institutions, and Social Experience in Post-Revolutionary British North America*. Montreal and Kingston: McGill-Queen's University Press, 2008.

Clarke, Isaac E. *Art and Industrial Education*. Albany, NY: J.B. Lyon, 1904.

Cochrane, Willard W. *The Development of American Agriculture: A Historical Analysis*. 2nd ed. Minneapolis: University of Minnesota Press, 1993.

Cohen, Marjorie Griffin. "The Decline of Women in Canadian Dairying." In Veronica Strong-Boag and Anita Clair Fellman, eds., *Re-thinking Canada: The Promise of Women's History*. Toronto: Copp Clark Pitman, 1991, 134–60.

– *Women's Work, Markets, and Economic Development in Nineteenth-Century Ontario*. Toronto: University of Toronto Press, 1988.

Cohoe, Margaret. "Kingston Mechanics' Institute, 1834–1850." *Historic Kingston* 32 (Jan. 1984), 62–74.

– "Kingston Mechanics' Institute to Free Library." *Historic Kingston* 33 (Jan. 1985), 42–55.

Cole, A.S., and H. Cole, eds. *Fifty Years of Public Work of Sir Henry Cole*. 2 vols. London: G. Bell, 1884.

Constant, Jean-François, and Michel Ducharme, eds. *Liberalism and Hegemony: Debating the Canadian Liberal Revolution*. Toronto: University of Toronto Press, 2009.

*Constitution and General Laws of the Farmers' & Mechanics' Institute of Streetsville in the County of Peel – Incorporated April 3rd, 1854*. Streetsville, ON: Weekly Review, 1858.

Cooper, John Irwin. *Montreal: A Brief History*. Montreal: McGill-Queen's University Press, 1969.

Cotgrove, Stephen F. *Technical Education and Social Change*. London: Allen and Unwin, 1958.

Courville, Serge. "Le marché des 'subsistences.' L'exemple de la plaine de Montréal au début des années 1830: une perspective géographique." *Revue d'histoire de l'Amérique française* 42 (autumn 1988), 193–239.

– "Villages and Agriculture in the Seigneuries of Lower Canada: Conditions of a Comprehensive Study of Rural Quebec in the First Half of the Nineteenth Century." In Donald H. Akenson, ed., *Canadian Papers in Rural History*, vol. 5. Ganonoque, ON: Langdale Press, 1986, 121–49.

Courville, Serge, and Normand Séguin. *Rural Life in Nineteenth-Century Quebec*. Canadian Historical Association, Historical Booklet No. 47. 1989.

Courville, Serge, and Normand Séguin, eds. *Atlas historique du Québec. La paroisse*. Sainte-Foy: Les Presses de l'Université Laval, 2001.

Craven, Paul, ed. *Labouring Lives: Work and Workers in Nineteenth-Century Ontario*. Toronto: University of Toronto Press, 1995.

Craven, Paul, and Tom Traves. "Dimensions of Paternalism: Discipline and Culture in Canadian Railway Operations in the 1850s." In Craig Heron and Robert H. Storey, eds., *On the Job: Confronting the Labour Process in Canada*. Montreal and Kingston: McGill-Queen's University Press, 1986, 47–74.

Crawford, Pleasance. "Some Early Niagara Nurserymen." In J. Burtniak and W.B. Turner, eds., *Agriculture and Farm Life in the Niagara Peninsula*. St Catharines, ON: Brock University, 1983, 63–90.

Cross, Michael S. *The Workingman in the Nineteenth Century*. Toronto: Oxford University Press, 1974.

Crowley, Terry. "Experience and Representation: Southern Ontario Farm Women and Agricultural Change, 1870–1914." *Agricultural History* 73 (spring 1999), 238–51.

– "Rural Labour." In Paul Craven, ed., *Labouring Lives: Work and Workers in Nineteenth-Century Ontario*. Toronto: University of Toronto Press, 1995, 13–102.

Curtis, Bruce. *Building the Educational State: Canada West, 1836–1871*. London, ON: Althouse Press, 1988.

– "Class, Culture and Administration: Educational Inspection in Canada West." In Allan Greer and Ian Radforth, eds., *Colonial Leviathan: State Formation in Mid-Nineteenth-Century Canada*. Toronto: University of Toronto Press, 1992, 103–32.

– "'Littery Merritt,' 'Useful Knowledge' and the Organization of Township Libraries in Canada West, 1840–1860." *Ontario History* 68 (Dec. 1986), 284–312.

– *The Politics of Population: State Formation, Statistics, and the Census of Canada, 1840–1875*. Toronto: University of Toronto Press, 2002.

– *True Government by Choice Men? Inspection, Education, and State Formation in Canada West*. Toronto: University of Toronto Press, 1992.

Dabney, Charles W. *Agricultural Education*. Albany, NY: J.B. Lyon, 1900.

Darroch, Gordon. "Scanty Fortunes and Rural Middle-class Formation in Nineteenth-Century Central Ontario." *Canadian Historical Review* 79 (Dec. 1998), 621–59.

Darroch, Gordon, and Michael Ornstein. "Ethnicity and Class: Transitions over a Decade: Ontario, 1861–1871." Canadian Historical Association, *Historical Papers* (1984), 114–37.

Dawson, J. William. *Contributions Toward the Improvement of Agriculture in Nova-Scotia; with Practical Hints on the Management and Improvement of Live Stock, etc.* 2nd ed. 1856.

– *First Lessons in Scientific Agriculture for Schools and Private Instruction*. Montreal: John Lovell, 1864.

– *On the Course of Collegiate Education, Adapted to the Circumstances of British America.* Montreal: H. Ramsay, 1855.

– *The Duties of Educated Young Men in British America.* Montreal: John Lovell, 1863.

Dean, Henry H. *Canadian Dairying.* Toronto: William Briggs, 1903.

Dembski, Peter Paul. "Sir John Carling." In *Dictionary of Canadian Biography*, vol. 14. Quebec and Toronto: Les presses de l'Université Laval and University of Toronto Press, 1988, 185–9.

Derry, Margaret. "Gender Conflicts in Dairying: Ontario's Butter Industry." *Ontario History* 90 (spring 1998), 31–48.

– *Horses in Society: A Story of Animal Breeding and Marketing, 1800–1920.* Toronto: University of Toronto Press, 2006.

– *Ontario's Cattle Kingdom: Purebred Breeders and Their World, 1870–1920.* Toronto: University of Toronto Press, 2001.

– "The Development of a Modern Agricultural Enterprise: Beef Cattle Farming in Ontario, 1870–1924." PhD thesis, University of Toronto, 1997.

Désilets, Andrée. "Jean-Charles Chapais [*père*]." In *Dictionary of Canadian Biography*, vol. 11. Quebec and Toronto: Les presses de l'Université Laval and University of Toronto Press, 1982, 175–7.

Dickinson, John, and Brian Young. *A Short History of Quebec.* 3rd ed. Montreal: McGill-Queen's University Press, 2003.

Dionne, Narcisse-E. *Les cercles agricoles dans la Province de Québec.* Quebec: L. Brousseau, 1881.

Dodds, Philip. *The Story of Ontario Agricultural Fairs and Exhibitions 1797–1967.* Picton, ON: Picton Gazette Publishing Company, 1967.

Dougall, James. *The Canadian Fruit-culturist; or, Letters to an Intending Fruit-grower.* Montreal: John Dougall & Son, 1867.

Douglas, A.G., trans. *Traduction libre et abrégé des leçons de chimie données par le chevalier H. Davy.* Montreal, 1820.

Dowbiggin, Ian. "John Seath." In *Dictionary of Canadian Biography*, vol. 14. Quebec and Toronto: Les presses de l'Université Laval and University of Toronto Press, 1998, 918–19.

Drummond, Ian. *Progress without Planning: The Economic History of Ontario from Confederation to the Second World War.* Toronto: University of Toronto Press, 1987.

Dumont, Michelline. *Girls' Schooling in Quebec, 1639–1960.* Historical Booklet No. 49. Ottawa: Canadian Historical Association, 1990.

Dunbar, Willis. *The Michigan Record of Higher Education.* Detroit: Wayne State University Press, 1963.

Dunbar, Willis, and George May. *Michigan: A History of the Wolverine State.* Grand Rapids, MI: W.D. Eerdmans Publishing Company, 1980.

Duncombe, Charles. *Doctor Charles Duncombe's Report upon the Subject of Education Made to the Parliament of Upper Canada, 25th February 1836.* Toronto: M. Reynolds, 1836.

Dunlop, William. *An Address delivered to the York Mechanics' Institute March, 1832.* York: W.J. Coates, 1832.

Eadie, J. "The Napanee Mechanics' Institute." *Ontario History* 68 (1976), 209–21.

Eales, Walter. *A Lecture on the Benefits to be Derived from Mechanics' Institutes; delivered in the Toronto Mechanics' Institute, February 5, 1851.* Toronto: J. Stephen, 1851.

Easterbrook, W.T., and H.G.J. Aitken. *Canadian Economic History.* Toronto: University of Toronto Press, 1988.

Ellis, W.S. *A Report on Elementary Technical Education for Ontario.* Kingston, ON: Daily News, 1900.

Evans, A.M. "Andrew Smith." In *Dictionary of Canadian Biography*, vol. 13. Quebec and Toronto: Les presses de l'Université Laval and University of Toronto Press, 1994, 961–3.

Evans, Keith. *The Development and Structure of the English Educational System.* London: University of London Press, 1975.

Evans, William. *A Treatise on the Theory and Practice of Agriculture, Adapted to the Cultivation and Economy of the Animal and Vegetable Productions of Agriculture in Canada.* Montreal: Fabre, Perrault, 1835.

– *Agricultural Improvement by the Education of Those Who are Engaged in it as a Profession.* Montreal: Courier Office, 1837.

– *Agriculture in Lower Canada.* Montreal: Montreal Gazette, 1856.

Fahmy-Eid, Nadia. "Ultramontanisme, idéologie et classes sociales." *Revue d'histoire de l'Amérique française* 29, no. 1 (1975), 49–68.

Fair, Ross D. "Gentlemen, Farmers, and Gentlemen Half-farmers: The Development of Agricultural Societies in Upper Canada, 1792–1846." PhD thesis, Queen's University, 1998.

Fecteau, Jean-Marie. *Un nouvel ordre des choses: la pauvreté, le crime, l'État au Québec, de la fin du XVIIIe siècle à 1840.* Montreal: VLB éditeur, 1989.

Ferry, Darren. "'The Original Ideas has been considerably amplified.' Culture, Authority, and the Emergence of a Liberal Social Order in the Central Canadian Mechanics' Institute Movement, 1828–60." In Nancy Christie, ed., *Transatlantic Subjects: Ideas, Institutions, and Social Experience in Post-Revolutionary British North America.* Montreal and Kingston: McGill-Queen's University Press, 2008, 439–74.

– *Uniting in Measures of Common Good: The Construction of Liberal Identities in Central Canada, 1830–1900.* Montreal: McGill-Queen's University Press, 2008.

Fisher, Berenice M. *Industrial Education: American Ideals and Institutions.* Madison: University of Wisconsin Press, 1967.

Fowke, Vernon C. *Canadian Agricultural Policy.* Toronto: University of Toronto Press, 1946.

Frayling, Christopher. *Royal College of Art: One Hundred and Fifty Years of Art and Design.* London: Barrie and Jenkins, 1987.

French, Goldwyn S. "Egerton Ryerson and the Methodist Model for Upper Canada." In Neil McDonald and Alf Chaiton, eds., *Egerton Ryerson and His Times.* Toronto: Macmillan, 1978, 45–58.

Friedland, Martin L. *The University of Toronto: A History*. Toronto: University of Toronto Press, 2002.

Friel, H.J. *Inaugural Address at the Opening of the Winter Course of Lectures before the Ottawa Mechanics' Institute and Athenaeum, October 2nd, 1855*. Ottawa: Citizen, 1855.

Friesen, Gerald, and Lucy Taksa. "Workers' Education in Australia and Canada: A Comparative Approach." *Labour/Le travail* 38 (Nov. 1996), 170–97.

Frost, Stanley Brice. *McGill University, for the Advancement of Learning, 1801–1895*. Montreal: McGill-Queen's University Press, 1980.

Frost, Stanley Brice, and Robert H. Michel. "Sir William Christopher Macdonald." In *Dictionary of Canadian Biography*, vol. 14. Quebec and Toronto: Les Presses de l'Université Laval and University of Toronto Press, 1998, 689–94.

Fruit Growers' Association of Ontario. *20th Annual Report*. Toronto: The Association, 1889.

Fussell, G.E. "The Agricultural Revolution, 1600–1850." In Melvin Kranzberg and Carroll Pursell, eds., *Technology and Western Civilization*, vol. 1. New York: Oxford University Press, 1967, 128–42.

Gagan, David. "Land, Population, and Social Change: The 'Critical Years' in Rural Canada West." *Canadian Historical Review* 59 (1978), 293–318.

Gagen, Robert F. "History of Art Societies in Ontario." In J. Castell Hopkins, ed., *Canada: An Encylopaedia of the Country*, vol. 3. Toronto: Linscott Publishing Co., 1898, 360–5.

Gagnon, Robert. *Histoire de l'École polytechnique de Montréal, 1873–1990*. Montreal: Boréal, 1991.

– "Les discours sur l'enseignement pratique au Canada français, 1850–1900." In M. Fournier, Y. Gingras, and O. Keel, eds., *Sciences et médecine au Québec: perspectives sociohistoriques*. Quebec: Institut québécoises de recherche sur la culture, 1987, 19–39.

– "Urgel-Eugéne Archambeault (Archambault)." In *Dictionary of Canadian Biography*, vol. 13. Quebec and Toronto: Les Presses de l'Université Laval and University of Toronto Press, 1994, 22–3.

Gagnon, Serge. "François Pilote." In *Dictionary of Canadian Biography*, vol. 11. Quebec and Toronto: Les Presses de l'Université Laval and University of Toronto Press, 1982, 689–91.

– "Napoléon Aubin." In *Dictionary of Canadian Biography*, vol. 11. Quebec and Toronto: Les presses de l'Université Laval and University of Toronto Press, 1982, 34–7.

Gaitskell, C.D. *Art Education in the Province of Ontario*. Toronto: Ryerson Press, 1948.

Galarneau, Claude. *Les collèges classiques au Canada français*. Montreal: Fides, 1978.

Garner, A.D., and E.W. Jenkins. "The English Mechanics' Institutes: The Case of Leeds." *History of Education* 13 (1984), 139–52.

Gattinger, F.E. *A Century of Challenge: A History of the Ontario Veterinary College*. Toronto: University of Toronto Press, 1962.

Gentilcore, R. Louis, ed. *Historical Atlas of Canada, Volume II: The Land Transformed, 1800–1891.* Toronto: University of Toronto Press, 1993.

Gibbons, Robert. *Address Delivered before the Agriculture and Arts Association of Ontario at the Twenty-Fifth Annual Provincial Exhibition at Toronto, 1874.* Toronto: The Globe, 1974.

Gidney, R.D., and W.P.J. Millar. *Inventing Secondary Education: The Rise of the High School in Nineteenth-Century Ontario.* Montreal: McGill-Queen's University Press, 1990.

– *Professional Gentlemen: The Professions in Nineteenth-Century Ontario.* Toronto: University of Toronto Press, 1994.

Gigault, G.A. "Agriculture in the Province of Quebec." In J. Castell Hopkins, ed., *Canada. An Encyclopaedia of the Country,* vol. 5. Toronto: Linscott Publishing Co., 1899, 48–52.

Gilmour, James M. *Spatial Evolution of Manufacturing: Southern Ontario, 1851–1891.* Toronto: University of Toronto Press, 1972.

Gingras, Yves, and Robert Gagnon. "Engineering Education and Research in Montreal: Social Constraints and Opportunities." *Minerva* 26, no. 1 (spring 1988), 53–65.

Girod, Amury. *Conversations sur l'agriculture, par un habitans de Varennes.* 1834.

Goddard, Nicholas. "The Development and Influence of Agricultural Periodicals and Newspapers, 1780–1880." *Agricultural History Review* 31, no. 2 (1983), 116–31.

Goldin, Claudia, and Lawrence Katz. *The Race between Education and Technology.* Cambridge, MA: Harvard University Press, 2008.

Goodwin, W.L. "A School of Science." *Canada Educational Monthly* 9 (1887), 85–8.

Goulet, Denis, and Frédéric Jean. "Duncan McNab McEachran." In *Dictionary of Canadian Biography,* vol. 15. Quebec and Toronto: Les Presses de l'Université Laval and University of Toronto Press, 2005, 639–43.

Graff, Harvey J. "Respected and Profitable Labour: Literacy, Jobs and the Working Class in the Nineteenth Century." In Gregory S. Kealey and Peter Warrian, eds., *Essays in Canadian Working Class History.* Toronto: McClelland and Stewart, 1979, 58–82.

Greer, Allan. *The Patriots and the People: The Rebellion of 1837 in Rural Lower Canada.* Toronto: University of Toronto Press, 1993.

– "The Patterns of Literacy in Quebec." *Histoire sociale/Social History* (Nov. 1978), 295–35.

Guildford, Janet. "Coping with De-industrialization: The Nova Scotia Department of Technical Education, 1907–1930." *Acadiensis* 16 (1987), 69–84.

Guillet, Edwin C. *In the Cause of Education: Centennial History of the Ontario Educational Association 1861–1960.* Toronto: University of Toronto Press, 1960.

Guillet, Valère. *Un petit système d'agriculture.* Montreal: La Bibliothèque canadienne, 1829.

Gundy, H.P. "Hugh Christopher Thomson." In *Dictionary of Canadian Biography,* vol. 6. Quebec and Toronto: Les Presses de l'Université Laval and University of Toronto Press, 1987, 772–4.

Hamel, Thérèse, Michel Morisset, and Jacques Tondreau. *De la terre à l'école: histoire de l'enseignement agricole au Québec, 1926–1969.* Montreal: Hurtubise HMH, 2000.

Hamelin, Jean, ed. *Les travailleurs québécois 1851–1896*. Montreal: Les Presses de l'Université du Québec, 1973.

– *L'histoire de l'Université Laval. Les péripéties d'une idée*. Sainte-Foy: Les Presses de l'Université Laval, 1995.

Hamelin, Jean, and Pierre Poulin. "Pierre-Joseph-Olivier Chauveau." In *Dictionary of Canadian Biography*, vol. 11. Quebec and Toronto: Les presses de l'Université Laval and University of Toronto Press, 1982, 177–87.

Hamelin, Jean, and Yves Roby. *Histoire économique du Québec 1851–1896*. Montreal: Editions Fides, 1971.

Hamilton, Gillian. "The Decline of Apprenticeship in North America: Evidence from Montreal." *Journal of Economic History* 60 (Sept. 2000), 627–64.

– "The Market for Montreal Apprentices: Contract Length and Information." *Explorations in Economic History* 33 (1996), 496–523.

*Hamilton & Gore Mechanics' Institute. Exhibition of Fine Arts, Manufactures, Curiosities, etc.* Hamilton, 1855.

Hann, Russell. *Farmers Confront Industrialization: Some Historical Perspectives on Ontario Agrarian Movements*. Toronto: New Hogtown Press, 1975.

Hardy, René, and Normand Séguin. *Forêt et société en Mauricie*. Montreal: Boréal Express, 1984.

Hardy, René, and Normand Séguin, eds. *Histoire de la Mauricie*. Sainte-Foy: IQRC, 2004.

Harris, Robert. "Art in Quebec and the Maritime Provinces." In J. Castell Hopkins, ed., *Canada: An Encyclopaedia of the Country*, vol. 3. Toronto: Linscott Publishing Co., 1898, 353–9.

Harris, Robin S. *A History of Higher Education in Canada (1663–1960)*. Toronto: University of Toronto Press, 1976.

Harris, Robin S., and Ian Montagnes, eds. *Cold Steel and Lady Godiva*. Toronto: University of Toronto Press, 1974.

Harvey, Fernand. *Révolution industrielle et travailleurs*. Montreal: Boréal, 1978.

Hatvany, Matthew G. *Marshlands: Four Centuries of Environmental Change on the Shores of the St. Lawrence*. Ste-Foy: Les Presses de l'Université Laval, 2003.

Heaman, E.A. *The Inglorious Arts of Peace: Exhibitions in Canadian Society during the Nineteenth Century*. Toronto: University of Toronto Press, 1999.

Heap, Ruby. "Un chapitre dans l'histoire de l'éducation des adultes au Québec: les écoles du soir, 1889–1892." *Revue d'histoire de l'Amérique française* 34, no. 4 (1981), 597–625.

Hedrick, Ulysses P. *A History of Agriculture in the State of New York*. Albany: New York State Agricultural Society, 1933.

Heron, Craig. *Working in Steel: The Early Years in Canada, 1883–1935*. Toronto: McClelland and Stewart, 1988.

Hewitt, Martin. "Science as Spectacle: Popular Scientific Culture in Saint John, New Brunswick, 1830–50." *Acadiensis* 18 (1988), 91–119.

– "Science, Popular Culture, and the Producer Alliance in Saint John, N.B." In Paul
   Bogaard, ed., *Profiles of Science and Society in the Maritimes prior to 1914*. Fredericton,
   NB: Acadiensis Press, 1990, 243–75.
– "The Mechanics' Institutes of Prince Edward Island." *Island Magazine* 21 (1987),
   27–32.
Hincks, Sir Francis. *Reminiscences of His Public Life*. Montreal: William Drysdale, 1884.
Hind, Henry Youle, ed. *Eighty Years' Progress of British North America*. Toronto: L. Nichols,
   1865.
– *Narrative of the Canadian Red River Exploring Expedition of 1857 and of the Assiniboine
   and Saskatchewan Exploring Expedition of 1858*. 2 vols. London: Longman, Green,
   Longman and Roberts, 1860.
Hinton, D.A. "Popular Science in England, 1830–1870." PhD thesis, University of Bath,
   1979.
Hodgetts, J. E. *From Arm's Length to Hands-on: The Formative Years of Ontario's Public
   Service, 1867–1940*. Toronto: University of Toronto Press, 1995.
– *Pioneer Public Service: An Administrative History of the United Canadas, 1841–1867*.
   Toronto: University of Toronto Press, 1955.
Hodgins, J. George, and Alex T. Machattie. *Report of an Inquiry in Regard to Schools of
   Technical Science in Certain Portions of the United States*. Toronto: Hunter, Rose, 1871.
Hodgins, John George. *Documentary History of Education in Upper Canada from the Passing
   of the Constitutional Act of 1791 to the Close of the Reverend Doctor Ryerson's Administration
   of the Education Department in 1876*. 28 vols. Toronto: Warwick Brothers and Rutter,
   1894–1910.
– *The Establishment of Schools and Colleges in Ontario, 1792–1910*. 3 vols. Toronto: L.K.
   Cameron, 1910.
Holman, Andrew. *A Sense of Their Duty: Middle-class Formation in Victorian Ontario Towns*.
   Montreal and Kingston: McGill-Queen's University Press, 2000.
Holmes, Alexander. *A Brief History of Dairy Education at Home and Abroad from 1832 to
   1892*. Middlesbrough, England: Jordison, 1892.
Hopkins, J. Castell. "Canadian Arts and Art Schools." In J. Castell Hopkins, ed., *Canada:
   An Encyclopaedia of the Country*, vol. 3. Toronto: Linscott Publishing Co., 1898,
   398–400.
– *Historical Sketch of the Ontario Department of Agriculture. June 1912* (reprint from
   *Canadian Annual Review*, 1910). Toronto: s.n., 1912.
Houston, Susan E., and Alison Prentice. *Schooling and Scholars in Nineteenth-Century
   Ontario*. Toronto: University of Toronto Press, 1988.
Hudon, François. "Joseph-Xavier Perrault." In *Dictionary of Canadian Biography*, vol. 13.
   Quebec and Toronto: Les Presses de l'Université Laval and University of Toronto
   Press, 1994, 828–30.
– *L'action agronomique au Québec: son histoire, son oeuvre*. Quebec: L'Ordre des agro-
   nomes du Québec, 1987.

Hughes, Everett C. "Industry and the Rural System in Quebec." In Marcel Rioux and
    Yves Martin, eds., *French-Canadian Society* (Toronto, 1964), 76–85.
Hurt, R. Douglas. *American Agriculture: A Brief History.* Ames: Iowa State University Press,
    1994.
Innis, Harold A. "The Wheat Economy." In Harold A. Innis and Mary Q. Innis, eds.,
    *Essays in Canadian Economic History.* Toronto: University of Toronto Press, 1956,
    273–9.
Innis, Harold A., ed. *The Dairy Industry in Canada.* Toronto: Ryerson Press, 1937.
Irwin, Thomas W. "Government Funding of Agricultural Associations in Late
    Nineteenth Century Ontario." PhD thesis, University of Western Ontario, 1997.
Isbister, John. "Agriculture, Balanced Growth, and Social Change in Central Canada
    since 1850: An Interpretation." *Economic Development and Social Change* 25 (July 1977),
    673–97.
James, Charles Canniff. "History of Farming in Ontario." In A. Shortt and A. Doughty,
    eds., *Canada and Its Provinces*, vol. 18. Toronto: Publishers Association of Canada,
    1914, 551–82.
–   *The Teaching of Agriculture in our Public Schools, delivered in Boston to Farmers' National
    Congress, 1899.* S.l.: s.n., 1899.
–   *The Teaching of Agriculture in the Public Schools. Special Bulletin of the Department of
    Agriculture.* Toronto: Warwick and Sons, 1892.
Jarrell, Richard A. "Governmental Response to Technological Innovation: Leadership
    or Reaction?" In Brian Elliott, ed., *Technology, Innovation and Change.* Edinburgh:
    Centre of Canadian Studies, 1986, 29-48.
–   "Henry Youle Hind." In *Dictionary of Canadian Biography*, vol. 13. Quebec and Toronto:
    Les Presses de l'Université Laval and University of Toronto Press, 1994, 471–4.
–   "Justin de Courtenay and the Birth of the Ontario Wine Industry." *Ontario History*
    103, no. 1 (spring 2011), 81–104.
–   "L'Ultramontanisme et la science au Canada français." In M. Fournier, Y. Gingras,
    and O. Keel, eds., *Sciences et médecine au Québec: perspectives sociohistoriques.* Quebec:
    Institut québécois de recherche sur la culture, 1987, 41–68.
–   "Science and the State in Nineteenth Century Canada: Nova Scotia Discovers
    Agriculture." In Paul Bogaard, ed., *Profiles of Science and Society in the Maritimes.*
    Fredericton, NB: Acadiensis Press, 1990, 221–42.
–   "Science and the State in Ontario: The British Connection or North American
    Patterns?" In Roger Hall, William Westfall, and Laurel Sefton MacDowell, eds.,
    *Patterns of the Past: Interpreting Ontario's History.* Toronto: Dundurn Press, 1988,
    238–54.
–   "Science as Culture in Victorian Toronto." *Atkinson Review of Canadian Studies* 1, no. 1
    (1983), 5–12.

- "Science Education at the University of New Brunswick in the Nineteenth Century." *Acadiensis* (spring 1973), 55–79.
- "Some Aspects of the Evolution of Agricultural and Technical Education in Nineteenth-Century Ireland." In Peter J. Bowler and Nicholas Whyte, eds., *Science and Society in Ireland: The Social Context of Science and Technology in Ireland.* Belfast: Institute of Irish Studies, 1997, 101–17.
- "The Influence of Irish Institutions upon the Organization and Diffusion of Science in Victorian Canada." *Scientia Canadensis* 9, no. 2 (1985), 150–64.
- "The Rise and Decline of Science in Quebec, 1824–1844." *Histoire sociale* 9, no. 19 (1977), 77–91.
- "The Social Functions of the Scientific Society in 19th-Century Canada." In R. Jarrell and A. Roos, eds., *Critical Issues in the History of Canadian Science, Technology and Medicine.* Thornhill, ON: Scientia Press, 1983, 31–44.

Jean, Bruno. "Edouard-André Barnard." In *Dictionary of Canadian Biography*, vol. 12. Quebec and Toronto: Les Presses de l'Université Laval and University of Toronto Press, 1990, 57–60.

- *Les idéologies éducatives agricoles (1860–90).* Montreal: s.n., 1977.

Johnson, F. Henry. "A Colonial Canadian in Search of a Museum." *Queen's Quarterly* 77 (summer 1970), 217–30.

- "The Fate of Canada's First Art Museum." *Queen's Quarterly* 78 (summer 1971), 241–9.

Johnston, Charles M. *E.C. Drury: Agrarian Idealist.* Toronto: University of Toronto Press, 1986.

Johnston, James F.W. *Elements of Agricultrual Chemistry and Geology.* New York: Wiley and Putnam, 1842.

- *Notes on North America, Agricultural, Economical, and Social.* Edinburgh: William Blackwood, 1851.

- *Report on the Agricultural Capabilities of the Province of New Brunswick.* Fredericton, NB: J. Simpson, 1850.

Jolois, J.-J. *Joseph-François Perrault (1753–1844) et les origines de l'enseignement laïque au Bas-Canada.* Montreal: Presses de l'Université de Montréal, 1969.

Jones, Elwood H. "Adam Fergusson." In *Dictionary of Canadian Biography*, vol. 9. Quebec and Toronto: Les Presses de l'Université Laval and University of Toronto Press, 1976, 251–2.

Jones, Robert Leslie. "French-Canadian Agriculture in the St. Lawrence Valley, 1815–1850." *Agricultural History* 16 (1942), 137–48.

- *History of Agriculture in Ontario, 1613–1880.* Toronto: University of Toronto Press, 1946.

Judd, William W., ed. 1976. *Minutes of the London Mechanics' Institute (1841–1895).* London, ON: London Public Libraries, 1976.

Katz, Michael B. *The People of Hamilton, Canada West: Family and Class in a Mid-Nineteenth-Century City.* Cambridge, MA: Harvard University Press, 1975.

Katz, Michael B., Michael J. Doucet, and Mark J. Stern. *The Social Organization of Early Industrial Capitalism.* Cambridge, MA: Harvard University Press, 1982.

Kealey, Gregory S., ed, with intro. *Canada Investigates Industrialism: The Royal Commission on the Relations of Labor and Capital, 1885* (abridged). Toronto: University of Toronto Press, 1973.

– "Labour and Working-Class History in Canada: Prospects for the 1980s." *Labour/Le travail* 7 (1981), 67–94.

– "The Orange Order in Toronto: Religious Riot and the Working Class." In Gregory S. Kealey and Peter Warrian, eds., *Essays in Canadian Working Class History.* Toronto: McClelland and Stewart, 1979, 13–34.

Kealey, Gregory S., and Bryan D. Palmer. *Dreaming of What Might Be. The Knights of Labor in Ontario, 1880–1900.* Toronto: New Hogtown Press, 1987.

Keane, Patrick. "A Study in Early Problems and Policies in Adult Education: The Halifax Mechanics' Institute." *Histoire sociale/Social History* 8 (1975), 255–74.

Kechnie, Margaret C. *Organizing Rural Women: The Federated Women's Institutes of Ontario, 1897–1919.* Montreal and Kingston: McGill-Queen's University Press, 2003.

Kelly, Kenneth. "The Transfer of British Ideas on Improved Farming to Ontario during the First Half of the Nineteenth Century." *Ontario History* 63 (June 1971), 103–11.

Kelly, Thomas. *A History of Adult Education in Great Britain.* Liverpool: Liverpool University Press, 1970.

– *George Birkbeck, Pioneer of Adult Education.* Liverpool: Liverpool University Press, 1957.

Kerr, D.G.G. *Sir Edmund Head, a Scholarly Governor.* Toronto: University of Toronto Press, 1954.

Kerr, Donald, and William J. Smyth. "Agriculture, Balanced Growth, and Social Change in Central Canada since 1850: Some Comments toward a More Complete Explanation." *Economic Development and Social Change* 28 (April 1980), 615–22; reply by J. Isbister, 623–5.

Killan, Gerald. *David Boyle: From Artisan to Archaeologist.* Toronto: University of Toronto Press, 1983.

Klotz, Otto. *A Review of the Special Report of the Minister of Education on the Mechanics' Institutes of Ontario.* Toronto: Willing and Williamson, 1881.

Kristofferson, Robert. *Craft Capitalism: Craftworkers and Early Industrialization in Hamilton, Ontario, 1840–1872.* Toronto: University of Toronto Press, 2007.

Kuhn, Madison. *Michigan State: The First Hundred Years, 1855–1955.* East Lansing: Michigan State University Press, 1955.

[Lachlan, Robert]. *Address of the Directing President of the Western District Agricultural and Horticultural Society.* Sandwich, UC: H.C. Grant, 1838.

Lamonde, Yvan. *Gens de parole. Conférences publiques, essais et débats à l'Institut Canadien de Montréal 1845–1871.* Montreal: Boréal, 1990.

– *Histoire sociale des idées au Québec (1760–1896)*. Montreal: Fides, 2000.

– "Inventaire des études et des sources pour l'étude des associations 'littéraires' québécoises francophone au XIXe siècle (1840–1900)." *Recherches sociographiques* 16, no. 2 (1975), 261–75.

– "Le membership d'une association du XIXe siècle. Le cas de l'Institut canadien de Longueuil (1857–1860)." *Recherches sociographiques* 16, no. 2 (1975), 219–40.

– *Les bibliothèques de collectivités à Montréal (17ᵉ–19e siècles): sources et problèmes*. Montreal: Bibliothèque nationale du Québec, 1979.

– "Liste alphabétique de noms de lieux où existèrent des associations 'littéraires' au Québec (1840–1900)." *Recherches sociographiques* 16, no. 2 (1975), 277–80.

Landon, Fred. "The Agricultural Journals of Upper Canada (Ontario)." *Agricultural History* 9 (1935), 167–75.

– *Western Ontario and the American Frontier*. Toronto: Ryerson Press, 1941.

Landry, A.C.P.R. *Traité populaire d'agriculture théorique et pratique*. Montreal: Imprimerie canadienne, 1878.

Langelier, Jean-Chrysostome. *Traité d'agriculture à l'usage des écoles et des praticiens*. Quebec: J. Dussault, 1890.

Langevin, Jean. *Réponses aux programmes de pédagogie et d'agriculture pour les diplômes d'école élémentaire et d'école modèle*. Quebec: Joseph Darveau, 1862.

Larivière-Derome, Céline. "Un professeur d'art au Canada au XIXᵉ siècle: l'abbé Joseph Chabert." *Revue d'histoire de l'Amérique française* 28, no. 3 (1974), 347–66.

La Rue, Hubert. *Petit manuel d'agriculture à l'usage des écoles*. 2nd ed. Quebec. C. Darveau, 1872.

Lawes. J.B., et al. *The Soil of the Farm*. New York: Orange Judd, 1883.

Lawr, D. A. "Agricultural Education in Nineteenth-Century Ontario: An Idea in Search of an Institution." In Michael B. Katz and Paul H. Mattingly, eds., *Education and Social Change: Themes from Ontario's Past*. New York: New York University Press, 1975, 169–92.

– "The Development of Ontario Farming, 1870–1914: Patterns of Growth and Change." *Ontario History* 64 (1972), 239–51.

Layton, David. *Science for the People*. New York: Science History Publications, 1974.

Leacy, F.H., M.C. Urquhart, and K.A.H. Buckley, eds. *Historical Statistics of Canada*. Ottawa: Statistics Canada, 1983.

Leake, Albert H. *Education and Industrial Efficiency*. Toronto: L.K. Cameron, 1906.

– *The Means and Methods of Agricultural Education*. Boston: Houghton, Mifflin, 1915.

Lebon, Wilfrid. *Histoire du Collège de Sainte-Anne-de-la-Pocatière*. 2 vols. Quebec: Charrier & Dugal, 1948–9.

Lebrun, Isidore. *Tableau statistique et politique des deux Canadas*. Paris: Treutel et Weurtz, 1833.

*Le cinquantenaire de l'Ecole d'agriculture de Sainte-Anne de la Pocatière. Les 20 et 21 décembre 1909*. Quebec: Dussault & Proulx, 1910.

[Leclerc, Nazaire-A.]. *Catechisme d'agriculture ou la science agricole mis à portée des enfants par * * ** Quebec: Darveau, 1868.

Lee, Matthew. "Birkbeck, George (1776–1841)." In H.C.G. Matthew and Brian Harrison, eds., *Oxford Dictionary of National Biography*. Oxford: Oxford University Press, 2004. www.oxforddnb.com.ezproxy.library.yorku.ca/view/article/2454

Lessard, Renald. "Louis Gugy." In *Dictionary of Canadian Biography*, vol. 7. Quebec and Toronto: Les Presses de l'Université Laval and University of Toronto Press, 1988.

Létourneau, Firmin. *Histoire de l'agriculture (Canada français)*. Montreal: Imprimerie Populaire, 1950.

Linteau, Paul-André, René Durocher, and Jean-Claude Robert. *Histoire du Québec contemporain*. Montreal: Boréal Express, 1979.

Little, J.I. *Crofters and Habitants: Settler Society, Economy and Culture in a Quebec Township, 1848–1881*. Montreal: McGill-Queen's University Press, 1991.

– *State and Society in Transition: The Politics of Institutional Reform in the Eastern Townships 1838–1852*. Montreal and Kingston: McGill-Queen's University Press, 1997.

Lortie, Léon. "Jean-Baptiste Meilleur." In *Dictionary of Canadian Biography*, vol. 10. Quebec and Toronto: Les Presses de l'Université Laval and University of Toronto Press, 1972, 504–9.

Loudon, J.C. *Encyclopedia of Agriculture*. 2 vols. London: Longman, Hurst, 1825.

*Lovell's Montreal Directory for 1842–3*. Montreal: Lovell, 1842.

MacKenzie, Ann. "Edward William Thomson." In *Dictionary of Canadian Biography*, vol. 9. Quebec and Toronto: Les Presses de l'Université Laval and University of Toronto Press, 1976, 788–9.

– "George Buckland." In *Dictionary of Canadian Biography*, vol. 11. Quebec and Toronto: Les Presses de l'Université Laval and University of Toronto Press, 1982, 132–3.

– "William Graham Edmundson." In *Dictionary of Canadian Biography*, vol. 8. Quebec and Toronto: Les Presses de l'Université Laval and University of Toronto Press, 1985, 266–8.

Macleod, Donald. "Practicality Ascendant: The Origins and Establishment of Technical Education in Nova Scotia." *Acadiensis* (spring 1986), 55–92.

MacLeod, Roy, ed. *Days of Judgement: Science, Examinations and the Organization of Knowledge in Late Victorian England*. Driffield: Nafferton, 1982.

Madill, Alonso. *A History of Agricultural Education in Ontario*. Toronto: University of Toronto Press, 1937.

Magnan, Jean-Charles. *Le monde agricole: précurseurs et contemporains*. Montreal: Les Presses libres, 1972.

Maheux, Arthur. "P.-J.-O. Chauveau, promoteur des sciences." *Mémoires de la Société royale du Canada* 1, 4e série (1963), 87–103.

Male, George A. *Education in France*. Washington, DC: U.S. Department of Health, Education, and Welfare, 1963.

Marcus, Alan I. *Agricultural Science and the Quest for Legitimacy: Farmers, Agricultural Colleges, and Experimental Stations, 1870–1890*. Ames: Iowa State University Press, 1985.

Marks, Lynne. *Revivals and Roller Rinks: Religion, Leisure, and Identity in Late Nineteenth-Century Small-Town Ontario.* Toronto: University of Toronto Press, 1996.

Marti, Donald B. "The Purposes of Agricultural Education: Ideas and Projects in New York State, 1819–1865." *Agricultural History* 45 (Oct. 1971), 271–83.

– "To Improve the Soil and the Mind: Agricultural Societies, Journals, and Schools in the Northeastern States, 1791–1865." PhD thesis, University of Michigan, 1979.

Martin, Carol. *A History of Canadian Gardening.* Toronto: McArthur and Company, 2000.

Martin, George H. *The Evolution of the Massachusetts Public School System.* New York, 1923.

Mayeur, Françoise. *Histoire générale de l'enseignement et de l'éducation en France.* Tome III. Paris, 1981.

McCalla, Douglas. *Planting the Province: The Economic History of Upper Canada 1784–1870.* Toronto: University of Toronto Press, 1993.

– "Railways and the Development of Canada West, 1850–1870." In Allan Greer and Ian Radforth, eds., *Colonial Leviathan: State Formation in Mid-Nineteenth-Century Canada.* Toronto: University of Toronto Press, 1992, 220–9.

McCallum, John. *Unequal Beginnings: Agriculture and Economic Development in Quebec and Ontario until 1870.* Toronto: University of Toronto Press, 1980.

McDonald, Neil, and Alf Chaitton, eds. *Egerton Ryerson and His Times.* Toronto: Macmillan, 1978.

McDougall, Elizabeth Ann Kerr. "Henry Esson." In *Dictionary of Canadian Biography*, vol. 8. Quebec and Toronto: Les Presses de l'Université Laval and University of Toronto Press, 1985, 272–3.

McEachran, D., and Andrew Smith. *The Canadian Horse and His Diseases.* Toronto: James Campbell, 1867.

McEvoy, H., ed. *The Province of Ontario Gazetteer and Directory.* Toronto: Robertson and Cook, 1869.

McGuire, Susan. "Portrait of the Pastor: Henry Esson Was the Guiding Force behind the Montreal Mechanics' Institute." *Quebec Heritage News* (Nov./Dec. 2008). www.atwaterlibrary.ca/sites/default/files/Portrait_of_the_pastor.pdf

McInnis, R.M. "A Reconsideration of the State of Agriculture in Lower Canada in the First Half of the Nineteenth Century." In Donald H. Akenson, ed., *Canadian Papers in Rural History, vol. 4.* Gananoque, ON: Langdale Press, 1982, 9–49.

– *Perspectives on Ontario Agriculture 1815–1930.* Gananoque, ON: Langdale Press, 1992.

– "Some Pitfalls in the 1851–1852 Census of Agriculture of Lower Canada." *Histoire sociale* 14 (May 1981), 217–31.

– "The Changing Structure of Canadian Agriculture, 1867–1897." *Journal of Economic History* 42, no. 1 (March 1982), 191–8.

McKay, Ian. "The Liberal Order Framework: A Prospectus for a Reconnaissance of Canadian History." *Canadian Historical Review* 81 (2000), 617–45.

McKillop, A.B. *Matters of Mind: The University in Ontario 1791–1951.* Ontario Historical Studies Series. Toronto: University of Toronto Press, 1994.

McNairn, Jeffrey L. *The Capacity to Judge: Public Opinion and Deliberative Democracy in Upper Canada, 1791–1854.* Toronto: University of Toronto Press, 2000.

McQueen, James. "The Development of the Technical and Vocational Schools of Ontario." MA thesis, Columbia University, 1934.

*Mechanics' Institutes, and the Best Means of Improving Them. Prize Essays.* Toronto: Hunter, Rose, 1877.

Meilleur, J.-B. *Cours abrégé de leçons de chymie, contenant une exposition précise et méthodique des principes de cette science, exemplifiés.* Montreal, 1833.

– *Mémorial de l'éducation du Bas-Canada.* Montreal: J. Rolland, 1860.

Ménard, Johanne. "L'institut des artisans du comté de Drummond, 1856–1900." *Recherches sociographiques* 16, no. 2 (1975), 207–18.

Millar, John. *Education for the Twentieth Century.* Toronto: William Briggs, 1901.

– *Technical Education. Report of a Visit to the Schools of Massachusetts, and Opinions on the Subject of Technical Education.* Toronto: Warwick Bros. and Rutter, 1899.

Millard, J. Rodney. *The Master Spirit of the Age: Canadian Engineers and the Politics of Professionalism, 1887–1922.* Toronto: University of Toronto Press, 1988.

Mills, James. "Agricultural Education in Ontario." In J. Castell Hopkins, ed., *Canada: An Encyclopaedia of the Country,* vol. 5. Toronto: Linscott Publishing Co., 1898, 93–6.

Mills, James, and Thomas Shaw. *The First Principles of Agriculture.* Toronto: J.E. Bryant, 1890.

Mondelet, Charles. *Letters on Elementary and Practical Education.* Montreal: John James Williams, 1841.

Morgan, Henry J. *Canadian Parliamentary Companion.* Montreal: s.n., 1869.

– *The Canadian Men and Women of the Time: A Handbook of Canadian Biography of Living Characters.* Toronto: W. Briggs, 1912.

Morton, Desmond. *Working People.* Montreal: McGill-Queen's University Press, 2007.

Morton, William L. *Henry Youle Hind, 1823–1908.* Toronto: University of Toronto Press, 1980.

Mulaire, Bernard. "Joseph Chabert." In *Dictionary of Canadian Biography,* vol. 12. Quebec and Toronto: Les Presses de l'Université Laval and University of Toronto Press, 1990, 170–1.

Murray, Heather. *Come, Bright Improvement! The Literary Societies of Nineteenth-Century Ontario.* Toronto: University of Toronto Press, 2002.

Nadeau, Jean-Guy. "Joseph-Charles Taché." In *Dictionary of Canadian Biography,* vol. 12. Quebec and Toronto: Les Presses de l'Université Laval and University of Toronto Press, 1990, 1012–15.

Naylor, R.T. *The History of Canadian Business 1867–1914. II. Industrial Development.* Toronto: Lorimer, 1975.

Nesmith, Tom. "The Philosophy of Agriculture: The Promise of the Intellect in Ontario Farming, 1835–1914." PhD thesis, Carleton University, 1988.

Nish, Elizabeth, ed., *Debates of the Legislative Assembly of United Canada, 1841–1867.* Montreal: Presses de l'Ecole des hautes études commerciales, 1970–93.

Norrie, Kenneth, Douglas Owram, and J.C. Herbert Emery. *A History of the Canadian Economy.* 3rd ed. Scarborough, ON: Nelson, 2000.

O'Brien, Lucius. "Art Education – a Plea for the Artizan." *Rose-Belford's Canadian Monthly & National Review* 15 (1879), 584–91.

Olmstead, Alan, and Paul Rhode. *Creating Abundance: Biological Innovation and American Agricultural Development.* Cambridge: Cambridge University Press, 2008.

Ontario Agricultural Commission. *Canadian Farming: An Encyclopaedia of Agriculture being the Report of the Ontario Agricultural Commission.* Toronto: C. Blackett Robinson, 1881.

Orwin, Christabel S., and Edith H. Whetham. *History of British Agriculture 1846–1914.* London: Longmans, 1964.

Osborne, Brian S. "Trading on the Frontier: The Function of Peddlers, Markets, and Fairs in Nineteenth-Century Ontario." In Donald H. Akenson, ed., *Canadian Papers in Rural History,* vol. 2. Gananoque, ON: Langdale Press, 1980, 59–81.

O'Sullivan, Austin, and Richard A. Jarrell. "Agricultural Education in Ireland before 1914." In Norman McMillan, ed., *The Revolutionary Force in Irish Education.* Carlow: Tyndall Publications, 2000, 376–404.

Ouellet, Fernand. *Histoire économique et sociale du Québec, 1760–1850: structures et conjoncture.* Montreal: Fides, 1966.

– *Le Bas-Canada: 1791–1840: changements structuraux et crise.* Ottawa: Editions de l'Université d'Ottawa, 1976.

Palmer, Bryan D. *A Culture in Conflict: Skilled Workers and Industrial Capitalism in Hamilton, Ontario, 1860–1914.* Montreal: McGill-Queen's University Press, 1979.

– "'Give Us the Road and We Will Run It': The Social and Cultural Matrix of an Emerging Labour Movement." In Gregory S. Kealey and Peter Warrian, eds., *Essays in Canadian Working Class History.* Toronto: McClelland and Stewart, 1979, 106–24.

– *Working-Class Experience: Rethinking the History of Canadian Labour, 1800–1991.* Toronto: McClelland and Stewart, 1992.

Parr, Joy. *The Gender of Breadwinners: Women, Men, and Change in Two Industrial Towns 1880–1950.* Toronto: University of Toronto Press, 1990.

Parvin, Viola E. *The Authorization of Textbooks for the Schools of Ontario 1846–1950.* Toronto: University of Toronto Press, 1965.

Pentland, H. Clare. *Labour and Capital in Canada, 1650–1860.* Toronto: J. Lorimer, 1961.

Perrault, Joseph-François. *Traité d'agriculture adapté au climat du Bas-Canada.* Quebec: Fréchette, 1831.

Perron, Marc-A. "Fréderic-M.-F. Ossaye." In *Dictionary of Canadian Biography*, vol. 9. Quebec and Toronto: Les Presses de l'Université Laval and University of Toronto Press, 1976, 612–13.

– *Un grand éducateur agricole. Edouard-A. Barnard 1835–1898*. S.l., s.n., 1955.

Perron, Normand. "Genèse des activités laitières, 1850–1960." In Normand Séguin, ed., *Agriculture et colonisation au Québec. Aspects historiques*. Montreal: Boréal Express, 1980, 113–40.

Phillips, W.G. *The Agricultural Implement Industry in Canada: A Study of Competition*. Toronto: University of Toronto Press, 1956.

Poirier, Pascal. *Institut Canadien-français d'Ottawa. Réminiscences*. Ottawa: A. Bureau et frères, 1908.

Pomfret, Richard. *The Economic Development of Canada*. Toronto: Methuen, 1981.

*Premier congrès des cercles agricoles Saint-Isidore, laboreur*. Montreal: Eusèbe Senécal et Fils, 1887.

Prentice, Alison. *The School Promoters: Education and Social Class in Mid-Nineteenth Century Upper Canada*. Toronto: University of Toronto Press. 2004.

Prost, Antoine. *Histoire de l'enseignement en France, 1800–1967*. Paris: A. Colin, 1968.

[Proulx, Narcisse.] *Les écoles d'agriculture de la Province de Québec vengées*. Ste-Anne-de-la-Pocatière: Firmin H. Proulx, 1877.

Provancher, Léon. "Les écoles d'adultes." *Naturaliste canadien* 5, no. 4 (1873), 105–10.

Province du Québec. *Rapport préliminaire de la commission agricole*. Quebec: Elzéar Vincent, 1888.

Québec (Province) Législature. *Débats de l'Assemblée législative du Québec*. Quebec: La Législature, 1964–68.

Rafferty, Oisin Patrick. "Apprenticeship's Legacy: The Social and Educational Goals of Technical Education in Ontario, 1860–1911." PhD thesis, McMaster University, 1995.

Ramirez, Bruno. *On the Move: French-Canadian and Italian Migrants in the North Atlantic Economy, 1860–1914*. Toronto: McClelland and Stewart, 1991.

Ramsay, Ellen L. "Art and Industrial Society: The Role of the Toronto Mechanics' Institute in the Promotion of Art, 1831–1883." *Labour/Le travail* 43 (spring 1999), 71–103.

*Rapport du comité chargé par le Conseil d'Agriculture, P.Q., de visiter L'Ecole d'agriculture de l'Etat de Michigan à Lansing, E.U. et L'Ecole d'agriculture d'Ontario à Guelph. Présenté à l'Assemblée du 12 décembre 1883*. Quebec, 1883.

Rea, K.J. *A Guide to Canadian Economic History*. Toronto: Canadian Scholars' Press, 1991.

Reaman, G. Elmore. *A History of Agriculture in Ontario*. 2 vols. Don Mills, ON: Saunders, 1970.

Reid, Thomas Wemyss, ed. *Memoirs and Correspondence of Lyon Playfair*. London: Cassell, 1899.

*Report of the General Committee of the Mechanics' Institute of Montreal (1854)*. Montreal, 1855.

*Report of the Kingston School of Mining and Agriculture. Submitted to the Annual Meeting, April 18ᵗʰ, 1894.* Kingston, ON: British Whig Office, 1894.

*Report of the Proceedings of the Second Annual Meeting of the Permanent Central Farmers' Institute of Ontario.* Grimsby, ON: Independent Steam Job Office, 1889.

Richards, Stewart. "Agricultural Science in Higher Education: Problems of Identity in Britain's First Chair of Agriculture, Edinburgh 1790–c 1831." *Agricultural History Review* 33, no. 1 (1985), 59–65.

Richardson, Lynn E. "James Young." In *Dictionary of Canadian Biography*, vol. 14. Quebec and Toronto: Les Presses de l'Université Laval and University of Toronto Press, 1998, 1087–9.

Ritchie, T. "Henry Ruttan." In *Dictionary of Canadian Biography*, vol. 10. Quebec and Toronto: Les Presses de l'Université Laval and University of Toronto Press, 1972, 636–7.

Robert, J.-C. "William Evans." In *Dictionary of Canadian Biography*, vol. 8. Quebec and Toronto: Les Presses de l'Université Laval and University of Toronto Press, 1985, 277–9.

Robertson, James W., and Albert H. Leake. *Macdonald Manual Training Schools in Canada. The Ottawa Manual Training School.* Toronto: s.n., 1901.

Robertson, John Ross. *Landmarks of Toronto.* Toronto: J.R. Robertson, 1899.

Robins, Nora. 1981. "The Montreal Mechanics' Institute: 1828–1870." *Canadian Library Journal* 38, no. 6 (Dec. 1981), 373–9.

– "'Useful Education for the Workingman': The Montreal Mechanics' Institute, 1828–70." In Michael R. Welton, ed., *Knowledge for the People: The Struggle for Adult Learning in English-Speaking Canada, 1828–1973.* Toronto: OISE Press, 1987, 20–34.

Romney, Paul. "Charles Fothergill." In *Dictionary of Canadian Biography*, vol. 7. Quebec and Toronto: Les Presses de l'Université Laval and University of Toronto Press, 1988.

Ross, Alexander M., and Terry Crowley. *The College on the Hill: A New History of the Ontario Agricultural College, 1874–1999.* Toronto: Dundurn Press, 1999.

Ross, George. *The School System of Ontario (Canada), its History and Distinctive Features.* New York: Appleton and Co, 1896.

Rossiter, Margaret. 1975. *The Emergence of Agricultural Science: Justus Liebig and the Americans, 1840–1880.* New Haven, CT: Yale University Press, 1975.

Rouleau, T.-G. *Notice sur l'Ecole normale Laval de Québec pour l'Exposition de Chicago.* Quebec: L. Brousseau, 1893.

Roy, Fernande. *Progrès, harmonie, liberté: le libéralisme des milieux d'affaires francophones à Montréal au tournant du siècle.* Montreal: Editions Boréal, 1998.

Royle, E. "Mechanics' Institutes and the Working Classes." *Historical Journal* (1971), 305–21.

Russell, Sir E. John. *A History of Agricultural Science in Great Britain 1620–1954.* London: Allen and Unwin, 1966.

Ryerson, Egerton. *First Lessons on Agriculture; for Canadian Farmers and their Families.* Toronto: Copp, Clark, 1870.

– *Inaugural Address on the Nature and Advantages of an English and Liberal Education ...
delivered at the Opening of Victoria College*. Toronto: By order of the Board of Trustees
and Visitors, 1842.

– *Report on a System of Public Elementary Instruction for Upper Canada*. Montreal: Lovell
and Gibson, 1847.

– *The Educational Museum and School of Art and Design for Upper Canada with a Plan of the
English Educational Museum, &c*. Toronto: Lovell and Gibson, 1858.

– *The Story of My Life*. Toronto: W. Briggs, 1883.

Sabourin, Hélène. "La chambre des arts et manufactures: les quinze premières années,
1857–1872." MA thesis, Université du Québec à Montréal, 1989.

Samson, Daniel. *The Spirit of Industry and Improvement: Liberal Government and Rural-
Industrial Society, Nova Scotia, 1790–1862*. Montreal and Kingston: McGill-Queen's
University Press, 2008.

"Samuel Passmore May." In *Appleton's Cyclopaedia of American Biography*. New York: D.
Appleton and Co., 1887–89.

Sandwell, R.W. "Rural Reconstruction: Towards a New Synthesis in Canadian History."
*Histoire sociale/Social History* 27 (May 1994), 1–32.

– "The Limits of Liberalism: The Liberal Reconnaissance and the History of the Family
in Canada." *Canadian Historical Review* 84 (2003), 423.

Saunders, William. *Report on Agricultural Colleges and Experimental Stations, with Suggestions
Relating to Experimental Agriculture in Canada*. Ottawa: s.n., 1886.

Savard, Pierre. "William Sheppard." In *Dictionary of Canadian Biography*, vol. 15. Quebec
and Toronto: Les Presses de l'Université Laval and University of Toronto Press, 2005.

Scadding, Henry. *Toronto of Old: Collections and Recollections Illustrative of the Early
Settlement and Social Life of the Capital of Ontario*. Toronto: Adam, Stevenson, 1873.

Scottish Commission on Agriculture. *Report of the Scottish Commission on Agriculture to
Canada 1908*. Edinburgh. W. Blackwood, 1909.

Sears, William P., Jr. *The Roots of Vocational Education: A Survey of the Origins of Trade and
Industrial Education Found in Industry, Education, Legislation and Social Progress*. New
York: Wiley, 1931.

Seath, John. *Education for Industrial Purposes: A Report*. Toronto: L.K. Cameron, 1911.

– *Manual Training and High School Courses of Study*. Toronto, 1901.

Séguin, Maurice. *La 'nation canadienne' et l'agriculture (1760–1850)*. Trois-Rivières:
Boréal Express, 1970.

Séguin, Normand, ed. *Agriculture et colonisation au Québec. Aspects historiques*. Montreal:
Boréal Express, 1980.

Selman, Gordon, and Paul Dampier. *The Foundations of Adult Education in Canada*.
Toronto: Thompson Educational Publishing, 1991.

Shapin, Steven, and Barry Barnes. "Science, Nature and Control: Interpreting
Mechanics' Institutes." *Social Studies of Science* 7 (1977), 31–74.

Sheets-Pyenson, Susan. *John William Dawson: Faith, Hope, and Science.* Montreal: McGill-Queen's University Press, 1996.

Sissons, C.B. *Egerton Ryerson: His Life and Letters.* Toronto: Clarke, Irwin, 1947.

Smith, Walter. *Technical Education and Industrial Drawing in Public Schools.* Montreal: Gazette Printing Co., 1883.

Smyth, Delmar McCormack. "The Gradual Emergence of Ontario's Community Colleges." In H. Oliver, M. Holmes, and I. Winchester, eds., *The House that Ryerson Built.* Toronto: OISE Press, 1984, 159–77.

*Société d'agriculture de Québec, établie sous la sanction de son Excellence le Gouverneur-en-chef. Règles de la Société.* Quebec: s.n., 1818.

*Special Report of the Minister of Education on the Mechanics' Institutes (Ontario)* [by S.P. May]. Toronto: C. Blackett Robinson, 1881.

Squair, John. *John Seath and the School System of Ontario.* Toronto: University of Toronto Press, 1920.

Stamp, Robert M. "Ontario at Philadelphia: The Centennial Exposition of 1876." In Neil McDonald and Alf Chaiton, eds., *Egerton Ryerson and His Times.* Toronto: Macmillan, 1978, 302–17.

– "The Campaign for Technical Education in Ontario, 1876–1914." PhD thesis, University of Western Ontario, 1970.

*Statuts de la Société Saint-Jean-Baptiste de la Cité de Québec.* Quebec, 1873.

Stirling, J. Craig. "Postsecondary Arts Education in Ontario, 1876–1912." In Harold Pearse, ed., *From Drawing to Visual Culture: A History of Art Education in Canada.* Montreal: McGill-Queen's University Press, 2006, 86–102.

– "Postsecondary Arts Education in Quebec from the 1870s to the 1920s." In Harold Pearse, ed., *From Drawing to Visual Culture: A History of Art Education in Canada.* Montreal: McGill-Queen's University Press, 2006, 47–84.

Talman, J.J. "Agricultural Societies of Upper Canada." *Ontario Historical Society Papers and Records* 27 (1931), 545–52.

Tanner, Henry. *First Principles of Agriculture.* London, 1878.

Taylor, Jeffery. "Professionalism, Intellectual Practice, and the Educational State Structure in Manitoba Agriculture, 1890–1925." *Manitoba History* 18 (1989), 36–45.

Templé, Edmond-Marie. *Méthode nationale de dessin: cours préparatoire.* Montreal, 1886.

Têtu, H., and C.-O. Gagnon, eds. *Mandements, lettres pastorales et circulaires des évêques de Québec,* vol. 4. Quebec: A. Coté, 1888.

*The British Farmer's and Farm Labourer's Guide to Ontario, the Premier Province of the Dominion of Canada.* Toronto: C. Blackett, 1880.

"The Grenfell Mechanics' and Literary Institute Minute Book, 1892–95." *Saskatchewan History* 17 (1964), 105–10.

*The Quebec Guide: Comprising an Historical and Descriptive Account of the City and Every Place of Note in the Vicinity.* Quebec: W. Cowan, 1844.

Thibault, Norbert. *De l'agriculture et du rôle des instituteurs dans l'enseignement agricole.* Quebec: P.G. Delisle, 1871.

Thompson, Samuel. *Reminiscences of a Canadian Pioneer for the Last Fifty Years.* Toronto: Hunter, Rose, 1884.

[Thomson, H.C.]. *The Prompter, a Series of Essays on Civil and Social Duties.* Kingston, ON: H.C. Thomson, 1821.

*Toronto Mechanics' Institute Catalogue of Books in the Library.* Toronto: Toronto Mechanics' Institute, 1862. (Copy in Baldwin Room, Toronto Reference Library.)

Trudel, Jean. "L'Art Association of Montreal: les années d'incertitude, 1863–1877, part 1." *Journal of Canadian Art History* 29 (2008), 116–45; part 2, 29 (2009), 93–113.

True, Alfred Charles. *A History of Agricultural Education in the United States, 1785–1925.* Washington, DC: United States Government Printing Office, 1929.

– *A History of Agricultural Extension Work in the United States 1785–1923.* Washington, DC: United States Government Printing Office, 1928.

Tulchinsky, Gerald J.J. *The River Barons: Montreal Businessmen and the Growth of Industry and Transportation 1837–53.* Toronto: University of Toronto Press, 1977.

Tylecote, Mabel. *The Mechanics' Institutes of Lancashire and Yorkshire before 1851.* Manchester: Manchester University Press, 1957.

Vernon, Foster. "The Development of Adult Education in Ontario, 1790–1900." EdD thesis, University of Toronto, 1969.

Vézina, Raymond. "Napoléon Bourassa." In *Dictionary of Canadian Biography*, vol. 14. Quebec and Toronto: Les Presses de l'Université Laval and University of Toronto Press, 2000, 185–9.

Vincent, David. *Literacy and Popular Culture. England 1750–1914.* Cambridge: Cambridge University Press, 1989.

Walden, Keith. *Becoming Modern in Toronto: The Industrial Exhibition and the Shaping of a Late Victorian Culture.* Toronto: University of Toronto Press, 1997.

Wallace, W. Stewart. 1927. *A History of the University of Toronto, 1827–1927.* Toronto: University of Toronto Press, 1927.

Webber, Jeremy. "Labour and the Law." In Paul Craven, ed., *Labouring Lives: Work and Workers in Nineteenth-Century Ontario.* Toronto: University of Toronto Press, 1995, 105–201.

Wells, Gaye. "Mechanics' Institutes in Ontario, 1831–1895." Unpublished research paper, University of Toronto Library School, 1974.

Whitcombe, Charles E. *The Canadian Farmer's Manual of Agriculture: The Principles and Practice of Mixed Husbandry as adapted to Canadian Soils and Climate.* Toronto: Willing and Williamson, 1879.

White, Richard. *The Skule Story: The University of Toronto Faculty of Applied Science and Engineering, 1873–2000.* Toronto: Faculty of Applied Science and Engineering, University of Toronto, 2001.

Wilson, Sir Daniel. *On the Practical Uses of Science in the Daily Business of Life: The Inaugural Lecture to the Evening Courses of Lectures for Working Men.* Toronto: C.B. Robinson, 1881.

Wiseman, John A. "Phoenix in Flight: Ontario Mechanics' Institutes, 1880–1920." *Canadian Library Journal* 38, no. 6 (Dec. 1981), 401–5.

– "Silent Companions: The Dissemination of Books and Periodicals in Nineteenth-Century Ontario." *Publishing History* 12 (1982), 17–50.

Wood, Henry Trueman. *A History of the Royal Society of Arts.* London: Murray, 1913.

Wood, J. David. *Making Ontario: Agricultural Colonization and Landscape Re-creation before the Railway.* Montreal and Kingston: McGill-Queen's University Press, 2000.

Wood, L.A. *A History of Farmers' Movements in Canada.* New ed. Toronto: University of Toronto Press, 1975.

Wrightson, John. *Agricultural Textbook, Embracing Soils, Manures, Rotation of Crops, and Live Stock, Adapted to the Requirements of the Syllabus of the Science and Art Department, South Kensington. Illustrated.* London, 1877.

– *The Principles of Agricultural Practice as an Instructional Subject. Illustrated.* London, 1888.

Wykes, David L. "Robert Bakewell (1725–1795) of Dishley: Farmer and Livestock Improver." *Agricultural History Review* 52, no. 1 (2004), 38–55.

Young, Arthur. *A Tour in Ireland, 1776–1779.* 2 vols. Dublin: James Williams, 1780.

Young, C.R. *Early Engineering Education at Toronto, 1851–1919.* Toronto: University of Toronto Press, 1958.

Young, John ('Agricola'). *The Letters of Agricola on the Principles of Vegetation and Tillage: Written for Nova Scotia, and Published First in the Acadian Recorder.* Halifax, 1822.

Zeller, Suzanne. *Inventing Canada: Early Victorian Science and the Idea of a Transcontinental Nation.* Montreal: McGill-Queen's University Press, 2009.

– "Roads not Taken: Victorian Science, Technical Education, and Canadian Schools, 1844–1913." *Historical Studies in Education* 12 (2000), 1–28.

# Index